P9-DBI-965

A "Washington Merry-Go-Round" of Libel Actions

A "Washington Merry-Go-Round" of Libel Actions

Douglas A. Anderson

Nelson-Hall nh Chicago

Library of Congress Cataloging in Publication Data

Anderson, Douglas A.

A Washington "Merry-go-round" of libel actions.
Bibliography: p.
Includes index.
1. Trials (Libel)—United States. 2. Libel and slander—United States. 3. Journalistic ethics—United States. 4. Pearson, Drew, 1897-1969. 5. Anderson, Jack, 1922- I. Title.
KF221.L5A5 346'.73'034 79-18126
ISBN 0-88229-547-0 (Cloth)
ISBN 0-88229-746-5 (Paper)

Manufactured in the United States of America

10 9 8 7 6 5 4 3 2 1

To

Claudia, Laura, and Mary

Contents

Preface ix

1. The "Merry-Go-Round" and Its Men 1

Pearson—The Man 4 *Anderson—The Man 12*

2. The Muckraking "Merry-Go-Round" and Its World 16

The Column Is Launched 16 *The Current-Era "Merry-Go-Round" 20* *The Column's Muckraking Heritage 22* *Muckraking Role of "Merry-Go-Round" Writers 24* *The Controversial Columnists 30* *A Profile in Libel 44*

3. The "Merry-Go-Round" and Its Libel Law Boundaries 55

Common Law Origins 58 *Defenses against Libel Actions 61* *Common Law Cornerstones 65* *A Trend Emerges 68* *A National Standard Is Born 71* *Post-*Sullivan *Developments 74* *The Current State of the Press 95*

4. Initial Libel Challenges to the "Merry-Go-Round"—MacArthur and Sweeney 99

Sweeney's Sixty-Eight Libel Suits 102 *The Sweeney Suits—Their Effects on Pearson and Libel Law 124*

5. The "Merry-Go-Round" and the Years of Common Law Defenses 128

Cases Involving Public Officials 129 *Cases Involving Public Figures 143* *Cases Involving Private Persons 169* *Pearson—A Courtroom Regular 179*

6. The "Merry-Go-Round" and the Years of Protection for "Robust, Wide-Open" Reporting 181

Cases Involving Public Officials 182 *Cases Involving Public Figures 207* *Pearson and Anderson Remain Active in the Courts 218*

7. Fighting Back: Men of the "Merry-Go-Round" as Plaintiffs 219

A Refusal to Be Intimidated 244

8. The "Merry-Go-Round": Cursed, Sued—but Successful 245

Effects of Evolving Libel Law on the Column 254 *Effects of the Column on Evolving Libel Law 257*

Appendix 263

About the Notes 266

Notes 268

Selected Bibliography 322

Index 339

Preface

It is unlikely that any American syndicated newspaper column has been involved in as many libel actions as the "Washington Merry-Go-Round." The reason is simple: the late Drew Pearson, a pioneer in Washington-based investigative reporting, and Jack Anderson, his successor, are among the twentieth century's most prominent muckrakers; their aggressive reporting has obviously done little to endear them to the innumerable public officials who have found themselves unflattered subjects.

Nearly one thousand editors across the country, when they open their morning mail, know that the envelope from the United Feature Syndicate contains often embarrassing, and usually exclusive, revelations about some of the nation's most powerful people. The "Merry-Go-Round" column, which seldom exceeds three double-spaced typewritten pages, assumes much larger proportions when removed from the envelope, set in type, and placed on a newspaper opinion page. It is no coincidence, then, that Pearson and Anderson have found themselves in the courts so often since the column's 1932 inception.

Through the years, "Merry-Go-Round" writers have probably broken more major stories, been cursed by more public officials, and read by more citizens than any other syndicated columnists. Their disclosures have helped send congressmen to jail, played a major role in crumbling a Republican administration, and "retired" many elected officials from public office. When a column—every day for nearly a half century—criticizes, ridicules, or exposes wrongdoing among the country's elite, the columnist can logically expect to defend himself against lawsuits. How have writers of the "Merry-Go-Round" column fared in their defense? That is the subject of this book.

As most journalists are aware, the United States Supreme Court is involved in a continuing effort to define the proper relationship between the need for a vigorous, uninhibited press, as symbolized by the "Merry-Go-Round," and the legitimate interest in redressing wrongful injury by defamation. When the Court held in 1964 (in *New York Times Co.* v. *Sullivan*) that a state cannot, under the First and Fourteenth Amendments, award damages to a public official for defamatory falsehoods relating to his official conduct unless he proves "actual malice"—that the statement was made with knowledge of its falsity or with reckless disregard for the truth—it nevertheless did not put all questions to rest. Despite the increased protection given the press in the landmark ruling, and in expansion of the rule that was to follow, several questions still have no fixed answers: How far can the news media go in reaching into the private lives of public officials or figures? How is a public figure defined? What precautions must a journalist take when discussing a person who does not fall into the public official or figure category?

These questions have been particularly pertinent to "Merry-Go-Round" writers during the past half century. Any columnist who specializes in investigative reporting must be cognizant of libel law boundaries. It would take very few court losses, considering the astronomical damages often sought, to put a column out of business. A muckraking writer must be extremely careful to stay within the court-sanctioned libel law limits.

The purposes of this book, then, are: (1) to trace the development of the law of libel as it has applied to public officials and public figures during the period of the "Washington Merry-Go-Round" column; (2) to trace the scores of libel actions brought against and by writers of the "Merry-Go-Round" since the column's inception; (3) to examine the various defenses and legal strategies employed by "Merry-Go-Round" legal counsel; (4) to determine the effects on the column of libel law evolution, particularly the constitutional privilege established in *New York Times Co.* v. *Sullivan;* and (5) to determine the effects, if any, of libel suits involving the column on the development of the law. The book begins with a sketch of the lives and careers of the "Merry-Go-Round" writers who figure so large in this legal account.

A major contribution of this book is the compilation of legal actions initiated by and against "Merry-Go-Round" writers, thus adding to the historical and legal significance of the controversial, muckraking column. Significant libel cases —both reported and unreported—that involved the column have been examined, complete with legal issues, defenses, and the courts' decisions and reasoning. Facts and holdings from similar "Merry-Go-Round" cases have been synthesized. The findings should have implications for students of communication law and press freedom as well as members of the working media who have a responsibility to discuss public figures, events, and issues of public concern in the "uninhibited, robust, and wide-open" manner that the *New York Times Co.* v. *Sullivan* case was grounded upon.

It must be emphasized, however, that this book's list of "Merry-Go-Round" suits is not all-encompassing; because of the national circulation of the column and the fact that most of the cases were unreported, examining all the suits would be next to an impossible task. Every effort, however, was made to locate all reported decisions; all cases filed in the Federal District Court for the District of Columbia; all cases mentioned, but not cited, in Pearson-Anderson literature; and all unreported cases suggested by attorneys who worked with Pearson and Anderson. One further caveat should be mentioned: material gathered from personal interviews is, of course, susceptible to less than precise recollections on the part of those interviewed.

* * *

The writer would like to express his gratitude to Dr. Harry W. Stonecipher, School of Journalism, Southern Illinois University at Carbondale, for his valuable advice in the development of this book. Appreciation is also expressed to Drs. Robert Trager, George Brown, and M. Browning Carrott, all of SIU-C; Dr. Ralph Johnson, *Toledo* (Ohio) *Blade* editorial writer; Dr. Warren T. Francke, Department of Communication, the University of Nebraska at Omaha; and Cate Peterson, a talented English-journalism major at UNO, for their suggestions and help.

Formal thanks should be given to Tyler Abell, a Washington, D.C., attorney, who, as Drew Pearson's stepson, is editor of the Pearson diaries. Abell was especially helpful in directing the writer to longtime friends of the late Pearson who were in positions to offer particular insights into the muckraker. Abell also graciously granted the writer permission to examine and utilize the not-yet-public Pearson papers in the Lyndon Baines Johnson Library, Austin, Texas.

Gratitude is extended the Mellett Fund for a Free and Responsible Press, an independent nonprofit corporation established through a bequest from Lowell Mellett to the Newspaper Guild, which awarded the writer a research grant, thus making financially possible the travel involved in gathering information for this book.

Credit goes to Kathie Lee, Omaha, for typing the manuscript.

A private debt of gratitude is owed to the writer's wife, Claudia, who made many personal sacrifices and provided much-needed encouragement, and to Laura and Mary, two young girls who likely thought their father lived at school rather than at home.

1

The "Merry-Go-Round" and Its Men

Drew Pearson liked to relate that the postal service once delivered, directly to his door, a letter addressed merely to "The S.O.B."—no city was named.[1] The letter was sent to him shortly after President Harry S Truman so crudely described him.[2] The syndicated muckraking columnist and cofounder of the "Washington Merry-Go-Round" newspaper column was unruffled.[3] A few days after Truman delivered the epithet, Pearson countered on his regular radio broadcast:

> These are the days, Mr. President, when the world can use a lot of brotherhood. So I'm going to take those initials, Mr. President, and use them proudly, in an entirely different way. I would like to suggest that in the future, we . . . make them mean "servants of brotherhood" and that we form a new militant crusading order of servants of brotherhood.[4]

Episodes such as this have made the "Merry-Go-Round" column the most widely read of its day. A Louis Harris survey, conducted just prior to Pearson's death on September 1, 1969, indicated that the muckraker was the best-known columnist in the United States.[5] *Time* magazine once claimed that Pearson was involved in more controversy than any other journalist of his time.[6] Jack Anderson, who inherited the column upon Pearson's death, is similarly categorized. He has, for example, been labeled "the most celebrated practitioner of the muckraking tradition"[7] and the "outstanding muckraker of the times."[8]

Pearson operated on the theory that notoriety was as good as fame. He constantly told his reporters that controversy was "good for the column. If you write a column like ours, you've got to be controversial. People will read you even if they hate you."[9] The columnist, in fact, often told friends that, when he died, he wanted to be buried on his Potomac farm under the inscription, "Here Lies an S.O.B."[10] By the middle 1940s, Pearson had a proven track record of noteworthy controversies. He had been called a "liar" by President Franklin D. Roosevelt; sued by Gen. Douglas MacArthur for $1,750,000 in libel damages for portraying the war hero as a "swaggering strutter," among other things; and officially dropped by the Washington Social List for getting into "too many controversies."[11]

The *National Review,* through the years, was likely as critical of the muckraking columnist as any other publication. In a 1961 editorial the magazine claimed that Pearson was guilty of so many factual mistakes in his columns that his corrections had become "second nature." The editorial said in part:

> Mr. Pearson exercises his incompetence with noteworthy consistency: always, that is, to the detriment of conservatives. It is a pattern; and patterns are not accidents; someone wills them. And Mr. Pearson mounts his attack in such a way—in the last days of a campaign, and with surreptitious distribution—that the victim cannot defend himself. Again a pattern, not an accident; someone wills it. Out of the patterns of willful distortion and furtive attack emerges the unassailable conclusion: Mr. Pearson is a liar and a coward.[12]

The *Congressional Record* also includes several feverish outcries directed at the columnist. In what was likely the most colorful anti-Pearson blast ever on the Senate floor, seventy-five-year-old Sen. Kenneth McKellar of Tennessee took the muckraker to task. The title over the *Congressional Record* entry gives an indication of the tone of the criticism: "Personal Statement About A Lying Human Skunk."[13]

McKellar was extremely irritated with a "Merry-Go-Round" column in which Pearson denounced the senator's record in Congress, giving particular emphasis to the Tennessean's nasty temper and patronage policies. To add frosting to the cake, Pearson referred to the senator as a "blustery mountaineer" and a "hillbilly." McKellar warmed to the task quickly:

> I digress long enough to say that I do not know Pearson; but really he is an ignorant ass, is he not? (laughter) I was not born in the mountains. I never lived in a mountain country in my life; and yet this ignorant, blundering, lying ass, who makes his living by lying on Senators and other public men, seems to think there is something discreditable about mountains, or about being born in the mountains.

McKellar went on to explain that three things did arouse his temper, including lying. He said that "if ever there was an opportunity for my temper to be aroused by plain lying, it would be aroused by the plain lying of this so-called Washington columnist, I believe he is called. He is just an ignorant liar, a pusillanimous liar, a peewee liar, and he is a paid liar."

The senator was so enraged that he could not resist piling insult upon insult while he had the floor. He delayed going to the men's room during his frenzied tirade; when he finally finished, he quickly went to the rest room, fainted, and needed a doctor.[14]

Sen. Theodore Bilbo of Mississippi once became so irritated with a Pearson column critical of Walter Reed General Hospital that he strongly lashed out at the muckraking columnist.

Judging from the parenthetical interjection in the *Congressional Record,* Bilbo entertained his colleagues quite well:

> Mr. President, it is not only generally known, but it is universally admitted that Drew Pearson is the biggest and most notorious liar in America today. Not only is Pearson recognized as being the biggest liar, but he is also recognized as being the most perfect smear artist of the press and radio. He will go down in history as Drew Pearson the sponge (laughter), because he gathers slime, mud, and slander from all parts of the earth and lets them ooze out through his daily contributions to a few newspapers which have not yet found him out.[15]

What manner of man provoked such hostile, outspoken reactions?

Pearson—The Man

Andrew Russell Pearson was born December 13, 1897, in Evanston, Illinois, the son of Paul Martin Pearson, a college speech teacher, and Edna Wolfe Pearson. Young Pearson spent most of his boyhood in Swarthmore, Pennsylvania, where his father taught at the Quaker college.[16] He attended Phillips Exeter Academy in New Hampshire, and then Swarthmore College, from which he was graduated Phi Beta Kappa in 1919.[17] At Swarthmore, Pearson edited the college newspaper and was involved in numerous extracurricular activities. During vacations from prep school and college, he worked on his father's Chautauqua circuit. He started as a member of the tent crew, was promoted to motion picture operator, then to advance man, and ultimately to lecturer.[18]

When Pearson graduated from college, his father got him a job in Serbia with the American Friends Service Committee; his salary was six dollars a month. Pearson found plenty to keep him busy in a country badly ravaged during the First World War. He had an advantage over most of his fellow Quakers who were city bred: he had spent several childhood summers on the Kansas farms of relatives, and this farm background helped make him resourceful. As a result, he was very popular with the country's peasants. One of the devastated Balkan villages he helped rebuild was named for him: Pearsonavatz.[19]

The columnist's experiences in Serbia (now a constituent republic of Yugoslavia) were extremely gratifying to him. He always kept in touch with the Yugoslavs, maintaining a solid relationship with the country's ambassador during the decades after he left the country. In the 1960s the Pearsons returned to Yugoslavia; the columnist met with President Tito and several friends he had made there four decades earlier. The columnist and his wife also visited Pearsonavatz, where some of the houses he had helped build were still standing.[20]

After returning to America in 1921, Pearson taught industrial geography for a year at the University of Pennsylvania. For the next few years (with a year out in 1924 to teach geography at Columbia University), Pearson traveled widely as a newspaperman, seaman, and lecturer in Europe and the Far East.[21] Ernest Cuneo, Washington, D.C., lawyer and writer, who was a student of Pearson's at Columbia, remembers him as being "very conscientious and thorough." Cuneo, in fact, sees Pearson's training in economic geography and his service with the Friends as helping to uniquely equip him for his writing career. Cuneo believes that Pearson "took his Quaker concern and put it into journalism."[22]

In 1925, the muckraker married the Countess Felicia Gizycka, daughter of Eleanor (Cissy) Patterson, owner-publisher of the *Washington Times-Herald,* and granddaughter of Joseph Medill, founder of the *Chicago Tribune.*[23] Drew and Felicia, however, were divorced in mid-August 1928.[24] At about this time, Pearson was gaining a strong entrance to Washington journalism. His first Washington job was as foreign editor of David Lawrence's *United States Daily,* which later evolved into *U.S. News & World Report.*[25] He then moved on to the Washington bureau of the *Baltimore Sun.*

In 1931, Pearson and Robert S. Allen anonymously published their book *Washington Merry-Go-Round,* which was critical of the Herbert Hoover administration. Pearson was working for the *Sun* when his authorship of the book became known. He was given the opportunity to resign his post but, true to his nature, chose to be fired. Apparently he had an ulterior motive. It had been speculated that government officials had brought pressure on the *Sun* to discharge Pearson, and, by forcing the newspaper to fire him, he became the "Dred Scott of a freedom of the press controversy which won national notice."[26]

In 1932, Pearson and Allen launched a column with the same name as the book. Obviously the controversy helped boost their new venture.

With the column going well, Pearson remarried in 1936. His new bride, Luvie Moore, a movie critic for the *Times-Herald,* had one son, Tyler Abell, by a previous marriage.[27] Cissy Patterson remained cordial toward Drew and his new family for a time. The *Times-Herald* published the "Merry-Go-Round" until the columnists' New Deal tastes began to irritate Mrs. Patterson. Pearson then moved the column from his former mother-in-law's paper to the *Washington Post,* where it has since remained.[28] The switch brought about conflicting stories. Publisher Patterson announced in a bold front-page story that she had gotten rid of Pearson and Allen because of their "poisonous attempts" to "smear" General MacArthur. The columnists, on the other hand, explained that they had given the publisher six months' notice, and that she had distorted the MacArthur issue. Pearson and Allen put together an advertisement, giving their side of the story, but no Washington publisher would carry it.[29]

The *Post* has traditionally published the "Merry-Go-Round" on one of the comic pages. A letter to the editor in a November 1956 edition of the *Post,* in fact, claimed this was a good place for it. The writer explained that Pearson's "predictions" were wrong so often, they were generally more entertaining than the rest of the comics on the page.[30]

Pearson did not seem to mind negative references of this nature; they amused him. He was able to capitalize on his reputation as a muckraking, not-always-accurate columnist, not only in the journalistic world, but in a sideline interest as well. He used his name in connection with a product he produced on his eight-hundred-acre farm overlooking the Potomac River and the Chesapeake and Ohio Canal. Robert C. Jensen, a *Washington Post* staff writer, described it:

> He [Pearson] put out a rich soil product called "Drew Pearson's Muck," which was billed as being "packaged by the best muckraker in the U.S." The muck was taken from the bottom of an old canal on his farm. [It was also marketed] under the name of "Drew Pearson's Best Manure," with such advertising slogans as "better than in the column," and "all cow, no Bull."[31]

Though the manure idea was a good one—from a publicity angle—it was far from a financial success.[32]

The Maryland farm was the columnist's only real hobby. He spent his spare weekends there and liked the idea of being a "country squire." George Vournas, a Washington, D.C., attorney and long-time Pearson friend, once related to the Pearson family over dinner that the muckraker's first loyalty was to the column, his second to the radio broadcast, his third to his wife and family, his fourth to the farm, and his fifth to Vournas. Mrs. Pearson immediately retorted that this was incorrect. Vournas, anticipating that Luvie would claim she came first, was in for a surprise. Mrs. Pearson explained that her husband's cows on the Maryland farm rated third, and she was really only fourth.[33]

Pearson, it seems, had the unusual ability to spread his energy across many areas. He worked day and night. Catnaps got him through the days; he seldom slept more than four consecutive hours at night. He spent so much time on the telephone during the afternoon gathering information that he was forced to do most of his writing at night.[34] It was not unusual—in fact, commonplace—for the columnist to work sixteen to twenty hours a day, seven days a week. He was also very secretive, often having two or three of his reporters working on the same story—without any of them knowing about the others. He did not totally confide in anyone. Though he discussed pending libel suits extensively with his attorneys, he would say little or nothing about the litigation to his reporters. The columnist had an encyclopedic memory. He sometimes gave a reporter instructions on a small card, and he could conjure up the image of it months later—expecting his instructions to have been fulfilled.[35]

Though Pearson kept his reporters extremely busy, he cultivated an immense number of personal sources. If information came from a source he genuinely trusted, he often published it as literal truth without further checking. This, of course, was sometimes to his chagrin. Still, the columnist was generally very careful about checking copy before allowing it to be distributed by the syndicate.[36]

Naturally, a muckraker like Pearson was the victim of hundreds of complaints, many by telephone. The columnist, however, mastered his butler's voice; if he answered his home telephone and did not recognize the voice of the caller, he said Mr. Pearson was not home. This proved frustrating to the real butler, whom callers sometimes berated, thinking he was the columnist putting on an act.[37]

Though Pearson received scores of complaints, some justified, he printed a retraction only occasionally. Instead, if threatened by a subject of one of his columns, he was more likely to reinvestigate, dig up some even more damaging information, and then print it.[38] Pearson readily absorbed most of the harsh remarks cast in his direction–including those by various presidents—but some of the criticisms cut deeply. He felt, however, that he had to be able to take it because in his business one did not go around "writing nice things" about everyone.[39]

Pearson often lost his temper, but he was basically softhearted, and his displeasure with the individual involved quickly evaporated. In his middle years, Pearson was described as

> a tall, tweedy, disarmingly mild-mannered fellow, with thinning light brown hair, a spare moustache and earnest mien; he looks like a shy, quizzical cow college professor—except for his wary blue eyes. The mild manner camouflages a

> tough, diamond-hard core. . . . Though more conservative newsmen have tried to laugh him off as a Fearless Fosdick of journalism, none can match his hard work or his arm-long record of newsbeats.[40]

It was likely his hard work and willingness to "tell all" about people in power that accounted for his wide following.

Pearson was not one to write beautiful prose; his crisp paragraphs read "like jottings on an envelope in a lurching taxicab." According to *Time* magazine:

> It's not how he says it, but what he says: a brand of ruthless, theatrical, crusading, high-voltage, hypodermic journalism that has made him the most intensely feared and hated man in Washington. It is the kind of journalistic vigilance that keeps small men honest, and forces bigger men to work in an atmosphere of caution that frequently cramps their style. . . . Like oldtime muckrakers Lincoln Steffens and Ida M. Tarbell, Pearson hates wickedness. But these reformers had more time to draw a bead on it, and never needed, or thought they needed, seven sensations a week to stay in business.[41]

Pearson, however, did not do it alone. He had an able partner during the column's first decade: Robert S. Allen.

Allen, like Pearson, had a strong background for the journalistic endeavor. Born on July 14, 1900, in Latonia, Kentucky, Allen gained newspaper experience as early as age thirteen, working as a copyboy for the *Louisville Courier-Journal*. He attended the University of Kentucky before lying about his age and joining the army. He served in France and returned a second lieutenant. In 1919 he enrolled as a sophomore at the University of Wisconsin. He graduated in 1921 and worked on the *Madison Capital-Times* and *Wisconsin State Journal*. He continued to serve in the National Guard, attaining the rank of captain. In 1923 and 1924 he studied in Munich and served as correspondent for the *Christian Science Monitor* and the United Press. Allen returned to America and accepted a job with the *Monitor's* Washington bureau. He was made bureau head in 1930; his salary was $150 a week. Though apparently reasonably happy with his job, he always felt he was writing "under wraps." This set the stage for his coauthorship of *Washington Merry-Go-Round* and subsequent column adventure.[42]

Allen went on active duty with the army during World War II, but Pearson continued to turn out the column daily. Though his methods irked many of his competitors as well as public officials, most respected his ability, if not his practices. In 1944, for example, in a poll of Washington newsmen, Pearson was acclaimed the most influential capital correspondent. In terms of "reliability, fairness, and ability to analyze the news," however, he was rated tenth.[43]

Though his successor, Anderson, has received a Pulitzer Prize, that diadem always eluded Pearson.[44] For his disclosures involving Sen. Thomas Dodd of Connecticut and Rep. Adam Clayton Powell, Jr., of New York (both of which centered upon fiscal malfeasance), Pearson was voted a Pulitzer Prize in reporting. The Pulitzer trustees overruled their editorial committee, however, and awarded the honor to someone else.[45]

Despite Pearson's tiger-behind-the-typewriter image, his "Quaker conscience" led him to make several humanitarian gestures: Freedom Balloons, the Friendship Train, and his celebrated exclusive interviews with the Soviet Union's Nikita Khrushchev in the summer of 1961—a time when world tensions were high.[46].

It was Pearson's idea—carried to fruition in 1951—that balloons with friendship messages be launched across the Iron Curtain to citizens in satellite nations.[47] In 1947 the columnist organized a Friendship Train that traveled across the United States, picking up food and money to be sent to needy Europeans. The train started in Los Angeles; Pearson donated $10,000 of his own money to launch it. The drive was widely publicized and caught on rapidly; it exceeded the columnist's highest hopes.[48] Americans contributed $40 million worth of food, enough to fill approximately seven hundred boxcars, all of which was shipped to France and Italy.[49] Pearson believed the project achieved two major goals:

Western Europe was made aware that the United States cared, and President Truman was made to realize that the American people were willing to sacrifice.[50]

For his efforts with the special train, Pearson was named "Father of the Year." Gen. Dwight Eisenhower, president-elect of Columbia University, presented the columnist with a silver medal.[51] The columnist was also awarded the Bernardo O'Higgins Order of Merit by the government of Chile for his instrumental role in the Friendship Train Project.[52] The muckraker was even included among twenty-four candidates for the 1949 Nobel Peace Prize. The only other American nominated was Eleanor Roosevelt.[53] When told of Pearson's nomination, President Truman remarked that he could not categorically say the government had not nominated Pearson, but he assumed that the columnist probably had nominated himself.[54]

Pearson worked into his seventies, with undying zeal for reporting. He was sophisticated but did not let that interfere with his enthusiasm for his job. Throughout his career, he maintained the energy and drive of a young journalist just out of college.[55]

After being regarded as one of the country's most influential political columnists for thirty-seven years, Pearson died of a heart attack on Monday, September 1, 1969, at Georgetown University Hospital, Washington, D.C.[56] He was praised as a "muckraker with a Quaker conscience. In print he sounded fierce, in life he was gentle, even courtly. . . . [He] did more than any man to keep the national capital honest."[57] At Pearson's funeral, former senator Wayne Morse, Democrat of Oregon, eulogized the columnist as "more than a journalist." Morse said Pearson was a "citizen-statesman dedicated to the service of mankind."[58]

When Pearson died, his was the most widely read political column in the United States. It was published in more than six hundred newspapers—nearly twice as many as its closest competitor, the David Lawrence column.[59] Pearson left the column in experienced hands, however. His designated successor, Anderson, had been with the column more than two decades.

Anderson—The Man

Jack Northman Anderson was born in Long Beach, California, on October 19, 1922, to Orlando N. Anderson, a native of Utah, and the former Agnes Mortensen, who had moved to America from Denmark at the age of fifteen. The family settled in Utah when Jack was two years old. He grew up in Cottonwood, a small town outside Salt Lake City. One of Anderson's first jobs was with the *Murray Eagle,* a weekly newspaper near his home. He started there when he was twelve years old. He was also editor of his junior and senior high school newspapers, while working for fifteen cents per column inch as a stringer for the *Salt Lake Tribune.*[60]

Anderson attended the University of Utah in 1940–41 and then, like many other young Mormons, became a missionary. He traveled in the South, primarily in Georgia, Florida, and Alabama, seeking converts to the church. Mormon missionaries travel at their own expense, so Anderson's mother went to work as a taxi driver to help meet financial obligations.[61] Anderson returned to Salt Lake City two years later, in 1943, and shortly thereafter enlisted in the Merchant Marine. After seven months, he resigned his commission and earned status as a war correspondent for the *Deseret News.* He did some minor reporting in China until he was drafted into the U.S. Army. He was discharged from the army in 1946 and returned to the United States.

Though Anderson had heard of Pearson, he had never read him until he got out of the service. A friend had suggested to him that, since he wanted to be a Washington reporter, he should seek a job from the nation's foremost muckraker.[62] Pearson hired Anderson as a part-time assistant in December of 1947. Though Anderson was only twenty-four, he already had twelve years of newspaper experience. His salary: $50 a week. Within a few weeks he was elevated to full-time assistant and paid $100.[63]

The year after Anderson went to work for Pearson, the young reporter met Olivia Farley, an FBI employee. In 1949 they were married.[64] By 1954, Anderson had become somewhat disgruntled with his "Merry-Go-Round" duties; he had been with Pearson seven years and had received little public credit for his work. The young reporter told Pearson he intended to quit the column to take a position as *Parade* magazine's Washington correspondent. Pearson quickly suggested that Anderson take the *Parade* job and work for the "Merry-Go-Round" as well. He promised that Anderson would eventually have a joint by-line and finally "inherit" the column. Anderson got his by-line—though it took twelve years. As an indication of Pearson's tight payroll, Anderson's *Parade* salary for part-time work soon outstripped his "Merry-Go-Round" earnings. In 1963, for example, Anderson earned $11,400 from Pearson and $28,500 from *Parade*. Still, Anderson loved his "Merry-Go-Round" work and thought it best to remain.[65]

As might be expected, Anderson had other opportunities to leave the "Merry-Go-Round" after he made a name for himself in Washington. One publishing syndicate, in fact, gave him an opportunity to launch his own column. The syndicate, however, wanted him to provide strong opposition to Pearson and the "Merry-Go-Round." Though Anderson could have made $75,000 a year (compared to the $14,000 Pearson was then paying him), he turned down the offer. It was a matter of loyalty. "What I learned about Washington, I learned from Drew," Anderson explained. "I never would have started a column to rival him."[66]

The warm personal attributes of Anderson are often mentioned—in contrast to the aggressive muckraker perception held by many.[67] Professionally, Anderson sees himself as more of a muckraker than Pearson, whom he has labeled more of a "backroom reporter."[68] However, Anderson has apparently not been star-struck by his skyrocketing fortunes:

> In public, Jack was the relentless muckraker bent on exposing wrongdoing whatever the human consequences.

> In private, he was a big softy whose wife once said she had seen him lose his temper only once in more than twenty years of marriage. In most people, there is at least some connection between their public posture and their private nature. But in Jack Anderson, there was virtually none.[69]

Anderson's associates are strong believers in their boss and what the column stands for. Les Whitten once expressed satisfaction with his "Merry-Go-Round" job during an interview with *Life* magazine:

> This job gives me a chance to do what I wanted to do all my life, knock the bleeding crap out of people who are corrupting this country and there are plenty of them. We only catch chips of the truth. But I don't think that's frustrating: to get the whole truth, you've got to be God.[70]

This type of philosophy apparently is pervasive among the "Merry-Go-Round" staff today.

Anderson's writings are often vividly descriptive. Emphasizing the columnist's writing style and favorite adjectives, one journalist wrote:

> Few corporate executives, generals and government officials are mentioned in the column, which is instead peopled by titans, tycoons, potentates, panjandrums, moguls, magnates, high-muck-a-mucks, bigwigs, brass hats and czars . . . . Anderson's characters rarely have something to say, state or comment upon; they whine, huff, snort, grump, mutter, bare their fangs, or worse.[71]

Though his sometimes trite, but always understandable style has its critics, Anderson is unconcerned. He sees himself as an investigative reporter, not an intellectual political analyst.[72]

Anderson was, of course, on the ground floor of several Watergate revelations. Charles Colson, Watergate participant and former special White House counsel to President Nixon, admitted in his book *Born Again* that he had once proposed an investigation of Anderson because the White House considered the reporter its "arch nemesis." Colson revised his opinion of the muckraker after a television debate between the two. Colson wrote that, though Anderson "had blasted me for years in his syndicated column," the muckraker showed true compassion by approaching Colson's wife offstage before the debate and offering financial help to the family, if needed, while her husband was serving his prison sentence. Colson said that he "did not learn until later what a deeply religious man Jack Anderson is, a side he has kept out of the news."[73] Anderson later confirmed Colson's account. "Sure, I offered to help," he said. "If his wife had called asking financial help, I would have gladly given it." The call, however, never came.[74]

Though Pearson's and Anderson's names constantly come up in discussions of America's foremost muckraking journalists, both men, on occasion, have exhibited the personal attributes of humanitarians. Given the unique writing styles and personalities of Pearson and Anderson, it is little wonder that the "Merry-Go-Round" is the most widely circulated column of its type in the world.

2

The Muckraking "Merry-Go-Round" and Its World

The "Merry-Go-Round" syndicated opinion column, which appears daily in more than nine hundred newspapers,[1] has been described as unquestionably providing "more average folks with their view of the federal government than any [other] column in existence."[2] Though aggressive reporting is the trademark of the muckraking column, it is also known for its "sacrifice of fact to fancy when the crusading spirit is upon it."[3] Its spicy language has been categorized as "colloquial, irreverent, and not always grammatical."[4]

The Column Is Launched

The anonymously published book *Washington Merry-Go-Round*, coauthored by Robert Allen and Drew Pearson in 1931, was basically a muckraking compilation of facts and anecdotes about President Herbert Hoover and other government and society leaders in Washington, D.C. When authorship of the book was made known, however, Allen lost his job as chief of the Washington bureau of the *Christian Science*

Monitor, and Pearson was fired as State Department correspondent for the *Baltimore Sun.*[5] The "Merry-Go-Round" column, which first appeared on November 17, 1932, evolved from the initial Pearson-Allen book and its follow-up, *More Merry-Go-Round,* which was published in 1932. Allen later wrote of the "experimental" nature of the muckraking column, "After the 1932 Presidential campaign we had decided to try our hand at an innovation in Washington reporting—a column which offered the type of material and verve that our book did."[6]

Initially, newspaper syndicates showed little interest in a daily "Merry-Go-Round." Finally, Karl Bickel of United Feature Syndicate agreed to "experiment" with the column. Samples were sent to most of the nation's editors, but few were impressed. At the end of the first few months, in early 1933, only 6 newspapers had subscribed. However, the number ballooned to 270 by May 1934.[7] It began to appear that Bickel had made a sound decision, and it was equally obvious that Pearson's and Allen's financial resources were bound to rise considerably above the twenty-five dollars a week each received after they first signed with the syndicate.[8] Both the title and content of the column rapidly became known across the country.[9] Pearson and Allen sparked a journalistic trend toward interpretive and investigative reporting of national affairs on a more intense scale than ever before practiced.[10]

The significance of the early "Merry-Go-Round" was pointed out in a book published in 1944 by Charles Fisher, then a writer for the *Philadelphia Record.* The volume evaluated many of the primary syndicated columnists of the day and praised the "Merry-Go-Round" for being the first truly national Washington-based column.

> Whatever its record of accurate prophecy and interpretation, the "Merry-Go-Round" is a production of some historic importance in American journalism. It was one of the great factors in the change in the coverage of national politics which began with the New Deal. It pried so assiduously into

> doings behind the white marble and boiled shirt facade of the Capital, made public so many of the stories which had been circulated with relish in the National Press Club but kept reverently off the news wires, that other news-gathering agencies were compelled to follow suit.[11]

Pearson and Allen saw advantages in the syndicated column. They claimed that, under a single employer, the paid employee must follow the mandates of his immediate superior; with hundreds of employers (client newspapers), however, chances were better that they would get their points to the public in one paper or another.[12]

Nevertheless, controversy surrounded the column from its beginning. The "Merry-Go-Round" consistently supported New Deal measures; therefore, many conservative editors would have preferred not to publish it. Because of the instant popularity of the enterprise, however, editors who rejected the column faced the possibility that a competing newspaper might carry it.[13]

By 1939 the "Merry-Go-Round" was being heralded as the most widely circulated column in the world "which specializes in giving the hotfoot to dignitaries."[14] It proved so popular that in December 1944, the Bell Syndicate offered Pearson $80,000 a year for his articles—$20,000 more than United Feature was paying. Pearson quickly agreed. In 1944 the column was carried by 508 daily and Sunday newspapers.[15] By 1948 the subscribers had risen to nearly six hundred, with more than 20 million readers.[16]

In the early days of the column, Pearson and Allen divided the work. Pearson generally covered the State Department and diplomatic corps. Allen concentrated on the Congress, the Supreme Court, and such miscellanea as labor unions.[17] Their methods, however, differed greatly. Allen chose to gather his news rather informally. Schooled as a "beat man," he continued the practice, though he had gained a certain prestige as coauthor of the column. Pearson also gathered material effectively, but in another style. His reporting "was done largely in dinner clothes or tails." He picked up a great deal of information "moving decorously in the world of fashion."[18]

Despite their antithetical approaches, the men worked effectively together. One national magazine in 1939 made vivid their compatibility:

> Pearson, son of a Quaker professor, is smooth, Anthony Edenish, complex and a Boy Scout at heart. . . . One might suspect him of being a teacher, a deacon, or a dentist, never a news hound. Allen, an ex–Army sergeant, is bombastic, scornful, and outwardly uncomplicated. . . . He fumes and swears and tears off in all directions, exactly the type one would expect to be a bang-up reporter.[19]

From its inception, the "Merry-Go-Round" was a nemesis of government officials. Even in the early years it was not unusual for Pearson or Allen to discover his telephone was being tapped. Pearson, in fact, always assumed that his telephone conversations were being intercepted. Therefore, when he wanted to leak a story that was not true, he would sometimes arrange for a friend to call in order that the two could discuss the fictitious subject.[20] Surveillance, however, did not seem to greatly bother Pearson and Allen during this time. One magazine article simply said: "It amuses them to know they have the federal government biting its nails."[21]

The team of Pearson and Allen was broken up as World War II erupted. Allen reenlisted in the army, where he rose to the rank of colonel. After the war, he apparently had no strong desire to return to the column. The two agreed to end the partnership; Pearson consented to pay Allen $45,000 over a six-year period in overdue allowances.[22]

Pearson, growing more aggressive with the years, continued to expose. *Newsweek* illustrated the columnist's "Merry-Go-Round" style:

> Pearson devoted himself to uncovering corruption in government, feuding with his numerous enemies and promoting a wide variety of personal and political cases with a missionary zeal. In the process he managed to create his own powerful yet electric form of journalism, a highly personal mix of gossip, sentimentality and investigative reporting.[23]

The column built a reputation for "hard-hitting reporting, liberal politics—and often irresponsible techniques."[24]

No one appeared to be neutral toward Pearson; people seemed to greatly respect or despise him. This became evident whenever a particularly controversial topic or individual was dissected. For example, when Pearson and Jack Anderson published their series of columns in the middle 1960s alleging fiscal malfeasance on the part of Sen. Thomas Dodd of Connecticut, most members of the Senate chose to ignore it, at least initially. The *Nation,* in an editorial, praised Pearson and Anderson for their efforts. The editorial pointed to the irony of the circumstances immediately following the "Merry-Go-Round" allegations: the Department of Justice launched an investigation, but not of Dodd; instead, it centered upon the columnists' use of Dodd's files. The editorial claimed that "this seems an odd reaction to charges of such gravity." The editorial further praised Pearson:

> Drew Pearson practices a difficult but necessary kind of journalism. He does not have the power of subpoena nor the right to cross-examine under oath. What he does have are a capable leg man—Jack Anderson—numerous contacts, a good news sense and courage. Sometimes he misses, but there is no denying the unique service he has performed in an age in which newsmen play it safe more often than not.[25]

Such incidents and comments illustrate the mixed reactions of people and institutions toward the controversial column. Recipients of the sharp criticisms of "Merry-Go-Round" writers choose to belittle or ignore the column. Others, as evidenced by the *Nation's* editorial, are appreciative of the service.

The Current-Era "Merry-Go-Round"

When Anderson took control of the column upon Pearson's death in September 1969, the inheritor claimed it would be somewhat different. "Basically Drew was issue-oriented," Anderson told a national newsmagazine. "He had his heroes and villains and painted issues in blacks and whites.[26] Anderson's remarks, however, should not be interpreted as harsh criticism of his mentor. He always looked upon Pearson as a father figure. Pearson's death came as a shock to his junior associate. Anderson felt numb; to this day he has no clear recollection of the first month after he assumed control of the column. He recalls, however, that he felt an "awesome responsibility."[27]

Time, in a generally complimentary cover story on Anderson, referred to the modern "Merry-Go-Round" as a "mish-mash with an uneven history." Reference was made to the "dry spell" of news scoops immediately after Pearson's death, when the column often zeroed in on trivial items. This dearth of news did not last long, however, thanks to the actions of the American government and the International Telephone and Telegraph Company that Anderson uncovered.[28]

Former "Merry-Go-Round" reporter Brit Hume outlined the differences in the column after Anderson took it over:

> Under Pearson, the column had been an unpredictable mix of muckraking, crusading, and personal commentary. Corrupt officials had gone to jail because of Pearson's reporting and countless stories had been told that never would have without him. Even Pearson's enemies conceded that his mere presence made honest men of many officials who might otherwise not have been. . . . He was an international celebrity and one of the journalistic giants of the century. . . . Pearson was tendentious, an arch-liberal, at times a careless reporter.[29]

Anderson, in contrast, was described as "sort of a pastel character."

When Anderson took over the column, he refrained from writing opinion, depending instead on investigative reporting in its pure sense. Though Anderson has often been credited with bringing more of a sense of fairness to the column, he, like Pearson, has his critics. Oliver Pilat, a Pearson biographer, wrote that Anderson is no match for his predecessor. Pilat predicted that, without the "knight-errant mantle of his predecessor," Anderson will remain merely a "muckraker, compared to Drew Pearson, muckraker-crusader."[30]

Anderson, meanwhile, is proud of the fact that, though he may not be as colorful as his mentor, the "Merry-Go-Round" continues as "a court of last resort for the voiceless, the little people." More than three hundred letters are received by the column daily; many contain news tips. The "Merry-Go-Round" under Anderson is regarded as one of the most influential columns in the country, mainly because the "self-styled investigative reporter gives it an inside-Washington flavor readily absorbed in the hinterland."[31]

The Column's Muckraking Heritage

Pearson and Anderson are routinely categorized as muckrakers. It is important, however, to understand what the label implies. Historical purists place the dates 1902–1912 on muckraking's literary tombstone, but "Merry-Go-Round" columns since 1932 make it plain that this type of reporting endures.

To fully appreciate muckrakers of Pearson's and Anderson's caliber, it is necessary to analyze the historical link between their writings and those of earlier periods. The modern era's breed can trace its literary name to the turn of the twentieth century, when President Theodore Roosevelt first applied the label to crusading journalists. In a speech on April 14, 1906, at the laying of the cornerstone of the U.S. House of Representatives office building in Washington, Roosevelt described reform journalists as "muckrakers."[32]

The President recalled John Bunyan's description in *Pilgrim's Progress* of the man with the muckrake. The man could look no way but downward, with a muckrake in his hands. Invited to abandon his rake and join the search for the celestial crown, he chose to continue raking the filth of the floor. Roosevelt said the muckraker "typifies the man who in this life consistently refuses to see aught that is lofty, and fixes his eyes with solemn intentness only on that which is vile and debasing."

It did not take long for the "muckraking" label to be affixed to reformers who were engaged in denouncing corruption, "whether or not they deserved the odium explicit in the President's application of the epithet."[33]

It would be erroneous to assume, however, that muckraking suddenly developed at the turn of the twentieth century. Though the name was coined then, there is ample evidence of waves of exposure during the nineteenth century. The *New York Times* exposé of the Boss Tweed scandal shortly after the Civil War is a prime example. Frederic Hudson of the *New York Herald* credited the *Times* with the utter annihilation of the Tweed ring. In 1873, he wrote that "there has been nothing equal to the result thus obtained in the history of journalism."[34]

Emphasizing the existence of nineteenth-century investigative exposure, journalism educator Warren T. Francke wrote:

> While overshadowed by the Muckraking Era . . . the sensational, crusading, muckraking, investigative exposures of the nineteenth century have not been entirely ignored. To a great extent, changing genre, changing conceptual terms and changing social conditions served to separate common journalistic experience. From time to time, the enduring line of reportorial experience has been reknotted.[35]

Regardless of their antecedents, progressive era investigative journalists of exposure transformed muckraking into a national phenomenon.

Almost overnight, it appears, muckraking works began to dominate many of the mass-circulation magazines. The phenomenon, unknown on a national scale in 1901, was spreading rapidly by 1903 and by 1904 was "shaking the nation's magazine journalism with revelations and challenges."[36]

The muckraking movement waned during the 1920s. People for the most part were war weary and satisfied with America. The *New Republic* and the *Nation* were among the few magazines that continued the muckraking tradition during those years.[37]

Pearson's and Allen's "Merry-Go-Round" column, in turn, helped keep muckraking alive in the pre-World War II years. One writer emphasized the importance of the column:

> Mixing gossip and muckraking, the columns and broadcasts of Drew Pearson from the 1930s onward achieved con-

siderable public influence despite mild support from the mass audiences for muckraking. Then, after the war, muckraking books began appearing in increasing numbers.[38]

Pearson and Allen also carried on their muckraking crusade during the depression years with four books: *Washington Merry-Go-Round* (1931), *More Merry-Go-Round* (1932), *The Nine Old Men* (1936), and *Nine Old Men at the Crossroads* (1937).[39]

America looked ahead to better days after World War II, but its goal was never carried to the ultimate because of the subsequent cold war. Muckraking enjoyed a slight revival as Pearson continued his "Merry-Go-Round" writing and as several exposes of other authors made their appearance on the market.[40] In addition to the popular column, Pearson and Anderson coauthored two books during this period: *U.S.A.—Second-Class Power?* (1958) and *The Case Against Congress* (1968). Both belong in the muckraking category.

Social upheavals in the 1960s and Watergate revelations in the 1970s have spurred a modern upsurge in muckraking. Writings of the late Pearson, Anderson, and other contemporary muckrakers can be compared with those of the most prominent progressive era practitioners. Many of the governmental, societal, and business issues that so dominated the classical period's writings are found among the primary themes of today's journalists of investigative exposure.

Muckraking Role of "Merry-Go-Round" Writers

The "Merry-Go-Round" syndicated newspaper column's primary writers, the late Pearson and Anderson, are so matter-of-factly characterized as journalists of exposure that one recent book simply labeled the column, "Muckrakers, Inc."[41] Anderson, together with consumer advocate Ralph Nader, have been termed "at least as devastating in their attacks on corruption and privilege as the [Lincoln] Steffenses and [David Graham] Phillipses of an earlier period."[42]

One link between Pearson and Anderson and the progressive era muckrakers is the "use of tantalizing gossip and slangy language"—which may have helped to swell the column's subscriber list to its present total of nearly one thousand newspapers.[43]

Another link between past and present muckrakers is their shared, genuine concern for the welfare of the nation. The criticism leveled by the early muckrakers was a result of "pride in their nation and their awareness of forces which conceivably could endanger her well being."[44] S. S. McClure wrote: "For the new patriotism is not that which shuts its eyes and boasts, fires rockets and fails to vote. It is that which sees the truth, faces and fights any enemy of the country, at home or abroad, or in any disguise."[45]

Contemporary muckrakers, such as "Merry-Go-Round" writers, also believe that their exposure of government wrongdoing is in the best interests of society. Anderson has been described as a "Robin Hood-type sophisticated heckler," who is hard on the powerful and the champion of the "little man." Though he makes politicians uneasy, he does not particularly enjoy it:

> At times I have wished I were in another business. When my staff and I do a job we are dealing with senators and Cabinet members. They are charming and nice. It would be much more pleasant to write only "good" things about them. Politicians are an insecure lot. And, they feel even more insecure around me. I don't want them to feel this way, but I won't let them bribe me with their friendship, either. Even the honest ones have done something they don't want to be made public. I don't get any enjoyment out of exposing people, but it is my responsibility.[46]

Homage was also paid Pearson as "watchdog" for the public. Some persons who were close to the columnist feel that he performed a unique public service: he kept government officials honest for fear of exposure. Nothing could stop Pearson from printing a story he believed to be true and in the public interest. It is possible that a healthy respect for Pearson's lethal pen deterred many officials from abusing their office.[47]

Pearson gloried in the name "muckraker." Anderson wrote the day after his mentor died:

> Drew Pearson was a muckraker. Of all the names he was called during four decades as Washington's top investigative reporter, muckraker was the one he liked best. It was symbolic of his career as a columnist, fighting the powerful and the privileged when he found them using the government to advance themselves.[48]

An editorial in the *New York Times* the same day vividly linked Pearson to the progressive era muckrakers:

> Drew Pearson was a descendent of the tradition made famous by such earlier practitioners as Lincoln Steffens and Upton Sinclair. For 36 years until his death at 71, his column adapted the untiring and often merciless skill of investigative political reporting, known popularly as muckraking.[49]

The *Times* editorial said Pearson's targets were determined neither by ideology nor by concern over the hostilities of popular figures or special interest groups. Despite occasional lapses in accuracy, Pearson "served an important cause in exposing violations of ethical and legal standards."[50]

It would be misleading, however, to assume that Pearson was so highly regarded by all people. One writer made the distinction obvious:

> Some considered him [Pearson] a talented practitioner of one of the loftiest forms of journalism—scourging the venal and corrupt in public life. Others abominated him as a skilled exponent of one of the basest forms of journalism—assassinating the character of selfless public servants through falsehood and distortion.[51]

No matter how others regarded him, however, Pearson took his role as a muckraker seriously. He once remarked that his job as a newspaperman was "to spur the lazy, watch the weak and expose the corrupt."[52]

Every congressman with "something to hide" likely feared Pearson. One biographer said "nobody ever hit Congress harder or more persistently than Drew Pearson." Representatives Ernest Bramblett of California, Walter Brehm of Ohio, Andrew May of Kentucky, and J. Parnell Thomas of New Jersey were sent to jail for fiscal wrongdoing, largely as a result of Pearson columns. The muckraker was also among the leaders in disclosing details of money manipulations of Sen. Thomas Dodd and Rep. Adam Clayton Powell.[53] Anderson, in fact, labeled the list of those exposed by his mentor as "almost a Who Was Who in America." In addition to the congressmen Pearson helped send to jail, Anderson cited the three Senate investigations of Sen. Joseph McCarthy that were sparked by the muckraker's disclosures.[54]

Pearson was constantly exposing and crying for reform in his columns. He called for Medicare, better meat inspection, oil pipeline safety, and health warnings for cigarettes—all before these causes became fashionable. He used the "Merry-Go-Round" to push for legislation he favored. However, Pearson carried his influence one step further: he often instructed his legmen to "warn committee members of reprisals if they voted wrong."[55]

The columnist was not afraid to write a story other reporters would not. He was first to report that Gen. George S. Patton had slapped a battle-fatigued recruit during the invasion of Sicily, a story other newsmen were aware of but withheld from print.[56] Nor did Pearson have any qualms about ignoring the unwritten rule then observed by the Washington press corps that the drinking habits of politicians were not authentic examples of news.[57]

Historians who specialize in twentieth-century muckrakers have repeatedly cited Anderson as the "outstanding muckraker of the times."[58] *Time,* in a recent cover story, concurred:

> Though obviously a creature of the muckraking philosophy, Anderson is in a class by himself. Unlike the ideologues who write for small or specialized publications, he has a mass audience. . . . Partly because he has triumphed over the frustrations suffered by others [he has no editor or publisher to directly second-guess his judgment], fellow muckrakers, almost to a man, hail Anderson as a hero.[59]

Anderson has broken several "big stories" since inheriting the column. His office-issued biography claims he was first to report that federal law-enforcement agencies were spying on American citizens; the first to write that the CIA has attempted to assassinate foreign leaders, including Cuban premier Fidel Castro; the first to report (February 1975) that the United States was contemplating military intervention in the volatile Middle East; the first to implicate John Mitchell and H. R. Haldeman in the Watergate scandal; the first to report that "hush money" had been offered Watergate defendants; and the first to report that President Nixon had no prior knowledge of the Watergate break-in, but had participated in the cover-up. His effects have also been felt in congressional circles. He takes credit for driving senators Dodd, George Murphy (a Republican from California), and Marlow Cook (a Republican from Kentucky) out of office. His series of columns also led to the resignation of Postmaster General Ted Klassen in the middle of his term.[60]

The muckraker gained widely heralded popularity in 1972, on the heels of two key disclosures. He linked International Telephone and Telegraph and the federal government with behind-the-scenes dealings regarding an antitrust settlement, and he was the first to report the United States "tilt" toward Pakistan in the Indo-Pakistan War. In fact, he become something of a national celebrity. His office was flooded with congratulatory mail and job applications of young, aspiring journalists.[61] A *Life* magazine article pointed to the irony of this: Anderson is not a flashy, perpetual-motion go-getter. Rather, he leads a "pristinely ascetic personal life, eschewing drink, tobacco and raucous living."[62]

Time emphasized the general change in attitude toward Anderson and the "Merry-Go-Round":

> Anderson may now be taken a little more seriously in Washington. His industriousness and courage have never been questioned, and the latest series of columns prove that his information pipelines indeed run deep.[63]

Former Anderson employee Brit Hume articulated that his boss's handling of the Indo-Pakistan affair "showed that muckraking, if accurate, will attract both the attention and praise of the rest of the media."[64]

Though Anderson was riding a high tide of popularity in early 1972 and would once again reach unprecedented heights with various Watergate revelations, things did not look so promising to "Merry-Go-Round" employees after the columnist claimed that Democratic vice-presidential aspirant Thomas Eagleton of Missouri had a long record of drunken-driving tickets. Anderson was unable to produce hard evidence to substantiate his charge. The columnist felt a particular despair after the incident. Hume said his boss had "risen to a position of fame and credibility never before achieved by a muckraking journalist and, almost overnight, he had lost it."[65]

Anderson has indeed worked diligently toward the cultivation of a more respectable product. He is succeeding, at least in the opinion of *Newsweek:*

> Despite . . . occasional slips, Anderson is generally credited with producing a fairer and more factual column than Pearson, who, for all his straitlaced ethics, occasionally rode ideological hobby horses and pursued personal vendettas.[66]

Though Anderson has continued to rake muck after inheriting the column, his methods are somewhat different from Pearson's. For example, Pearson did seldom check out a story with its subject, fearing he might lose the "scoop."[67] Anderson, on the other hand, believes that a "fundamental rule" of good journalism is always to go to the source to verify or disprove information. He gives his subjects a chance to respond to his charges. Denial on the part of the source would, of course, not necessarily prevent Anderson from printing information if other evidence were overwhelming.

In addition, Anderson has often said that he is more careful than Pearson in checking facts. He contends that "a fact doesn't become a fact until it can be proved." He once said:

> One must have documentation or an adequate number of sources to persuade a court [when involved in a libel action].

> Our rule is if we can bring three witnesses to court who are creditable, that should be enough to convince a court. We won't accept as a fact something just because somebody tells us it is. . . . It is only a lead for us until we can document it. . . . We would not use gossip. . . . I think gossip is unverified information; once we check it out it is no longer gossip.[68]

The muckraker operates on the theory that official government spokesmen are not going to tell him anything the government does not want him to know. He once said: "I have never known an official to call a press conference to confess his errors and mistakes. If I want to write what they want me to write I can look at their elaborate press kits."[69]

Anderson has broken many major stories, but his influence is difficult to measure, as was the case with the progressive era muckrakers. Though no laws have been passed as a result of his column, a number of former incumbents are now "retired" because of him.[70] Also, his influence has spread beyond his "Merry-Go-Round" writings and the books he coauthored with Pearson. Since 1952, for example, Anderson has either written or coauthored six others: *McCarthy: The Man, the Senator, the "Ism"* (1952); *The Kefauver Story* (1956); *Washington Exposé* (1967); *American Government . . . Like It Is* (1972); *The Anderson Papers* (1973); and *Confessions of a Muckraker* (1979).[71]

The Controversial Columnists

Naturally, Pearson's and Anderson's vivid writings have led to a number of controversies. Pearson physically tangled with Senator McCarthy and lobbyist Charles Patrick Clark. Most presidents from Franklin Roosevelt to Richard Nixon verbally chastised the columnist. Anderson, too, has been controversial. His battles with the Nixon administration resulted in litigation.

Pearson's relations with McCarthy were extremely volatile. In December 1950, at Washington's fashionable Sulgrave Club, the previously impersonal clash between the two came to a physical confrontation. Explaining that Pearson and

McCarthy had been hating each other for some time—at a distance—*Time* reported that

> the action started before the entree [it was a dinner party], and it had a certain air of grandeur: in their line, Pearson and McCarthy are the two biggest billygoats in the onion patch, and when they began butting, all present knew history was being made.[72]

The senator was apparently the aggressor. Encountering Pearson in the cloak room after the meal, McCarthy grabbed the columnist by the arms. There are varying reports of what happened next—but in characteristic fashion each claimed the next day that he had not been hurt by the other. McCarthy said he had "slapped Pearson with his open hand and knocked him down." One energetic McCarthy friend claimed the senator had lifted the columnist "three feet off the floor" with a solid punch. Pearson's story? He insisted that the senator had kicked him in the groin, twice—but that it hadn't hurt.[73]

When the story about the encounter spread through the press, reactions were mixed. Some twenty-four senators telephoned their congratulations to McCarthy, while the Wisconsin senator's office reportedly received one hundred fifty congratulatory telegrams.[74] Most people, however, made light of the incident. For Christmas, Pearson got a pair of miniature boxing gloves from his secretaries.[75] President Truman also saw humor in the encounter. He commented that he "enjoyed seeing those two skunks piss on each other."[76]

Just days after McCarthy slapped Pearson, the senator unleashed verbal barrages at the columnist. As usual, McCarthy attempted to link his adversary with the Communist party. Using his Senate shield from libel, McCarthy encouraged "loyal" Americans to notify newspapers carrying the Pearson column that they didn't want this "Moscow-directed character assassin being brought in to their homes to poison the well of information at which their children drink." In a vehement chastisement, which took up nearly eight pages in the *Congressional Record,* McCarthy mixed his remarks about Pearson with statements made by others. In one form or another, each of the remarks labeled Pearson a liar.[77]

The Wisconsin senator claimed that

> only a man as diabolically clever as Pearson could continue to maintain his huge reading and listening audience after being so completely and thoroughly labeled an unprincipled liar and a fake. It is impossible for me to understand how so many reputable newspapermen can buy the writings of this twisted, perverted mentality which so cleverly sugarcoats and disguises his fiendishly clever, long-range attempts to discredit and destroy in the minds of the American people all of the institutions which make up the very heart of this Republic.

After verbally linking Pearson to the Communist party, McCarthy tempered his remarks with the fact that the columnist had never actually signed up as a member of the party, nor had he ever paid dues.

As his psychological clincher, McCarthy insisted that Pearson was a Communist because he was continually criticizing the House Un-American Activities Committee:

> I ask those who are skeptical as to whether Pearson actually has been doing a job for the Communist Party to stop and review Pearson's record over the past ten years. You will find that he has always gone all-out to attack anyone who is attempting to expose individual and dangerous Communists, while at the same time he goes through the fakery of criticizing Communism and Communists generally. The heads of the House Un-American Activities Committee have always been his targets.

In concluding his vituperative rantings, McCarthy said he did not feel guilty about using his Senate shield against libel because Pearson did essentially the same thing. McCarthy claimed that most of the columnist's property had been "conveyed away to his wife" in order that it not become subject to judgments for libel. McCarthy said he would consent to repeat his remarks off the Senate floor if the muckraker would allow the properties to be applied toward payment of any future damages he might be assessed.

While McCarthy publicly placed the "Communist" label on Pearson, the Soviet press apparently saw things differently. Just months before McCarthy's blast, a Russian magazine published a strong attack against the columnist, calling him "the chained dog of monopolists of Wall Street." The official Soviet newspaper, *Pravda,* proclaimed that "the Pearson news cocktail is a mixture of one or two facts with a dose of anti-Soviet lying."[78] Thus, the columnist was being criticized by the Communist press for being a supreme capitalist while McCarthy, on the home front, was branding him a Communist.

Shortly after McCarthy chastised Pearson from the Senate floor, the American Veterans Committee called on the Eighty-second Congress to institute impeachment proceedings against the Wisconsin senator. The group issued a statement labeling the attack on Pearson "a threat to American freedom of expression."[79] The *New York Post,* meanwhile, editorialized that "McCarthy has . . . demanded that . . . newspaper and radio officials . . . suppress Pearson. This is as flagrant an attempt to intimidate the organs of free opinion as any ever undertaken in our history."[80]

In June 1952, Pearson had another brush with physical danger. Washington lawyer Charles Patrick Clark, a lobbyist for Franco's Spain, was the attacker. Pearson had earlier charged Clark with using "undue influence" to get Maine's Sen. Owen Brewster and Brooklyn Congressman Eugene Keogh to sponsor aid to Franco. Again, versions of the fight differed. Pearson claimed that Clark approached him while he was putting an after-dinner mint into his mouth at the Mayflower Hotel in Washington and "whammed me a helluva jolt on the neck." Clark, however, said he hit Pearson in the eye with his left fist, but swung and missed with his right. At the same time, he was reportedly yelling, "This is for [former Secretary of Defense James] Forrestal and Brewster and [Gen. Harry] Vaughan and Keogh and myself, you son of a bitch!" Pearson immediately charged to the office of the U.S. district attorney and swore out an assault warrant. Clark did not seem to mind terribly. *Time* magazine reported that he later "pranced about outside the Mayflower's main entrance, re-enacting the battle for the hotel doorman and passing senators."[81]

Though controversies such as these likely both irritated and amused Pearson, one troublesome episode cut much deeper; it involved America's first secretary of defense, James Forrestal. Forrestal committed suicide after resigning his defense post, and some critics believed Pearson and fellow journalist Walter Winchell were partly to blame because of their consistent attacks on the official. The columnists had questioned his emotional stability, his financial honesty, his patriotism, and "even his chivalry."[82] President Truman, however, had refused to take action against Forrestal because he did not want to appear subservient to the columnists' advice. Finally, in March 1949, Forrestal resigned. The "Merry-Go-Round" revealed that "Forrestal had run into the street from his home in Hobe Sound, Florida, shouting: 'The Russians are coming, the Russians are coming!' " This was the public's first notice of Forrestal's "psychotic break." He was admitted to Bethesda Naval Hospital for psychiatric care. Two months later, on May 22, 1949, he leaped to his death.[83]

Pearson devoted considerable space in his diary to his thoughts on the matter. He wrote that the former defense secretary really died "because he had no spiritual reserves. He had spent his entire life thinking only about himself." The columnist claimed that Forrestal's "passion was public approval," that he "craved it almost as a dope addict craves morphine. Toward the end he would break down and cry pitifully, like a child, when criticized too much." Pearson acknowledged that Forrestal was a loyal and patriotic American who had worked hard for his country, but "he seriously hurt the country he loved by taking his own life." Further, Pearson believed that Forrestal "did not know what the lash of criticism meant. He did not understand the give-and-take of the political arena."[84]

After Forrestal's suicide, there was widespread public reaction to treatment of the former defense secretary by columnists, particularly Pearson and Winchell. As a magazine for professional journalists pointed out, "members of Congress filled the *Congressional Record* with verbal scoldings of press and radio; letters-to-the-editor burned with indignation, and many columnists and editorial writers joined in the chorus."[85] The *Washington Post,* in fact, received several letters on the matter, some threatening to cancel subscriptions unless the "Merry-Go-Round" was dropped.

Meanwhile, President Truman, still chafing about Pearson's quick rebuttal to the "S.O.B." label the president had affixed on him, tried to make political hay out of the Forrestal suicide. Pearson wrote that Truman, at a staff conference, stated "that son-of-a-bitch Pearson got the best of me on the SOB thing, but I'm going to get the best of him on the Forrestal suicide. I'm going to rub it in until the public never forgets."[86]

Pearson's long-time nemesis, fellow columnist Westbrook Pegler, also got into the act. Pegler wrote that Forrestal was not merely a war casualty, as President Truman had said, but "was a victim of the wanton blackguardism and mendacity of the radio, which has been a professional specialty of Drew Pearson."[87] Pearson, who later filed a libel suit against Pegler for the remarks, claimed that his rival "virtually accused me of murdering Forrestal. Telegrams and telephone calls have been coming in singing the same song."[88]

The situation presented, on a national scale, the philosophical question of where the press should draw a dividing line: how far should it go "in its role as guardian of the nation's welfare and proper critic of the acts of its public officials?" *Time* declared that both Pearson and Winchell had overstepped "the bounds of accuracy and decency" and "both had strayed far from their responsibilities as journalists."[89]

As public reaction set in, Pearson reevaluated the role he might have played in the death. He wrote that "it looks like an organized campaign." The hurt was apparently deep. Pearson said that "people are repeating the charge that I killed Forrestal to the extent that I am almost beginning to lie awake nights wondering whether I did. Certainly a lot of people have convinced themselves that it is true."[90]

Pearson, however, thought that it was his duty to tell the country about any emotional shortcomings in a defense secretary, in spite of the man's popularity and even though Mrs. Pearson herself suggested he "lay off" a little. Drew repeatedly told her that the only way to get readers' attentions on important matters was to "hammer, hammer, hammer." The Forrestal columns were mentally difficult for Pearson to write, but he felt very strongly about telling the American people what he knew.[91]

Pearson's relations with American presidents during his muckraking career also merit examination. As might be expected, America's chief executives were never free from the columnist's wrath when the spirit or occasion moved him. His first major controversial brush with a president came in 1931, after *Washington Merry-Go-Round* was published. Parts of the book belittled President Hoover. Hoover, in turn, sought to learn who had written the book (it had been published anonymously). His discovery that Pearson and Allen were responsible did nothing to solidify relations between the men.[92] This was not, however, the first trouble between Pearson and Hoover. The columnist's negative attitude toward Hoover can be partially traced to the president's exclusion of Pearson from the guest list of a chartered ship carrying various American officials and members of the press to an international conference in South America. Angry, the columnist managed to wangle himself on board. Still, he did not appreciate the slight. But his success in joining the group further illustrates Pearson's aggressiveness and tenacity as a reporter. He always prided himself on his resourcefulness and ability to accomplish a task, no matter how great the odds.[93]

The columnist, though a New Deal liberal, thought nothing of attacking President Roosevelt in print.[94] As a result, his relations with FDR stopped short of cordiality. It was not until September of 1943, however, that Roosevelt blasted the columnist publicly. Pearson drew the president's wrath for stating in his column that Secretary of State Cordell Hull had long been anti-Russian. Coming during the middle of World War II, this did not set well with Roosevelt.

The president released his frustration in colorful style: he managed to describe Pearson as a "chronic liar" without once referring to the columnist by name. Told of FDR's remarks, Pearson replied: "I am complimented to join the long list of newspapermen whom the President has attacked. However, the Russians, being shrewd diplomats, were fully aware of Mr. Hull's long and consistent anti-Russian attitudes. It didn't take me to tell them about it."[95]

I. F. Stone, writing in the *Nation*, speculated that FDR, by labeling Pearson a "chronic liar," was using the columnist as an example of White House regard toward sometimes critical columnists. Indeed, the article labeled the president's attack "ill-tempered" and "unfair." The account also pointed to a *Washington Post* editorial that defended Pearson. The *Post* said it regarded the president's conduct as "unworthy" and "unbecoming" and a "gross libel on some fearless and necessary work by Mr. Pearson." Stone further said:

> Like the rest of us, Drew Pearson has made his quota of mistakes, but "chronic liar" is a strong term and the press corps has long memories. It easily recalls the many occasions on which the State Department—and the White House—has indignantly denied "Merry-Go-Round" stories which were later confirmed.[96]

Press observers at the time pointed out that, unlike Stone and the *Washington Post*, most of Pearson's colleagues did not rush to defend him, as would normally have been the case when a member of the press was openly criticized by a public official. *Time* simply said that Pearson was "not popular with his colleagues" and was "frequently guilty of colossal errors of fact."[97]

Pearson's experience with Roosevelt apparently did not intimidate him in his treatment of the next U.S. president, Harry S Truman.

Truman softly nudged the columnist in January of 1946 when he upbraided Pearson for telling a "whopper" on Mrs.

Truman. It seems that Pearson reported that the first lady had taken a private railroad car back to Washington after visiting in Missouri; the president said it wasn't a private car. *Newsweek* was philosophical about the presidential criticism. It said that "Pearson departed with this distinction: for whatever it may be worth, he is the only correspondent in Washington denounced personally by two Presidents."[98]

It was three years later, however, that Truman really berated the muckraking columnist. The president was addressing a meeting of the Reserve Officers Association at the Army-Navy Country Club, Arlington, Virginia. The dinner was in honor of Truman's military aide, Maj. Gen. Harry Vaughan, a man Pearson had often criticized in his column. Since Truman had already labeled Pearson a "liar," what he had to say did not come as a complete shock. After delivering some "nostalgic comments on the military life" of Vaughan, Truman got to the heart of the matter:

> Now, I am just as fond of and just as loyal to my military aide as I am to the high brass, and I want you to distinctly understand that any S.O.B. who thinks he can cause any of these people to be discharged by me by some smart-aleck statement over the air or in the paper, he has got another think coming. No commentator or columnist names any members of my Cabinet or my staff. I name them myself and when it is time for them to be moved on, I do the moving—nobody else.[99]

The news of the president's remarks was immediately made public. They did, however, create some touchy problems for a few people. For example, the official White House stenographer changed "any S.O.B." to "anyone." The original phrase, however, had already been noted by newsmen and made the Teletype rounds in a matter of minutes. Radio commentators, apparently fearful of the 1934 Communications Act's rule against profanity, "worked hard to keep their language more sedate than the President's."[100] The *Washington Post* made the story its front-page lead. Looking out for the most naive readers, the *Post* reported that "the President, in his address, used the letters S.O.B., which are often used as an abbreviation for profanity."[101]

The *New York Times* also carried the story on page one. In the body of the story was a comment issued by Pearson:

> If Mr. Truman is trying to discourage the right of fair comment, then he, too, has another think coming. The men on his staff are his business—even though the taxpayers have to foot the bill. But when his staff members accept medals from a military dictator [Pearson had earlier criticized Vaughan for accepting the decoration of the Order of San Martin from Argentina] whose principles this government has denounced, then it is the public's business and should be Truman's.[102]

Despite the rebuttal, Truman was apparently quite pleased with himself for placing the "S.O.B." label on the columnist. As reaction spread across the country, Truman said he found it "quite satisfactory."[103]

The *St. Louis Post-Dispatch*, for example, editorially said it understood the president's motives. In a one-paragraph editorial, the *Post-Dispatch* opined that,

> While it will be argued, we suppose, that Presidents cannot afford to be human and must always retain their tempers, we can well understand the President's use of the term S.O.B. as applied to a certain showman and think that, considering all the circumstances, it was very well applied. In this case Harry Truman does not need our sympathy, but if he wants it he has it.[104]

The *Washington Post* was editorially critical of Truman's remark. Claiming that the president, since his election, had grown "prodigiously both in public esteem and self-esteem," the editorial also said "it appears that it is 'vicious and unjustified' to attack a friend of the President."[105] Meanwhile, the Reverend Carl McIntire, president of the International Council of Christian Churches, publicly stated that Truman should "apologize to the American people" for using the "S.O.B." term.[106]

Pearson's relationship with Truman was stormy, to say the least. Both were peppery individuals; the columnist often regarded their verbal exchanges as "sparring" matches. Neither man brooded much about the other's remarks. In fact, Pearson sought an interview with Truman after he left the White House. The former president accepted, and the two men became friends again.[107]

Pearson got himself in trouble with the Eisenhower administration early. Some one hundred seventy-five newsmen had gathered to watch films of the first hydrogen bomb blast at Eniwetok in 1952. The administration, however, had placed a one-week hold on the film and information, so that magazines and newsreel producers could get an even break with the daily press. Before the week was up, Pearson carried a description of the "monstrous fireball" in his column. This, of course, broke the release, and other papers quickly followed. When criticized by press secretary James C. Hagerty, Pearson had a perfectly logical explanation—a clarification that showed the extent of his governmental news sources. The columnist explained that he did not purposely break the release date, because he did not even know about it; he had not attended the film showing. Rather, because he "had nothing better to write about," he had sent the column out to his subscribing newspapers before the film was even shown. Pearson later snapped, "Just because I pulled an April Fool scoop [it was April of 1954] is no reason for their accusations."[108]

A little more than two years later, Pearson reported that President Eisenhower had suffered a "mild relapse" of heart trouble while driving in a parade through Minneapolis. Pearson reported that Eisenhower's car "took off" from the motorcade and "sped" to the airport. He said in his column that the story would be denied by the administration. This prediction proved correct. Hagerty branded the column "the most amazing document of falsehood" that he had ever seen. According to the press secretary, it included at least "ten misstatements of fact." Though several other correspondents backed the administration's correction, Pearson refused to change his column. He simply stated, "My story was carefully checked, and I believe it to be true."[109] As *Newsweek* pointed out in connection with a similar incident, the columnist had been branded a "liar" by two Democratic presidents (FDR and Truman); the gesture by the Republican Eisenhower administration merely made it "bipartisan."[110] Though Eisenhower never came up with anything so sensational as "liar" or "S.O.B.," he did once say that he considered any newspaper that carried the "Merry-Go-Round" to be "irresponsible."[111]

Tyler Abell once described the columnist's relationship with Eisenhower as his worst with any president. Eisenhower did to Pearson what the muckraker had extreme difficulty tolerating—the president ignored him. Even when Drew wrote something that Eisenhower obviously resented or disliked, the president remained silent, refusing to be drawn into a controversy.[112]

The muckraking columnist, out of political bias, usually zeroed in on Republican administrations more than Democratic, but his relationship with John F. Kennedy was not particularly strong. The two men never cultivated a bond of friendship. Kennedy was, however, interested in the exclusive talks Pearson had had with Khrushchev during the summer of 1961.[113]

Pearson's relationship with Lyndon Johnson was another matter. Though he never hesitated to criticize the Texan, Pearson was basically pro-Johnson. They had first met as "New Dealers" in the 1930s. During the Johnson presidency, Pearson enjoyed ample access to the White House. The columnist's involvement with Johnson was his most interesting presidential relationship. Though Pearson had written some harsh things about LBJ when the latter was in the Senate, the criticism tapered off considerably after Johnson ascended to the White House. Pearson, approving LBJ's increasing liberalism during his years in the Oval Office, backed him almost one hundred percent. According to Abell,

> Johnson manipulated Drew. I don't think there was any question of it. He promised Drew things that he did not deliver. . . . Johnson was such a good manipulator that he

> would soft-soap Drew. . . . This goes back to the fact that Drew was basically softhearted. When people would approach Drew on a purely private basis, if they had any grounds, they could often talk him around.[114]

Still, the columnist truly admired Johnson, respecting him as a politician and friend. Mrs. Pearson, in fact, decided to put her husband's papers in the LBJ Library in Austin, Texas, because she felt "Drew would like them there."[115]

Given Pearson's preference for Democratic presidents, most people felt the columnist would come down hard on President Richard Nixon. The columnist had never had much of a personal relationship with Nixon, but he had been critical of the politician as early as 1948 when Nixon sought election to the U.S. Senate. As far as Pearson was concerned, Nixon was completely on the McCarthy side of the fence during the early 1950s and was an unprincipled, opportunistic politician.[116] However, the muckraker was not overly critical of President Nixon during his "honeymoon" months in the Oval Office, and during Nixon's first year as president, Pearson died.

Pearson's designated successor, Anderson, was not so lenient with the Republican leader. In his book, *An American Life*, Jeb Stuart Magruder, former special assistant to President Nixon, wrote that G. Gordon Liddy, former member of the "Plumbers," a special White House investigations unit, once came into his office to discuss a legal matter. At the close of the business conversation, Magruder said he "grumbled about some columns Jack Anderson had been writing that were embarrassing to the Administration."[117] Magruder went on to exclaim, "Boy, it'd be nice if we could get rid of that guy." Magruder went back to work, only to have his administrative assistant burst into his office with "a look of horror on his face." The assistant asked Magruder if he had told Liddy to kill Jack Anderson. Magruder wrote that he immediately dispatched his assistant to stop Liddy. The task was accomplished before Liddy got out of the building. A shaken Magruder then explained to the "Plumber" that he was "just using a figure of speech about getting rid of Anderson."[118]

This episode illustrates the stormy relationship between Anderson and the Nixon administration—a sometimes hostile coexistence that culminated in the courts. As the Watergate proceedings were winding down, on September 27, 1976, Anderson filed suit for $22 million in damages from Nixon and nineteen subordinates.[119] The suit, which was dismissed on April 4, 1978, by the Federal District Court for the District of Columbia, accused Nixon and his aides of conducting a five-year campaign to take away the columnist's First Amendment rights and destroy his credibility. It cited seventeen allegations of harassment, investigations, or surveillance by the CIA or the "Plumbers."

Though Anderson was deadly serious when he brought the action, he nevertheless poked fun at the Nixon administration and its attempts to discredit him. For example, the muckraker once ridiculed a Central Intelligence Agency surveillance of him. Anderson labeled the surveillance "a CIA farce, an exercise in domestic deviltry, a Mack Sennett comedy come true." The columnist revealed that he was tipped off that his home was under CIA surveillance; the source supplied the muckraker with the license numbers of the stakeout cars. Anderson then launched a counterattack:

> I unleashed my nine children to initiate their own surveillance of the surveillants. My junior sleuths not only located the cars but photographed them. On April 3, 1972, the men with the binoculars ceased their vigil, perhaps demoralized by the countersnooping of my Katzenjammer paparazzi. . . . Watch out, CIA! The kids on my block are ready for you![120]

Anderson also commented that "no President should be permitted to marshal the awesome powers of government against a reporter, not even for the grievous offense of embarrassing the White House."[121]

Obviously, when a column exists primarily to expose wrongdoing in high places, controversy, intrigue, emotional public reaction—and, of course, lawsuits—logically materialize. As one might expect, aggressive, muckraking "Merry-Go-Round" writers who specialize in telling of governmental, societal, and business deficiencies—and the men responsible for those shortcomings—have been involved in a number of noteworthy libel suits.

A Profile in Libel

Extensive controversies have centered around a host of lawsuits, mostly libel, brought against writers of the column. There is no complete list of Pearson or "Merry-Go-Round" lawsuits. There have been scores, but opinions as to their number vary. *Newsweek* reported that Pearson was involved in some fifty libel cases during his career.[122] Just before his death, the columnist said he could not recall how often he had been sued, but he estimated "maybe fifty times."[123] The *New York Times* Pearson obituary said the muckraker was sued, "maybe fifty times," mostly without success.[124] Pearson, in 1966, told a *Wall Street Journal* reporter that he had been sued for libel "about two dozen times."[125] The late columnist told Anderson that he had been involved in "about twenty-five" libel suits.[126] Other persons, including Pearson's step-son, Tyler Abell, a Washington, D.C., attorney, have indicated that there were so many suits they would not venture a guess as to their number.[127]

Though Anderson has carried on the muckraking practices of his predecessor, he has not been besieged with lawsuits. Since Pearson's death, Anderson has been actively involved in four suits as a defendant;[128] he has been a plaintiff in two others.[129]

Since most of the suits that involved the "Merry-Go-Round" were unreported, their precise number will perhaps never be determined. However, during the column's nearly half-century existence, its writers have undoubtedly been in more actions than any other American syndicated columnists. This book discusses 126 libel actions—including sixty-eight suits filed by Ohio Congressman Martin L. Sweeney—that involve the column.[130] To further illustrate the columnists' involvement in litigation, an additional nine nonlibel actions—such as copyright, invasion of privacy, even assault and battery—are examined.

It is little wonder "Merry-Go-Round" writers have been a party to so much litigation. By Pearson's own count in 1956, he had been publicly denounced by fifty-four senators and congressmen, called a liar by two presidents (Harry S Truman and Franklin D. Roosevelt), officially investigated a dozen times for news leaks, and called eight times before congressional committees.[131] On the other hand, various journalists elevated Pearson and Anderson to high status among the century's muckrakers.

Pearson was a pioneer in Washington-based investigative reporting. Thus, his unprecedented aggressive methods proved irritating and frustrating to many public officials who, not accustomed to such harsh treatment by the press, sought satisfaction in the courts. One magazine article in 1945 graphically told of the muckraker's relationship with officialdom:

> Among Washington officeholders, Pearson is one of the most hated and feared men, and concern over what he will print or say next has caused more stomach ulcers in high places than any other single course of worry. The concern is felt through all the levels of government, for Pearson has pipelines throughout the structure.[132]

Anderson and his staff have also assembled an extraordinary number of sources. Though Anderson has not been dragged through the courts to the extent his predecessor was, he is nevertheless quite aware of the pitfalls that await any slip of the pen he might make. In fact, it did not take Anderson long to realize that "Merry-Go-Round" writers must constantly look over their shoulder for fear of libel. The young journalist had been with Pearson only two years when he thought it wise to return to college for one refresher course: libel law.[133]

In view of criticism of the column in some quarters, Anderson's decision was logical. In an article published in 1944, Pearson was labeled "the main White House stooge and sewer-level rumor monger that he was when he and a former reportial consort [Robert S. Allen, Pearson's "Merry-Go-Round" partner for nearly a decade] stood fin over flapper above any other White House sycophants in history—past, present and undoubtedly future." The article went on to say that, since Allen had left the column, "Pearson now grinds out all by his own self a thousand words of festooned baloney each day and peddles it to about three hundred careless newspaper publishers."[134]

The author of the article claimed that Pearson had a built-in libel protection because, in order to sue the muckraker, the plaintiff would also have to sue a newspaper in which the column in question had been published. The writer reasoned that, since the action would have to be brought in the newspaper's jurisdiction, it would be difficult to get a guilty verdict: "What local politician wearing the robes of a judge is going to refuse a favor to the local newspaper which can make or break him at the next election? Lucky Drew!" Whether such observations were valid or not cannot be determined, but there were countless similar remarks.

Though Pearson was widely criticized, he was not without his admirers. Ernest Cuneo, a Washington, D.C., attorney and writer, once described the muckraker as a "Quaker with a concern." Cuneo said that, when Pearson felt he was right, he was as tenacious as a bulldog. He assumed libel actions were part of the fight. "He would stay until the absolute bulldog finish," Cuneo said.

Cuneo paid Pearson high tribute when he evaluated the muckraker's effects on American journalism: "I feel Drew Pearson had a greater impact on his times than Horace Greeley during the Lincoln era. Pearson was a great man. He was the most loyal, courageous, and dogged man I ever knew."[135]

Newsweek, however, once pointed out that "muckraking, Pearson style" often resulted in libel suits.[136] This same magazine, in an article on the top Washington by-lines, claimed that congressmen diligently read the "Merry-Go-Round," but

Pearson's frequent court appearances on libel charges kept him from being considered a "final source."[137] Lawsuits evolved from well-publicized Pearson battles with such notables as Gen. Douglas MacArthur, Senator McCarthy, Representative Sweeney, columnist Pegler, right-wing radio commentator Father Charles E. Coughlin of Michigan, Representative Keogh of New York, and Senator Dodd of Connecticut. While most columnists shy away from libel actions —as defendants as well as plaintiffs—Pearson's record is marked by an abundance of cases in which he filled both roles with equal aggressiveness.[138]

Pearson, who was not as thick-skinned as he would have liked others to believe, kept a small file of articles in which he was blatantly criticized. The muckraker, it appears, was always on the lookout for potentially libelous materials written about him. He also kept a file containing letters from many persons who felt they had been libeled by him. Pearson would normally write a pleasant letter to the individual saying, in effect, that he was standing by his statements.

Despite the fact that he was sued for libel more than any fellow syndicated columnist, Pearson had to pay damages only once during his lifetime.[139] The $40,000 he had to pay in the single loss, however, was minute compared to the millions of dollars collectively sought in the scores of suits filed against the muckraker. Pearson's nearly blemish-free record in defending libel actions is indeed amazing when one considers that for nearly four decades he produced a daily column in which he consistently castigated some of the most powerful men in the world.

Pearson nevertheless realized the expense of the plethora of legal actions that involved him. He once wrote in the *Saturday Evening Post*:

> When my wife wonders why we have not accumulated more worldly goods, I can only reply that from 1947 to 1955 I spent $340,000 on legal fees. This is because I defend newspapers and radio stations that buy my material, and I never settle a case in its preliminary stage.[140]

The columnist, however, was philosophical about his involvements in extensive libel litigation. For example, he once told Chicago's Headline Club that "there is always the danger of libel suits in muckraking. One must be cautious and obtain airtight evidence before one accuses."[141]

Threat of a suit did not intimidate him; in fact, it sometimes excited him.[142] The muckraker regarded each libel suit brought against him as an affront to his honor; therefore, he was particularly tenacious in his defense.[143] There were few things Pearson approached with more vigor than defending himself against libel suits.[144] The *Washington Post* once remarked on Pearson's near-romantic enjoyment of conflict:

> Drew Pearson glorified in his feuds. To him "liar" from Franklin D. Roosevelt and "S.O.B." from Harry Truman were akin to encomiums. He relished denunciations from the protected floor of Senate and House.[145]

The muckraker had so many suits filed against him that he seemed constantly preoccupied with them; they demanded so much of his time, money, and energy that they nearly put him out of business on more than one occasion.[146] Many of the suits were little more than poorly disguised efforts to silence the columnist through extended, costly legal battles. Some actions were likely filed against the muckraker with little hope of winning; they were, rather, attempts to make his revelations impotent and to discredit the column.[147] Pearson naturally recognized these suits for what they were—time-consuming, money-draining ordeals. Still, he defended each of them to the end. He often allowed a pending action to absorb his thoughts and actions for up to half a day, but he had the remarkable capacity to "juggle twenty balls at the same time." Though he gave libel actions considerable thought and attention, to say nothing of money, he managed to keep the copy flowing for his daily column and regular radio broadcasts.[148]

Naturally it took more than a strong desire and willingness to expend time and money to successfully defend the suits; a knowledge of libel law was required. The columnist was the recipient of outstanding legal advice during his career, but he also had a sound understanding of libel law himself. Some of his friends contended, in fact, that Pearson knew more about libel law and its application than did most attorneys.[149]

Though the muckraker did not talk much about his involvements in libel actions, his friend Cuneo felt that Pearson contributed significantly toward the evolution of American libel law. Cuneo considered Pearson "the best expert on libel law in the country." Like the sailor who learns about the sea from day-to-day experiences, the columnist developed a firm grasp of libel law. For both, it was a matter of survival.[150]

A *Time* cover article on Pearson in 1948 said:

> Cagey Drew Pearson, a match for most libel lawyers, brags that he has not yet paid a judgment (though his attorneys' fees are huge). He will work for hours to make an item libel-proof or tone down the libel until it is not worth suing over. Editors seldom ask Pearson for proof. They know he will fight the case for them if they are sued. It is not altruism on his part. He cannot afford to lose many suits and stay in business.[151]

The muckraker stayed abreast of libel law developments. His interest in the law is illustrated by a letter he sent to Joseph Tumulty, a Washington attorney, regarding a case that the columnist felt was similar to one in which he was involved: "Undoubtedly in looking up cases on libel and Fascism, you have run across the case of *Consolidated Press* v. *New York World Telegram* in the New York Supreme Court. I believe it is written up in the *New York Law Journal* for January 31, 1938, page 507."[152]

Former secretary of state William P. Rogers, who worked with Pearson in a number of libel actions, recalled that the columnist "knew libel law, but he also let his attorneys handle his cases." Though the columnist was very active in gathering facts that might aid his defense, he did not tell his attorneys how to try a case.[153]

In addition to his sound knowledge of libel law, Pearson possessed an "internal instinct" on whether or not an individual he had criticized in his column might sue. Despite the threat of libel hanging over his head, Pearson often gambled on the unwillingness of people to file suits. He harassed or needled some individuals, appearing at times to be provoking the subject into suing. The columnist would, when he felt his information accurate, "take off" on an individual and "hit him from all directions, never being particularly concerned about a libel suit." As a general rule, if Pearson "really wanted somebody," he would not hesitate to print anything he felt pertinent.[154]

Pearson's vast involvement in litigation led him to think that he was capable of defending himself, without benefit of counsel. In fact, at the dinner table, the columnist often mentioned that one day he wanted to try his own libel case. Pearson's stepson Abell responded with the saying that only a fool has himself for a client, but Pearson "was a great one for rushing in where angels feared to tread."[155] The columnist's yearning to try a case himself, however, resulted in a blow to his ego.

Pearson's wife once parked his yellow Buick convertible near the entrance of Washington's Mayflower Hotel. While inside, Mrs. Pearson heard a crash, looked out, and, to her dismay, saw that a vehicle driven by a Mayflower parking attendant had shoved her car nearly to the front door of the hotel. The columnist, who had eaten lunch at the hotel on a regular basis for decades, demanded that the Mayflower buy him a new car. The hotel's insurance company countered that it would pay to repair the automobile. The stubborn Pearson, however, reacted by filing a suit seeking $6,000 in damages.[156] Pearson was told by his attorneys to negotiate a settlement with the insurance company, but the muckraker was intent on personally presenting his case to a jury.

His life as a lawyer, however, was unspectacularly short-lived. When initially addressing the jury, he asked if any of them had relatives who worked for insurance companies. The case was "thrown out almost before he closed his mouth." A mistrial was declared "before three seconds had elapsed."

The columnist ended up settling with the insurance company for much less than he could have received before taking his case to trial.[157]

Pearson's reluctance to take the advice of legal counsel also spread to his involvement in cases as a plaintiff. When the columnist decided to sue someone—despite the overwhelming probability that he would not be successful—he forged ahead with his plans. His attorneys continually told him he should not get involved in litigation as a plaintiff, but most of their appeals fell on deaf ears.[158] His good friend Cuneo echoed the attorneys: "I used to tell him time and again that the best story in the world was not worth the biggest libel suit. But he did not take my advice. . . . He had a concern. He walked the trails of the earth to help his fellow man; journalism became his instrument."[159] Mrs. Pearson also opposed her husband's so recklessly pursuing libel suits on his own. She felt one had to defend against them, but initiating them merely resulted in an unnecessary drain of time, money, and energy.[160]

Why have writers of the "Merry-Go-Round" column been so successful in defending against libel actions? The results would appear to defy the odds, especially in view of the public perception of the column. For example, William L. Rivers, in *The Opinion Makers*, said that "almost anything that smacks of wrong-doing is likely to get a wild ride on the 'Merry-Go-Round.' "[161] And the *Wall Street Journal* called the column "a collection of hard news, gossip, and prophecy that alternately delights or enrages Washingtonians, depending on its target for the day."[162] Such a reputation, it seems, would not be particularly conducive to winning libel actions initiated by some of the most prestigious men in the country.

Excellent legal advice has been a major factor in the column's astonishing success ratio in the courts. Pearson had the services of John Donovan as in-house counsel for nearly twenty-five years. Pearson once flatly labeled Donovan "the best libel law man in town,"[163] and others, including Washington, D.C., trial attorney F. Joseph Donohue, ranked him among the best-informed libel attorneys in the country. Donohue described Donovan as the "master of the technique of delay."[164] Abell said that his stepfather had great respect for Donovan's procedural abilities.[165]

Donovan's function was to examine libel complaints against the muckraker and handle all pretrial proceedings and filings. It was not unusual for a Pearson libel case to drag through the courts four or five years; dockets would be crammed with up to a dozen pages of defense motions. Thousands of pages of motions to dismiss, motions to reconsider, and answers to complaints were filed in some of the more important cases. This was Donovan's specialty. The time, energy, and money required to cope with such tactics overwhelmed some plaintiffs; their frustration is likely the reason so many of the suits against the columnist were dropped or dismissed before going to trial.[166]

Nevertheless, defending Pearson against libel actions was a full-time job. During the early 1950s, Donovan found litigation against his employer so heavy that he periodically sent a memo to the muckraker capsulizing the state of his legal affairs. On one occasion, Donovan listed fourteen pending actions involving the columnist.[167]

In addition to his role once a suit was filed, Donovan regularly read the "Merry-Go-Round" before distribution, often suggesting that certain passages be eliminated or "toned down." Pearson depended on his attorney a great deal; it was not uncommon for the columnist to get hold of Donovan before daylight to seek advice or offer opinions on pending actions.[168]

Pearson and Donovan met regularly to discuss strategy for pending libel actions. Donovan sometimes visited the columnist two or three times a day when a particularly worrisome case was pending.[169] The muckraker spared no expense—of money or energy—in defending against libel suits. He wanted, above all else, to maintain his integrity as a reporter. Though few of the suits filed against Pearson ever went to trial, when one did, the muckraker and Donovan generally selected a trial attorney who practiced in the geographical area where the case was to be heard; they chose a man with a proven record of success.

Once a case reached trial, Pearson made every effort to attend all the proceedings, despite the fact that doing so cut significantly into his writing time. Mrs. Pearson also attended many of her husband's trials; the columnist felt she was good luck.[170]

Pearson, of course, was extremely fortunate to have paid damages in only one case during his lifetime. A number of settlements would certainly have put him out of business. He carried no libel insurance because he did not want an insurance company constantly looking over his shoulder examining the content of his columns.[171]

Anderson has enjoyed the same kind of success in the courts as his late mentor, though he has been involved in far fewer cases. A number of factors help to explain why Anderson has not been sued as often as Pearson, but the most obvious reason is that columnists today have the advantage of functioning in a more liberal legal climate. In *New York Times Co.* v. *Sullivan* in 1964, the U.S. Supreme Court held that a state cannot, under the First and Fourteenth Amendments, award damages to a public official for defamatory falsehoods relating to his official conduct unless he proves "actual malice"—that the statement was made with knowledge of its falsity or with reckless disregard for the truth.[172] This holding obviously made libel battles for crusading, muckraking reporters much less demanding. Though the Court in 1974 retreated from the protection that the press had gained through a series of increasingly liberal decisions following *Sullivan,* newsmen still enjoy more legal freedom than they did prior to 1964.[173]

Like his predecessor, Anderson does not carry libel insurance. He explored the possibility, but decided it was too expensive. When insurance companies look at his fifty million circulation, the type of writing the column specializes in, and the important persons the column often deals with, premiums are placed at a lofty rate. Libel suits do not fascinate Anderson to the extent they did Pearson; still, the inheritor is very careful with his facts. He diligently checks each column for accuracy before it is distributed by the syndicate. However, his capable attorney, Warren Woods, does not read them ahead of time.[174]

Anderson categorizes most libel suits filed against him as "public relations": actions that allow subjects to claim that the column was wrong—as evidenced by their filing suit. Anderson has labeled the case filed by Senator Dodd an example.[175] The columnist said the facts he developed concerning Dodd were "overwhelming, but the Senate Ethics Committee 'pulled their punches.' In post-Watergate times, our disclosures would have led to criminal convictions."

Anderson does mirror Pearson's desire, on occasion, to file suit against others. Like Pearson's attorneys, Woods attempts to dissuade his client from entering into litigation as a plaintiff. But Anderson sometimes disregards him.

Libel suits involving writers of the "Merry-Go-Round" column are indeed multitudinous and captivating, but when one considers the backgrounds, styles, aggressiveness, pride, and muckraking heritage of Pearson and Anderson, it is little wonder they have found themselves in the courts so many times.

3

The "Merry-Go-Round" and Its Libel Law Boundaries

Like all journalists, writers of the syndicated "Merry-Go-Round" column must operate within the confines of existing libel law—or pay the consequences. Writers of the column have been labeled "liars" and "S.O.B.'s" by American presidents, accused of such destructive writing as to cause a federal official to leap to his death, verbally assaulted on the libel-proof congressional floor, physically attacked by irate officials, and made primary targets of government surveillance. Obviously, men who have stirred controversy to such an extreme must be particularly careful to stay within the boundaries of the constantly developing American libel law.

As the uneven, but perpetual, emergence of this legal phenomenon has taken place since the column's 1932 inception, writers such as the late Drew Pearson and Jack Anderson have been afforded both greater and lesser protection under the law. Though all journalists live under libel law and consequently must keep pace with its fluctuations, the obligation is particularly imperative to those who specialize in muckraking and investigative reporting. Journalists who pursue this type of writing are prone to find themselves in the courts, contending that what they have written is legally justified. Victims of the investigative genre conversely argue with equal intensity that there is a definite—albeit fuzzy—line that separates the permissible from the forbidden.

It is within these all-important libel guidelines that writers of the often entertaining, usually surprising, but always controversial column have operated in the decades since 1932. The law has been anything but static during this period, as evidenced by the remarks of one of America's most prominent legal scholars, the late Dean Prosser:

> There is a great deal of the law of defamation which makes no sense. It contains anomalies and absurdities for which no legal writer ever has had a kind word, and it is a curious compound of a strict liability imposed upon innocent defendants, as rigid and extreme as anything found in the law, with a blind and almost perverse refusal to compensate the plaintiff for real and very serious harm. The explanation is in part one of historical accident and survival, in part one of the conflict of opposing ideas of policy in which our traditional notions of freedom of expression have collided violently with sympathy for the victim.[1]

Despite the subtleties and complexities of libel law, however, the U.S. Supreme Court has been involved in a continuing effort to define the proper relationship between the need for a vigorous press and the legitimate interest in redressing wrongful injury by defamation. Muckraking writers, such as Pearson and Anderson, have of course found themselves enmeshed in this unceasing struggle.

Though the right of the press to criticize government and public officials has been generally accepted as a free press cornerstone since around 1800, it took nearly two centuries for the First Amendment's protection to be applied to civil libel cases. The law of libel was not nationalized until 1964. In *New York Times Co.* v. *Sullivan,* the U.S. Supreme Court held that a state cannot, under the First and Fourteenth Amendments, award damages to a public official for a defamatory falsehood relating to his official conduct unless he proves "actual malice"—that the statement was made with knowledge of its falsity or with reckless disregard of whether it was true or false.[2] The "actual malice" articulation in *Sullivan* is normally referred to as the *Times* rule.

The stabilization of American libel law, allowing a protection for falsehoods about public officials and figures so long as the writer does not act in reckless disregard for the truth, actually resulted from a slow evolution.[3]

Development in the law of libel is an on-going process. Even today, with a constitutionally protected freedom to discuss public officials and figures, many questions have no sure answers. How far can newspapers go when reaching into the private lives of public officials or figures? How is a public figure defined? What precautions must a journalist take when discussing a person who does not fall into the public official or figure category? Questions such as these have been considered repeatedly by the courts, particularly during the past half century.

It has been stated that one of the afflictions of the American press is that reporters and editors know so little about the law of libel.[4] This, however, is understandable. It is a complex subject, as evidenced by Dean Prosser's remarks, and a subject with which journalism educators and legal scholars alike have difficulty keeping pace.

Many editors are able to articulate some off-the-cuff remarks about libel per quod, libel per se, truth, and the absolute defenses. When the decision must be made to publish or not to publish, however, the problem becomes more acute. To compound the problem, legislators, courts, and legal scholars have done relatively little to clear up the murky libel waters.[5]

Robert Phelps and E. Douglas Hamilton, authors of a comprehensive book dealing with the subject, claim that, though most newspapermen tremble when the word *libel* is mentioned, many fears stem merely from lack of knowledge. They say this lack causes many editors to grow timid when dealing with a controversial story. According to Phelps and Hamilton:

> The timidity displayed in covering local news, where most of the danger of libel occurs, compared with the thunder about Cuba, Red China and the Soviet Union is ample proof that what critics call Afghanistanism is rampant. While social and economic factors contribute to this timidity, the reporters' and editors' lack of a working knowledge of libel is an important cause.[6]

It is essential, therefore, that journalists who continually deal with controversial subjects, writers such as those of the "Merry-Go-Round," have at least a basic understanding of libel law.

Common Law Origins

Defamation, made up of the twin torts of libel and slander, is generally held to mean "that which tends to injure 'reputation' in the popular sense; to diminish the esteem, respect, goodwill or confidence in which the plaintiff is held, or to excite adverse, derogatory or unpleasant feelings or opinions against him."[7] The distinction between libel (written defamation) and slander (oral defamation) used to be clearer than it is today. With the emergence of the electronic media—and their pervasive influence—the old supposition that slander is less harmful than libel has largely disappeared. Laws differ, but most state legislatures have decided that many defamatory spoken words on radio and television flow from scripts and should be treated as libels. This distinction is significant for columnists who also serve as electronic media commentators.

Libel and slander share various characteristics. In Illinois, for example, common law slander and libel include five classes of words:

> (1) Those imputing the commission of a criminal offense; (2) those imputing infection with a communicable disease of any kind which, if true, would tend to exclude one from society; (3) those imputing inability to perform or want of integrity in the discharge of duties of office or employment; (4) those prejudicing a particular party in his pro-

> fession or trade; and (5) defamatory words, which though not in themselves actionable, occasion the party special damages.[8]

Though Prosser admits that the courts have not been harmonious in dealing with defamation cases, he nevertheless contends that libel involves the idea of disgrace.[9] Libel has also been defined as:

> The unconsented and unprivileged communication to a third party of a false idea which tends to injure plaintiff's reputation by lowering the community's estimation of him, or by causing him to be shunned or avoided, or by exposing him to hatred, contempt or ridicule.[10]

A more complete definition might be:

> Reputation is said in a general way to be injured by words which tend to expose one to public hatred, shame, obloquy, contumely, odium, contempt, ridicule, aversion, ostracism, degradation, or disgrace, or to induce an evil opinion of one in the minds of right-thinking persons and to deprive one of their confidence and friendly intercourse in society.[11]

Some writers have simply said that "a publication is libelous of any person if it identifies him to any reader and its natural effect is to make readers generally think worse of the person identified."[12] *Black's Law Dictionary* defines libel in its most general sense as "any publication which is injurious to the reputation of another."[13]

Under common law, libel was divided into two categories: libel per se and libel per quod. Some words have been considered automatically defamatory because of the belief that their publication automatically causes injury. Black says of libel per se that the words must be

> of such character that an action may be brought upon them without the necessity of showing any special damage, the imputation being such that the law will presume that any one so slandered must have suffered damage.[14]

Libel per se, however, was altered in *Gertz* v. *Robert Welch, Inc.*,[15] when the Court held that a state could not permit recovery of presumed or punitive damages where liability was not based on a showing of knowledge of falsity or reckless disregard for the truth. The *Gertz* ruling, at least as it applies to media defamation of a private person, has altered the libel per se concept. Under traditional libel per se, when false charges were made that an individual had committed a crime, that he had some loathsome disease, that a woman was unchaste, or words were used that tended to injure a person in his trade, business, office, or occupation, the person defamed could collect damages without proof of negligence or reckless disregard of the truth.[16]

On the other hand, libel per quod includes:

> Publications which are susceptible of two reasonable interpretations, one of which is defamatory and the other is not, or publications which are not obviously defamatory, but which become so when considered in connection with innuendo, colloquim, and explanatory circumstances.[17]

Thus, during the first half of the twentieth century, a period in which Pearson did much of his writing, there was particular emphasis in the courts on the fact that libel would be determined by the interpretation of the words.

Journalism educator Clifton Lawhorne stressed the importance of word interpretation:

> It was generally held that words must be interpreted in their plain and ordinary sense. When words could be interpreted in only one way, it became the duty of the judge to rule whether they constituted libel per se. But if words were ambiguous or could, in the light of extrinsic facts, be interpreted in more than one way, it was the job of jurors, in finding fact, to determine if they constituted libel per quod.[18]

Certain requirements, however, must be met before there is a cause for action: there must be publication to a third person; this publication must have a damaging effect on an individual's reputation or good name; and there must be identification of the person allegedly defamed. If one of these elements is missing, there is no libel.[19]

Prior to the Supreme Court's landmark *New York Times Co.* v. *Sullivan* decision, a publisher printed materials susceptible of a defamatory meaning at his risk. Prosser summarized the common law doctrine of strict liability for the publication of false defamatory matter:

> The effect of this strict liability [for defamatory publications] is to place the printed, written or spoken word in the same class with the use of explosives or the keeping of dangerous animals. If a defamatory meaning, which is false, is reasonably understood, the defendant publishes at his peril, and there is no possible defense except the rather narrow one of privilege.[20]

Defenses against Libel Actions

Before *Sullivan,* when the majority of the Pearson suits were filed, most libel actions were defended under statutory and common law provisions, which may be absolute or qualified.[21] An absolute defense against libel actions exists regardless of the publication motive; a qualified or conditional defense is one that is complete only if the publisher meets certain other standards. Phelps and Hamilton list seven common law or statutory defenses. Absolute defenses are consent or authorization, self-defense or right of reply, privilege of participant, and the statute of limitations. The remainder are conditional: truth, fair comment and criticism, and privilege of reporting.[22] The *Times* "actual malice" rule is used so extensively today that the pre-1964 defenses developed through state statutes and the common law are not pervasively cited.[23] Nevertheless, they are available. (The *Times* rule will be discussed at length when the *Sullivan* case is examined below.)

A summary of absolute common law and statutory defenses:

Consent or authorization—This defense can be cited if the plaintiff was aware the story was about to be printed, but consented to its publication. This, obviously, is not likely to happen often—particularly when one considers the volatile issues writers of the "Merry-Go-Round" often deal with.

Self-defense or right of reply—This defense can be utilized when the victim of an attack in the press refutes the allegations. The individual countering the original story, however, must be careful not to overextend his protection. The reply must be related to the original publication and cannot be a separate personal attack.

Privilege of participant—This defense protects words spoken in legislative, judicial, or other official proceedings. This defense is not particularly valuable to muckrakers who communicate their opinions primarily through newspaper articles. On the other hand, several political figures were able to rely on this privilege to speak out freely—and sometimes viciously—against Pearson on the protected floors of the House and Senate.

Statute of limitations—This defense bars suits after a certain period of time. With only five exceptions—Arkansas, Delaware, Hawaii, New Mexico, and Vermont—the statute of limitations on libel is one, two, or three years.

A summary of conditional common law and statutory defenses:

Truth—This is an absolute defense in a number of states, but in others only truthful statements that are published for "justifiable ends" or "good motives" (the *conditions*) are protected. Truth is not frequently used as a defense; it is often illusory and difficult to prove. Pearson, nonetheless, did cite it on a few occasions.

Fair comment and criticism—This defense gives the reporter the right to articulate his *opinions* on matters of public interest, e.g., reviews of books, plays, movies; editorials on public subjects; and personal viewpoint columns. Fair comment and criticism, however, does not protect misstatement of *facts*. This defense is valuable to columnists, like "Merry-Go-Round" writers, who specialize in opinion writing.

Privilege of reporting—Since so much news evolves from governmental proceedings, this defense is commonly used. It gives the press a conditional privilege to make *fair* and *accurate* reports of what happens during public meetings and to report the contents of official reports. Phelps and Hamilton point out, however, that in order for this defense to be successful, it must meet certain conditions. For example, it must be plain to the reader that the article is a report, that it is fair and accurate, that there is no extraneous libelous matter, and that it is published without malice.[24]

Obviously, conditional privileges are severely limited in comparison to those that are absolute. According to Prosser:

> The condition attached to all such qualified privileges is that they must be exercised in a reasonable manner and for a proper purpose. The immunity is forfeited if the defendant steps outside of the scope of the privilege, or abuses the occasion. Thus qualified privilege does not extend . . . to the publication of irrelevant defamatory matter with no bearing upon the public or private interest which is entitled to protection.[25]

If a defendant is unable to successfully utilize any of the absolute or conditional defenses—and a judge or jury holds against him—he can still explore the possibilities of mitigating factors. Such claims will not, of course, keep the court from assessing damages—but they can be helpful in slicing damage payments. He can, for example, show that, though he published the libel, he harbored no ill will toward the plaintiff. A newsman might claim that the plaintiff already had such a bad reputation that his article did not appreciably lower the plaintiff's esteem in the eyes of others. If the newspaper printed a retraction—a clear admission that a mistake was made—this could also mitigate damages. Or if the newsman relied on a reliable source—such as one of the wire services—he could cite this factor to show that he had no reason to believe that what he published was not true.[26]

If a defendant is held liable for a defamatory publication, the types of damages that may be assessed against him are: (1) compensatory or general—compensation for injury to reputation; (2) special or actual—the tangible monetary loss (which must be established) suffered by the plaintiff as a result of a false statement; (3) punitive or exemplary—"smart money" used to punish past libelous conduct and to discourage similar future conduct; and (4) nominal—token damages awarded in libel actions where there has been no serious harm to a plaintiff.[27]

Despite the common law defenses, prior to *Sullivan* the threat of a libel action as a result of discussing public officials obviously remained a cloud over journalists such as Pearson and Anderson, who almost daily scrutinized the actions of government leaders. According to historians Alfred H. Kelly and Winfred A. Harbison:

> The most controversial aspect of tort libel law [prior to the *Sullivan* case] was the threat to free and open criticism of public officials and other personages in the public eye. Newspapers, rival politicians, and other commentators who were guilty even of simple error in criticizing such persons very often laid themselves open to heavy suits for damages, a fact that quite conceivably had as great a deterrent effect upon free and open political criticism as had prosecutions for seditious libel in the eighteenth century.[28]

The threatening cloud existed because the U.S. Supreme Court, before 1964, never saw fit to decide directly the problem of reconciling the law of libel with the press guarantees of the First Amendment.

The Court, in numerous dicta, appeared to accept the proposition that libel laws were simply not affected by the First Amendment.[29] For example, in a 1931 case, *Near* v. *Minnesota*, the majority said:

> But it is recognized that the punishment for the abuse of the liberty accorded to the press is essential to the protection of the public, and that the common law rules that subject the libeler to the responsibility for the public offense, as well as for the private injury, are not abolished by the protection extended in our constitution.[30]

In a 1942 case, *Chaplinsky* v. *New Hampshire*, Justice Frank Murphy wrote for the majority:

> Allowing the broadest scope to the language and purpose of the Fourteenth Amendment [as it incorporated the First Amendment] it is well understood that the right of free speech is not absolute at all times, and under all circumstances. There are certain well-defined and narrowly limited classes of speech, the prevention and punishment of which

> have never been thought to raise any Constitutional problem. These include . . . the libelous. . . . It has been well observed that such utterances are no essential part of any exposition of ideas, and are of such slight social value as a step to truth that any benefit that may be derived from them is clearly outweighed by the social interest in order and morality.[31]

Thus, with the U.S. Supreme Court unwilling to establish a constitutional privilege for libel until 1964, the legal concept remained in flux. In the words of one libel scholar, "A patchwork of libel laws grew up from jurisdiction to jurisdiction, with some overall standardization but without national uniformity."[32]

Common Law Cornerstones

Two major decisions near the turn of the century—*Post Publishing Co.* v. *Hallam*[33] and *Coleman* v. *MacLennan*[34]—were often cited in discussions of privilege in libel opinions before *Sullivan* brought public libel under the umbrella of the First Amendment.

The *Hallam* case (1893) was based on an article that appeared in the *Cincinnati Post*. The story alleged that Theodore F. Hallam, a lawyer, had been paid to help swing votes in a Kentucky political convention to a rival candidate for the party nomination to Congress. Hallam, after a number of ballots at the convention, asked his supporters to vote for Albert S. Berry. The newspaper claimed that Berry, in return, had paid the food and drink bill that Hallam owed for entertaining his delegates on a river cruise. Judge (later President) William H. Taft refused to concede that the untrue statements printed in the story were privileged. The Post Publishing Company, indeed, had been unable to prove the story. Taft obviously thought that a statement of fact had to be proved.[35] He wrote:

> The existence and extent of privilege in communications are determined by balancing the needs and good of society against the right of an individual to enjoy a good reputation. The privilege should always cease where the sacrifice of

> the individual right becomes so great that the public good to be derived from it is outweighed. . . . The danger that honorable and worthy men may be driven from politics and public service by allowing too great latitude in attacks upon their characters outweighs any benefit that might occasionally accrue to the public from charges of corruption that are true in fact, but are incapable of legal proof.[36]

Fifteen years after *Hallam*, however, the Kansas Supreme Court chose to adopt a more liberal stance toward protection of the press.

The *Coleman* case (1908) involved an action for libel by C. C. Coleman, attorney general of Kansas, against F. P. MacLennan, owner and publisher of the *Topeka State Journal.* The suit was brought based on an article in MacLennan's newspaper stating facts relating to Coleman's official conduct in connection with a school fund transaction. The article drew allegedly defamatory conclusions about Coleman's actions. The Kansas Supreme Court affirmed a lower court decision in favor of MacLennan. The court held that the story was written in good faith and therefore privileged, although the matters in the article were conceivably untrue in fact and derogatory to the character of the candidate.[37]

Kansas Supreme Court Justice Rousseau Burch wrote for the majority:

> Anyone claiming to be defamed by the communication must show actual malice, or go remediless. This privilege extends to a great variety of subjects and includes matters of public concern, public men, and candidates for office. Under a form of government like our own there must be freedom to canvass in good faith the worth of character and qualifications of candidates for office, whether elective or appointive, and by becoming a candidate, or allowing himself to be the candidate of others, a man tenders as an issue to be tried out publicly before the people or the appointing power his honesty, integrity, and fitness for the office to be filled.[38]

Thus, before the twentieth century's first decade had elapsed, two distinct rules of privilege had been formally articulated by the courts.

Though the *Hallam* and *Coleman* cases "did not originate the rules of privilege they adopted, they did become the opinion leaders in defining the privilege of discussing public officials without liability for libel." One journalism educator put the cases in historical perspective:

> Perhaps because of their deliberately careful and studied reasoning . . . [the cases] were later cited in case after case by state courts accepting one or the other of the two rules of privilege. The first, in promoting the doctrine of fair comment and criticism, presented a most logical case for limiting privilege to protect officials' right to a good name. The second, in advancing the doctrine of honest belief in truth, just as forcefully promoted a wide privilege of discussion to protect the public's right to know. Judges in each state had meaningful precedents upon which to balance the two interests that were being protected.[39]

Before *Sullivan*, states were categorized according to the libel formulas they followed. Suits against Pearson and Anderson were not always brought in the District of Columbia (where their attorneys were most familiar with existing libel laws). Lack of conformity in jurisdictional formulas made it more difficult for their lawyers to defend against actions in other geographic areas.

The narrow rule, that privilege was confined to comment and criticism based on actual facts, was known as the majority view. This view was consistent with the theory advanced in *Hallam*. From 1900 until the end of World War II, this view was adopted by decisions in twenty-one states and the territory of Hawaii.[40] Meanwhile, courts in sixteen states adopted the *Coleman* liberal rule—excusing false statements about officials that ordinarily would be libelous, provided the statements were published without malice and with probable cause for believing them true.[41] Courts in four states had not defined any doctrine of privilege or fair comment prior to the end of World War II.[42] Still other jurisdictions, including the District of Columbia, occupied a "middle ground," leaving room for a more liberal interpretation of privilege in libel cases where there were no charges of crime or gross immorality.[43]

After World War II, however, with a growing emphasis on free discussion, the libel-free privilege of discussing public officials and figures was extended. This liberal judicial trend was noticeable even in jurisdictions that retained the narrow view of privilege.[44] Emphasis began to be placed on free comment; honest mistakes were more readily excused.[45] Despite this trend toward liberalization, jurisdictional differences remained glaring. A chain libel suit filed in the late 1930s and early 1940s by Ohio Congressman Martin L. Sweeney against newspapers carrying a "Merry-Go-Round" column, for instance, provides an excellent example of how different jurisdictions approached the case due to the absence of a national libel law.[46]

A Trend Emerges

Meanwhile, journalists and scholars were beginning to advocate a federal rule that would protect misstatements of fact. A writer in a 1949 edition of the *Columbia Law Review* concluded that the state of libel law was complicated and extremely difficult to apply.

> The most needed development [in the law of defamation], however, is wider acceptance of the rule that there is a conditional privilege to make misstatements of fact. Most of the uncertainty of the law arises from the difficulty of disentangling comment, statements of motives, and statements of fact; this uncertainty would be avoided if all comments and statements about political officers and candidates were conditionally privileged. Such a rule would provide needed encouragement to those who wish to speak out honestly and with due care in the public interest, and the conditional character of the privilege would guarantee adequate protection to officers and candidates.[47]

Though there was no constitutional privilege to protect crusading newspapermen before 1964, the press was, according to scholar David Riesman, hardly at a great disadvantage.[48] Riesman and other scholars contended that large newspapers possessed an impressive control of publicity that could be used to intimidate judges and juries. Furthermore, it was often considered "bad form" for a politician to file a libel suit; he was supposed to be able to "take it."[49] Riesman wrote:

> The number of verdicts for defendants and awards of nominal damages seem to indicate that juries, nurtured in American cynicism about politicians, are in fact inclined to give even a large newspaper defendant the benefit of any doubt. Juries do not appear to manifest resentment against a press whose politicking and gossiping are entertaining. . . . In libel cases, moreover, pleading, practice and substantive law are filled with technicalities and traps for the unwary. Lawyers for the large newspapers are specialized, but the plaintiff's lawyer is apt to be inexperienced.[50]

Still other writers toward the end of the first half of the twentieth century were highly critical of American libel laws. The primary criticism was that the state-by-state differences failed to consider the "big picture." There was little orderly development of libel laws applicable to the entire country. What legislation there was tended to be "sporadic and piecemeal."[51] Though this haphazard development and application of libel laws prior to *Sullivan* received much criticism, judicial and legislative inertia for the most part preserved the "antiquities peculiar to the common law."[52]

Two U.S. Supreme Court decisions in the 1950s, however, offered a ray of hope to proponents of a constitutional privilege for misstatement of fact. For example, in *Beauharnais* v. *Illinois,*[53] the Court sustained an Illinois criminal libel statute as applied to a publication held to be both defamatory of a racial group and liable to cause violence and disorder. Almost as an afterthought, however, Justice Felix Frankfurter was careful to observe that the Court "retains and exercises authority to nullify action which encroaches on freedom of utterance under the guise of punishing libel." Further, he said, "discussion cannot be denied and the right, as well as the duty, of criticisms must not be stifled." In an accompanying footnote, Frankfurter said that "public men, are, as it were, public property."[54]

In *Barr* v. *Matteo,*[55] a 1959 case, the Court voted to sustain William G. Barr's plea for absolute privilege in defense of an alleged libel. Barr was a government official; the ruling thus established absolute immunity for public officials to criticize official conduct. Justice John Marshall Harlan, writing for the majority, said:

> The reasons for the recognition of the privilege have been often stated. It has been thought important that officials of government should be free to exercise their duties unembarrassed by the fear of damage suits in respect of acts done in the course of those duties—suits which would consume time and energies which would otherwise be devoted to governmental service and the threat of which might appreciably inhibit the fearless, vigorous, and effective administration of policies of government. . . . There must indeed be means of punishing public officers who have been truant to their duties; but that is quite another matter from exposing such as have been honestly mistaken to suit by anyone who has suffered from their errors.[56]

Barr v. *Matteo* thus provided an indication that the Court might place some form of privilege—absolute or, more likely, conditional—under the protection of the First Amendment.

As America entered the 1960s, it was becoming increasingly apparent that there was a need for a national libel standard, a solidifying solution that would bring all states under uniform guidelines. The *Matteo* decision, indeed, indicated that the logical thrust to nationalize libel law was imminent.

That it took nearly 200 years for the U.S. Supreme Court to be on the verge of formulating a constitutional privilege for libel law is, however, not particularly surprising. The Court's gradual philosophical development in this important area was consistent with its historical past. Supreme Court scholar Robert McCloskey, for example, wrote that

> new jurisprudence cannot be reached by a series of leaps and bounds. The Court's great successes in establishing jurisdiction have never been attained that way. We need only

> recall by way of example the slow and gingerly steps [Chief Justice John] Marshall took from *Marbury* to *Cohens* v. *Virginia* to confirm the Court's supremacy over the states, or the almost painfully gradual accumulation of precedents that led finally to substantive due process in the late nineteenth century. It is in the nature of courts to feel their way along.[57]

Amid the liberalism often associated with the Kennedy administration and the Warren Court, as America evolved from the slow-paced 1950s, the stage was set. Some people speculated that the increasingly liberal Court would enter the libel arena. It would be in keeping, at any rate, with the Court's reputation for activism.

The formal nationalization of the law of libel, as mentioned earlier, finally came in *New York Times Co.* v. *Sullivan* in 1964. The *Sullivan* decision extended to writers increased legal protection from libel suits when discussing public officials. This measure was undoubtedly well received by muckraking columnists, such as those of the "Merry-Go-Round," whose primary function was to perform a "watchdog" role over government and its officials.

A National Standard Is Born

L. B. Sullivan, one of three elected commissioners of Montgomery, Alabama, brought suit against the *New York Times,* alleging that he had been libeled by a *Times* advertisement that included false statements. The advertisement in question, entitled "Heed Their Rising Voices," filled a full page in the March 29, 1960, *Times.* It began by stating that "as the whole world knows by now, thousands of Southern Negro students are engaged in widespread nonviolent demonstration in positive affirmation of the right to live in human dignity as guaranteed by the U.S. Constitution and the Bill of Rights." Detailed was police action directed against students who participated in a civil rights demonstration and against a leader of the civil rights movement, Dr. Martin Luther King, Jr. The text appeared over the names of sixty-four persons, many widely known for their activities in public affairs, religion, trade unions, and the performing arts.[58]

Of the ten paragraphs of text in the advertisement, the third and a portion of the sixth were the basis of Sullivan's libel claim. The third paragraph read:

> In Montgomery, Alabama, after students sang "My Country, 'Tis of Thee" on the State Capitol steps, their leaders were expelled from school, and truckloads of police armed with shotguns and tear-gas ringed the Alabama State College campus. When the entire student body protested to state authorities by refusing to re-register, their dining hall was padlocked in an attempt to starve them into submission.

The offending part of the sixth paragraph read:

> Again and again the Southern violators have answered Dr. King's peaceful protests with intimidation and violence. They have bombed his home almost killing his wife and child. They have assaulted his person. They have arrested him seven times—for "speeding," "loitering," and similar "offenses." And now they have charged him with "perjury" —a felony under which they could imprison him for ten years.[59]

Sullivan contended that the word "police" in the third paragraph referred to him as the Montgomery commissioner who supervised the police department. As to the sixth paragraph, he contended that, since arrests are ordinarily made by the police, the reference to "they" would be read as referring to him. Thus, he argued, the paragraph would be read as accusing the Montgomery police, and hence him, of answering Dr. King's protests with "intimidation and violence." It was acknowledged that some of the statements contained in the two paragraphs were inaccurate.[60]

An Alabama trial judge submitted the case to the jury under instructions that the statements in the advertisement were libelous per se and were not privileged, so that the defendants might be held liable if the jury found they had published the advertisement and that the statements were made "of and concerning" Sullivan. The jury found for Sullivan;

the Alabama Supreme Court affirmed. Sullivan was awarded $500,000, the full amount sought.[61]

The rule of fair comment in Alabama was like that of the majority of the jurisdictions in America. It limited the privilege to the expression of defamatory opinions based on facts that could be established as true. In *Sullivan,* the defendants were unable to establish the truth of several of the particulars alleged.

It was amid these circumstances that the U.S. Supreme Court, on March 9, 1964, unanimously held that a public official would have to prove that the defendant acted with "actual malice"—that the statement was made with knowledge of its falsity or with reckless disregard of whether it was true or false—in order to collect damages.[62] The Court further indicated that the rule had been basically adopted by a number of state courts that had adhered to the views forwarded in the Kansas case of *Coleman.*[63]

The Court is naturally aware of the political considerations of any given situation or case. Author Harry Kalven, Jr., amplified this general theory and applied it to the *Sullivan* decision:

> The court, compelled by the political realities of the case to decide it in favor of the *Times,* yet equally compelled to seek high ground in justifying its result, wrote an opinion that may prove to be the best and most important it has ever produced in the realm of free speech.[64]

Kalven then converted the *Sullivan* decision into the following syllogism:

> The central meaning of the [First] Amendment is that seditious libel cannot be made the subject of government sanction. The Alabama rule on fair comment is closely akin to making seditious libel an offense. The Alabama rule therefore violated the central meaning of the Amendment. . . . The drama of the *Times* case then is that the Court, forced to extricate itself from the political impasse that was presented to it, did so by returning to the essence of the First Amendment to be found in its limitations on seditious libel.[65]

The majority opinion, written by Justice William Brennan, Jr., contained skillful and logical reasoning. Drawing a parallel to the *Matteo* decision, the Court emphasized that citizens should have the same opportunity to criticize government and public officials:

> Such a privilege for criticism of official conduct is appropriately analogous to the protection accorded a public official when he is sued for libel by a private citizen. . . . It would give public servants an unjustified preference over the public they serve, if critics of official conduct did not have a fair equivalent of the immunity granted to the officials themselves.[66]

Though *Sullivan* settled the libel uniformity problem with finality, the case nevertheless raised a great many questions. The Court, to complicate matters, had no desire to delve into them. Justice Brennan wrote:

> We have no occasion here to determine how far down into the lower ranks of government employees the "public official" designation would extend for purposes of this rule, or otherwise to specify categories of persons who would or would not be included. . . . Nor do we here determine the boundaries of the "official conduct" concept.[67]

Despite these questions, which would be left for future decisions, the Court had nationalized its "actual malice" rule.

In libel cases that followed the historic *Sullivan* ruling, the Court not only extended, refined, and amplified the "actual malice" concept, but a decade later narrowed the protection given the press in defamation suits.

Post-*Sullivan* Developmemts

Less than one year after *Sullivan,* the Court extended the "actual malice" doctrine to prosecutions for criminal libel.[68] James Garrison, the district attorney of Orleans Parish, Louisiana, during a dispute with the eight judges of the criminal district court of the parish, held a press conference at which he issued a statement disparaging their judicial conduct. The primary charge alleged to be defamatory was his attribution of a large backlog of pending criminal cases to the inefficiency, laziness, and excessive vacations of the judges. He also said the judges, by refusing to authorize disbursements to cover the expenses of undercover investigations of vice in New Orleans, had hampered his efforts to enforce the vice laws.[69] As a result, he was tried without a jury before a judge from another parish and convicted of criminal defamation under the Louisiana Criminal Defamation Statute. The Louisiana Supreme Court affirmed. The U.S. Supreme Court, however, reversed, holding that the Constitution limits state power to impose sanctions for criticism of the official conduct of public officials in criminal cases, as in civil cases, to false statements concerning official conduct made with knowledge of their falsity or with reckless disregard of whether they were false or not.[70]

Furthermore, the Court said Garrison's accusations that concerned judges' official conduct did not become private defamation because his statements might also have reflected on the judges' private character. The Court said it was inevitable that any criticism of the manner in which a public official performs his duties would tend to affect his private, as well as his public, reputation. The Court further elaborated:

> The *New York Times* rule is not rendered inapplicable merely because an official's private reputation, as well as his public reputation, is harmed. The public official rule protects the paramount public interest in a free flow of information to the people concerning public officials, their servants. To this end, anything which might touch on an official's fitness for office is relevant. Few personal attributes are more germane to fitness for office than dishonesty, malfeasance, or improper motivation, even though these characteristics may also affect the official's private character.[71]

The Court then quoted from the *Coleman* decision:

> Manifestly a candidate must surrender to public scrutiny and discussion so much of his private character as affects his fitness for office, and the liberal rule requires no more. But in measuring the extent of a candidate's profert of character it should always be remembered that the people have good authority for believing that grapes do not grow on thorns nor figs on thistles.[72]

After *Garrison,* the Court did not consider another major libel case until 1966.[73] In *Rosenblatt* v. *Baer,*[74] the Court extended the *Times* standard to public employees who hold positions of responsibility for the control of public affairs. Frank Baer was the former supervisor of a county recreation area who was employed by and responsible to three county commissioners. He brought the civil libel action in a New Hampshire state court against Alfred Rosenblatt, who, in his newspaper column, allegedly criticized the fiscal management of the area under Baer's direction. Baer obtained a jury verdict for $31,500 in damages; the Supreme Court of New Hampshire affirmed.[75] The U.S. Supreme Court granted certiorari, being concerned basically with the question of whether Baer was a "public official" within the constitutional privilege established in *Sullivan.* The Court reversed, emphasizing the strong interest in debate on public issues and concerning those persons in positions to significantly influence the resolution of the issues. The Court reasoned:

> It is clear, therefore, that the "public official" designation applies at the very least to those among the hierarchy of government employees who have, or appear to the public to have, substantial responsibility for or control over the conduct of governmental affairs.[76]

The Court cemented the "public official" designation of Baer by making use of his reasoning when he filed the suit: though he was not mentioned by name in the newspaper column, his role in the management of the area was so prominent that the public regarded him as the man responsible for its operations.[77]

The Court further expanded the *Times* rule in 1967 when it applied the "actual malice" test to a tort of "false light" invasion of privacy.[78] *Time, Inc.* v. *Hill* falls only indirectly into the pattern established by the *Sullivan* decision, for it was a privacy action brought by a person who was not within the public domain.[79] The case grew out of a *Life* magazine account of a play based on a 1952 incident in which James Hill and his family were held hostage in their home by three escaped convicts but were ultimately released unharmed. No violence occurred. The family changed residence to discourage publicity about the incident, which had caused extensive involuntary notoriety. A novel about the incident later appeared and was subsequently made into a play.

It was *Life's* review of this play that was the subject of the suit. The magazine described the play as a reenactment and used, as illustrations, photographs of scenes staged in the former Hill home. Alleging that the article gave the knowingly false impression that the play depicted the Hill incident, Hill sued for damages under a New York statute providing a cause of action to a person whose name or picture is used by another without consent for purposes of trade or advertising. Time, Inc., maintained that the article concerned a subject of general interest and was published in good faith.[80]

The Court reasoned that the subject of the *Life* article, the opening of a new play linked to an actual incident, was a matter of public interest. Drawing from the *Sullivan* decision, the Court said:

> Erroneous statement is no less inevitable in such a case [the *Life* article] than in the case of comment upon public affairs, and in both, if innocent or merely negligent, ". . . it must be protected if the freedoms of expression are to have the 'breathing space' that they 'need . . . to survive.' "[81]

In light of *Hill* and other decisions, it was becoming increasingly apparent that the *Times* rule would continue to play a pivotal role in libel actions, just as it had in the three years after the decision was handed down.[82] The Court, in fact, made a significant protraction of the "actual malice" rule in companion 1967 cases, *Curtis Publishing Co.* v. *Butts* and *Associated Press* v. *Walker*.[83] In these cases, the Court applied the "actual malice" standard to public figures. The Court heard the two cases to consider the impact of the *Times* decision on libel actions instituted by persons who were not public officials, but were public figures involved in issues in which the public had a justified and important interest.[84]

Briefly, the *Butts* case involved a libel action in federal court seeking compensatory and punitive damages for an article in the *Saturday Evening Post* in which Wallace Butts, athletic director at the University of Georgia, was accused of conspiring to "fix" a football game between his school and the University of Alabama. The article was based on an affidavit concerning a telephone conversation between Butts and Paul Bryant, head football coach at Alabama, which George Burnett, an Atlanta insurance salesman, had accidentally overheard because of an electronic error. Butts sought $5 million compensatory and $5 million punitive damages. The jury returned a verdict for $60,000 in general damages and $3 million in punitive damages. The trial court, however, reduced the total to $460,000.[85]

The *Walker* case grew out of the distribution of an Associated Press news dispatch giving an eyewitness account of a massive riot that erupted at the University of Mississippi because of federal efforts to enforce a court decree ordering the enrollment there of a Negro, James Meredith. The dispatch stated that Maj. Gen. Edwin Walker (retired), who was present on the campus, had taken command against federal marshalls sent there to effectuate the court's decree and to assist in preserving order. The article also described Walker as encouraging rioters to use violence and giving them technical advice on combating the effects of tear gas. Walker sued the Associated Press and more than a dozen other publications for a total of $33 million. His suit against AP was for $2 million. A jury awarded him $500,000 in compensatory damages.[86]

The U.S. Supreme Court upheld the *Butts* decision but reversed *Walker*. Of primary importance to libel law development, however, were the strong arguments of the Court to extend the *Times* rule. The Court reasoned that Butts occupied a position similar to Baer's, since Butts was charged with the important responsibility of managing the athletic affairs of a state university. It was apparent that Walker, a former Army officer, had thrust himself into the vortex of the controversy.[87]

The Court said that both Butts and Walker commanded a substantial amount of independent public interest at the time of the publications, and both should be labeled "public figures" under ordinary rules.[88] The Court continued:

> We consider and would hold that a "public figure" who is not a public official may also recover damages for a defamatory falsehood whose substance makes substantial danger to reputation apparent, on a showing of highly unreasonable conduct constituting an extreme departure from the standards of investigation and reporting ordinarily adhered to by responsible publishers.[89]

It was then reasoned by the Court that "extreme departures" had taken place in the *Butts* case. Evidence showed that the story was in no sense "hot news" and that, although editors of the magazine had ample opportunity to investigate fully the serious charges, elementary precautions were ignored.[90]

This negligent procedure was in contrast to the Walker dispatch, which required "immediate dissemination." In this instance, there was nothing in the series of events to give "the slightest hint of a severe departure from accepted publishing standards."[91] Chief Justice Earl Warren extolled the virtues of the *Butts* decision, terming the extension of the "actual malice" rule to public figures a "manageable standard, readily understood, which also balances to a proper degree the legitimate interest traditionally protected by the law of defamation."[92]

Though the Court neatly brought both public officials and figures under the "actual malice" test, some lower courts apparently had difficulty applying the test, even in the most obvious circumstances. For example, later in the 1967 term, the U.S. Supreme Court reversed a West Virginia lower court decision that awarded damages to a court official who alleged that, during his reelection campaign, he was libeled by three editorials, all highly critical of his official conduct.[93] The Court held that the failure of the newspaper to check with the official on his alleged use of intimidation to get what he wanted did not constitute "actual malice."[94]

Meanwhile, the Court continued to build a definition of "reckless disregard." Though never establishing a concrete definition, the Court sought to furnish meaningful guidance for the outer limits of the protection. In *Garrison,* it will be recalled, the Court emphasized the necessity of showing that a false publication was made with a "high degree of awareness of . . . probable falsity."[95] In *Butts,* Justice Harlan's opinion stated that evidence of either deliberate falsification or reckless publication "despite the publisher's awareness of probable falsity" was essential to recovery by public officials in defamation cases.[96]

In *St. Amant* v. *Thompson,*[97] however, the Court laid a third brick in the structure of definition:

> There must be sufficient evidence to permit the conclusion that the defendant in fact entertained serious doubts as to the truth of his publication. Publishing with such doubts shows reckless disregard for truth or falsity and demonstrates actual malice.[98]

The *St. Amant* case grew out of a televised speech in Baton Rouge, Louisiana, in which Phil St. Amant, a candidate for United States senator, alleged that money had changed hands illegally between Herman A. Thompson, an East Baton Rouge Parish deputy sheriff, and E. G. Partin, the president of a local union. St. Amant had obtained his information from a local Teamsters Union member.[99] Thompson promptly filed suit for defamation; the trial judge ruled in Thompson's favor and awarded $5,000 in damages. The Louisiana Court of Appeals reversed, but the Supreme Court of Louisiana reversed the appeals court, holding there was sufficient evidence that St. Amant had recklessly disregarded whether the statements about Thompson were true or false. The U.S. Supreme Court, however, capped this judicial tangle by reversing Louisiana's highest court, holding that there was not sufficient evidence to prove that St. Amant had entertained "serious doubts . . . as to the truth of his publication."[100]

The U.S. Supreme Court did not hear any more major libel cases until 1970. However, during the three-year interim after

St. Amant, lower courts continued to observe the "breathing space" the *Times* "actual malice" rule allowed the media. The steady expansion of the *Times* standard in the late 1960s led several courts to speculate that a private individual involved in an event of public interest would logically fall under the "actual malice" umbrella.[101]

Refinement of the *Times* doctrine by the U.S. Supreme Court also continued, as illustrated by a 1970 case, *Greenbelt Cooperative Publishing Assn., Inc.* v. *Bresler,*[102] and three cases handed down together during 1971: *Monitor Patriot Co.* v. *Roy,*[103] *Ocala Star-Banner* v. *Damron,*[104] and *Time, Inc.* v. *Pape.*[105]

In *Greenbelt Cooperative,* Charles Bresler, a prominent real estate developer and builder in Greenbelt, Maryland, brought a libel suit against the publishers of a small weekly newspaper, the *Greenbelt News Review.* Bresler, who was also a state legislator, was engaged in negotiations with the Greenbelt City Council to obtain certain zoning variances that would allow the construction of high-density housing on land owned by him. At the same time, however, the city was attempting to acquire another tract of land owned by Bresler for the construction of a new public high school. Extensive litigation concerning compensation for the school site seemed imminent unless there should be a price agreement between Bresler and city authorities. Obviously, the concurrent negotiations provided both parties considerable bargaining leverage. Two news articles in consecutive weekly editions of the local newspaper stated that at the public meetings some people had characterized Bresler's negotiating position as "blackmail." The case went to trial, and the jury awarded Bresler $5,000 in compensatory damages and $12,500 in punitive damages. The Maryland Court of Appeals affirmed.[106]

The Supreme Court reversed, reasoning that the case involved reports of public meetings concerned with local matters of importance. The Court said that "the very subject matter of the news reports, therefore, is one of particular First Amendment concern."[107] The Court held that the word "blackmail," in these particular circumstances, was not slander when spoken, and not libel when reported in the newspaper:[108]

> It is simply impossible to believe that a reader who reached the word "blackmail" in either article would not have understood exactly what was meant. . . . Even the most careless reader must have perceived that the word was no more than rhetorical hyperbole, a vigorous epithet used by those who considered Bresler's negotiating position extremely unreasonable. . . . To permit the infliction of financial liability upon the petitioners for publishing these two news articles would subvert the most fundamental meaning of a free press, protected by the First and Fourteenth Amendments.[109]

Thus, the Supreme Court made it vividly clear that more than lip service would be paid First Amendment protection. The three 1971 decisions dealing with libel handed down by the Court further emphasized this position.

In *Monitor Patriot,* the Court held that, as a matter of constitutional law, a charge of criminal conduct, no matter how remote in time or place, could never be irrelevant to an official's or a candidate's fitness for office for purposes of application of the "knowing or reckless disregard" rule of *New York Times Co.* v. *Sullivan.*[110] The suit grew out of a "Merry-Go-Round" column, written by Pearson, that discussed an upcoming New Hampshire election. The column spoke of political maneuvering in the primary campaign, referred to the criminal records of some of the candidates, and characterized Alphonse Roy, one of the candidates, as a "former small-time bootlegger."[111] Roy sued, but, on appeal, the Supreme Court made it clear that "the syllogistic manipulation of distinctions between 'private sectors' and 'public sectors,' or matters of fact and matters of law, is of little utility in resolving questions of First Amendment protection."[112]

The *Ocala Star-Banner* case grew out of a story printed in the small daily newspaper that served four counties in rural Florida. In 1966, the paper carried a story to the effect that Leonard Damron, then the mayor of a nearby community and candidate for county tax assessor, had been charged in a federal court with perjury, and that his case had been held over until the following term of court. The story, however, was false. It had been the mayor's brother, James Damron, who had been so charged.[113] Damron was awarded $22,000 compensatory damages by a jury. The Florida Court of Appeals affirmed.[114] The Supreme Court reversed, reasoning that the lower courts had erroneously interpreted the *Times* doctrine. Both lower courts contended that the defamatory publication revealed that Damron's official conduct or the manner in which he performed his duties were not the basis for the inaccuracy, and therefore did not fall under the protection of the *Times* rule.[115]

The Supreme Court insisted, however, that public discussion about the qualifications of a candidate for elective office presents "what is probably the strongest possible case for application of the *New York Times* rule." The Court said that under any test it could conceive, the charge that a local mayor had been indicted for perjury was relevant to his fitness for office.[116] This case serves as a solid example of how far the Court was willing to go in 1971 to protect the press.

Pape grew out of a *Time* magazine quote of a summary of a 1961 Civil Rights Commission report. In a discussion of "police brutality and related private violence," the report had mentioned the case of *Monroe* v. *Pape*[117] and gone on to list some of the allegations in a civil rights complaint James Monroe had filed against certain Chicago policemen, headed by Deputy Chief of Detectives Frank Pape. *Time* quoted from the summary without indicating that the charges were Monroe's and not the independent findings of the commission. Pape sued for libel. The district court granted *Time*'s motion for summary judgment, but the court of appeals reversed, holding that there had to be a trial to decide whether *Time*'s failure to make clear that it was reporting no more than allegations showed "actual malice" under the *Times* rule.[118] The Supreme Court, after determining that *Time* had taken a number of precautions to insure authenticity of the article, held that the circumstances did not show that the magazine had engaged in a "falsification" sufficient in itself to sustain a jury finding of "actual malice."[119]

> *Time*'s omission of the word "alleged" amounted to the adoption of one of a number of possible rational interpretations of a document that bristled with ambiguities. The deliberate choice of such an interpretation, though arguably reflecting a misconception, was not enough to create a jury issue of "malice" under *New York Times*. To permit the malice issue to go to the jury because of the omission of a word like "alleged," . . . would be to impose a much stricter standard of liability on errors of interpretation or judgment than on errors of historic fact.[120]

Though these 1970-71 Supreme Court cases continued to expand the *Times* doctrine, the series of libel decisions favorable to the press after *Sullivan* reached its climax in *Rosenbloom* v. *Metromedia, Inc.*[121] With the 1971 *Rosenbloom* decision, which made the "actual malice" rule applicable to "all discussion and communication involving matters of public or general concern, without regard to whether the persons involved are famous or anonymous,"[122] the press, in regard to defamation liability, ascended to what was likely its most protected position ever.

Rosenbloom presented the question of whether the *Times* "knowing or reckless falsity" standard applied in a state civil libel action brought, not by a public official or a public figure, but by a private individual for a defamatory falsehood uttered in a radio news broadcast about George Rosenbloom's involvement in an event of public or general interest.[123]

Rosenbloom was a distributor of nudist magazines in the Philadelphia metropolitan area. In response to citizen complaints, a special police squad initiated a series of enforcement actions under the city's obscenity laws. The police searched Rosenbloom's home and the rented barn he used as a warehouse, seizing the inventory of magazines and books they found.[124] Radio station WIP broadcast news stories at 6:00 P.M. and 6:30 P.M. on October 4, 1963, reporting the seized books as "obscene." At 8:00 P.M. when the item was broadcast for a third time, WIP corrected the sentence to read "reportedly obscene." Rosenbloom subsequently brought an action in federal district court, claiming that the magazines he distributed were not obscene; he therefore sought injunctive relief prohibiting further police interference with his business. Station WIP reported the lawsuit. This series of stories did not identify Rosenbloom by name but said that "the girlie-book peddlers say the police crackdown and continued reference to their borderline literature as smut and filth is hurting their business."[125]

A jury in state court acquitted Rosenbloom of the criminal obscenity charges under instruction of the trial judge that, as a matter of law, the nudist magazines he had been distributing were not obscene. Rosenbloom then filed a libel suit against station WIP. He claimed the station's unqualified characterization of the books as "obscene" in the two early broadcasts describing the controversy constituted libel per se and was proved false by his subsequent acquittal.[126] The jury returned a verdict for Rosenbloom and awarded $25,000 in general damages and $725,000 in punitive damages. The district court reduced the punitive damages to $250,000. The court of appeals, emphasizing that the broadcasts concerned matters of public interest, reversed.[127]

A plurality of the U.S. Supreme Court, affirming the reversal, concluded that the *Times* standard of knowing or reckless falsity applied to actions brought by a private individual for a defamatory falsehood when the individual was involved in an event of public or general interest.[128] The Court's plurality relied on standards established in *St. Amant:* it concluded that, though the radio station news reports characterized Rosenbloom's business as "the smut literature racket," there was no evidence to support a conclusion that the station "in fact entertained serious doubts as to the truth" of its reports.[129]

Justices John Marshall Harlan and Thurgood Marshall both dissented. They cited many factors that were to be incorporated into the majority *Gertz*[130] decision that the Court handed down some three years later. Both justices were bothered by the lack of a general rule of application first established in the 1964 *Sullivan* decision. In its place, the plurality had imposed a case-by-case examination of situations to determine what constituted an event of public concern.[131] Justice Harlan advocated measures that would become part of the majority opinion in *Gertz*:

> When dealing with private libel, the States should be free to define for themselves the applicable standard of care so long as they do not impose liability without fault; . . . a showing of actual damage should be requisitive to recovery for libel and . . . it is impermissible, given the substantial constitutional values involved, to fail to confine the amount of jury verdicts in such cases within any ascertainable limits.[132]

Justice Marshall was equally emphatic in his dissenting belief that the condition for privilege—that the defamation must not be published with "reckless disregard"—offered inadequate protection for both of the basic values at stake:

> In order for particular defamation to come within the privilege there must be a determination that the event was of legitimate public interest. That determination will have to be made by courts generally and, in the last analysis, by this Court in particular. Courts, including this one, are not anointed with any extraordinary prescience. . . . The danger such a doctrine portends for freedom of the press seems apparent. The plurality's doctrine also threatens society's interest in protecting private individuals from being thrust into the public eye by the distorting light of defamation.[133]

Marshall also made known his feelings about excessive judgments for damages:

> The unlimited discretion exercised by juries in awarding punitive and presumed damages compounds the problem of self-censorship that necessarily results from the awarding of huge judgments. . . . The threats to society's interest in freedom of the press that are involved in punitive and presumed damages can largely be eliminated by restricting the award of damages to proved, actual injuries.[134]

The strong dissents in *Rosenbloom* were ominous for the press. One writer said: "The decision in that case [*Rosenbloom*] held the seeds of its own destruction. By then it had become clear that the protection to defamation defendants had gone too far."[135] The public interest test laid down in *Rosenbloom* was open to extremely broad interpretation in the lower courts. A law review commentary made the ramifications glaring: "It became clear that the media could fabricate their own privilege; most anything they published became a matter of public interest because of the publication."[136]

Even before the *Rosenbloom* judgment was handed down, however, *Gertz* v. *Robert Welch, Inc.*[137] was in the courts. The *Gertz* decision is particularly significant in terms of momentum; for nearly a decade after the landmark *Sullivan* case, libel decisions had moved toward greater press protection. The circumstances in *Gertz,* however, supplied the avenue for retrenchment; the case marked a retreat from the *Rosenbloom* principles. In applying the privilege, *Gertz* focused, not on whether the publication concerned an event of public interest, but upon the pre-*Rosenbloom* status of the person defamed.

Elmer Gertz, a well-known Chicago attorney, brought a diversity libel action in the U.S. District Court, Northern District of Illinois, against Robert Welch, Inc., publisher of *American Opinion,* a John Birch Society magazine. After a Chicago policeman named Richard Nuccio was convicted of murder, the victim's family retained Gertz to represent them in civil litigation against Nuccio. The *American Opinion* article alleged that Nuccio's murder trial was part of a Communist conspiracy to discredit the local police, and it falsely stated that Gertz had arranged Nuccio's "frame-up," implied that Gertz had a criminal record, and labeled him a "Communist-fronter."[138] The district court jury awarded Gertz $50,000 in the libel action, but the district judge, deciding that the article dealt with a public issue and that the knowing or reckless falsehood rule therefore applied, entered judgment for the magazine. The U.S. Court of Appeals, Seventh Circuit, affirmed, and Gertz appealed.[139]

The U.S. Supreme Court reversed, holding that a publisher or broadcaster of defamatory falsehoods about an individual who is neither a public official nor a public figure may not claim the *Times* "actual malice" protection against liability for defamation on the ground that the statements concerned an issue of public or general interest.[140] The Court said one could become a public figure only by thrusting oneself "to the forefront of particular public controversies in order to influence the resolution of the issues involved," or by assuming a role "of especial prominence in the affairs of society."[141] Gertz, then, was not labeled a public figure because he had not thrust himself into the limelight of the controversy and "had achieved no general fame or notoriety in the community."[142] The Court reasoned that private individuals are more vulnerable to injury than public officials and public figures, and therefore more deserving of recovery.[143]

The Court went on to refute the *Rosenbloom* plurality opinion, which left it for judges to determine if an issue was of "general or public interest." The Court said that an accommodation of the competing values at stake in defamation suits by private individuals allows states to impose liability on a less-demanding showing—presumably negligence—than that required by the *Times* doctrine. However, the Court made it clear that the states "may not permit recovery of presumed or punitive damages, at least when liability is not based on a showing of knowledge of falsity or reckless disregard for the truth."[144]

Justice Harry Blackmun was the "swing man" in *Gertz*. Acknowledging that the Court had been sadly fractionated in *Rosenbloom*, Blackmun emphasized that it was important for the Court to come to rest in the defamation area, to clearly define a majority position that would eliminate the "unsureness engendered by *Rosenbloom*'s diversity."[145] Thus he went along with the *Gertz* majority. Justice Brennan dissented, emphasizing that *Rosenbloom*, in which the public or private nature of the individual hinged on whether he was involved in an event of public or general interest, struck a better accommodation than *Gertz* did between avoidance of media self-censorship and protection of individual reputations.[146] Brennan quoted from *Time, Inc.* v. *Hill,* where the Court said that matters of public or general interest do not suddenly become less so merely because a private individual did not 'voluntarily' choose to become involved."[147]

One law review commentary emphasized three major developments in the *Gertz* opinion that substantially depart from the reasoning of *Sullivan* and its progeny:

> (1) adoption of a constitutional balancing test which weighs the First Amendment interest in the institutional autonomy of the media against the state's interest . . .; (2) reformulation of the "public figure" concept; and (3) significant alteration of the common law rules governing damages in libel actions.[148]

Though *Gertz* withdrew some of the press protection afforded by *Rosenbloom,* the Court gave something in return to the media. According to one law review commentary, *Gertz* "increased the media's measure of protection from libel judgments by requiring all defamation plaintiffs to prove actual damages"—thus virtually eliminating media libel per se—"and by restricting awards of punitive damages to cases in which the plaintiff established knowing or reckless falsehood."[149] While private plaintiffs need only prove some degree of fault as determined by the particular state, the standard of proof required of public officials remains unchanged by *Gertz.* Thus, the *Rosenbloom* plurality was not completely overturned.

It has been logically concluded that *Gertz* created a two-tiered constitutional standard for libel laws, the first tier being the *New York Times* privilege when the defamation involves persons with public status, the second tier being the *Gertz* rule, a lesser protection for the media when injury is claimed by plaintiffs of private status.[150]

One writer developed two explanations for the Court's retreat in *Gertz:* (1) the Court's membership had changed (Justices Lewis Powell and William Rehnquist replaced Justices Hugo Black and John Marshall Harlan); and (2) under *Rosenbloom,* the lower courts had overextended the *Times* standard with the implied acquiescence of the U.S. Supreme Court.[151]

Legal counsel for Gertz was naturally pleased with the outcome:

> The Supreme Court has, through its own process of common law evolution, under the umbrella of the First Amendment to the Constitution, brought the law of defamation into more traditional tort lines.[152]

The attorney went on to explain that no longer would a plaintiff be able to collect damages merely upon showing that the defendant had said something bad about him; still, those who have suffered actual harm have the benefit of a forum to receive compensation.[153]

Though the effects of *Gertz* were uncertain, the Court forged ahead with another far-reaching decision less than two years later. In *Time, Inc.* v. *Firestone,*[154] the Court defined as a private person a woman who was married to a member of a wealthy industrial family, was a party to a divorce trial which resulted in significant media coverage, and whose appearances in the printed press were frequent enough to warrant her subscribing to a press clipping service and holding several press conferences in the course of the proceedings.

The case grew out of divorce proceedings involving Mary Alice Firestone and her husband, the scion of a wealthy industrial family. On the basis of newspaper and wire service reports and information from a bureau chief and a stringer, *Time* magazine published an item reporting that the divorce was granted "on grounds of extreme cruelty and adultery." Actually, the marriage was dissolved only on the ground of extreme cruelty. The divorce court never ruled Ms. Firestone had been guilty of adultery. Ms. Firestone sued and was awarded a $100,000 libel judgment, which was affirmed by the Florida Supreme Court. The U.S. Supreme Court remanded the case back to the Florida courts, holding that there was no evidence of fault presented to the jury, nor was there a finding of fault as specified in *Gertz*.[155] The Court, however, ruled that the *Times* rule, requiring a showing of "actual malice," was inapplicable to this case because Ms. Firestone was neither a public official nor public figure, based on the definition advanced in *Gertz:*

> For the most part those who attain this status [public figure] have assumed roles of especial prominence in the affairs of society. Some occupy positions of such persuasive power and influence that they are deemed public figures for all purposes. More commonly, those classed as public figures have thrust themselves to the forefront of particular public controversies in order to influence the resolution of the issues involved. In either event, they invite attention and comment.[156]

The *Firestone* majority stated that Ms. Firestone—

> did not assume any role of especial prominence in the affairs of society, other than perhaps Palm Beach society, and . . . did not thrust herself to the forefront of any particular public controversy in order to influence the resolution of the issues involved in it.[157]

Though *Time* used two arguments in its defense—Ms. Firestone was a "public figure" within the *Times* standard, and the article constituted a report of a judicial proceeding—the Court would not accept either defense.

The Court was just as adamant in rejecting the "judicial proceeding" argument as it had been in determining Ms. Firestone was not a "public figure." Justice Rehnquist emphasized that little would be gained by extending this blanket judicial proceeding privilege:

> The details of many, if not most, courtroom battles would add almost nothing toward advancing the uninhibited debate on public issues thought to provide principal support for the decision in *New York Times* [v. *Sullivan*]. . . . There appears little reason why these individuals [private persons] should substantially forfeit that degree of protection which

> the law of defamation would otherwise afford them simply by virtue of their being drawn into a courtroom.[158]

The Court also brushed aside the defense argument that a rational interpretation of an ambiguous document is constitutionally protected under the *Pape* decision. In *Pape,* the Court had been applying the *Times* standard to test whether the defendant had acted in reckless disregard of the truth, since Pape was a public figure.

Though *Gertz* and *Firestone* disturbed the press, a decision handed down by the U.S. Supreme Court on April 18, 1979, is potentially devastating. The case, *Herbert* v. *Lando,*[159] grew out of the Vietnam turmoil. In March of 1971, Lt. Col. Anthony Herbert gained national attention when he publicly charged two superior officers with covering up war crimes. Herbert said, in documents filed with the U.S. Army Criminal Investigations Division, that he had witnessed numerous atrocities while commanding a battalion in Vietnam. He cited the murders of four North Vietnamese prisoners of war by South Vietnamese police in the presence of an American adviser who failed to interfere. The killings allegedly occurred on February 14, 1969—thus Herbert labeled them the "St. Valentine's Day Massacre."

The colonel claimed that the Army was covering up his charges; he was abruptly relieved of his command. Herbert became a national celebrity. *Life* magazine did a flattering story; the *New York Times* published a laudatory article headlined, "How a Supersoldier Was Fired From His Command." Barry Lando, an associate producer of CBS Weekend News, was among those who interviewed Herbert and wrote complimentary stories. In 1972, when Lando became producer of CBS's documentary news program "60 Minutes," he decided to further investigate Herbert's charges. Lando conducted extensive interviews and laborious time-consuming research. Among other things, he concluded that the Army had done a reasonably thorough job of investigating Herbert's charges, that the superior officer to whom Herbert said he reported on February 14, 1969, was not in the country on that date, and that Herbert himself had, on occasion, engaged in intimidating behavior around prisoners of war. Lando produced and edited a report on Herbert for the February 4, 1973, "60 Minutes" program which was narrated by correspondent Mike Wallace. Lando then wrote an article for *Atlantic Monthly* magazine that was critical of the colonel.

Herbert sued Lando, Wallace, CBS, Inc., and the Atlantic Monthly Co., for $44,750,000 in damages for injury to his reputation and for impairment of his book, *Soldier*, as a literary property. Herbert contended that Lando had deliberately distorted the record through selective investigation, "skillful editing," and one-sided interviewing. During a one-year period, Lando responded to pre-trial discovery questions that required twenty-six sessions. The transcript totaled 2,903 pages. In addition, Lando introduced into evidence 240 exhibits which included transcripts of his interviews, some of his notes, videotapes of interviews and a series of drafts of the "60 Minutes" telecast.

When asked questions relating to his beliefs, opinions, intent and conclusions in preparing the program, however, Lando refused to answer. He cited the First Amendment. In attempting to determine Lando's state of mind—his personal beliefs—Herbert's attorneys hoped to prove the defendants had acted in "reckless disregard for the truth." A public figure must meet a heavy burden to prove actual malice, Herbert's attorneys reasoned. Thus, they felt justified in probing and analyzing Lando's thought processes.

The District Court held for Herbert, but the Second Circuit Court of Appeals reversed, holding that an inquiry into a journalist's thought processes violated the First Amendment. The appeals court majority emphasized that journalists "must constantly probe and investigate," must formulate views at every step, and must always question conclusions. The court said that if plaintiffs were allowed to probe into reporters' or editors' thought processes, journalists would tend "to follow the safe course of avoiding contention and controversy—the antithesis of the values fostered by the First Amendment."[160]

The U.S. Supreme Court, however, voted 6–3 to reverse. Justice Byron R. White, who wrote the majority opinion, said that "contrary to the views of the Court of Appeals, according an absolute privilege to the editorial process of a media defendant in a libel case is not required, authorized or presaged by our prior cases." The justice wrote that this privilege would "substantially enhance the burden of proving actual malice contrary to the expectations" of cases such as *Sullivan* and *Butts*. White stated:

> We are thus being asked to modify firmly established constitutional doctrine by placing beyond the plaintiff's reach a range of direct evidence relevant to proving knowing or reckless falsehood by the publisher of an alleged libel, elements that are critical to plaintiffs such as Herbert. The case for making this modification is by no means clear and convincing, and we decline to accept it.[161]

White disregarded contentions that the decision would have a "chilling" effect on the press and would make them avoid controversy. He wrote that permitting plaintiffs such as Herbert "to prove their cases by direct as well as indirect evidence is consistent with the balance" struck by prior Supreme Court libel decisions. Indeed, the majority said libel suit plaintiffs should be given the opportunity to probe defendants' states of mind during pre-trial questioning. White wrote:

> If the publisher in fact had serious doubts about accuracy, but published nevertheless, no undue self-censorship will result from permitting the relevant inquiry. Only knowing or reckless error will be discouraged; and unless there is to be an absolute First Amendment privilege to inflict injury by knowing or reckless conduct, which respondents do not suggest, constitutional values will not be threatened.[162]

Thus, *Gertz, Firestone,* and *Lando* (though their effects on the media are not yet completely clear) have definitely dampened press freedom after nearly a decade when the press enjoyed ever-expanding "breathing space" in the aftermath of the historic *Sullivan* decision.

The Current State of the Press

There has been a great deal of speculation on the effects of *Gertz*. One writer theorized that the decision would not likely spur a great increase in defamation suits instituted by private individuals because of time and expense involved. However, he predicted "an increase in the percentage of successful private citizen litigants, if the states promulgate less stringent standards for establishing liability."[163]

Gertz definitely marked a retrenchment from the standard established in *Rosenbloom*. One writer aptly categorized the decision when he said, "The Court took two modest steps forward and one large step backward." More specifically:

> It [the *Gertz* Court] enhanced press protection by holding that First Amendment interests preclude the states from imposing liability without fault and from awarding presumed or punitive damages, at least absent a showing of reckless or knowing falsity. But the Court severely constricted press protection by refusing to apply the *Times* privilege to persons who, although not public officials or public figures, are involved in matters of public or general concern.[164]

The jury is still out on the primary effects of *Gertz* on the media; therefore, it is only safe to conclude that in actions by private individuals the press has more protection than it did before *Sullivan*, but less than it came to assume after *Rosenbloom*.[165]

The *Gertz* Court made a "substantial departure from the broad, issue-oriented, protective approach" the Warren Court utilized when handing down *Sullivan*. One law review commentary emphasized that:

> The constitutional principle which emerges from *Gertz* is that the societal role of the press—as an independent institution—requires that it enjoy some measure of immunity from punishment for error in the full scope of its operation. . . . The Court solidified the distinction between "public" and "private" persons—not because the media interest was less demanding, but because the state interest was more

> compelling. Whether the resulting rules will afford more or less protection is largely a matter of speculation, but . . . the Court has retreated from the idea that the First Amendment rights of the press occupy a preferred position in the law of libel.[166]

The uncertainty of the *Gertz* ramifications extends to scholars, journalists, attorneys, and the courts themselves. Contrary to Justice Blackmun's intentions to solidify the law of libel, *Gertz* has not brought an air of certainty to the ever evolving concept.

It has been pointed out that there are now three distinct categories in libel actions: (1) public officials and figures who fall under the *New York Times* standard; (2) private plaintiffs, who must show merely fault to receive actual damages and "actual malice" to receive presumed or punitive damages if the publication deals with a matter of general or public concern; and (3) private libels, which continue to be dealt with under established common law principles of various states.[167]

Lower courts are also apparently having difficulty defining a "public" person. Though no single definition has emerged, an examination of lower court decisions shows: (1) persons who actively seek publicity for themselves or their cases will be considered public figures; (2) those who thrust themselves to the forefront of public controversies are public figures; and (3) those who accept a role in society where one can expect publicity cannot claim to be private individuals.[168] Despite these general observations, the *Gertz* criteria remain muddled. The distinction between a private person and public figure is still so loosely defined that the press cannot be sure in which categories their news subjects belong.[169]

To further complicate matters, the negligence standard, presumably established in *Gertz*, has received various interpretations from the state courts. Though at least two states—Indiana and Colorado—have clung to the *New York Times* actual malice standard, diverse standards have been adopted in other jurisdictions ranging from—

> gross negligence to ordinary negligence and [application of] . . . a variety of tests, including "clear and convincing evidence" (Florida), "reasonable ground" to believe in the truth (Illinois), "conduct of the reasonably careful person under the circumstances" (Kansas), "negligent failure to exercise due care" (Ohio), and "a preponderance of evidence" (New York).[170]

Obviously, the full impact of *Gertz* will not be known until the courts have more opportunity to fully interpret the far-from-concrete standards the case established.[171]

Meanwhile, media practitioners continue to grope in a libel sea of relative ambiguity and uncertainty. Based on various interpretations of *Gertz* in the lower courts, it appears that many judges are operating on the philosophy Justice Potter Stewart adopted when searching for a definition of obscenity: "[all I can say is that] I know it when I see it."[172]

Definitions for "public figures," "negligence," and "private persons" present an equal dilemma in the libel area. Though most newspaper editors may think they know a public figure "when they see one," the courts might not agree.

Therefore, it is apparent that a study of libel law produces conflicting emotions. Two libel authorities have, for example, written:

> The picture that emerges from this study of libel is one that heartens and at the same time appalls the observer. He is heartened at the trend in the law toward more freedom to speak out on public affairs [pre-*Gertz*]. He is appalled by the possible use of that freedom to wreck an innocent man's reputation.[173]

The fact remains, however, that from its earliest beginnings, the law of defamation has evolved by the balancing of conflicting interests.[174] The balancing is nowhere more apparent than in *Gertz,* where the right of the press to publish articles of public or general interest was weighed against the state's interest in redressing wrongful injury through defamation. Though it is a reasonable assumption that this balancing will continue, only future Supreme Court justices hold the answer to which interest will ultimately prevail. Thus, muckraking writers of the "Merry-Go-Round" column must constantly keep the ever evolving libel law in perspective, always realizing that to cross over the permissible-forbidden line established by the Court could result in significant monetary and credibility loss.

4

Initial Libel Challenges to the "Merry-Go-Round" —MacArthur and Sweeney

"Merry-Go-Round" columnists were confronted early with the specter of a formidable libel suit plaintiff. Drew Pearson and Robert S. Allen's column had been in existence less than two years when a $1,750,000 suit was filed in the Supreme Court for the District of Columbia.[1] Gen. Douglas MacArthur, army chief of staff, brought the action. The general charged that certain "Merry-Go-Round" columns had given the impression that he was guilty of conduct unbecoming an officer—that the columns held him up to ridicule and contempt.

According to MacArthur's complaint, the columns alleged that he was trying to succeed himself as chief of staff. The general also claimed that the articles had wrongly questioned his eviction of the "bonus Army."[2] Further, MacArthur alleged that the columnists had falsely accused him of leading a drive to remove Harry H. Woodring, assistant secretary of war.[3]

Pearson later wrote that it was President Franklin D. Roosevelt who actually persuaded MacArthur to file suit:

> The President was so irked that he took several minutes to tell the Cabinet that he wanted to put us out of business. . . . Frankly, it gave me a jolt to learn that the president of the United States would encourage a libel suit against two newspapermen who had supported the chief goals of his administration.[4]

The columnist, however, did not let the suit intimidate him; dozens of subsequent libel actions in later decades can be used as a measuring stick of his continued aggressive reporting.

Newsweek magazine used a feature approach to the *MacArthur* suit. The article said that Pearson and Allen had, in essence, charged MacArthur with sponsoring a bill to give retired chiefs of staff a twenty-one gun salute, and with soliciting a socially prominent person to help him get promotions. Using a feature approach, the *Newsweek* article said that, had Pearson and Allen reported on the suit, it might have read:

> The handsome and bemedaled chief of staff, Gen. Douglas MacArthur, who was "the hero of the Bonus Battle," last week slapped libel suits totaling $1,750,000 on Drew Pearson, the tall, handsome, and professorial-looking correspondent; on Eleanor (Cissy) Patterson, owner-manager of the *Washington Herald*, who was Pearson's mother-in-law while he was married to the Countess Felicia Gizycka; and on swashbuckling and hotheaded Bob Allen, co-author of the "Merry-Go-Round."[5]

Newsweek's story said that the suit was "one of the most resounding thwacks ever aimed at the Fourth Estate by a high government official." The article also noted that the libel suit was the first "ever filed against the column despite the fact that for eighteen months it has been distributing chatty and gossipy lowdown on capital higher-ups."[6]

An article in the *Literary Digest*, meanwhile, predicted that MacArthur's suit would possibly illustrate "how far a gossip columnist may go in this fertile field of officialdom":

> The legal latitude of a columnist is a thing most of Washington wants to know. While there are all shades of gossip "colyums," the essential nature of most is to print back-stage and back-stairs talk which fails to get into regular news dispatches because it is trivial, or undignified. It ranges all the way from intimate personalities—"keyhole stuff"—to disconnected by-products of straight news reporting.[7]

The article declared that many of the "more venturesome" Washington columnists were "treading easier" until the *MacArthur* suit was decided. The magazine further stated that, "if carried to a final determination," the *MacArthur* suit would "draw the line legally between what is and what is not privileged in the activities in Washington."[8]

The general, however, eventually dropped the suit, paying Pearson's and Allen's legal fees, when it appeared that some even more damaging material about him would come out at the trial.[9]

In some respects, the MacArthur episode established the tenor for the controversial "Merry-Go-Round" column—that no man or institution is immune from its muckraking attacks—and launched an amazing number of court confrontations in which Pearson was involved.

Naturally, the columnist did not get off so quickly—or so cheaply—in the majority of libel suits filed against him and his column. Rather, he was forced to expend a tremendous amount of money and energy to defend himself. He relied primarily on common law libel defenses.[10] Though these defenses did not provide as much protection as the "actual malice" rule articulated by the U.S. Supreme Court in 1964,[11] Pearson and his attorneys—through ingenuity, tenacity, pride, and libel law scholarship—made up for whatever theoretical and uniform protection was lacking in common law libel. Possibly no case in American legal history so vividly illustrates the various pre-1964 nonuniform jurisdictional libel law applications as the Sweeney chain suit.

Sweeney's Sixty-Eight Libel Suits

Newspapers of the late nineteenth and early twentieth centuries, which published primarily locally written columns and news dispatches, merely had to verify close-at-hand facts to steer clear of the libel arena. But as technological advances led to state, national, and international news coverage through press associations and feature syndicates, the possibility of chain libel suits became a fear among newspaper executives. No longer was it possible for a local editor to verify the accuracy of thousands of words compiled from dozens of sources.[12] The threat of devastating chain libel proceedings became real when Ohio congressman Martin L. Sweeney brought sixty-eight lawsuits against various newspapers, based upon publication of an allegedly libelous "Merry-Go-Round" column.[13] Filed in jurisdictions coast to coast and border to border, the suits created a huge headache for Pearson. Fortunately for him—and his finances—most of the cases were dismissed in their early stages. Through it all, however, the columnist claimed he could prove the truth of his column.

Because of the extensive nature of the case, Pearson maintained a voluminous file of correspondence with editors and attorneys involved in the various suits. Nearly three boxes of Sweeney materials are in the Pearson papers in the Lyndon Baines Johnson Library in Austin, Texas. Separate folders were kept regarding each case; it was a tremendous chore that must have detracted greatly from the time Pearson was able to devote to his "Merry-Go-Round" column. Amazingly, however, the muckraker personally answered the majority of correspondence concerning the chain case. Letters often transmitted a personal point of view; he was obviously very concerned about the outcome of the cases. In reality, his future depended upon it. The suit was, after all, an obvious attempt to bankrupt the column.[14] Pearson's wife, Luvie, certainly viewed the action as a massive effort to put her husband out of business. She traveled to many of the pretrial sessions, as did the columnist.[15]

To compound Pearson's problem, Sweeney threatened to sue more newspapers than he actually did. For example, Roy Anderson, editor of the *Ketchikan Chronicle* in Alaska, sent a letter to the columnist informing him of a threatened suit. Pearson responded, half in jest: "Thanks for your fine letter. I, too, hope you are not sued, though, if you are, at least Mr. Allen and I can then boast that our papers have been sued from Alaska to Panama. Sweeney has already brought suit against the *Panama American*."[16] Pearson also elaborated on the status of the case:

> Most of our editors have felt that there was not one chance in a hundred of Sweeney collecting even six cents in any city in the United States, even Ohio cities. You can imagine, for instance, the chance of an Alaskan jury, which probably never heard of Sweeney, finding that he had been hurt in so remote an area from his own Congressional district. . . . Naturally we have been most distressed at these suits, not because we as individuals are sued, but because of the nuisance involved to our editors and newspapers. So far, however, our editors and publishers have been grand and have stood behind us 100 percent.[17]

Pearson said he felt that most editors realized that the Sweeney action was "sort of a test case and that if Sweeney is able to get away with a blanket suit against all subscribers to a newspaper column, then all columns will be subject to this sort of drive against freedom of the press."[18]

The muckraker made a concerted effort to keep papers that had been sued by Sweeney abreast of developments in various jurisdictions. He continuously updated lists of newspapers that had been sued, attorneys defending the cases, amounts of money being sought by Sweeney, jurisdiction of cases, and other pertinent particulars. Pearson also carried on an extensive correspondence with George Carlin of the United Feature

Syndicate, distributor of the column, regarding progress in the various cases.

The action itself evolved from a December 23, 1938, "Merry-Go-Round" column that Sweeney claimed charged him with opposing the appointment of a federal district judge because the latter was a Jew. The column that the congressman objected to was five paragraphs in length. Sweeney claimed that the following excerpts were false:

> A hot behind-the-scenes fight is raging in Democratic congressional ranks over the effort of Father [Charles E.] Coughlin to prevent the appointment of a Jewish judge in Cleveland.

After explaining who the proposed appointee was, the column said that the appointment had also aroused the "violent opposition of Representative Martin L. Sweeney," who "was known as the chief congressional spokesman of Father Coughlin. [Father Coughlin, a Roman Catholic priest with a considerable national following, was sometimes accused of being anti-Semitic. See note 20 *infra* for more details.] Basis of the Sweeney-Coughlin opposition is the fact that [proposed appointee Emerich] Freed is a Jew, and not born in the United States." The columnists then mentioned other possible appointees and reasons they had been eliminated from consideration, and concluded, "Irate, Representative Sweeney is endeavoring to call a caucus of Ohio Representatives December 28 to protest against Freed's appointment."[19] The battle lines were drawn. Sweeney vociferously objected to the allegations; Pearson staunchly stood by the remarks.[20]

When the House returned from Christmas recess in 1939, Sweeney wasted little time in recounting his reaction to the column:[21]

> This article is a deliberate falsehood, and I cannot let this occasion pass without meeting the challenge of Drew Pearson and Robert S. Allen, who have more than once published in their "Washington Merry-Go-Round" malicious falsehoods concerning members of Congress in their official capacity.[22]

Sweeney went on to emphasize that, during his eight years in Congress, he had noticed that it was not uncommon for members of the body "to rise to a question of personal privilege to indict the abuse of a free press on the part of these well-known columnists."[23]

In an effort not to arouse all journalists, Sweeney emphasized that he had "wholesome respect for the members of the Fourth Estate," but "it is unfortunate that the sins of a few members of this exalted profession bring discredit at times upon some very fine men and women who are engaged in the field of journalism."[24]

The congressman labeled the column a "sounding board" for the Roosevelt administration. He announced that he was suing certain newspapers that had published the column; further, he said he was confident the courts of the country would verify his claims. Sweeney stated that he had obtained his former colleague in the House, John J. O'Connor of New York, as counsel.[25]

In all but one of the reported *Sweeney* cases the action was dismissed.[26] However, many suits required numerous briefs and motions before final action was taken; a complaint brought by Sweeney in the District of Columbia is an example.[27] The suit was filed against the United Feature Syndicate, Inc., distributors of the "Merry-Go-Round" column; Eleanor Patterson, publisher of the *Washington Times-Herald* which carried the column; Pearson; and Allen.[28] One of the documents in the case was the extensive deposition of Ernest Cuneo, a Washington, D.C., attorney and personal friend of Pearson, on behalf of the defendants, taken in January of 1941.[29] William A. Roberts of the law firm Roberts & McInnis, representative for the defendants, posed questions for Cuneo. Because of the multitude of *Sweeney* cases in which Roberts & McInnis was involved, Roberts asked that Cuneo's deposition be provided for each jurisdiction.[30] Counsel for Sweeney naturally objected, but the questioning continued.

After attorneys for the defendants filed a motion for judgment on the proceedings, Sweeney's lawyers immediately filed an opposition.[31] The congressman's attorneys objected to the statement by defense lawyers that the case filed in the District of Columbia represented but "one link in a chain":

> While defendants might lightly assert, as they do in this motion, that the complaint constitutes but "one link in a chain" of libel suits, it will readily be seen that this cause of action reaches to the very fountain-head from which streamed the matter complained of and which ultimately became the basis of libel actions filed in other jurisdictions.[32]

It was emphasized that the column was distributed to approximately three hundred twenty-five newspapers. Though Pearson's attorneys claimed that the article complained of was not libelous per se, Sweeney's lawyers countered:

> There appears to be but one question at issue, and that is whether it is libelous per se to falsely accuse a public official of religious and racial hatred in the performance of his official duties.[33]

It was further stated that "there can be no question but that the publication complained of would serve to damnify the plaintiff in the eyes of 4,081,242 Jews in this country."[34]

Though the vast majority of jurisdictions that heard the various *Sweeney* cases ruled that Pearson's remarks were not libelous per se, the congressman's counsel was able to list nine instances in which the case was not dismissed on the ground that the words were not libelous per se.[35] A quote, in fact, was taken from one of the nine examples, an unreported Illinois decision, *Sweeney* v. *Illinois Publishing and Printing Co., et al.:*

> It is one of the fundamentals of our institutions that neither race nor creed shall disqualify one from holding public office. The article in question in effect charges plaintiff with being unworthy of his position as a Congressman of the United States in making the Jewishness of Emerich Burt Freed a test of his qualifications to hold office.

A second paragraph from the Illinois decision was also quoted:

> Freedom of the press does not mean irresponsibility for newspaper publishers, and that freedom will best be preserved through the exercise of care by the publishers in verifying slanderous statements before publishing them.[36]

Thus, attorneys for the plaintiff argued that no special damages had to be set forth because it was clear that the words complained of were libelous per se.[37] Despite the marshaling of evidence by Sweeney's attorneys, however, the District Court for the District of Columbia granted the defense motion for a judgment on the proceedings.[38] The case was appealed to the court of appeals, which affirmed.[39]

The appeals court emphasized that it was not actionable to publish erroneous and injurious statements regarding political conduct and views of public officials so long as no charge of crime, corruption, or gross immorality was made. The court said that "such a publication is not 'libelous per se.' "[40] This ruling, however, was more than just another relatively liberal judgment.

Associate Justice Henry Edgerton, writing for the court, articulated some enlightened views on the First Amendment and libel actions:

> Cases which impose liability for erroneous reports of the political conduct of officials reflect the obsolete doctrine that the governed must not criticize their governors. Since Congress governs the country, all inhabitants, and not merely the constituents of particular members, are vitally concerned in the political conduct and views of every member of Congress.[41]

Edgerton further stated that the "protection of the public requires not merely discussion, but information." Acknowledging that errors of fact are inevitable, particularly in regard to a man's mental states and processes, Edgerton continued:

> Information and discussion will be discouraged, and the public interest in public knowledge of important facts will

> be poorly defended, if error subjects its author to a libel suit without even a showing of economic loss. Whatever is added to the field of libel is taken from the field of free debate.[42]

Pearson was naturally elated with the outcome. In fact, he wasted little time in spreading the word to his newspaper clients. The muckraker dispatched a memo to newspaper editors and attorneys involved in various Sweeney cases.[43]

This particular opinion was later cited in *New York Times Co.* v. *Sullivan* as recognizing that "erroneous statements are inevitable in free debate" and thus deserving of protection.[44]

Sweeney was not even able to get a favorable verdict in his home state of Ohio. The congressman filed suit in the Common Pleas Court of Summit County for the "Merry-Go-Round" article published in the *Akron Beacon Journal.* The trial court sustained a defense demurrer; the plaintiff then appealed.[45] The Ohio Court of Appeals carefully examined what it termed "a comprehensive classification" of matters considered libelous per se under Ohio state law. These included:

> (1) An offense indictable at law, involving in its perpetration moral turpitude or visitable with an infamous punishment; or (2) an offensive disease or other disgrace of a social character, importing the exclusion of its victim from reputable society; or (3) in the case of a woman, lack of chastity or her lack of standing in society as a woman; or (4) conduct which would be calculated to injure the person in his calling, business, trade or profession; or (5) matters which would bring him into ridicule, hatred, or contempt.[46]

The court stated that Sweeney claimed the "Merry-Go-Round" column in question included words that fell in the fourth and fifth categories.

Judge Arthur Doyle, however, quickly dismissed this contention. He stated that the claimed libel was directed

> solely to the activities of the congressman as a public officer and does not impute to him any conduct in his calling,

> business, trade or profession. The publication does not speak of the congressman as a lawyer.[47]

Secondly, Judge Doyle said that, when the words of ridicule or contempt relate solely to political views or arguments on questions of public interest and do not attack the character of a person, they are not actionable without proof of special damages.

Emphasizing the give-and-take inherent to discussion of matters in the political arena, the Ohio court said that opposition by a congressman to the appointment of a person to high public office for reasons of creed did not violate either the moral code or the "laws of the land." Drawing an interesting parallel, the court said that, if it were to rule in favor of Sweeney, it could also be said that the framers of the U.S. Constitution violated the moral code when they advocated portions of the document that limit the office of the presidency to natural-born citizens, or promoted the provision that no person can serve in Congress who has not been a U.S. citizen for seven years.[48]

Sweeney received similar treatment in the District Court for the Southern District of Texas.[49] The court said that decisions from other states were helpful but not controlling, since the case would have to be decided under Texas law. The court examined Texas libel law and granted the motion of defense attorneys to dismiss.[50] The court recognized that the general rule in Texas was that a statement concerning a public official, in order to be libelous per se, had to be of such a character as, if true, would subject him to removal from office.[51]

The court sought to answer the primary question: What effect would the publication have on the mind of an ordinary reader, or what construction would he put upon it?[52] The Texas court then borrowed reasoning from the only reported case in which it was held that the "Merry-Go-Round" column in question was libelous per se.[53] In that case, the Second Circuit Court of Appeals had given "due weight and effect" to the time and place of publication. In applying similar reasoning to readers in southern Texas, however, the district court reached quite a different decision. In what was likely the strongest rejection of Sweeney's complaint in the reported cases, District Court Judge James Allred stated:

> It seems to me this Court should not close its eyes to the fact that the "ordinary reader" of defendant *Corpus Christi Caller-Times* probably never heard of Congressman Sweeney before the publication, didn't remember his name five minutes afterward and did not care whether he opposed the appointment of Freed, or on what grounds.[54]

Allred further emphasized that the publication "hardly conveyed the impression" that Sweeney was anti-Semitic or un-American. Saying that "ordinary readers" around Corpus Christi were "fortunately tolerant and skeptical, especially as to political matters," he said they subscribed to the "general principle recognized by statute and decisions" that newspapers could publish what they wanted concerning a public officer so long as they did not falsely charge him with conduct that could conceivably subject him to removal from office.[55]

Allred, however, was not content to halt his opinion at this point. He continued to stress that public officials were subject to critical evaluation by the press:

> While a public officer or candidate cannot be libeled any more than any other citizen, he cannot go about with his feelings on his sleeve. Public officials and candidates are legitimate subjects for news and comment. While they cannot be libeled, they must reconcile themselves to occasional "yarns" which, however hurtful to their feelings, are not actionable.[56]

The judge emphasized that, while a newspaper cannot make untrue and libelous statements and comments ascribing corruption to a public official, a newspaper publisher could certainly avail himself of the qualified privilege of fair comment on matters of public interest, without establishing a perfect defense of truth. Further, Allred said that Texas courts, while always careful to protect the rights of a citizen to his good name, "have, with equal zeal, progressively recognized the right of newspapers to make reasonable and fair comment on the acts of public officials."[57]

Utilizing similar reasoning, the Federal District Court for the Southern District of Idaho granted a defense motion to dismiss in *Sweeney* v. *Capital News Publishing Co.*[58] District Court Judge Charles Cavanah succinctly stated:

> No special damages are alleged, and the inquiry on the motion to dismiss is whether the words of the article, on their face, without explanation or extrinsic proof, would tend to impeach the honesty, integrity, virtue or reputation of the plaintiff and thereby expose him to public hatred, contempt and ridicule as defined by the statute of this State.

To resolve the question, the definition of libel under Idaho statutes was examined:

> A libel is a malicious defamation, expressed either by writing, printing, or by signs or pictures, or the like, tending to blacken the memory of one who is dead, or to impeach the honesty, integrity, virtue or reputation, or publish the natural or alleged defects of one who is alive, and thereby to expose him to public hatred, contempt or ridicule.[59]

Judge Cavanah emphasized that a "careful study and analysis of the words" of the column was necessary, for they could not be made libelous per se by innuendo or statements of conclusions.[60] Upon examination of the column, Cavanah could find nothing libelous per se. He claimed that a congressman had a right to oppose any person who was being considered for a federal judgeship, and that to do so had no tendency to impair Sweeney's reputation.[61]

Meanwhile, the Tennessee Supreme Court was unable to find the words complained of to be libelous per se.[62] The court affirmed a lower court judgment that had sustained a demurrer by the defendant. The Tennessee Supreme Court, in an opinion written by Chief Justice Grafton Green, said that Sweeney's counsel had made a "strong argument," but the court could not agree with their contentions:

> The declaration contains no innuendo. Describing plaintiff as "the chief congressional spokesman of Father Coughlin" is not in itself libelous. The appellation *Father* indicates that Father Coughlin is a priest of the Catholic church, and to act as spokesman for an ordained member of the clergy imputes no disgrace nor any reflection on the spokesman's character. We can not take judicial notice of derelictions on the part of Father Coughlin, if he has been guilty of such.[63]

Green further reasoned that opposition of a congressman to the selection of a federal judge on grounds of creed or place of birth did not necessarily reflect "on the personal, professional, or official character of that congressman."[64]

Chief Justice Green pointed out that Sweeney could just as easily have opposed the appointment of Freed as a matter of political party policy, something perfectly natural and acceptable in a democratic society. Green also stated that much of Sweeney's argument would have been "more appropriate" if it had set out special damages.[65]

On the federal appeals level, the Court of Appeals for the Third Circuit affirmed a lower court judgment dismissing Sweeney's complaint against the Philadelphia Record Co. and two other corporations.[66] The circuit court heard all three appeals together to consider the controlling question of whether the dismissed complaints had stated any cause of action. The court held that they had not, thus affirming the lower court decisions.[67]

The court considered whether the words were libelous per se from three perspectives: whether they libeled the plaintiff as a congressman, as a member of the bar, or as a private citizen. Circuit Court Judge John Biggs wrote that there was "nothing in the published matter which connects the plaintiff . . . with the legal profession."[68] Further, under Pennsylvania law, to libel a public official the misconduct asserted "must be of a criminal nature or at least would warrant the removal of the public officer from his office."[69] It was decided that the "Merry-Go-Round" article did not abuse these criteria. The court also reasoned that the words were not libelous per se against Sweeney even in a purely private capacity. In a satiric gesture toward the Ohio congressman's stance, the court said:

> At the most the appellant is charged with being a bigoted person who, actuated by a prejudice of an unpleasant and undesirable kind, opposed a foreign born Jew for a judicial appointment. Let us assume that it was stated in the alleged libel that the plaintiff opposed the appointment of a candidate simply because he was an Eskimo born above the Arctic Circle. We think that this example makes obvious the absurdity of the plaintiff's position. Eskimos are not being persecuted. Jews [it was during World War II] are being widely persecuted. We think that it is the connotation of persecution, which when carried into the matter published concerning the plaintiff, gives it the fallacious aspect of being libelous per se.[70]

The column did not allege that Sweeney persecuted foreign-born Jews; rather, according to the court, it merely said that he opposed one for a federal judgeship.[71]

Though the "Merry-Go-Round" column of which Sweeney complained was repeatedly held to be not libelous per se in various jurisdictions, there was one notable exception. The Court of Appeals for the Second Circuit, by a divided vote, held that the column in question was libelous per se under the law of New York. In *Sweeney* v. *Schenectady Union Publishing Co.*, the circuit court reversed the case and remanded it back to the Northern District of New York, which had dismissed Sweeney's complaint on the ground that no cause of action had been pleaded.[72]

The circuit court majority reasoned that, in places where Jews made up a sizable portion of the population, as was the case in New York, it might be taken for granted that there would be an appreciable number of people who would hate or hold in contempt one who discriminated against a Jew merely because he was a Jew. The majority, Judges Harrie Chase and Learned Hand, with Charles Clark dissenting, felt the complaint was sufficient and that the column should be required to meet its merit and face trial.[73] The circuit court relied on the doctrine of *Erie Railroad Co.* v. *Tompkins,* in which the U.S. Supreme Court held that there was no federal common law, and that in diversity of citizenship cases, the federal courts had to follow state law, whether it was statutory or common.[74] Based on this, the Second Circuit court paid no attention to decisions in other jurisdictions that had held for Pearson. Judge Chase simply said that other rulings were "inconclusive."[75]

New York libel law, as stated in *Kimmerle* v. *New York Evening Journal, Inc.,* made libelous per se the publication of—

> words which tend to expose one to public hatred, shame, obloquy, contumely, odium, contempt, ridicule, aversion, ostracism, degradation, or disgrace, or to induce an evil opinion of one in the minds of right-thinking persons, and to deprive one of their confidence and friendly intercourse in society.[76]

Basing their reasoning on this law, the majority stated that "in a country still dedicated to religious and racial freedom decent, liberty-loving people" were greatly offended by the "narrow-minded injustice of the bigots who see individuals only en masse and condemn them merely because their ancestors were of a certain race or they themselves are of a certain religion."[77] In New York, therefore, where there were a substantial number of Jews, any person categorized as a bigot would be held up to ridicule, scorn, and contempt. The majority emphasized that free speech was freedom to tell the truth and comment fairly upon facts, but not "a license to spread damaging falsehoods in the guise of news gathering and its dissemination."[78]

The most historically significant portion of the *Schenectady* case, however, is Judge Clark's dissent. Clark wrote that there should be no libel against public officials unless statements were both false and unfair, and unless the aggrieved official proved special damages. Clark found the defense of truth, despite its seeming fairness, an inadequate practical safeguard. He argued, in effect, that the press should have more latitude in discussing a public official than a person who held no public office. Clark stated:

> It would be a fine world to live in if only tolerance were so usual that a charge of the lack thereof against a public official could be so presumptively untrue that it would seem on its face unfair and libelous. But in our present world we must not take the naive view that what ought to be is, and that whoever suggests the contrary is a slanderer; for if we do, we shut off all healthy criticism of prejudice, and allow bigotry full scope to act with impunity.[79]

Clark also said that the majority opinion was particularly frightening because "its broad sweep would take in comments found day after day in the most conservative newspapers."[80]

Carrying the majority decision to its ultimate extreme, Clark cautioned that minority comment on labor, religious, and political views, and activities of public officials would become "hazardous." He said that "the uncertain threat of suit, invited by a rule at once so vague and so extensive, is a restriction on freedom of the press almost as direct as a rule of clear liability."[81] This bold dissent served as impetus for the U.S. Supreme Court to grant *certiorari* to review the decision.[82]

The *Schenectady* case brought to attention the sticky dilemma of balancing the right of the individual to his good name against the social need for free speech. One law review commentary of the times pointed to the special nature of the case:

> This conflict between individual rights and the needs of a democratic society is accentuated when a public official claims to have been libeled. His position makes him a subject of constant discussion because of the special interest

> of the community in those who govern it. Some limits must nevertheless be imposed, since wholly unrestricted publication of false charges would exact of the public servant too high a price for the privilege of service.[83]

Indeed, the Second Circuit court's decision was widely criticized. For example, a note in a law review disagreed with the majority's reasoning. The author claimed that the court based its decision on New York law that concerned only "general social relations," not libels involving public officials.[84]

A note in the 1942 edition of the *Yale Law Journal* used the *Schenectady* decision as a springboard to advocate a law that would give the press more protection when discussing public officials. Using reasoning that would later surface in the *Gertz* decision,[85] the author contended:

> Freedom of expression is impeded to the extent that reports . . . cannot be published without threat of liability. This is especially true with respect to statements concerning public officials. . . . Accustomed to read both good and bad reports of its officers, the public may reasonably be expected to know that both are likely to be biased and exaggerated. . . . Moreover, through ready access to the press and special immunity from liability for their own utterances, public officials have more opportunity than private individuals to make effective denial of unfavorable reports and to counterattack with impunity. Since the net effect of charges against them can thus be diminished by methods not available to other persons, it seems fair and perhaps necessary to restrict the category of statements sufficient to support a presumption of damage in political libel actions.[86]

This same author wrote that, though the majority decision may have been "induced by a belief that charges of anti-Semitism tend to inflame and divide public opinion," it was nevertheless "questionable whether courts should use actions for libel as a means of embarking upon censorship of the press."[87]

Congressman Sweeney, meanwhile, was elated with the *Schenectady* decision: he reported to his colleagues on August

6, 1941, the outcome of the case and entered a copy of the decision in the *Congressional Record*.[88] Sweeney, however, also made known his feelings about the majority of decisions around the country. The congressman largely blamed New Deal-appointed judges. He pointed to one suit filed in the District Court for the Northern District of West Virginia:

> Not a scintilla of evidence was presented showing that I opposed the individual seeking the judgeship on the grounds that he was a Jew or on any other grounds. The record in this case should be a textbook on evidence in every law school in this country to demonstrate the power of the press and the cowardice of the judiciary in seeking to protect the press and the authors of the article who boast of their close connection to the White House.[89]

Sweeney made note of the relationship the "Merry-Go-Round" columnists supposedly enjoyed with the Roosevelt administration:

> Can it be that Messrs. Pearson and Allen have such political strength with the present administration that they are able to thwart the ends of justice? Time alone will tell and we will be watching carefully the action of the district attorney's office.[90]

The congressman then urged his colleagues to read the Second Circuit's *Schenectady* decision. In reference to Clark's dissent, Sweeney said they should "scrutinize the dissenting opinion rendered by another New Deal judge [to] determine whether or not the cause of tolerance in the United States is promoted by such dictum."[91]

The following spring the U.S. Supreme Court reviewed the case. The *New York Times,* with double and triple-deck banner headlines chronicling war news daily on page one, diligently followed, on inside pages, the progress of the *Schenectady* suit. In its brief filed before the Court, the Schenectady Union Publishing Co. asserted that "the right to criticize our rulers distinguishes our way of life from that of the dictatorships; it is our major corrective and without it the democratic mode is impossible."[92] The brief further declared that what the circuit court's decision "means in practical effect is that comment on matters of public interest, and particularly on public officials, is now—of all times—to become a dangerous thing."[93] It was also contended that under reasoning employed by the circuit court, it would be "equally libelous to say of Representative Sweeney that he opposed Freed for office because he was a Yankee, a Southerner or of English extraction."[94]

Several parties filed briefs in support of the publishing company; Pearson had enlisted the aid of various groups and newspaper publishers around the country. Included were the American Jewish Committee, the B'nai B'rith, the Jewish Labor Committee, the American Jewish Congress,[95] the American Civil Liberties Union,[96] and the New York State Publishers Association.[97]

Jonathan Daniels, editor of the *Raleigh News and Observer* in North Carolina, was among the newspapermen who sent a letter to the muckraker indicating an appreciation for the importance of the case. The letter said in part:

> I was very much interested in your letter with regard to the Sweeney case and your suggestion that we file a brief amicus curiae stressing the effect which this decision would have upon the freedom of the press. Normally my inclination is never to stick our nose in the courthouse unless somebody pulls us there. . . . In this case, however, we are definitely interested in the outcome . . . as all newspapermen should be.[98]

Though Pearson undoubtedly felt gratification from the support he received from journalists around the country, the U.S. Supreme Court's decision proved equally frustrating.

During oral arguments, Morris Ernst, counsel for the Schenectady Union Publishing Co., told the Court that a man may oppose the appointment of a Jew to public office without being anti-Semitic. Ernst told the Court that "many persons not opposed to my particular minority are opposed to the appointment of members of it to public office. It may be that they can be called cowards, but not anti-Semites.[99] Sweeney's counsel, O'Connor, countered with: "The newspaper did not merely accuse Sweeney of anti-Semitism. The article charges Sweeney with practicing un-Americanism in his official capacity." O'Connor then injected some emotional statements in reply to Ernst's remark that a public official should be "thick skinned." O'Connor said: "We contend that public officials are supposed to be thick-skinned to the truth, not falsehood. What decent Jew . . . would not hold Sweeney in contempt if he opposed Freed on the ground he was a Jew?"[100]

Though the Court would not receive another opportunity for twenty-two years to consider the constitutional limitations upon the power to award damages for libel of a public official,[101] it delivered no momentous decision. The justices were equally divided, splitting their vote four to four, with Justice Robert Jackson taking no part.[102] The lower court decision therefore stood. The case was sent back to the Northern District of New York for trial, at which the truth or falsity of the statement was to be made the issue. The Supreme Court did not issue a formal opinion, and the reasons for Justice Jackson's withdrawal and the individual stands of the other eight justices were not made public.[103]

Pearson, irritated with the High Court deadlock, instructed his attorneys to conduct a search for tie-vote precedents. Tenacious in his belief that the Court should have made a clear-cut decision, the muckraker helped his attorneys draft a preliminary legal brief. Emphasizing the lack of jurisdictional uniformity in American libel law, Pearson and his lawyers wrote that, if the Supreme Court denied a petition for rehearing,

> there will continue to emerge, as there has up to now, a crazy quilt of conflicting rulings in the realm of federal constitutional law and of charges made against national legislators. It is because the attorneys in all these other Sweeney cases urgently recognize the need for guidance by this Court that they have joined in this petition for rehearing.[104]

The Schenectady Union Publishing Company made one final effort by officially petitioning for reconsideration. The Court, however, denied the motion, with Justice Jackson again taking no part.[105]

American libel law might have been dramatically altered had Jackson participated. Nothing, however, changed; the Supreme Court could no more agree on whether nonmalicious false statements concerning public officials should be constitutionally protected than could the courts of the various jurisdictions in which Sweeney filed suit.

Pearson had, however, made every effort to force a Supreme Court decision. In this regard, he earned the respect of Paul L. Gross, general manager of the *Schenectady Union Star*. The muckraker always claimed he would help any client newspaper involved in a libel suit because of one of his columns; the *Schenectady* case was no exception.

In a letter to Pearson, Gross said he certainly had not "enjoyed" his involvement in the libel suit. Since he had to get "mixed up in one," however, he wrote that he would rather Pearson and Allen involve him in it "than any other two fellows" he knew. Gross thanked Pearson for his willingness to retain trial counsel. Gross labeled it "another very generous act."[106]

Despite the columnist's efforts, however, the glaring fact remained: America still had no uniform libel standard in regard to defenses against defamation actions brought by public officials.

The confusion of libel law application during the pre-1964 era is further illustrated by another Sweeney case, *Sweeney* v. *United Feature Syndicate*.[107] The same Second Circuit court affirmed a judgment upon a jury verdict for the defendant in a case appealed from the Southern District of New York. Two questions considered on appeal were: (1) whether the trial court erroneously left to the jury the determination of whether or not the "Merry-Go-Round" column in question was libelous per se and (2) whether it was an error for the judge to refuse to charge that the article was libelous per se.[108] The circuit court scrutinized the instructions given by the trial judge to the jury and concluded that they were accurate and appropriate. Judge Chase elaborated:

> Though perhaps more artistic language might have been chosen, the plain meaning of these instructions to the jury was that if it was found from the evidence that the article was false and libelous under the definitions of "libel per se" as contained in the charge and, as to which as a definition no fault has been found, the plaintiff was entitled to recover unless certain defenses, which are beside the issue on this appeal, were made out.[109]

Sweeney's counsel had argued that it was an error to submit the case to the jury since the circuit court's decision in *Schenectady* had held that the words were libelous per se.

Judge Chase, however, carefully explained the distinction between the two cases:

> There [in the *Schenectady* case] we were dealing only with an appeal from the dismissal of the complaint before trial on the ground that without the allegation of special damages no cause of action had been stated and, of course, assumed that the publication, interpreted as alleged, was false. Here there was no preliminary attack upon the sufficiency of the complaint.[110]

Chase emphasized that it was the "settled rule" in the courts of New York that when there was an "innocent interpretation" of words used in their setting in the territory in which the publication occurred, it was for a jury to decide if the article was defamatory.[111]

It is indeed a credit to Pearson's courage and confidence that he escaped financial disaster as a result of the Sweeney cases. By 1943, however, after thousands of man-hours, dollars, and depositions, all the suits had been dismissed. The muckraker had not personally paid a penny to Sweeney in damages. A handful of client newspapers, however, agreed to pay settlements. According to a list compiled by Pearson's office, the following newspapers agreed to settlements of $200 or less: the *Eldorado Times* of Arkansas, the *Turlock Journal* of California, the *Chelsea Record* of Massachusetts, the *Bristol Herald Courier* of Virginia, and the *Milwaukee Sentinel.* The *Reading Eagle* (Pennsylvania) apparently made the largest settlement: $900.

Newspaper executives were, however, in constant touch with Pearson regarding possible settlements. Since the columnist was not named a defendant in most of them, he was in a position merely to offer advice and legal resources at his disposal. Though a few newspapers did settle out of court, Pearson was obviously against it, as shown in a letter he sent to an Arkansas editor: "Thanks for your letter . . . regarding possible settlement of the Sweeney case. I note that there is a possibility of settling for $100. While I cannot make any decision for you, it might be helpful to tell you of some of our experience in other cases similar to this."

Pearson went on to recount various Sweeney suits, including one in which a newspaper refused to settle for fifty dollars—because the publisher was "pretty sore at Sweeney's blackmail tactics, and decided to stand pat."[112]

By late 1942 the muckraker was growing increasingly confident about ultimate success. An Arizona attorney wrote the columnist about possible settlement of a Sweeney action against the *Prescott Courier*. Pearson quickly responded that only a few newspapers had settled with the Ohio congressman—all for very small amounts of cash. The columnist mentioned the only case that had caused him extensive worry in this regard, which involved the *Milwaukee Sentinel*:

> We had word that Sweeney had been looking forward to Milwaukee, and once before when the paper suggested the possibility of a settlement [in 1941] Sweeney held out for $20,000. However, two days before the pre-trial hearing Sweeney called the attorney in New York and suggested a settlement of $300. The attorney countered with $200 which Sweeney promptly accepted.[113]

Pearson pointed out, however, that most settlements had been for even less.

The muckraker said that Sweeney offered to settle a case in Charleston, West Virginia, for $5—but was refused. According to the columnist, the same situation developed in Huntington, West Virginia. Pearson claimed the "only real settlement" that Sweeney ever received was from the Reading newspaper, which was being sold. The muckraker wrote that the paper's owners settled for $900 "in order to sell the paper" and "clean up back liabilities." Pearson said he had not been consulted in the matter. The columnist indicated, however, that he felt sure Sweeney was "very much fed up" with the pending suits.[114]

Realizing that a dismissal of all pending cases was imminent, Pearson wrote the same Arizona attorney in December of 1942:

> If nothing else has developed regarding a settlement of the Sweeney case, I suggest that you hold everything. Sweeney's attorney in Washington has approached us with a proposal to settle all the suits at once. Lawyers are now discussing the matter, and I have reason to feel optimistic about the outcome. The only settlement we will consider is one without any payment of any case whatsoever by any newspaper or by me.[115]

Pearson eventually got what he wanted. An agreement between the muckraker and Sweeney was reached on January 12, 1943.

In a memo to interested editors and attorneys, Pearson wrote that all cases that had not yet been resolved in court would be dismissed. Pearson and Sweeney also agreed that they would not "in any manner whatsoever give favorable or unfavorable publicity, or aid, assist, abet, or cause to be aided, assisted, or abetted, any persons (or) organizations . . . in giving publicity . . . to this settlement."[116] The agreement did not, however, preclude giving information to client newspapers, law reviews, or trade journals.

Pearson emphasized that "no apology or payment of any kind was involved." He said he had been anxious to "terminate the headache of having these remaining suits hang over newspapers' heads, even though most editors and publishers did not seem particularly worried by them." The columnist also thanked newspapermen and attorneys for their help:

> I should like at this time to tell you how much I appreciated your support and cooperation in this, the biggest chain libel suit in history. While it was unfortunate that such a suit should have been brought against the "Washington Merry-Go-Round" and its client newspapers, nevertheless, many editors with whom I have talked feel that sooner or later a test case of this kind was sure to arise involving the right of fair comment on a public servant, and that this case has been a very important one for freedom of the press.[117]

Pearson showed remarkable foresight in closing the memo. He wrote that the decision by the District of Columbia Court of Appeals, which upheld the right of comment regarding a public servant even if the remarks were untrue—unless they connoted criminal action—would "stand forth as a great landmark for freedom of the press."[118] The columnist was, of course, referring to the suit Sweeney had brought against Pearson, Allen, and Cissy Patterson of the *Washington Times-Herald*—a case that was to be cited in the historic *Sullivan* decision of 1964.

The Sweeney Suits—Their Effects On Pearson and Libel Law

The Sweeney chain libel suit can possibly best be described as a concerted, massive effort to bankrupt the "Merry-Go-Round" column. Filed by Ohio right-wing congressman Sweeney, the sixty-eight suits sought aggregate damages of untold millions.[119] Filings in jurisdictions across the country further frustrated the column's writers and attorneys. Extensive depositions had to be taken in several of the suits, local counsel had to be retained in jurisdictions far removed from the nation's capital, and Pearson had to appear personally in several of the cases. Possibly, however, Sweeney and his counsel, former New York congressman O'Connor, underestimated the combat readiness and tenacity of muckraker Pearson. The columnist refused to let the suits cripple his energy or financial resources.

By the time most of the Sweeney suits were in the courts, Pearson's partner, Allen, was on active duty with the army. Therefore, Pearson shouldered the total burden of assisting his attorneys. As would become his trademark in later years, however, the muckraker did more than simply maintain his defenses; he fought back in the courts, filing a $500,000 libel suit on his and Allen's behalf against O'Connor and Sweeney.[120] The suit provides good background on the Sweeney chain libel case. As a basis of Pearson and Allen's claim, the success of the column was cited:

> The column has been published continuously for more than eight years and has been noted throughout that period for the industry, resourcefulness, accuracy and courage of its authors in the reporting of news, particularly that relating to political and governmental subjects. It has grown steadily in circulation because of the confidence of newspaper readers and editors in the integrity of its authors and in the substantial accuracy of their reports. This column, the plaintiffs' reputation as its authors, and the existing contracts for its distribution constitute business assets of great value to the plaintiffs.[121]

Pearson and Allen provided background information on O'Connor that put the chain libel suit in a different light. The plaintiffs contended that, as early as 1938, Sweeney's lawyer O'Connor had "conceived a violent antagonism to the plaintiffs" about columns they had written concerning his policies and actions.[122] At that time, O'Connor had allegedly sent to all newspapers that published the "Merry-Go-Round" a letter in which he threatened to file libel suits. Pearson and Allen's complaint further alleged that O'Connor had circulated the letters "for the purpose of intimidating the said newspapers and preventing the publication and diminishing the acceptance and influence" of the column.[123] The columnists also contended that, though no law suits were ever filed, the former New York congressman "nevertheless persisted in his opposition and expressed antagonism" toward the columnists "in his intention to drive them from the practice of their profession."[124]

The complaint further alleged that, after the "Merry-Go-Round" column on Sweeney was published, O'Connor, "maliciously and with intent to injure the plaintiffs, induced the defendant Sweeney to commence suits."[125] The columnists further stated that O'Connor, on his letterhead, sent a form letter to more than one hundred "influential" persons across the country, asking for recommendations of competent local attorneys willing to undertake a suit against "the above named newspaper" on an "attractive contingent basis." O'Connor would furnish such an attorney "a copy of the article, our complaint, and all other information."[126]

O'Connor explained that he understood the reluctance on the part of some attorneys to take part in proceedings against local newspapers, particularly if the lawyers had political ambitions, but he emphasized that "these two writers must be brought to a halt some day."[127]

The columnists further asserted that the multitude of suits represented an attempt to drive them out of business:

> The defendants have deliberately and with malice employed every possible technical means to harass, burden, obstruct, and delay the plaintiffs and the United Feature Syndicate, Inc., and the newspapers in which the news articles of the plaintiffs are published in procuring the final determination of the said suits and they have further publicly stated their intention of commencing suits against all newspapers publishing the news article. . . . The defendants, and particularly the defendant O'Connor, have demanded and procured unreasonable continuances of cases assigned for trial so as to cause a simultaneous or nearly simultaneous trial of the actions and thus render impossible the adequate defense.[128]

The columnists likely gained much pleasure from filing the suit, but they were no more successful than Sweeney had been in his efforts. O'Connor moved for judgment on the proceedings; Judge Jennings Bailey granted it.[129]

Though none of the parties or attorneys in the vast Sweeney litigation reaped a financial windfall, the cases did have an appreciable effect on the ever evolving American libel law. Lack of a uniform standard in the libel law had long been a topic of conversation among American legal scholars, but the well-publicized Sweeney chain suit brought the dilemma to the forefront. Several law review commentaries dealt with the massive suit,[130] thus alerting scholars across the country to the inconsistencies in the law; newspapers published progress reports of some of the most prominent chain cases;[131] editors across America were alerted to the dangers of a chain suit in an increasingly technological business;[132] the nation's congressmen became aware of the ramifications of jurisdictional discrepancies in dealing with libel suits involving public officials;[133] and, perhaps most important, the U.S. Supreme Court, though it could not reach a majority decision, for the first time in its history squarely confronted the question of the possibility of constitutional limitations upon the power to award damages for libel of a public official.[134]

Pearson's unceasing quest to uphold his integrity as a reporter through tireless and costly litigation also became apparent. This near fanaticism to keep a clean record in libel suits initiated against him became increasingly evident during ensuing decades. Scores of public officials, public figures, and private persons would file libel actions against the muckraker, but, like Sweeney, they would discover that the combination of perseverance, money, power of the press, and skillful legal maneuvering through available defenses would prove to be a nearly unbeatable trump hand for the columnist.

5

The "Merry-Go-Round" and the Years of Common Law Defenses

Though Drew Pearson and his "Merry-Go-Round" emerged triumphant in two early major libel confrontations, with Gen. Douglas MacArthur and Ohio congressman Martin L. Sweeney, the muckraker's outspoken, aggressive, and sometimes careless reporting stamped him a prime target for additional actions. From the late 1930s until his death, not a year passed that Pearson did not find himself in the courts. His adversaries varied; they included gubernatorial candidates, state attorneys general, lobbyists, military officers, industrial millionaires, fellow columnists, even a cigar and newspaper vendor. The subjects of the allegedly libelous columns also varied, ranging from bribery of public officials to innuendo suggesting the unchastity of a woman.

Common law libel defenses were utilized shrewdly by Pearson's attorneys during the pre-1964 years.[1] For a defendant to be successful in the courts, it was essential that he make effective use of such common law defenses as privilege of a participant, truth, privilege of reporting, fair comment and criticism, consent or authorization, self-defense or right of reply, and the statute of limitations.[2] Fortunately for Pearson, he had several capable attorneys, most notably John Donovan, who joined the columnist as house counsel after World War II to mastermind the intricate procedural filings that were so important during the common law defense years.

Despite the lack of constitutional protection and uniformity in pre-1964 American libel law, Pearson logged an amazing success record in the courts. The feat takes on added proportions when one considers the controversial subject matter with which the columnist dealt and the powerful people he allegedly libeled. Various pre-1964 libel cases in which "Merry-Go-Round" writers were defendants are examined in this chapter. For organizational purposes, cases have been grouped by status of the plaintiffs: public officials, public figures, and private individuals.[3]

Cases Involving Public Officials

In one of the most widely publicized Pearson libel cases, Fred N. Howser, attorney general of California, brought a $300,000 action against the columnist.[4] The suit evolved from two Pearson broadcasts, originating in the District of Columbia, that were carried by radio stations in California and nine other Western states. Essentially, the muckraker charged Howser with having accepted a bribe, a statement that was clearly defamatory per se.[5]

Howser's duties as attorney general included representing the state in litigation concerning California's interest in and title to offshore territory within three miles of its coastline, including an area normally referred to as "the tidelands oil land."[6] Thus, Howser based the first of two counts on an April 25, 1948, broadcast, which included:

> Los Angeles: Fred Howser, the California Attorney who has been lobbying for tidelands oil, is in serious trouble in his own State. He is under investigation for alleged friendship with the big gamblers.

> Governor Warren wants a very thorough probe and is determined to let the chips fall where they may even if it means the indictment of his own Attorney General.[7]

The California official based his second count on a September 12, 1948, broadcast, which said in part:

> Long Beach, California, exclusive: Fred Howser, California's attorney general and other leader of the Tidelands Oil Lobby, seems headed for trouble. New evidence is being placed before a grand jury in Mendocino County . . . regarding Howser's ex-agents who were caught protecting gamblers. So far, Howser has denied any connection. But regarding another separate case, I hold in my hand a sworn affidavit, stating that in September, 1946, when Howser was Long Beach district attorney and a candidate for State Attorney General, he accepted twelve $100 bills passed on to him from a well known Long Beach gambler. That $1200 was nothing less than protection money—in other words, a bribe!—received by the man who is now trying to persuade the nation that the Federal government should hand back its submerged oil lands to California and Louisiana, where, incidentally, they would be subject to more bribes.[8]

Pearson pleaded truth and qualified privilege. The latter, under California law, allowed defamatory statements concerning a public official or candidate for public office even if the statement was untrue, provided it was uttered in good faith and without malice.[9]

As his trial attorney Pearson retained William Rogers, who later became attorney general in the second Eisenhower administration and secretary of state during the first portion of the Nixon administration. Rogers offered evidence tending to show that, at a time when the plaintiff was a candidate for public office, Joseph A. Irvine, a bookmaker, turned over an envelope to James T. Mulloy, who was then employed to deliver it intact to Howser. The envelope allegedly contained twelve $100 bills. Pearson said Mulloy delivered it to Howser, explaining that it was being sent with compliments of Irvine.[10]

The jury was ultimately persuaded by Rogers and witnesses for the defendant that Pearson's statements were true and that they were made without malice.[11] The court reasoned that, since the truth of the publication had been established, the finding was a complete defense to the action and, standing alone, necessitated judgment for the muckraker. District court judge Alexander Holtzoff said that, once truth had been shown, "privilege became insignificant," and a new trial should be granted "only if to do so would promote the ends of justice."[12] When Howser did petition for a new trial, the court denied the motion, reasoning that the parties had been given full opportunity to present their contentions and had been afforded a fair trial.[13]

Utilizing truth as a defense is at best risky; a jury can go either way. Rogers undoubtedly realized this. According to one long-time Pearson friend, Washington, D.C., attorney George Vournas, Rogers had already begun laying the groundwork for an appeal should the jury have held for Howser. Vournas, however, confidently told Rogers not to bother, that the outcome was a "sure thing."[14]

Pearson and Rogers, though cautiously optimistic about the decision, likely did not place it in the "sure thing" category. The columnist, for example, kept voluminous files on the case, the oil lobby, and even public reactions to Howser's suit. Rogers remembers the case as one that could have put Pearson in dire financial straits had he lost. But the muckraker remained composed and gracious: "After I summarized my argument to the jury and before we got the verdict, Drew told me that he was very happy with the way I handled the case—regardless of the outcome." According to Rogers, this was unique: "Most clients don't compliment you until *after* they get a favorable verdict."[15] *Time* magazine, after Pearson won the case, commented that the columnist had kept intact his record of never losing a libel suit.[16]

True to his nature, however, Pearson did not merely defend himself against Howser's suit; he filed a counter slander suit seeking $500,000 in damages.[17] In the unreported but related case, Pearson alleged that Howser, in April of 1950, in the presence of two reporters, insinuated that the columnist had induced two men to commit perjury during the course of certain "notorious proceedings" in California. Pearson claimed that by virtue of Howser's remarks he had been "brought into disgrace" and the value of his news articles, writings, and radio broadcasts had been "diminished."[18] Howser's attorneys countered that the complaint failed to state a claim upon which relief could be granted, that the remarks were true, and that they were fair and bona fide comment upon matters of public interest.[19]

The case dragged on for several months before Pearson's attorneys sought to consolidate it with the then pending suit Howser had filed against Pearson. Warren Woods, who filed the request, said it was evident that the time and expense of the court, plaintiff, and defendant in both actions would be saved if they were consolidated in order that depositions could be taken at the same time.[20]

Howser's attorneys, however, filed an opposition to the motion to consolidate. It was emphasized that the two actions involved an alleged libel and an alleged slander:

> The subject matter of the two alleged torts is entirely different. There is no connection of any kind between the two, other than the identities of the parties to the litigation. There is no question of fact and no question of law common to either action. A recital of the facts will clearly establish the accuracy of these conclusions.[21]

Furthermore, it was claimed that Pearson was attempting to consolidate the two suits "to defeat a just result in the libel action by confusing it with the slander suit."[22] Judge Burnita Matthews denied the motion to consolidate.[23]

Two months later, Pearson was acquitted of Howser's charges, but the instant case remained alive. There were additional filings; on December 11, 1951, however, both parties agreed the case should be dismissed with prejudice.[24]

In a libel case brought against Pearson by Daniel T. Duncan, engineer and promoter for Buzzard's Roost power project in Greenwood County, South Carolina, the muckraker utilized essentially the same common law defenses that he did in *Howser.*[25] Duncan sought damages totaling $200,000 for an allegedly libelous "Merry-Go-Round" column published on November 25, 1938.[26] Pearson wrote that one of the reasons some 1938 voters "turned sour" on New Deal policies was that the administration in Washington had been inconsistent and lax. Pearson went on to cite the Public Works Administration's Buzzard's Roost power project in Greenwood County. Pearson said that "instead of promoting goodwill for Roosevelt in South Carolina, the project has turned a lot of people against him."[27]

The columnist then listed the reasons: while "bare subsistence" wages were being paid truck drivers and other laborers, Duncan was making 6 percent of the total contract, or about $180,000. Pearson further charged that various local officials had received funds from the federal grant.[28] In his complaint, Duncan alleged that the article was calculated to bring him into disrepute with the government administration, that it implied he was dishonest and had been guilty of fraud.[29]

Pearson claimed that he had the right to publish and comment upon matters of public interest, and the statements were true. Pearson further said that the article was published without malice in a bona fide desire to acquaint the public with matters of general interest concerning the use of public funds.[30] The U.S. District Court for the Eastern District of South Carolina held for Pearson; Duncan appealed, and the Fourth Circuit affirmed.[31] Part of the grounds for Duncan's appeal centered upon the facts that the district court had not admitted as evidence a previous column Pearson had written concerning the official, nor had it admitted correspondence between the two men. Duncan, in his appeal, made reference to a September 6, 1938, "Merry-Go-Round" column in which it was written that many PWA project workers did not vote in national elections and that Duncan was "opposed to any candidate whom the president favors."[32] Duncan then sent a letter to Pearson, explaining that he was, in fact, "strongly Roosevelt." Pearson responded with a cordial letter.[33] The circuit court contended that the September 6 column was obviously not actionable and no malice could have been inferred from it. The court, exercising judicial restraint, said that "only where the evidence is clearly admissible or where there has been abuse of discretion in excluding it, should an appellate court interfere."[34]

On the surface, it would appear that Pearson and his attorneys did not have to work particularly hard in defending against Duncan's action. This, however, was not the case. The muckraker accumulated two bulky folders of correspondence with attorneys and friends concerning the suit; he obviously spent considerable time in helping to prepare his defense.

An Oregon public official also noticeably taxed Pearson's finances and energy. Stanley Earl, a Portland city commissioner, filed at least three suits in the late 1950s against Pearson or newspapers that carried his column.[35] Earl, who was first elected to the Portland City Commission in 1952, was later reelected. He had long been active in Oregon public life, serving on the War Man Power Commission, West Coast Region, during World War II and on the Governor's Post-War Advisory Committee.[36] Essentially, Earl sought damages for two "Merry-Go-Round" columns.

In his $500,000 suit brought in the District of Columbia, the Portland city commissioner cited a March 2, 1957, column in which Pearson reported on Sen. John McClellan's investigating committee on teamster racketeering. The muckraker stated that the committee called Jim Elkins, a man "with something of an underworld history," as its star witness. The columnist also said that Earl was a good friend of Elkins's and had begun his career as a bouncer in one of Elkins's brother's "after-hours joints," had once been jailed "for strongarm tactics in union activities," and had once written a letter attempting to get a pardon for Elkins after he was "thrown into an Arizona jail for assault with intent to kill."[37] Pearson cited an example of the alleged Elkins-Earl tie. He said that when Elkins "bossed Portland's pinball industry," Earl, as a councilman, proposed legal pinball machines. Elkins, however, was "squeezed out" of the pinball racket, and "with sudden righteousness," Earl reportedly "attacked pinballs as a vicious gambling device."[38]

Earl, in his complaint, also cited a March 15, 1957, "Merry-Go-Round" column. In this article, Pearson reported that his associate, Anderson, had called Earl "in order to learn the truth about his alleged role as a champion of clean government."[39] Pearson recounted Anderson's telephone interview with Earl. The commissioner became irritated, according to Pearson, and his "conversation became so ludicrous that Anderson terminated the interview."[40]

Counsel for Pearson listed seven defenses: (1) the articles were published in good faith without malice, with good motives, and for justifiable ends; (2) the complaint failed to state a claim upon which relief could be granted; (3) the articles were true; (4) the columns were a fair and substantially accurate report of the Senate investigation hearings; (5) the columns were fair comment concerning a matter of public interest; (6) Earl failed to deliver to Pearson a demand for a correction or retraction as required by the laws of Oregon; and (7) the columns were published in the ordinary course of business, without actual intent to defame Earl and with "reasonable and probable cause for believing" them true.[41] Earl's attorneys possibly felt the defenses were solid. At any rate, exactly ten months after the Portland official filed the action, he voluntarily dismissed it with prejudice.[42]

Earl also brought suit in his native Oregon.[43] The action, filed in the Circuit Court for Coos County, is particularly interesting for two reasons: it was one of the most publicized trials in Coos Bay history, and it was the first libel case in which Anderson became personally involved, though he was not named as a defendant. The Portland commissioner sought $250,000 in damages against Times, Inc., owner of the *Coos Bay Times,* and Sheldon Sackett, editor and publisher of the newspaper.[44]

Forest W. Amsden, now a Portland television executive, was executive editor of the *Coos Bay Times* when the suit was filed, and he remembers it vividly.[45] According to Amsden, the Pearson suit added to a general uproar over vice in Portland and attracted considerable public interest for this reason.[46] The Coos Bay case went to trial less than one year after the action was filed, but, like most suits in which Pearson was involved, it included numerous procedural filings. Shortly after the suit was filed, in fact, the defendant newspaper corporation moved for a change of judge on the belief that Dal M. King, the judge assigned to hear the case, was prejudiced against the defendant.[47] King granted the motion the same day it was made; William S. Fort, a circuit court judge of the Second Judicial District of Oregon, was assigned to hear the case.[48]

Defense attorneys subsequently moved for dismissal, claiming that the columns clearly constituted fair comment and criticism upon matters of public concern, and that they were "substantially true."[49] The motion was denied and the case set for trial. Less than one month before the trial date, however, the defendant sought a change of venue to Lane County.[50] Helen W. Johnson, vice-president of Times, Inc., signed an affidavit explaining the reason for the request. She claimed that the *Times* was

> widely known as a forceful, crusading newspaper and as such has made many enemies in Coos County. It has been outspoken editorially against vice conditions and other situations and has stepped on many toes, including many residents of Coos County. The friends and relatives of the interests criticized will carry grudges against this newspaper even though they may be carried unconsciously. The newspaper has been

> outspoken in political campaigns and many political grudges are carried against the newspaper.[51]

Johnson also emphasized the "controversial" nature of publisher Sackett. Further, she said that Coos County residents were "likely to be violent in their liking or hating of the paper or of the publisher."[52]

Earl's attorneys objected to the change of venue, claiming that it would cause inconvenience to the plaintiff's witnesses and could cause further delay.[53] The following day, attorneys for Times, Inc., sought a postponement of the trial.[54] Earl, however, objected.[55] Despite the plethora of motions, the case moved quickly through the Coos County system. One week after Earl objected to the motion to postpone, Judge Fort denied the motion for a change in venue, but granted the motion for postponement; he reset the trial for April 7.[56]

The trial lasted nearly a week. Anderson flew to Coos Bay from the nation's capital to testify. He contended that information printed in the column had been ascertained primarily from a telephone interview he conducted with Earl. Anderson, getting his first taste of libel suit involvement, read from his notes the conversation he had with Earl. Earl's counsel, meanwhile, attempted to show that the libelous portions of the columns evolved from Anderson's questions—his words—rather than Earl's answers. The columnist, noticeably irritated, retorted that he was not in the habit of answering his own questions. "As a reporter, I ask questions; I don't answer them," claimed Anderson.[57]

In any event, on April 12, the jury reached a verdict. It voted eleven to one for the defendant. Amsden always wondered why Earl chose the Coos Bay paper to sue. One of the approaches taken by the newspaper corporation's attorney, William Walsh, was to ask the Coos Bay jury, "Why are they trying to wash all their filthy Portland linen in our clean Coos County courtroom?" Amsden said he was sure the major reason the newspaper won the case was the jury's perception that a Portland politician was trying to persecute a Coos County newspaper.[58]

Another Oregon public official, former office holder and candidate for the Democratic gubernatorial nomination Lew Wallace, brought a $250,000 libel suit against Pearson in February of 1956 for allegations made in the "Merry-Go-Round" column and in two radio broadcasts during the previous month.[59] Pearson had claimed, according to the complaint, that Wallace had written a letter to President Eisenhower urging him to "exert pressure" on the secretary of the interior to award a mining patent to a certain family.[60] The complaint emphasized that Pearson's column was "meant and intended to convey that plaintiff was and is guilty of conduct unbecoming to one who has held public office in the past."[61]

Pearson's personal attorney, Donovan, filed a motion to dismiss on the ground that the complaint failed to state a claim upon which relief could be granted.[62] Donovan contended that the words complained of were not libelous per se and that there was no allegation of special damage or economic loss. As was often the case, the columnist's attorney emphasized that the plaintiff was a "politician," that he had held various state offices in Oregon and was at the time of the writing a candidate for office.[63]

As primary support, Donovan quoted from *Sweeney* v. *Patterson*, in which the court of appeals made it clear that it was not actionable to publish erroneous or injurious statements regarding political conduct and views of public officials, "so long as no charge of crime, corruption, gross immorality or gross incompetence is made and no special damage results."[64] Donovan also cited another Sweeney chain libel case in support of his motion. A district court judge in Texas was quoted:

> While a public officer or candidate cannot be libeled any more than any other citizen, he cannot go about with his feelings on his sleeve. Public officials and candidates are legitimate

> subjects for news and comment. While they cannot be libeled, they must reconcile themselves to occasional "yarns" which, however hurtful to their feelings, are not actionable.[65]

Wallace's attorneys objected to the motion for dismissal, claiming that, since Pearson did not refer to Wallace as a candidate for political office, the Sweeney cases cited as controlling were "not to the point."[66]

The Oregon man's attorneys contended that charges of dishonesty were libelous per se even when the words used merely intimated "a suspicion of dishonesty. It has been held clearly libelous to make a written charge of conspiracy to defraud, cheat, or swindle."[67] After examining Donovan's motion, however, the district court ordered that it be granted and the complaint dismissed because "the publication is not libelous per se and there is no allegation of special damage or economic loss."[68]

A similar case, filed some two years later against the columnist, involved Arthur J. McGonigle, Pennsylvania gubernatorial candidate. He sued the muckraker for $300,000.[69] Pearson quickly jumped to the offensive; he issued a statement bristling with confidence:

> A lot of people in Pennsylvania had been wondering why McGonigle, having threatened to sue on Sept. 30, waited 30 days before going ahead with it. If he had really wanted a prompt showing of the truth, he could have filed immediately and we could have taken depositions before this. As I said before, I shall be glad to meet Mr. McGonigle in court.[70]

Pearson's strong public statement is illustrative of his confident and tenacious attitude when defending himself against libel actions.

McGonigle's charges evolved from a "Merry-Go-Round" column published in the *Reading* (Pennsylvania) *Times.* Pearson wrote that Pennsylvania Republican officials had selected McGonigle, "a relatively unknown pretzel manufacturer," over Harold Stassen, aide to President Eisenhower and negotiator for disarmament. The column said that Mc-

Gonigle had promoted himself as a "sound" man who had come up the hard way and had pieced together a successful bakery business from a $300 investment and bank loans. The muckraker, however, refuted McGonigle's claim:

> It happens that the true facts are a matter of court record and therefore not subject to argument.
>
> They show that McGonigle's business start was by no means the American success story but that pretzel manufacturer McGonigle got so twisted making a success of pretzels that he, his brother and their associates had to cough up $186,500, plus $50,000 in attorney's fees.[71]

Pearson then related details of a suit that was brought against McGonigle, his brother, and associates for allegedly selling Bachman Bakeries in Reading to a "fictitious purchaser." The columnist concluded:

> Putting up a good part of $186,500, plus $50,000 attorney's fees, was good business. For the McGonigles later sold Bachman Bakeries for a reported $3,500,000. It had cost them $5,140 plus $600 for fees and commissions.[72]

McGonigle denied the allegations; he attempted to refute, point for point, the muckraker's charges. The gubernatorial candidate, for example, stated in his complaint that he did not sell the company to himself for almost nothing and then "pay up" for having done so; that he was not involved in a court proceeding in 1957; and that he was not "in any wise at fault or responsible for or liable for any of the acts complained of" in the court proceedings Pearson erroneously recounted.[73]

Pearson's attorney, Donovan, moved for dismissal on the ground that the complaint failed to state a claim against the defendant upon which relief could be granted.[74] Donovan contended that the words complained of were not libelous per se and there had been no allegation of special damage or economic loss. It was emphasized that McGonigle was a "politician." As he did in his *Wallace* case brief, Donovan quoted from *Sweeney* v. *Caller-Times Publishing Co.*,[75] and further, he quoted from the turn-of-the-century *Coleman* decision:

> Under a form of government like our own there must be freedom to canvass in good faith the worth of character and qualifications of candidates for office, whether elective or appointive, and by becoming a candidate, . . . a man tenders as an issue to be tried out publicly before the people . . . his honesty, integrity, and fitness for the office to be filled.[76]

Donovan said Pearson did admit "two clerical errors": the federal case involving McGonigle, his brother, and associates was settled in 1947—not 1957; it was settled for $168,500, not $186,500, plus $50,000 attorneys' fees.[77] But Donovan claimed that the words did not charge McGonigle with crime, corruption, gross immorality, or gross incompetence, as required by the *Patterson* case.[78] Judge Matthew McGuire, however, denied the motion to dismiss.[79]

Donovan then utilized several common law defenses: fair and accurate report of judicial proceedings; fair comment upon matters of public interest; truth; publication in good faith with reasonable cause for believing the report true.[80] The case was set for trial, but McGonigle voluntarily dismissed it with prejudice.[81]

The muckraker elaborated on the dismissal in a letter to a Philadelphia attorney:

> I made no apology, no correction, and paid no settlement fee. The settlement was made just on the verge of an argument on our motion to dismiss, and in an earlier argument the Judge had indicated from the Bench that he attached considerable weight to our brief.

Pearson went on to explain that he was "never really worried about the outcome of the suit, although any libel suit can be tricky."[82]

The columnist also had little apparent difficulty defending himself against a libel action filed by Ernest K. Bramblett, a California congressman, who sought $500,000 in damages.[83] The complaint centered upon a "Merry-Go-Round" column of October 31, 1952, which concerned Bramblett's secretarial hiring practices. Pearson quickly grabbed the attention of his readers:

> One of the most interesting payrolls in the House of Representatives is that of Congressman Ernest Bramblett of Pacific Grove, California. Not only has his wife been on the payroll for five years without working in the office, but the Congressman has some other unique secretarial situations.[84]

The muckraker went on to give examples of women whose secretarial salaries had allegedly been doubled by Bramblett. Pearson charged that Bramblett had offered one secretary a salary boost from $2,400 to $5,000 a year, provided she would pay him $5,000 cash in advance. The secretary, according to Pearson, refused. The columnist made it clear, however, that the secretary had "declined to comment" on the allegation.[85]

The complaint further stated that Pearson meant that Bramblett "was and has been dishonest and corrupt in his capacity as a public official." The complaint charged that the column was "willfully and maliciously false and defamatory and unprivileged and known to be such by defendants when it was composed and caused to be published . . . through hatred, ill will, and malicious design and purpose."[86] The case, however, was not aggressively pursued. Docket entries were minimal; the suit was routinely dismissed on June 4, 1953.

Thus, Pearson enjoyed great success in defending himself against libel actions brought by public officials during the pre-1964 era. In many of these cases, the muckraker's primary attorney, Donovan, strongly emphasized the "public" nature of the plaintiffs' roles, constantly reiterating precedents that followed the liberal *Coleman* rule. That rule, articulated by the Kansas Supreme Court, excused false statements about public officials that ordinarily would be libelous, provided that the statements were published without malice and with probable cause for believing them true.

In those cases filed against the columnist in the District of Columbia, Donovan relied heavily on the *Patterson* decision, which established a relatively liberal approach to libel law defenses in that jurisdiction.[87] In all cases, however, Donovan attempted to get the complaints dismissed. If unsuccessful, he continued to inundate the court with procedural filings.

Pearson's greatest challenges in the pre-1964 period, however, came from plaintiffs who would logically be categorized as public figures. A man in this category, in fact, claimed the distinction of being the only libel plaintiff to win a damage suit against the columnist during his lifetime.

Cases Involving Public Figures

Norman Littell, former U.S. assistant attorney general, filed a $300,000 libel suit against Pearson and the Bell Syndicate, Inc., for a "Merry-Go-Round" column published in April of 1949. Littell, who had served in the government capacity from April of 1939 until November of 1944, was actively practicing law in Washington, D.C., when he filed suit against the muckraker.[88]

The cause of action was based on thirty-seven words of a "Merry-Go-Round" column, with particular emphasis on the last nineteen:

> The Justice Department is casting a quizzical eye on ex–Assistant Attorney General Norman Littell. They have reports that *Littell is acting as a propagandist for the Dutch Government, though he failed to register as a foreign agent.*[89]

Littell contended that the statement amounted, on its face, to an accusation of crime, that it represented an assault upon his integrity as a professional man to earn a living, and that it was libelous per se.[90]

Pearson's attorney Donovan denied that the article was libelous. He grounded his defense upon the following claims: (1) the article constituted a fair report of Justice Department action and was published without malice; (2) the statements of fact were substantially true and the statement of opinion represented reasonable, fair, and bona fide comment upon matters of public interest; (3) in its ordinary meaning and significance, absent innuendoes, the article complained of was true in substance; (4) it was published in good faith, without malice and in reliance upon trustworthy sources; and (5) Littell failed to state a claim upon which relief could be granted.[91]

Littell's counsel moved to strike the defenses, or to make them more definite. It was argued that the privilege that attached to a "fair report" of official proceedings could not be utilized when no official proceedings had been initiated, that "fair comment" could not be used when the statement in issue was a statement of fact, and where a crime was charged it was not enough to plead that the accusatory words had been used, or that another had used them.[92]

Attorneys for both parties exchanged briefs and motions for nearly a year before the district court issued a memorandum that struck the defenses of fair report of proceedings (the court said there was no report of "action" by the Justice Department) and all defenses except that which was grounded upon good faith and reliance on usually trustworthy sources. The memorandum said:

> A defamatory statement cannot be legally excused simply because the writer believed or relied upon trustworthy sources. However, evidence that the defendant acted in good faith, without malice, and in reliance upon trustworthy sources would be competent in connection with the plaintiff's claim for punitive damages even though it will not be a defense to his claim for compensatory damages.[93]

Pearson was allowed the opportunity to file an amended answer; counsel for the columnist did so.[94] Filings continued during the next several months; eventually, however, the case was scheduled for trial in the spring of 1953. It was consolidated with a second action Littell had filed against Pearson in 1950.[95]

Pearson's involvement in libel litigation during this period was indeed intense. The columnist and his primary attorney,

Donovan, were kept busy following the procedural progress of a handful of actions. Donovan sent a memo to Pearson informing him that the assignment commissioner's office in the district court had said that four pending cases against the columnist would soon be ready for pretrial hearings. With obvious reference to the column Littell had based his first complaint upon, Donovan said that when the former assistant attorney general's lawyers noticed that his two cases had been consolidated they would likely " 'cast a quizzical eye' on the order."[96]

Littell had filed the second suit less than one year after his first; it also sought $300,000 in damages.[97] The follow-up case grew out of a May 21, 1950, radio broadcast that concerned "pro-communist Washington lobbies." The muckraker began the broadcast with a slap at Senator McCarthy. He said that it had been four months since McCarthy first made his charge that there were 207 card-carrying Communists in the State Department, and during the interim the senator had failed to produce a single card-carrying Communist "or any other type of communist." Pearson said, however, that there were "some interesting pro-communist lobbies" in Washington. He then suggested that a committee look into some activities at the Polish Embassy in order to

> ascertain how, after Gerhardt Eisler [Pearson identified him as an undercover representative of Comintern, an organization of the Communist Party] was spirited out of New York on the Polish steamer Batory, an attorney arranged for Polish communists to board the returning steamship and interview the crew ahead of U.S. officials who wanted to find out how Eisler escaped.[98]

Next came paragraphs that aroused Littell:

> That attorney was a former high official of the Justice Department, and because, unlike McCarthy, I believe in naming names without Congressional immunity, that gentleman is Norman Littell.
>
> His activities and that of others could be a start in ascertaining what lawyers, lobbyists, Congressmen, ex-members

> of the Truman Committee, or sons-in-law, or anyone else, are working for the communists or the fascists, for Poles, or Peron, or Franco, or for any government which does not believe in letting democracy live.[99]

Littell claimed that the column conveyed "the impression to a wide audience" that he was a Communist, thereby injuring his reputation.[100]

The consolidated cases gained considerable attention in Washington as the trial approached. One extraordinary feature of the suits was that Littell had been a friend of Pearson's. The former government official liked to relax by chopping wood in the country; he had often visited Pearson's Maryland farm and spent hours at his hobby. Mrs. Pearson believed that the things her husband wrote about Littell were actually "not that shattering." She thought there were "any number of things he wrote that I thought would bring down the house—but they never did. It was always 'silly' things that resulted in libel suits."[101]

Pearson, however, instinctively realized that his perfect record in defending against libel suits was at stake. An entry in his diary dated April 27, 1953, was ominously prophetic:

> Started the Littell trial. Unfortunately I had a lecture engagement at the University of Florida, Gainesville. This is the first time I have ever been absent during any part of a libel suit, and I am superstitious.[102]

In subsequent diary entries during the course of the trial, the columnist's anxiety was apparent. He was even concerned about the trial judge—excongressman Charles McLaughlin. He wrote that McLaughlin "seemed like a nice and friendly person," but the muckraker indicated that he was "suspicious" that Littell's trial attorney, Edward Bennett Williams, who taught law at Georgetown University, "may have a sort of access to McLaughlin."[103] In another diary entry during the trial proceedings, however, the columnist wrote that he felt confident McLaughlin was "leaning over backward to be fair with both sides."[104]

On May 15, 1953, the jury held for Littell in the 1949 case, thus handing Pearson his first (and only) libel suit loss during his lifetime.[105] In the consolidated case that was filed in 1950, however, the jury announced that it could not agree upon a verdict. Judge McLaughlin ordered that the jurors be discharged from further consideration of the case.[106] The jury awarded Littell $50,000 in the Dutch case, plus $1 in punitive damages. Pearson eventually settled with Littell for $40,000. To make the payment, he had to mortgage his Potomac, Maryland, farm.[107]

After the jury awarded damages to Littell, Pearson reflected on his earlier instincts about the case: "I confess when I first took a look at the jury, composed of rather complacent, self-righteous, middle-class people, I had grave misgivings about the outcome of this suit."[108]

The columnist was extremely depressed with the verdict. He returned to his office with a sour look on his face. William Neel, one of his long-time employees, asked the columnist if he would like to take a boat ride to relax. Pearson's wife said she thought it was a "capital" idea; she telephoned her housekeeper to prepare some fried chicken. That night, Mr. and Mrs. Pearson stretched out atop the boat's cabin and stared at the stars. The columnist was depressed and deflated. The depression, however, likely resulted more from an ego than a monetary concern. It was doubly difficult for him to lose because he had always felt he "had" Littell.[109]

Mrs. Pearson also felt her husband should not have lost the case. She attributed the loss partly to the fact that Littell had Williams, a widely respected attorney, as his trial counsel. Mrs. Pearson said she had attended many jury trials involving her husband's libel suits, but she knew the *Littell* case was a "disaster" as soon as it got underway.[110]

Pearson instructed his attorneys to appeal the decision. To add fuel to the fire, just days after the judgment, the muckraker wrote another column directed at Littell that the former assistant attorney general believed was libelous. As a result, he sent out letters to various newspapers that had carried the column, asking for retractions. This, of course, touched off a flurry of correspondence from editors and publishers to Pearson. Before further action was taken on this third possible suit, however, the columnist and Littell made an agreement that stipulated the payment by Pearson for damages in the first action, the dropping of his appeal, and a dismissal of the second consolidated suit.

The muckraker then told his subscribing newspaper editors that no retraction would be necessary, that he and Littell had settled their differences. In a letter to the executive editor of the *Los Angeles Daily News,* Pearson elaborated upon the events behind the settlement. The columnist explained that he had decided to drop his appeal because Littell was "bombarding some of the newspapers in an effort to pressure me, and in order to save my newspapers further headaches, I have finally, at least to some extent, knuckled under."[111]

Viewed against the total picture, the $40,000 payment was a paltry sum. The columnist, however, did not look at it that way; it represented a black mark on his record. His good friend, tax attorney Randolph Paul, advised him to "take his licking and deduct it from his income taxes." Pearson followed the instructions, but he always regretted having the single blemish on his libel record.[112]

Some six years after the *Littell* cases, Pearson was again sued for libel concerning remarks allegedly related to the Foreign Agents Registration Act of 1938.[113] George Lincoln Rockwell, head of the "Committee to Impeach Governor Almond" of Virginia, filed suit against Pearson for a February 17, 1959, "Merry-Go-Round" column that centered upon activities of the group. The columnist wrote that the group headquartered at Rockwell's Arlington, Virginia, home. He described the headquarters as "one of the most virulent and vitriolic hate-nests in the U.S.A."[114] The columnist further wrote that the group had "contact with those investigated in connection with the bombing of the Atlanta synagogue, draws money from Arab sources, and even sends word of its activities to Col. Gamal Abdel Nasser of Egypt."[115] The muckraker, however, acknowledged that Nasser denied that he had anything to do "with the American hate-nest." The columnist also said that Rockwell had been supplying literature to James Madole, who was cited in 1954 by the House Un-American Activities Committee as "the would-be Fuehrer of the Nazi-style National Renaissance party, which attempts to maintain a uniformed 'elite guard' in the Hitler tradition." Pearson concluded by saying that "this is the background of the little group which is sending out thousands of petitions calling for the impeachment of the governor of Virginia."[116]

Pearson's attorney, John Donovan, quickly moved for dismissal on the ground that Rockwell's complaint failed to state a claim upon which relief could be granted.[117] The defendant's brief claimed that "the gist of a libel action is injury to reputation." According to Donovan, however, Rockwell did not claim damages for injury to his reputation, but for loss of wealthy former supporters of his activities.[118] Donovan then emphasized that Rockwell, in his complaint, had confined himself to a single paragraph in the "Merry-Go-Round" column. Pearson's comment that the group "draws money from Arab sources" was the basis for the libel action. Rockwell claimed the words were libelous per se, since they charged him with a crime under the Foreign Agents Registration Act of 1938.[119] Donovan, however, said that the words were not actionable per se since they did not expressly charge Rockwell with a specific offense.

Counsel for the columnist emphasized that to be libelous per se the words in question could have only one meaning: charging Rockwell with an indictable offense. However,

> The words do not say Rockwell was acting as a propagandist for a foreign government, for a foreign political party or a foreign group and was required to register as a foreign agent. . . . Mere receipt of money does not make

> Rockwell an agent. Rather the test would be its use to spread foreign propaganda in the United States.[120]

Donovan also contended that the columnist clearly pointed out that the purpose of the group was to impeach Governor Almond; it was not an Arab movement—and Nasser's own newspaper denied that he had anything to do with the American group.[121]

Pearson's lawyer concluded his brief by saying that Rockwell's complaint did not state a cause of action for injurious falsehoods since it lacked an essential element for words alleged to be libelous per quod: special damages.[122] Judge Holtzoff agreed. On May 18, less than two months after Rockwell filed his complaint, the district court dismissed it.[123]

Several other pre-1964 libel cases in which Pearson was a defendant centered upon columns or broadcasts in which he allegedly tied an individual or group to some type of "un-American" stance, or to an activity that could be so perceived.[124] It is important to realize that when these suits were brought—during World War II and the subsequent cold war—"Americanism" was an emotional and explosive issue. Though, at least on the surface, some of the cases concern what today might be thought of as minor accusations, they took on larger proportions during this era.

Koehne v. *Radio Corporation of America* was a multimillion dollar class action suit brought in 1943 by Ira Chase Koehne, an attorney; Howard V. Broenstrup; and Frank W. Clark on behalf of more than two dozen others against RCA, several broadcasting outlets, and broadcaster Pearson.[125]

The suit evolved from a portion of the March 28, 1943, Pearson broadcast:

> The Justice Department: The American Civil Liberties Union has refused to help the 33 indicted Hitler agents, following which a new rival, The Citizens Civil Liberties Union, has been formed has an office [*sic*] at 1118 Bar Building. But there is something very peculiar about this new Civil Liberties Union. Its office also is the office of

> the attorney for Victor Braunstropt [*sic*], one of the alleged Hitler agents who is indicted.[126]

The gist of the sixteen-count complaint was that the entire paragraph was false: it implied, falsely, that because the well-known American Civil Liberties Union had refused to defend the class of member plaintiffs, the group was in such great need of assistance that it formed a "new rival" with offices at 1118 Bar Building; the broadcast falsely alleged that there was something "very queer, odious and/or, stigmatic" about the new rival; and the individuals who had been indicted in district court had not been accused of or charged with being Hitler agents, as the broadcast indicated.

Further, Koehne said he was libeled because his office at 1118 Bar Building had been referred to, even though the alleged "Citizens Civil Liberties Union" had not been formed to his knowledge and had never used his office as a headquarters. He was, instead, merely the attorney for Broenstrup, whose name Pearson had mispronounced and misspelled in his broadcast text. Koehne further alleged that the broadcast caused him grave injury in his person and property. Koehne claimed that each of the defendants had knowledge "of the foregoing wrongs conspired to be done" and that each of them had "power to prevent or aid in preventing the commission of" the alleged wrongs.[127]

Shortly after the suit was filed, defendants RCA, the Blue Network Company, Inc., the National Broadcasting Company, the Evening Star Broadcasting Company, and Pearson moved that the complaint be dismissed, or in the alternative, stricken.[128] There were subsequent filings in the action, but the case was eventually dismissed.[129]

The columnist also defended against a similar suit brought by Prescott Dennett, a Washington, D.C., resident and armed forces veteran. Dennett brought a $100,000 libel and slander suit in 1946 against Pearson, Radio Station WMAL, the Evening Star Broadcasting Company, the American Broadcasting Company, and the Serutan Company, Pearson's radio sponsor.[130] The plaintiff cited an April 16, 1944, radio broadcast by Pearson, which said in part:

> The Justice Department: Gerald K. Smith, one time Huey Long rabble-rouser tonight called a press conference to save the thirty indicted Hitler agents. Meanwhile, Prescott Dennett, one of the indicted gentlemen who used the frank of Congressmen Fish and Martin Sweeney to mail pro-Nazi propaganda all over the country, has faked an illness at Walter Reed Hospital in order to avert trial. However, the Justice Department informs me that the trial will proceed anyway.[131]

Dennett claimed that the words "has faked an illness at Walter Reed Hospital in order to avert trial" were defamatory and untrue.[132]

Counsel for Pearson contended that the complaint failed to state a claim upon which relief could be granted. The columnist's attorney utilized several common law defenses: truth, fair comment upon a matter of public interest in which Dennett was a participant, privilege for a report on judicial proceedings, and the statute of limitations.[133] The case proved easy to defend: attorneys for the plaintiff failed to aggressively pursue it, and it was dismissed on November 19, 1949, for want of prosecution.[134]

During World War II the muckracker was also sued for $100,000 in a libel suit brought by James J. Laughlin, an attorney for defendant Charles Smythe in a major sedition trial. In his complaint, Laughlin contended that Pearson, in a radio broadcast, essentially claimed that the attorney "would shortly be charged or indicted for conspiring with certain criminals."[135] The broadcast, aired on May 21, 1944, included the following:

> My last prediction: The Sedition Trial. The United States Government is now trying twenty-nine American citizens on the charge of sedition. This is one of the most serious cases of the entire war, for these men are charged with a conspiracy against their own country. However, a group of lawyers and defendants have stirred up such a commotion

> in the court room that one of them, James J. Laughlin, has been cited for contempt. Laughlin is the attorney for defendant Charles Smythe, and not long ago he also defended three bank robbers at Hyattsville, Maryland, one of whom had what appeared to be a perfect alibi. The records of a Florida jail showed that this bank robber was allegedly imprisoned there at the time that the Maryland robbery took place. . . . James Laughlin, turbulent attorney in the sedition trial, will be charged with conspiracy in connection with altering these prison records.[136]

In his defense, Pearson's attorney claimed that Laughlin's complaint failed to state a claim upon which relief could be granted, that the statements and prophesy were true, that the remarks constituted "reasonable, fair and bona fide comment upon matters of public interest," that the "statements of fact and opinion were published without malice" and with consent of the plaintiff. Further, Pearson's answer claimed that Laughlin, on several occasions, had "publicly announced that he was about to be indicted in Baltimore and that the imminence of such an indictment had been bruited about 'for the past eighteen months.' "[137] Procedural filings continued, but before a year had elapsed, Laughlin decided to drop the case.[138]

Another attorney involved in Capitol Hill–related legal affairs, Franklin Anderson, brought a $100,000 suit against Pearson, Allen, and Eleanor Patterson, owner of the *Washington Times-Herald,* in 1940.[139] The suit grew out of a "Merry-Go-Round" article published in the *Times-Herald* on October 5, 1939, under the headline "Fascists in Capitol." The column, in part, read:

> Congressmen are supposed to stick together. Traditionally the Houses of Congress are two big gentlemen's clubs. But today if you happen into the office of Representative Jacob Thorkelson of Butte, Montana, you may find him engaged with an attorney for William D. Pelley, of the Silver Shirts, who is suing Thorkelson's colleagues on the Dies Committee.
>
> The attorney is Franklin Anderson, retained by Pelley in a libel suit which the Silver Shirt chief has brought against

> all of the Dies Committee for statements made about him. Anderson is in and out of Thorkelson's office almost every day.
>
> Thorkelson is famous in Congress for his pro-Nazi-Fascist speeches. He is one of the most garrulous speakers in the House and a thorn in the side of his Republican colleagues, who don't know how to keep him quiet.[140]

The complaint alleged that the plaintiff was referred to as a "Fascist in Capitol" and that the defendants intended to convey to readers that Anderson was a Fascist engaged in un-American activities.[141]

Attorneys for Pearson and Allen moved that the case be dismissed on the ground that the complaint failed to state a claim upon which relief could be granted, that it appeared on the face of the complaint that the part of the article alleged to be libelous was not published of and concerning the plaintiff, and that the alleged defamation was not libelous per se. Defense attorneys also moved to strike from the complaint the statement that the writers intended to convey to readers that Anderson "was a Fascist engaged in un-American activities" on the ground that the words of the column were not susceptible to such a meaning.[142]

As was often the case in pre-1964 libel cases, Pearson's attorneys emphasized that innuendos and extrinsic facts were necessary to "color them [the words of the column] with a defamatory hue." It was further claimed that "it is elementary libel law that the article complained of must be read in its entirety and interpreted in its natural and reasonable sense.[143] A fair reading of the article, according to the defendants' brief, was that Congressman Thorkelson was the protagonist; his conduct was the subject of the comment.

> The only statements of and concerning the plaintiff in the article are that the plaintiff was an attorney for William D. Pelley; that he was retained by Pelley in a libel suit which Pelley had brought against all of the members of the Dies Committee for statements made about him; and that Anderson was in and out of Thorkelson's office almost every day.

> None of these statements could reasonably be construed as charging the plaintiff with being a Fascist, or as connecting him up with the reference to Fascists, in the caption of the article.[144]

It was also emphasized that, since the words upon which the suit was based were not libelous per se, there could be no cause of action unless the plaintiff pleaded and proved special damages, which he had failed to do.[145] Upon consideration of the motion to dismiss, the district court granted the request. It was dismissed with prejudice.[146]

Dr. Edward A. Rumely, secretary of the Committee for Constitutional Government, also became irritated with a Pearson broadcast with "un-American" overtones. Rumely filed a $200,000 suit against the muckraker in 1948.[147] The action evolved from a March 21, 1948, radio broadcast by Pearson that was carried by more than 225 radio stations. The broadcast transcript read in part:

> Attention, Price Daniel, Attorney General of Texas: Why, Mr. Daniel, is your Tidelands oil lobby associated with Edward Rumely, who served a jail sentence for being a German agent and who admits to spending $460,000 as a lobbyist? Incidentally, your Tidelands oil lobby, Mr. Daniel, has behind it a lot of the very same people who are also lobbying for Arabian oil and against Palestine.

On March 28, Pearson followed with this broadcast concerning Rumely:

> Austin, Texas: Well, my old friend Price Daniel, attorney general of Texas, has informed me that he had no idea his Tidelands oil lobby was associated with Edward Rumely, who served a jail sentence as a former German agent. I am delighted to accept this assurance even though ex-German agent Rumely is sending out one million copies of a speech by Texas Governor Jester on tidelands oil, plus three million other pieces of propaganda.[148]

Rumely claimed that the statements were understood to mean that he had been convicted of being disloyal and unfaithful to the United States, had been imprisoned as a German agent, had improperly and corruptly spent $460,000 in an effort to affect legislation pending before the Congress; that he was engaged in flouting the laws of government; and that he was sympathetic toward enemies of the United States. Rumely denied all the allegations, emphasizing that, though he had been convicted of conspiracy following World War I, he was given a full and unconditional pardon by President Calvin Coolidge, and that at no time did he engage in lobbying with respect to tidelands oil legislation.[149]

Attorneys for Pearson answered that the complaint failed to state a claim upon which relief could be granted, that the language complained of was true in substance, and that it was fair comment upon a matter of public interest in which Rumely was a participant.[150] Procedural motions continued, but like so many of the Pearson cases, the suit was eventually dropped. It was dismissed with prejudice on June 23, 1948.[151]

Though Pearson found himself in the courts on numerous occasions defending against those who accused him of falsely and maliciously portraying them in an "un-American" light, the columnist apparently had little difficulty in successfully defending himself. He often relied on the answer that the plaintiff failed to state a claim upon which relief could be granted, that the words complained of were not libelous per se, and perhaps most importantly, that they constituted fair comment upon matters of public interest. During this period of American history, practically any news story that even remotely concerned "un-American" motives or activities could logically be considered a matter of public interest.

Pearson, however, did not confine himself to comments concerning his ideas of "un-American" activities. Rather, nearly all people and institutions were potential targets of the muckraker, as evidenced by three suits initiated by military men.[152]

In an action brought during World War II, James G. Ware, a career naval officer, sought $200,000 in damages from

Pearson and Eugene Meyer, publisher of the *Washington Post,* for two articles that appeared in the *Post.*[153] Ware, commanding officer at Camp Peary, Williamsburg, Virginia, based his charges on a "Merry-Go-Round" column and a follow-up article written by a *Post* staff writer.[154]

The controversy started with Pearson's June 14, 1943, column, which the *Post* carried on page one. The muckraker wrote that Camp Peary had weathered various stormy controversies, "but most interesting is the story of the hogs of the commanding officer, Capt. J. G. Ware. Captain Ware is raising hogs on United States property."[155] Pearson wrote that Navy personnel manned the hog farm. He quoted Ware as saying that the meat was used primarily for barbecue recreational purposes on the post, but some of it did go to market in Richmond. The columnist, however, closed with this clincher: "Even so, with government land, government labor, and government machinery, it's a situation to make most hog raisers green with envy."[156]

As might be expected, the Department of the Navy quickly denied the allegations. The *Post* dutifully carried the denial on page one. It quoted Lt. Comdr. W. Marvin McCarthy:

> The hog farm was started as a ship's service activity to provide food for the officers and men and had grown out of the meat shortage. Only small amounts of meat are sold on the open market and all proceeds go into the ship's service fund. Many camps have their own gardens operated by the men to supply food for the officers' and men's messes.[157]

On the other hand, the article also quoted Pearson as reiterating his stand that the "hog heaven" was operated by Ware on government property, that enlisted personnel worked the farm, and that profits went directly to the captain.[158]

Ware charged that the column was false; Pearson's attorneys filed an answer, claiming that, absent innuendos, the—

> statements of fact contained therein are substantially true, and are entirely true except to the extent that either of said articles may be construed to mean that the plaintiff was carrying on the business of a hog farm for private profit,

> and the statements of opinion contained therein constitute reasonable, fair and bona fide comment upon matters of public interest and were published without malice.[159]

The brief further stated that Pearson had obtained his information from "trustworthy" sources and he believed it to be true at the time of publication. It was also emphasized that the muckraker had telephoned Ware, giving the captain an opportunity "to correct any possible misunderstanding with reference to the facts." Ware, however, made no effort to do so, and Pearson "submitted it for publication in the honest and reasonable belief that it was entirely true."[160]

Pearson's attorneys introduced an additional column, written by the muckraker, and published in the *Post* on December 16, 1943. It, too, was carried on page 1. The brief indicated that Pearson did so "in an effort to completely eradicate any misunderstanding which might have been caused by the previous articles."[161] The headline set the tone for the article: "Seabee Training in the U.S. Brings Miracles on the Battlefronts." The kicker-headline read: "Tribute to Capt. Ware and Seabees."[162] The column read like a press release for the Seabees—a group of men training to operate bulldozers; install water systems, telephones, and electric light plants; build cantonments; or even repair ships. These jacks-of-all-trades were trained at three camps, one of them being Camp Peary. The columnist paid particular tribute to Ware:

> These camps in themselves have been near miracles of construction. When Captain Ware turned up near Williamsburg, Va., in September, 1942, to command his new Seabee camp, he found nothing but thirty square miles of wilderness and swampland.[163]

Pearson then explained that Ware conceived the idea of raising hogs in order to provide extra meat for the Seabees, and "this led to reports that he was operating the farm for his own profit." The columnist carefully explained, however, that all of the proceeds went to the ship's service fund and to benefit the Seabees.[164] The muckraker, in what was obviously a poorly disguised retraction, added frosting to the cake:

> Morale, always difficult in any new organization, is now excellent. The training the Seabees get in the swamps of Virginia under a retired naval captain called back to active duty is one big reason for the feats of heroism and accomplishment in the southwest Pacific.[165]

Despite Pearson's December column, Ware's attorneys did not immediately drop the action. Trial was set for May 16, 1944. However, just two weeks before that date, attorneys for both parties agreed that the case should be dismissed.[166]

The *Ware* case possibly serves as an example of how quickly Pearson could "backtrack" when he sensed that the common law defenses might prove insufficient. On the other hand, it may illustrate his self-professed desire to be accurate and erase any misunderstandings that might evolve from his columns. At any rate, the muckraker was not immune to reversing himself in print if he felt compelled to do so.

The two other actions involving former military personnel grew out of a July 30, 1948, "Merry-Go-Round" column published in the *Washington Post* and other newspapers. Kenwood Ross, a former army officer, filed one suit, seeking $500,000 in damages.[167] The other was brought by Joseph B. Franzino, also a private citizen, who had served as an enlisted man in the army. He sought $200,000.[168]

In the column, Pearson had pointed to a "scandal" brewing in the army that had been "so far completely hushed up." The columnist said that black marketing of U.S. Army goods by "high-up officers of the 24th Infantry Division" had been uncovered. The man who turned in his superiors, however, was killed before he could testify. Pearson said the potential witness was killed "under mysterious circumstances." But "a subsequent court-martial fined the assistant chief of staff, Lt. Col. Kenwood Ross . . . $1,000 for selling Army rations." The column listed other army personnel who were fined for selling the rations. "Significantly, the only private involved,

Joseph B. Franzino, was the only man to go to jail. He got three years at hard labor plus a dishonorable discharge from the Army."[169]

In his complaint, Ross contended that the publication insinuated that he was "guilty of the murder of one Lt. Charles Vetter, or of aiding and assisting others in procuring this murder," that he was involved in one of the worst scandals in the U.S. Army, that he was one of the 24th Infantry Division officers engaged in the illegal sale for personal profit and gain of goods belonging to the army, and that he was fined $1,000 for selling army property. Ross claimed that all the information was false.[170]

Pearson's attorneys answered that the column, discarding innuendo, was privileged as a fair account of an army court martial; that it was published without malice; that it represented fair and bona fide comment upon matters of public interest; that, when read in its ordinary meaning and without connotations imputed in the innuendoes, it was true in substance; that it had been published in good faith and with reliance upon trustworthy sources; and that the plaintiff's complaint failed to state a claim upon which relief could be granted.[171] During the next two years, the case was not aggressively pursued. Finally, however, on February 27, 1952, the case was dismissed with prejudice by agreement of counsel for all parties.[172]

Franzino's complaint was similar. His attorneys charged that, though the columnist did not specifically say so, it was generally understood that the plaintiff was guilty of murder, or of aiding and assisting others in procuring the murder, that he was involved in one of the worst scandals in the United States Army, that he was engaged in the illegal sale for personal profit of goods belonging to the U.S. Army, and that he had been sentenced by an army court to three years' confinement in a prison. Attorneys for Franzino said that all of the allegations were "false" and were "known or should have been known by defendants to be false."[173] Furthermore, the complaint said that Franzino had "suffered humiliation, mental anguish and distress."[174]

Pearson's attorney then listed four defenses: when read in its ordinary meaning, absent innuendoes, the column was privileged as a fair account of an army court martial; that it was published without malice; that the statements constituted an opinion concerning a matter of public interest, published in good faith, without malice, and in reliance upon trustworthy sources; and that the defendant had failed to state a claim upon which relief could be granted.[175] The case, like most actions against the muckraker, never went to trial. It was dismissed with prejudice about one year after Ross's case was dropped.[176]

Since Pearson was willing to challenge military men in his columns, it is not surprising that, with equal zeal, he attempted to expose what he considered wrongdoing in high places–specifically, certain activities in the nation's capital. Three cases in particular attracted considerable attention and notoriety in Washington, D.C.[177]

Lobbyist John Monroe filed a million dollar libel suit against Pearson in 1943 for a "Merry-Go-Round" column published in the *Washington Post*.[178] He also filed a companion suit against Eugene Meyer of the *Post* in which he sought $350,000 in damages.[179] The cases were consolidated for trial purposes. Monroe charged that twenty-one statements in the "Merry-Go-Round" column that appeared in the *Post* on May 3, 1943, and three portions of a follow-up May 9, 1943, Pearson radio broadcast were false.[180] The column, among other things, named a number of distinguished persons who had been guests at Monroe's home. Pearson wrote that "probably most of these famous guests did not realize that they were being used as a front in connection with war contract lobbying."[181] Pearson went on to say that Monroe "had been sued a dozen times for debt," and that Monroe's home on R Street could be compared to "the notorious Little Green House on K Street of Harding's day."[182]

Monroe alleged that the "innuendo" of the article was that he was "seeking to conceal corrupt and unpatriotic war contract transactions, mysteriously and extravagantly negotiated" at his home; and that his R Street residence was a "rendezvous for persons involved in dishonest and unpatriotic transactions, and indulging in orgies of drinking, gambling and lewdness." Furthermore, Monroe claimed that the statement that he "had been sued a dozen times for debt" represented "malicious innuendo" that the plaintiff "habitually failed to pay his honest debts."[183]

The complaint also referred to part of the May 9, 1943, Pearson radio broadcast:

> The big red house on R Street: The House Military Affairs Committee investigating war lobbyist John Monroe and his mysterious house on R Street has a bear by the tail and can't let go. Last week many Congressmen, particularly Republicans, were worried sick that Monroe might name more guests who had come to his house for dinner. They repeatedly told him they did not want to know who his dinner guests were. Last week I gave the Military Affairs Committee some tips as to what they might investigate. Here are some more. See whether Monroe didn't appear before the Washington Rent Commission to help secure a reduction of rent for a colonel. A guest at the R Street house, who helps buy tanks for the army. Also look into Monroe's deal to buy a steam boiler from the New Orleans Public Service Co., and then sell it at a much higher price to the Aluminum Corporation. I think you will find that Donald Nelson stopped the deal—but especially, gentlemen, you might investigate whether one of your own colleagues, a Congressman from Louisiana, was not supposed to get a juicy commission.[184]

Monroe alleged that the radio broadcast included "innuendoes" that, taken in their entirety, implied that he "was dishonest, corrupt, indecent, and unpatriotic, and was engaged in practices which were questionable, unlawful and contrary to public policy."[185] Before filing the suit, Monroe demanded a retraction. Pearson, however, refused.[186]

Pearson's attorney, in answer to the complaint, contended that neither the broadcast nor the column, stripped of innuendo, was libelous, that when read in their entirety "in their ordinary meaning," the statements of fact were true, that the statements of opinion were "fair and bona fide comment upon matters of public interest," and that they were published without malice.[187]

Trial was scheduled for March, 1944. A lengthy trial was apparently expected: the judge presiding over the pretrial proceedings suggested that two alternate jurors be ordered to sit.[188] The trial lasted less than two weeks, however, as the jury held for Pearson and further stipulated that Monroe pay the costs of the columnist's defense.[189]

In what was possibly the most bizarre case involving the muckraker, Rumanian millionaire industrialist Nicolae Malaxa brought a $5 million libel suit in 1955; on September 27, 1960, however, he claimed as special damages loss of an additional $45 million, thus bringing the total damages sought to $50 million.[190] Docket entries alone in the case consumed more than eight pages. Ironically, after extensive pretrial proceedings, deposition taking, and filings, the case was dismissed in May of 1962 for lack of prosecution.[191]

Malaxa was born in Rumania in 1884, came to the United States in 1946, and was lawfully admitted for permanent residency in New York in September of 1953. He brought suit against Pearson based primarily on a January 13, 1952, "Merry-Go-Round" column that Malaxa claimed accused him of being "pro-Nazi and pro-Communist" and a December 15, 1955, column in which Malaxa said Pearson repeated his alleged libelous charges.[192] Malaxa's complaint also said that the 1955 column "cast doubt in the public mind as to the loyalty and fitness of Vice President Richard Nixon and [California] Congressman Pat Hillings."[193] Malaxa further alleged that Pearson's column prejudiced authorities against him. In essence, the industrialist contended that the muckraker's columns "were intended to accuse" him of "committing bribery; by innuendo to hold the plaintiff up to contempt and ridicule . . . and to suggest that plaintiff is not a fit person to be admitted to the United States."[194]

In the January 13, 1952, column, Pearson had quoted from a "confidential report" that showed that Malaxa had "various business dealings with the Communists." Despite this, Pearson said, Malaxa was on the list to get a special bill passed by Congress giving him permanent residence in the United States.[195] The "special report" consisted of a letter found in the purse of a federal agent. The columnist reported that the letter, dated May 11, 1948, was written to J. Edgar Hoover by Alan R. McCracken, acting director of the Central Intelligence Agency. It read in part:

> During 1937, Malaxa began his collaboration with the Nazi regime in Germany. He established close relations with German industralists, including Albert Goering, the brother of Herman Goering. Malaxa gave Albert Goering an interest in all his companies.[196]

According to the muckraker, the letter also said Malaxa had been paid $2 million by the Soviet government for a large pipe mill it had confiscated.[197]

Also entered as evidence by the plaintiff was a February 19, 1952, "Merry-Go-Round" column in which Pearson retracted remarks made against Malaxa. Pearson wrote that it was "embarrassing for a newspaperman who tried hard to be right to find out sometimes how wrong he can be."[198] The columnist explained that after publishing the January 13 column, he had received from the former prime minister of Rumania a letter explaining that his own cabinet, not the Communists, had made the payments to Malaxa for his steel mill. Pearson said that "further study of the voluminous records in the Malaxa case" also showed that Malaxa had fought both the Nazis and the Communists.[199] On February 24, 1952, the muckraker sent a letter of apology to Malaxa.[200] This apparently closed the Pearson file on the millionaire; the resolution was, however, only temporary.

On December 15, 1955, just one day before Malaxa was due to return to the United States after spending a year in Argentina, the muckraker again lashed out at the Rumanian. Entered as Exhibit D by the plaintiff in his complaint was a "Merry-Go-Round" column that appeared on the editorial page of the *New York Daily Mirror.* Pearson had written that "the story behind Malaxa and his many moves to pull wires in highup political places is probably the most amazing of any refugee entering this country."[201] The columnist cited a Malaxa-owned corporation that proposed to build a plant near Whittier, California, Vice President Nixon's hometown. Reference was made to help given Malaxa by Nixon. Pearson quoted from a letter dated September 14, 1951, in which Nixon asked a defense production administrator to "grant a quick tax write-off to Malaxa's firm."[202] The columnist closed with, "It will be interesting to see whether Malaxa is readmitted to the United States and for how long."[203]

The case dragged on for more than five years. As activity in the case began to wind down, however, Pearson's attorney filed a motion for summary judgment.[204] Lawyer Donovan claimed five defenses: (1) that the columns were privileged as a fair report and account of judicial, legislative, and administrative proceedings; (2) that the columns were privileged as fair comment upon a matter of public interest and concern; (3) that the columns were privileged in that Malaxa consented to publication of the 1951 report of his administrative proceedings, a copy of which he gave to Pearson; (4) that the matters complained of published by Pearson prior to December 15, 1955, were barred by the statute of limitations; and (5) that the matters complained of, absent innuendoes, were true, published in good faith without malice and for justifiable cause.[205]

Donovan further claimed that Malaxa brought the suit against Pearson to keep the columnist from writing anything further about him until the immigration authorities decided whether he could remain permanently in the United States.

In addition, Donovan contended that Malaxa had instructed his attorney not to press the suit during the course of administrative hearings and that he had no "serious intention" of prosecuting the case.[206]

By the early 1960s, docket entries in the case read like a never ending afternoon soap opera. Donovan, in a brief on Pearson's behalf, emphasized the extended nature of the proceedings: Malaxa's deposition had been taken three times through an interpreter, during the course of which he constantly changed his testimony; that Malaxa did not "press" the case in 1956, 1957, or 1958; that the millionaire, during one deposition, had claimed special damages, but refused to state what they were; that though Malaxa claimed Pearson's column had cost him $45 million in Argentine contracts, this was not an accurate assessment.[207] In a twenty-eight-page brief in support of his motion for summary judgment, Donovan cited countless precedents to support his contention.[208] Nevertheless, the case was scheduled for trial on May 29, 1962.

Malaxa, however, made one final attempt to delay the proceedings. Two weeks before the scheduled trial, the aging industrialist requested a continuance because of his failing health.[209] The request included a letter from a New York physician, which read in part:

> During the last year, [Malaxa's] general health has deteriorated greatly due to frequent attacks of angina pectoris. He has consulted many cardiologists for this condition but they have not been able to improve his condition.
>
> In view of the above mentioned angina, I have strongly advised Mr. Malaxa to avoid stress, strain or emotional outbursts which tend to increase the severity and frequency of his attacks. Strain in any form at this time is to be avoided at all costs.[210]

After nearly seven years of legal maneuvering, however, the case finally went to trial. Donovan and Pearson engaged F. Joseph Donohue, a man who had built a reputation in the District of Columbia as an outstanding trial attorney, to serve as the muckraker's trial counsel. Fully prepared, the defense attorneys entered the courtroom. When the case was called, however, Malaxa's attorney stood up and announced to the court that his client asked that the case be dismissed. Neither Pearson, Donovan, nor Donohue had any idea that this might occur; it came as a complete, albeit pleasant, surprise.[211]

The muckraker also emerged a victor in a libel case decided about one year later. In *Dall* v. *Pearson,*[212] the plaintiff sought $4 million in damages. Essentially, the column he complained about was an account of testimony he had given before a congressional committee. Pearson wrote that Dall attacked "political Zionist planners for absolute rule via a one-world government." Further, the muckraker claimed Dall proceeded into an anti-Semitic "diatribe" and attacked the Jews.[213]

Pearson's counsel, John Donovan, moved for summary judgment, claiming that the alleged defamatory statement was true and also constituted fair comment.[214] Dall, meanwhile, claimed that his testimony was not anti-Semitic, nor an attack on Jews. He said he did not use the word "Jews" and clearly did not attack all Jews; rather, he was concerned with only those who were Zionists and also non-Jews who were Zionists. The court refused to accept this argument, however, reasoning that "an attack on a group does not necessarily mean that it has to be an attack on every single individual member of the group."[215] Further, the court said that Dall had a First Amendment right to criticize any group in the community, no matter what their religious or racial views. The court emphasized, therefore, that when one criticizes or attacks a group, "he has no just cause for complaint if somebody said that he did."[216]

The district court then examined Dall's testimony and the "Merry-Go-Round" article. Though Dall claimed that Pearson's version was "distorted" and "inaccurate," the court noted that the account given was substantially true and that Pearson's comments were within the scope of fair comment.[217]

As for Dall's objection to Pearson's use of the word "diatribe," the court said that the word was merely a "popular characterization of an emphatic, intemperate, critical statement," and that this term, too, was within the scope of fair comment.[218] The district court then granted the motion for summary judgment.

Not all the libel cases in which Pearson was a defendant prior to 1964 were sensational. For example, the columnist was involved as a defendant in a District of Columbia case that fell into the "routine" category. In June of 1948, Silver Motors, Inc., a franchised dealer of Tucker Corporation, which manufactured automobiles for sale to the public through its franchised dealers, filed a $500,000 libel suit against Pearson and the American Broadcasting Company, Inc.[219] The complaint charged that on June 6, 1948, Pearson aired "a statement that the Justice Department . . . will commence an investigation into the Tucker Corporation's 'Dream Car' that will blow the new Chicago automobile firm higher than a kite." The complaint further alleged that Pearson's comments were understood by listeners to "mean that the said automobile would never be produced by the . . . Tucker Corporation" and that the product was merely "a dream and not an actuality."[220] The corporation insisted that, because of the broadcast, it had been "greatly harmed" and had "suffered cancellation of purchase orders and loss of good will."[221] The suit, however, was unspectacularly short-lived: it was dismissed without prejudice exactly six months after being filed.[222]

The *Silver Motors* case is, however, another illustration of the pioneer role Pearson assumed in the 1930s and 1940s. Automobile corporations today, thanks to Ralph Nader and other consumer groups and investigative news reporters, would not likely even dream of suing a newspaper or a reporter for printing comments about a proposed investigation into a particular car. But in the decades immediately before and after World War II, Pearson's aggressive and novel methods made him the target of many disgruntled officials and corporations. The columnist, however, also found himself in the courts defending against private individuals.

Cases Involving Private Persons

In a marathon case that spanned dozens of procedural motions, two jury trials, and more than five years, Mary G. Gariepy, a Michigan resident, brought a $450,000 defamation suit against Pearson for two radio broadcasts.[223] In the suit, which also named the American Broadcasting Company, Inc., as a defendant, Ms. Gariepy grounded her complaint partly on a January 30, 1949, broadcast that included:

> Detroit: The Justice and Treasury Departments have ordered the prosecution of Dr. Bernard F. Gariepy of Royal Oak, Michigan, in a strange income-tax case indirectly involving Father [Charles E.] Coughlin. Dr. Gariepy's defense is that Father Coughlin gave him $68,000 because of *alienation of affection* of Mrs. Gariepy by the radio priest. The Justice Department plans to prosecute Gariepy anyway.[224]

Ms. Gariepy also cited the following words in a February 6, 1949, Pearson broadcast: "Despite denials, the income tax case of Dr. Bernard F. Gariepy, indirectly involving Father Coughlin, will be brought to trial. When that trial takes place we will see who was really telling the truth."[225]

Ms. Gariepy, a Detroit anesthetist, married Dr. Gariepy in June of 1935. She obtained a divorce from him on September 13, 1943. The Reverend Mr. Coughlin, an ordained priest of the Roman Catholic Church, was pastor of a parish, the Shrine of the Little Flower, in Royal Oak, Michigan.[226]

Ms. Gariepy sought punitive, general, and special damages. Special damages were sought because she claimed her son was subjected to such "abuse, contumely and physical mistreatment" by peers at school and in his neighborhood that she was forced to withdraw him from the neighborhood school and send him to a boarding school a substantial distance from her residence. She alleged that this greatly increased her expense for his maintenance, support, and education. She further alleged that Pearson's remarks had placed "in jeopardy" her position as a professional anesthetist.[227]

A rough draft on a piece of copy paper preserved in the Pearson papers shows the columnist's initial reaction to the *Gariepy* suit:

> I have known that for sometime certain friends of Mrs. Gariepy have been trying to persuade her to file suit against me. It is interesting therefore that they were not able to do so until one year minus one day after my broadcast. Personally I welcome the suit, since it will give me a chance to clear up certain false innuendoes prevalent in the Detroit area. I have no doubt as to the outcome of the case.[228]

The allegedly libelous column on the Gariepy–Father Coughlin link naturally touched off a volatile reaction among some people and institutions.

The *Michigan Catholic* newsletter, in fact, headlined a release: "Time to Clear Air of Pearson Poison." The article said in part:

> Exposed two years ago by the *Saturday Evening Post* as an unscrupulous gossip monger, called by President Roosevelt a "chronic liar," voted by his Washington colleagues as the "most influential but least reliable" of their number, his continued presence on the airways is a sorry commentary on our supine tolerance of moral degradation.
>
> Pearson's vicious slander upon Father Charles E. Coughlin . . . was an insult equally . . . to all Catholic priests and to the Catholic people who revere their priests.
>
> We call upon the Federal Communications Commission to exercise its authority to clear the air of this nuisance. The FCC heretofore has silenced purveyors of "goat gland" nostrums and other quack remedies that menaced the physical health and welfare of the public.
>
> Will it do no less with this contaminator of character, an assassin of good name.[229]

A denial of the Pearson charges by Father Coughlin was printed in the same newsletter. The priest said that it was a "Pearsonian lie to affirm that I transacted any financial business or bestowed any funds or hush money to Dr. Bernard Gariepy."[230]

Dr. Gariepy and his ex-wife also issued denials. Dr. Gariepy said that during his testimony before IRS officials, "no charge of any kind was made against Father Coughlin, nor was his name mentioned in connection with the receipt by me, or payment to me, of any money, at any time or for any reason."[231] Ms. Gariepy said that, "On one occasion I spoke with Father Coughlin for about ten minutes in the rectory office about my divorce. That is the only time I ever met or spoke to him. He wouldn't know me if we passed in the street."[232]

The muckraker did not take the criticism directed toward him and his column by Father Coughlin lying down. Pearson was apparently concerned about sentiment in the Catholic community. Western Union distributed the columnist's reaction:

> I am afraid some people have misconstrued what I said about Father Coughlin as a reflection on other members of his cloth. This is most emphatically not the case. And I am sure that if you were fully familiar with my broadcasts you would concur.
>
> For instance while I have received mail criticizing me because of my statements on Father Coughlin I have also received much more mail praising my tribute to the late Father Flanagan.[233]

Pearson listed several other examples of "friendly" gestures toward the Catholic faith. The columnist said he could "recall all too vividly the cries and taunts of 'Pope-lover' hurled at me by a mob of Klansmen when I denounced the Klan in a radio broadcast from Atlanta, Georgia." Pearson also wrote that "criticism and censorship cuts both ways. It may cut at you and it may cut at me. I have had plenty of it, and expect to have plenty more."[234]

Meanwhile, in court proceedings, Pearson's attorneys utilized several common law defenses: fair reporting of executive and subsequent judicial proceedings, truth, and fair comment concerning a matter of public interest.[235] The columnist sought summary judgment. The district court rejected his defense that the broadcast was privileged because the allegations were never stated during a public hearing; rather, they were not "public" until Pearson's broadcast put them in that category. Had the statement concerning the tax suit been made public before Pearson's broadcast, then it would have been privileged.[236] Therefore, the question for the district court turned on whether or not the words could reasonably be understood to support "the innuendo of unchastity as charged in the complaint."[237]

The court reasoned that the term *alienation of affection,* as generally and commonly understood, "conveys the idea of a change in mental attitude and nothing more." The court said that, in their common meaning, the words did not connote any unchastity on the part of anyone. The legal meaning of the term, according to the court, was "a change in mental attitude of one spouse toward another, induced by a third party."[238] The district court then granted Pearson's motion for summary judgment, emphasizing that a reporter should not be subject to "strained and unusual" meanings of statements "to afford the basis for an evil innuendo," when the normal meanings of the words were not evil.[239] The battle, however, was far from over; Ms. Gariepy filed an appeal.[240]

The court of appeals reversed, holding that the question of whether the statement could be reasonably understood as implying that Ms. Gariepy had been an unchaste wife was a question for a jury.[241] Circuit Court Judge Henry Edgerton said Pearson's broadcasts could conceivably have been understood as implying that Ms. Gariepy was unchaste; therefore, a jury should be permitted to decide whether they actually were so understood.[242] Edgerton emphasized that only when the court could "say that the publication is not reasonably capable of any defamatory meaning" could it rule, as a matter of law, that the publication was not libelous.[243]

The case was eventually scheduled for trial in the district court in October 1954. Pearson, realizing that he would need an expert trial lawyer, conferred with his house counsel, Donovan. They decided on F. Joseph Donohue. The trial was held, but the jury could not agree upon a verdict. Therefore, on October 30, 1954, District Court Judge Jennings Bailey ordered that the jury be discharged from further consideration of the case.[244] Donohue talked with some of the jurors after they had been dismissed; he was told that only one person had refused to vote for the columnist.[245]

The muckraker then sent out a number of letters to newspaper clients. In part, he wrote:

> We finally went to trial in the *Gariepy* case. In brief, we had a hung jury—in other words, a mistrial. But on the whole it was encouraging from our point of view, because the jury voted eleven-to-one in my favor. They were out about a day and a half, but one lady refused to move. . . . I don't know whether the other side is going to bring a new trial or not. I hope they won't.[246]

As it turned out, Pearson was guilty of wishful thinking. Ms. Gariepy soon filed for another trial; it was scheduled for early the following year.

Meanwhile, attorneys Donovan and Donohue had decided to travel to Royal Oak to get Father Coughlin's deposition. On a bitter cold December day, the two lawyers and a clerk of the court arrived at the right-wing priest's home. Father Coughlin proceeded to berate Donohue for "bothering" him. The priest said that Donohue, a graduate of Catholic University in Washington, D.C., should have "known better" than to harass him. After some unfriendly exchanges, Donohue turned to the clerk and asked him to swear in the witness. Although Father Coughlin refused to swear to tell the truth, the deposition was taken. However, when Pearson's attorneys returned to Washington they moved that the deposition not be admitted as evidence. The court agreed and instructed that it be sealed.[247]

The second trial was started on January 27, 1955; it lasted less than one week. On February 2, the jury held for Pearson and ordered that Ms. Gariepy pay the costs of the defense.[248] Obviously unhappy with the result, Ms. Gariepy filed a motion to set aside the judgment and verdict and moved for a new trial. Exactly one month later Judge Edward Tamm overruled the motion.[249]

Pleased that the ordeal had come to a successful end for him, Pearson wrote a letter of appreciation to Donohue. The muckraker, in fact, often praised his attorneys. The letter to Donohue read in part:

> I would just like to repeat what I told you immediately after the trial and tell you what a magnificent job I think you did. My wife now says I will have a tough job keeping up with the things you said about me—and I agree with her.[250]

Although *Gariepy* was the most publicized pre-1964 Pearson libel case involving a private individual, the muckraker was involved in at least three others.

Ernest Howard of Washington, D.C., brought a libel action against the Washington Post Company, Pearson, and the Bell Syndicate. The suit, filed in 1949, sought $250,000 in damages.[251] The case evolved from a March 21, 1949, "Merry-Go-Round" column that said in part:

> North Carolina Blood Is Thick: Senator Clyde Hoey of North Carolina is on the Senate Expenditures Committee, now engaged in probing alleged political favoritism inside the RFC [Reconstruction Finance Corporation] whereby former Congressman Frank Hancock of North Carolina used his brother-in-law, Ernest Howard, inside the RFC, to arrange government loans for clients. This has netted various fees for Hancock. Although Senator Hoey is taking no part in the investigation, his committee is. And during the investigation Senator Hoey showed up as guest of honor at a luncheon given by Mrs. Ernest Howard, who is the wife of the one man under investigation and the sister of the other—Frank Hancock.[252]

This column was published eleven days after a picture of the luncheon cited by Pearson appeared in the *Post*. The cutline beneath the picture said that Mrs. Ernest Howard, president of the Columbia Heights Citizens Association, had as her guest at the dinner Sen. Clyde R. Hoey. Howard, however, complained.

> The plaintiff, Ernest Howard, is not the Ernest Howard of the R.F.C. The Mrs. Ernest Howard who attended the dinner of the Federation of Citizens Association and whose picture with that of Senator Clyde Hoey was published and circulated in *The Washington Post* on March 10, 1949, hereinbefore referred to, is not the wife of Ernest Howard of the R.F.C., but is the wife of the plaintiff in this action.[253]

Obviously, the case was one of mistaken identity. Howard claimed that his friends, associates, and acquaintances, as well as the general public, would "reasonably think and actually understand" that the article referred to him.[254]

Pearson's attorneys, John Donovan and James R. Murphy, answered that the complaint failed to state a claim upon which relief could be granted; that the article complained of was not of and concerning the plaintiff; that the words complained of constituted "reasonable, fair and bona fide comment upon matters of public interest" and were published without malice.[255] Mention was also made of a March 25, 1949, Pearson column that read in part:

> Senator Clyde Hoey of North Carolina: Apologies for getting the wrong Mrs. Ernest Howard with whom you were photographed the other day; and glad to know that the lady in the photograph was not the Mrs. Ernest Howard, wife of the RFC official, whom your committee is investigating. . . . Also apologies to Mrs. Ernest Howard of 1521 Monroe St., who sat beside Senator Hoey at a dinner given by the Citizens Association and who is not the wife of an RFC official. Also apologies to Mrs. Ernest Howard of 2744 Woodley Pl., who was not at the dinner but who is the wife of the RFC official.[256]

Pearson was apparently making a concerted effort to set the record straight.

The suit filed by Howard was not aggressively pursued; it was dismissed with prejudice on April 12, 1951. However, in 1950 Howard's wife had filed an action based on the same column, and this suit remained in the courts. Mrs. Howard sought $200,000 in damages.[257] The case dragged on for more than two years before Pearson's attorneys filed a motion for summary judgment. It was contended that there was no genuine issue of fact involved and that, as a matter of law, the publication complained of did not even pertain to the plaintiff:[258]

> Although as a matter of law it does not appear that the article is libelous even if it referred to the plaintiff, this motion is directed solely to the point that the article does not refer to the plaintiff. In view of the facts as shown by the pleadings and the deposition of the plaintiff, it is evident that the article does not contain matter "of and concerning" the plaintiff. Therefore, there is no necessity for discussion as to whether the article would be defamatory if it referred to the plaintiff because it is so clear that it does not.[259]

The brief went on to explain that the March 21 article described "another" Mrs. Ernest Howard, not the plaintiff. It was pointed out that the column referred to Mrs. Howard as the wife of an RFC official, the sister of former congressman Frank Hancock, and from North Carolina.[260] On the other hand, the plaintiff was not the wife of the Ernest Howard decribed in the article, but of an Ernest Howard who worked for the District of Columbia Fire Department; she was born and raised in Missouri, not North Carolina; and she was not the sister of, or in any way related to, excongressman Frank Hancock who was named in the article.[261] The brief also emphasized that the plaintiff was involved in numerous civic groups in the District of Columbia and was "well known locally because of her activities." It was stated that "it is inconceivable that her friends or acquaintances would even mistakenly think that the publication which she complains about referred to her."[262] It was further pointed out that neither the picture nor the cutline referred to anything in the Pearson column, nor did the Pearson column refer to the picture and cutline.[263]

Mrs. Howard's counsel opposed the motion for summary judgment, emphasizing that the case had been pending for more than two years, with the pretrial continued on "some occasions" at the request of the defendants. Further, the "attempted claim that the publication was not of and concerning the plaintiff . . . would be a matter of fact to be determined at the trial."[264] The motion for summary judgment was denied and trial scheduled. During subsequent pretrial proceedings, however, Pearson's attorneys further emphasized that the article complained of did not refer to the plaintiff, was not libelous, that Mrs. Howard had suffered no damage by reason of the article, and that the column had been published in good faith and without malice.[265] Like the action brought by Mr. Howard, Mrs. Howard's suit never went to trial. Instead, it was dismissed with prejudice.[266]

Some four years later, another private citizen, Sam Kefalos, operator of a newspaper and cigar stand and ticket sales agency for three bus companies in Bridgeport, Ohio, brought a two-count slander and libel suit against the columnist that sought $420,000 in damages.[267] The first count concerned a March 25, 1956, radio broadcast by Pearson, which said in part:

> Bridgeport, Ohio: Congratulations to Police Chief Ludwig Hoge for finally closing down the SLAS Club and the Acorn Club, now called the Pastime Poolroom, even though you did have a little trouble with Mayor George Britton in doing this.
>
> May I suggest that the mayor look a little carefully about his own office building. He might find some very interesting operations going on there. Also see why it is that Sam Kefalos who "seels" cigars at the bus terminal doesn't "seel" cigars out of one particular box.
>
> Also take a look upstairs over the bus terminal regarding certain things going on there.
>
> You made a start, Mr. Police Chief, but there is a lot to be done in Bridgeport.[268]

The complaint further alleged that Pearson, while conducting a crusade against alleged illegal underworld activities in the Wheeling, West Virginia, area, had told his listeners that the activities had moved across the river to Bridgeport. The complaint alleged that Pearson's listeners were led to believe that Kefalos was participating in illegal operations such as operating or condoning the operation of a place for prostitution and the operation of a lottery, all of which were in violation of the laws of Ohio.[269]

The second count was based on articles published in the *Wheeling News-Register* and the *Martin's Ferry* (Ohio) *Ledger*. The newspapers had quoted from the transcript of Pearson's radio remarks and informed readers that they could hear them on a local radio station.[270]

Pearson's attorney, Donovan, immediately moved to dismiss the action because it failed to state a claim against the columnist upon which relief could be granted. Donovan contended that the words complained of in the two counts were neither slanderous nor libelous per se. Neither charged the plaintiff with commission of a crime. It was emphasized that in Kafalos's first count, which referred to a March 18, 1956, broadcast, the plaintiff was not named, nor was the community of Bridgeport as a whole.[271] It was then stressed that, in determining whether the words were slanderous per se, accompanying innuendo stating their purpose must be disregarded: "If the words are not actionable in themselves, they cannot be made so by innuendo."[272]

Donovan then pointed out that the rule in the District of Columbia was that, where a court cannot hold that a publication, on its face, is actionable per se, then the plaintiff must allege and prove special damages. In essence, he said, the statements in question represented libel per quod; extrinsic circumstances and innuendo were needed to show that the words were defamatory; and special damages, therefore, had to be alleged and proved.[273]

However, Donovan said, there had been no allegation of special damages or economic loss. Pearson's attorney further emphasized that "the spoken words do not tend to injure Kefalos in his business as a news vendor, cigar seller, or ticket vendor."[274]

The district judge agreed with Donovan. Less than two months after Kefalos filed suit, it was ordered that the complaint be dismissed because the publications referred to in both counts were not actionable per se and there was no allegation of special damage or economic loss.[275]

Thus, Pearson's counsel skillfully utilized procedural maneuvers, appropriate common law defenses, and the relatively liberal libel law in the District of Columbia that an article was not libelous per se unless there were charges of crime or gross immorality. As a result, they managed to protect the columnist from heavy damages, even when private individuals were the plaintiffs.

Pearson—A Courtroom Regular

Pre-1964 libel cases in which Pearson was a defendant illustrate his near-romantic view of conflict. On every occasion, he staunchly defended his First Amendment rights to publish what he believed to be matters of public interest. As might be expected, his involvement in litigation was not limited to the libel arena. The muckraker, for example, was involved in a copyright suit[276] and an invasion of privacy case[277] as a defendant. He also became embroiled in a tax case with the federal government.[278]

In fact, Pearson, a pioneer in Washington-based investigative reporting, continuously found himself in the courts. Presidents denounced him, congressmen verbally crucified him on the libel-proof floors of their respective houses, and broadcast sponsors dropped him as a result of his volatile dealings with people in power.

Well-publicized accounts of some persons' "anti-Pearson" behavior and remarks possibly encouraged other public officials, public figures, and private individuals to file lawsuits. The columnist was, without doubt, a "marked man" during his entire writing career, particularly during the 1930s, 1940s, and 1950s, when he stood at the top of the list of America's controversial muckrakers.

Excluding the massive Sweeney chain libel suits,[279] Pearson was a defendant in at least twenty-six libel cases before 1964.[280] In addition, his writings led to at least three lawsuits against newspapers because they published his column.[281]

Though undoubtedly a defendant in more libel suits than any syndicated columnist of his time—he was, in fact, likely sued more times than any other American columnist in history—Pearson lost only one during his lifetime.[282] As emphasized earlier, the muckraker's success in defending against libel suits in the pre-1964 era is truly phenomenal when one considers that there was a lack of constitutional protection and little jurisdictional uniformity in libel law. The columnist repeatedly proved that common law libel defenses, if effectively utilized, could provide even muckraking investigative journalists with ample protection.

At any rate, as America ushered in the faster-paced 1960s, when the U.S. Supreme Court nationalized libel law and more syndicated columnists engaged in investigative reporting, it might have seemed reasonable that libel actions against the "Merry-Go-Round" column would taper off. For during this era, it became exceedingly difficult for public persons to collect damages in libel suits, and there were more "targets"—investigative reporters—for potential suits.

6

The "Merry-Go-Round" and the Years of Protection for "Robust, Wide-Open" Reporting

The landmark *New York Times Co.* v. *Sullivan* decision of 1964 changed libel law dramatically,[1] but contrary to what one might expect, it did not lead to a great decrease in libel suits against the "Merry-Go-Round." Writers of the controversial muckraking column have continued to find themselves in the courts. The *Sullivan* ruling gave reporters the constitutional protection to pursue public issues in an "uninhibited, robust, and wide-open" manner,[2] but irate subjects nevertheless retained the right to continue suing, no matter how remote their chances of recovering damages.

During the decade after *Sullivan,* the courts continued to expand protection for journalists when discussing public officials and figures.[3] It became increasingly difficult for "public persons" to prove what is labeled the *Times* "actual malice" rule—that the statement was made with knowledge of its falsity or with reckless disregard of whether it was true or false[4]—in order to collect damages. Ironically, however, a public official or figure brought all but one of the post-1964 libel cases that involved "Merry-Go-Round" writers as defendants.[5] Public persons—including congressmen, gubernatorial candidates, state-level officials, lobbyists, and legal counsel for powerful unions—who found themselves subjects of uncomplimentary columns were not intimidated by the odds against winning a libel suit; they continued to file.

As was the case with pre-1964 libel actions, however, the columnists and their attorneys continued to be successful in the courts. This chapter, then, will examine post-1964 libel cases in which writers of the "Merry-Go-Round" column were defendants.

Cases Involving Public Officials

United States Representative Eugene B. Keogh of New York filed three suits against Pearson between 1962 and 1964 seeking aggregate damages of $5 million.[6] These cases are particularly interesting because Keogh and his attorney, Philip Handelman of New York, proved as pertinacious as Pearson and his primary attorney, John Donovan. It is therefore not surprising that two of the suits dragged on for more than a decade—until nearly five years after Pearson's death.[7]

The first action, filed in 1962 in the District of Columbia, sought $2 million in damages. It named Pearson and the Washington Post Publishing Company as defendants. The suit was based on two "Merry-Go-Round" columns; Keogh's complaint said they were intended to convey that he took bribes that influenced his official actions and votes, and further, that he attempted to bribe a federal judge "but was spared from prosecution because of his close political association with the president and attorney general of the United States."[8] Keogh claimed that Pearson's columns included false and defamatory matter and that they were written with intent to injure him. Keogh further alleged that the *Washington Post*, in publishing the columns, was "grossly negligent and reckless" in view of the nature of the columns and "the writer's reputation among journalists."[9] The Washington Post Company relied on the *New York Times* "actual malice" rule in requesting summary judgment. The district court also took into consideration the then-recent *Garrison* v. *Louisiana* standard that reckless disregard constituted "false statements made with a high degree of awareness of their probable falsity."[10]

The district court denied the motion for summary judgment; four days later, however, the Post corporation filed a motion to reconsider. The court then decided to amend its earlier decision and permit the Post corporation to seek a ruling by the U.S. court of appeals.[11] Pearson also requested reconsideration, but his motion was denied for lack of standing. Attorneys for the columnist had failed to join the Post corporation in filing for summary judgment, so, the court reasoned, Pearson had suffered no injury by its denial.[12]

Emphasizing that conditions required by the U.S. Supreme Court to meet the "actual malice" test were not precisely clear, Judge Leonard Walsh of the district court said:

> This Court recognizes that these decisions weigh heavily against implying malice from the face of publication. However we do not believe that the decisions of the Supreme Court forbid such implication.[13]

Walsh also distinguished *Keogh* from the *Sullivan* and *Garrison* precedents. He said the defamatory material in *Keogh* was directed against a single individual, identified by name; in *Sullivan,* however, the plaintiff was not libeled by name. In *Garrison*, no one specific person was libeled; rather, statements were made against eight men of the parish in their capacity as judges. Secondly, according to Walsh, the allegations against Keogh were thought to be "more serious" than in *Sullivan* or *Garrison*.[14]

The district court was noticeably baffled with *Keogh* and the interpretation of precedents. Walsh, however, stood his ground that the standard for "actual malice" did not, "as a matter of law, dictate the necessary granting of a summary judgment." Nevertheless, he acknowledged that there existed "substantial ground for a difference of opinion as to the law." Thus, the district court certified the case for interlocutory appeal.[15]

The Circuit Court of the District of Columbia reversed.[16] In a decision that extended increased protection against libel judgments to newspapers carrying syndicated columns, the court ruled that there was no

> convincing, realistic basis for the position that newspapers in circumstances similar to the *Post*'s should bear greater responsibilities of verification [of syndicated columns] than the Supreme Court required of the *New York Times,* where information available from published articles in the *Times*' own files "demonstrated the falsity of the allegations."[17]

Circuit Court Judge J. Skelly Wright also considered the time and money that would be consumed if newspapers were required to verify the statements of a syndicated columnist, and the self-censorship that might result:

> We should be hesitant to impose responsibilities upon newspapers which can be met only through costly procedures or through self-censorship designed to avoid risks of publishing controversial material. The costliness of the process would especially deter less established publishers from taking chances and, since columns such as Pearson's are highly popular attractions, competition with publishers who can afford to verify or to litigate would become even more difficult.[18]

Though the instant case dealt specifically with the Washington Post Company's motion for summary judgment, Judge Wright took the opportunity to articulate some relatively liberal press freedom philosophies. Concerning the necessity of granting summary judgments when warranted, he said:

> In the First Amendment area, summary procedures are . . . essential. For the stake here, if harassment succeeds, is free debate. One of the purposes of the *Times* principle, in addition to protecting persons from being cast in damages in libel suits filed by public officials, is to prevent persons from being discouraged in the full and free exercise of their First Amendment rights with respect to the conduct of their government. The threat of being put to the defense of a lawsuit brought by a popular public official may be as chilling to the exercise of First Amendment freedoms as fear of the outcome of the lawsuit itself, especially to advocates of unpopular causes.[19]

The circuit court emphasized that, since *Barr* v. *Matteo*,[20] the Supreme Court had made it clear that public officials, including congressmen, were immune from liability for statements made in the course of their official duties. Thus, the court reasoned, it was only logical that "the other side of the coin is that public officials do not have the same protection from libelous statements as private victims."[21]

Before reaching its decision, the circuit court carefully examined the facts of the case. It discovered that three *Post* executives had read one or both of the Keogh columns before they were published, thus hardly leading one to believe that the newspaper had "recklessly" published the articles.[22]

Keogh, however, also attempted to introduce a series of excerpts from various magazine and newspaper articles by which he hoped to establish that Pearson's "reputation for accuracy and veracity" was such "that mere reliance upon his word is grossly negligent and reckless."[23] Keogh insisted that, since the column was so controversial, the failure of the *Post* to verify its accuracy before publication constituted "actual malice" under the *Times* definition.[24]

The circuit court was quick to stress, however, that Keogh's affidavits concerning Pearson's reputation for accuracy were clearly inadmissible because the allegations were "almost all hearsay."[25] In fact, the court made light of Keogh's attempt to discredit the columnist through derogatory news stories:

> Given its broadest possible significance, Keogh's affidavit shows only that Pearson had made erroneous statements on a very few prior occasions, and that he has a controversial reputation.[26]

The court said that "proof of isolated instances of inaccuracy" during a thirty-five-year writing career in which Pearson had published more than ten thousand columns, could not "be accorded significance."[27]

Judge Wright further supported the role of muckraking investigative reporters in a free press:

> It is highly unlikely, moreover, that the form of journalism engaged in by Pearson and other columnists could survive in the face of a rule requiring verification to negate recklessness. Pearson and his fellow columnists seek and often uncover the sensational, relying upon educated instinct, wide knowledge and confidential tips. Verification would be certain to dry up much of the stream of information that finds its way into their hands. Whether or not this would please a number of us is irrelevant. What matters is that a rule requiring verification in the absence of evidence that the publisher had good reason to suspect falsity would curtail substantially a protected form of speech.[28]

Despite the kind words for columnists such as Pearson, the court granted summary judgment for only the Post corporation; Pearson was left as a defendant. He died with the case still pending.

The second case filed by Keogh against the muckraker in the District of Columbia was also pending when Pearson died.[29] The New York congressman brought the 1964 suit for a "Merry-Go-Round" column headlined "The Franco Lobby." In this column, which appeared in the *Washington Post* on March 4, 1964, Pearson wrote that Spain's Francisco Franco, "the self-acclaimed opponent of communism," whose country traded with Fidel Castro's Cuba, received some $30 million in American military aid each year because of "one of the most amazing lobbies in the history of American government."[30] The muckraker wrote that Franco had friends within the Catholic church, in the business world, within the Pentagon, and in the Senate and the House of Representatives. Concerning Franco's House supporters, Pearson wrote:

> Franco has an ancient clique of Democrats working for him, now headed by Gene Keogh and John Rooney, both of Brooklyn. They consistently plug for more funds for Franco, even demand that his foreign aid be earmarked.[31]

Furthermore, the columnist claimed that Franco had the support of lobbyist Charles Patrick Clark, who had influence with key congressmen who voted funds for Franco.[32]

Keogh, through his attorney Handelman, claimed that the Pearson column was meant to convey that he had been "influenced in his official actions and votes by the receipt of money or other special favor" and had "championed the cause of a foreign nation and government to the detriment of the United States" for pecuniary or other special gain to himself.[33]

Pearson's attorney moved to dismiss the suit, contending that the column was clearly a comment on the administration of public affairs—the political views and conduct of public officials in the administration, in both houses of Congress, and in the Pentagon. Donovan emphasized that the column, on its face, made no charge nor imputation of crime, corruption, gross immorality or gross incompetency against Keogh; thus, under *Sweeney* v. *Patterson,*[34] it was not libelous per se. Donovan also pointed out that the congressman had not suffered any damage, nor had he lost his seat in Congress.[35]

Donovan contended that *New York Times Co.* v. *Sullivan*[36] was controlling—that Pearson's remarks concerning Keogh were protected by the First and Fourteenth Amendments.[37] Quoting from *Sullivan,* Pearson's counsel emphasized that discussion of military aid to Spain was certainly within the "profound national commitment to the principle that debate on public issues should be uninhibited, robust and wide open" and could sometimes include "unpleasantly sharp attacks on government and public officials."[38]

Meanwhile, Handelman insisted that the remarks concerning Keogh were libelous per se in so much as he was accused of being improperly influenced by a paid foreign agent in the casting of votes as a member of Congress.[39] As for the *Times* "actual malice" rule, Handelman claimed it could not be read "to vitiate a cause of action for malicious defamation."[40] Keogh's attorney further elaborated:

> The plaintiff here has alleged malice in no uncertain terms. Plaintiff proposed to show that the defendants, Pearson and Anderson, published this article entitled "The Franco Lobby"

> as a contrived and continuing attack upon Congressman Keogh, motivated among other things, by their malicious reaction to being named defendants in another libel action brought against them by Congressman Keogh, which is now pending in this very court, and has occupied a great deal of the time of plaintiff and defendants and their attorneys.[41]

Though considerable time had been expended on the second case as well, it was only the beginning. Filings continued by attorneys for both parties.

Early in 1965 Donovan made another attempt to get the case dismissed. He emphasized that Keogh had, at that time, three libel suits pending against the column, two in the District of Columbia and one in New York.[42] Donovan also mentioned an instance that occurred in open court on November 10, 1964, in which Handelman allegedly told Judge Edward Tamm that "he would file suit against Pearson every time he wrote about Congressman Keogh in the future."[43] More important, according to Donovan, Keogh could not produce any evidence of "actual malice" as defined by the *Sullivan* and *Garrison* decisions.[44] Pearson, meanwhile, in an affidavit, claimed that he had written the column in good faith and had not made any knowingly false statements with "reckless disregard" for the truth about Keogh's official conduct:

> I do not now and did not on March 4, 1964, bear any animus, ill will, hatred, hostility or actual malice towards Plaintiff. I know Plaintiff only as a public official, not personally. I did not intend to and "had no wanton desire" to harm or cause injury to Plaintiff through knowing falsehood or reckless disregard of the truth.[45]

Despite efforts by both parties, little progress was made in the case. As mentioned earlier, this suit and the 1962 action were both pending when Pearson died in 1969.

Tyler Abell, Pearson's stepson and executor of the estate, replaced Donovan as attorney of record and filed a suggestion of death to inform the court that defendant Pearson had died. Handelman, however, quickly substituted Luvie Pearson, the columnist's widow and collector of the estate, as the defendant. After numerous procedural filings during the next four years, District Court Judge William Jones called both parties together and asked if there were not a way to settle. The Pearson family was anxious to close the estate and agreed that it might be best to pay a settlement, though Abell later said he had hated to do it.[46]

It is possibly only fitting, however, that a man so absorbed in libel actions during a reporting career that spanned four decades was plagued by suits into his grave. Settlement of the *Keogh* case was among the final orders of business before Pearson's estate could be closed.[47] Ironically, although the *Keogh* case meant loss to the Pearson estate, American newspapers reaped real, if intangible, gains. As was emphasized earlier, the circuit court of the District of Columbia ruled in 1966 that newspapers could not be held legally responsible for writings by syndicated columnists about public officials unless the newspaper editors had reason to believe the facts untrue. Though a circuit court ruling does not officially become the position of the U.S. Supreme Court by virtue of the latter's denial of *certiorari*, other lower courts often adopt new principles that are allowed to stand by the high court. The *New York Times*, in fact, commented that the *Keogh* decision could create a "general acceptance of the immunity doctrine."[48] Clifton Lawhorne, journalism educator and author of a book dealing with the evolution of American libel law, agreed, writing that the court of appeals decision "would appear to be of extreme importance to newspapermen."[49]

There is, however, an additional aspect of irony to the *Keogh* cases: Pearson was beaten at his own game. Through the years he had discouraged many plaintiffs by perseverance and procedural patience. Keogh, equally tenacious and determined, also utilized an outstanding lawyer and dozens of procedural motions to keep the cases in the courts for more than a decade. The settlement, however, might never have materialized had Pearson still been alive.

Another libel suit settled after Pearson's death was brought by Alphonse Roy, a candidate for his party's nomination for a U.S. Senate seat. The case grew out of a "Merry-Go-Round" column that was published on September 10, 1960—only three days before the New Hampshire Democratic party's primary election—in the *Concord Monitor*.[50] The column referred to maneuvering in the primary campaign, mentioned the criminal records of several candidates, and characterized Roy, who had served as a U.S. marshal, as a "former small-time bootlegger."[51] Roy was not elected in the primary, and he subsequently sued the Monitor Patriot Company and the North American Newspaper Alliance (NANA), the distributor of the column, for libel.[52]

The defendants offered "truth" as their primary defense at the trial; evidence was presented on the issue of whether Roy had, in fact, been a bootlegger during the Prohibition era. The defendants also said they had "published in good faith, without malice, and with a reasonable belief in the probable truth of the charge, and on a lawful occasion."[53] In the course of instructions to the jury, the trial judge said that Roy was a "public official" by virtue of his candidacy in the primary. Therefore, he continued, under the *New York Times* "actual malice" rule, to find the defendant guilty would require a showing that the article was false and had been published with reckless disregard for the truth. The judge, however, said this condition would have to be met only if the libel concerned "official conduct," as opposed to "private conduct."[54] The judge further elaborated on this distinction; he said that if the charge directly concerned Roy's "fitness for office," it would fall within the concept of official conduct, but if it were merely a "bringing forward of the plaintiff's long forgotten misconduct in which the public had no interest, then it would be a private matter in the private sector."[55]

The trial judge instructed the jury that if it found the libel to be in the "public sector," the *Times* "actual malice" test would have to be met and the verdict would have to be in favor of the defendant. If the jury determined the publication to be in the "private sector," however, there were only two possible defenses: "lawful occasion" and "conditional privilege."[56] The jury returned a verdict that provided for a total of $10,000 in damages from both the newspaper and NANA. On appeal, the New Hampshire Supreme Court affirmed, holding that the trial judge properly sent to the jury the question of whether or not the alleged libel was "relevant" to Roy's fitness for office.[57]

The U.S. Supreme Court, however, reversed and remanded. The majority held that publications concerning candidates for public office "must be accorded at least as much protection under the First and Fourteenth Amendments as those concerning occupants of public office,"[58] that there should be no "syllogistic manipulation of distinctions between 'private sectors' and 'public sectors,' "[59] and that, as a matter of constitutional law, a "charge of criminal conduct, no matter how remote in time or place, can never be irrelevant to an official's or a candidate's fitness for office" for purposes of applying the *Times* "actual malice" rule.[60] Further, Justice Potter Stewart said the jury in the New Hampshire case had been misguided by the trial judge, and the case should be reversed and remanded.[61]

Justice Stewart spoke at some length on the trial judge's instructions, which imposed a "far less stringent" standard of proof than the knowing falsehood or reckless disregard test.[62] Borrowing reasoning from *Garrison*, Justice Stewart quoted with approval the following statement:

> To this end, anything which might touch on an official's fitness for office is relevant. Few personal attributes are more germane to fitness for office than dishonesty, malfeasance, or improper motivation, even though these characteristics may also affect the official's private character.[63]

Justice Stewart then emphasized that the trial judge's instructions "left the jury far more leeway to act as censors than is consistent with the protection of the First and Fourteenth Amendments in the setting of a political campaign."[64]

Justice Hugo Black, concurring in part, dissented from portions of the opinion that permitted the case to be tried again under a different set of jury instructions. He reiterated his belief that it was time for the Court to abandon the *Times* "actual malice" test and to "adopt the rule to the effect that the First Amendment was intended to leave the press free from the harassment of libel judgments."[65]

Pearson's tenacity when involved in libel suits is vividly illustrated through developments in the *Monitor Patriot* case. The columnist was on his deathbed shortly after the New Hampshire Supreme Court ruled for the plaintiff. While hospitalized, only days before his death, the muckraker instructed his stepson, Tyler Abell, that he wanted to appeal the decision to the U.S. Supreme Court. It was Pearson's last wish that the case be appealed, not settled. As was pointed out, the High Court accepted *certiorari,* reversed, and remanded. Rather than go through the expense of extended litigation in New Hampshire, Abell decided to settle the case. Abell emphasized, however, that had his stepfather been alive, the case would have been allowed to run its course.[66] As was the situation with *Keogh*, though Pearson's family had to make a settlement payment to Roy, the case made a contribution to press freedom. One journalism educator, for example, emphasized that *Monitor Patriot* was important because it helped to answer the question of what period of an official's past life is open to press examination.[67]

Monitor Patriot and *Keogh* are examples of how costly it was for Pearson to defend against libel actions. As in scores of previous cases, the columnist was forced to spend thousands of dollars during the proceedings. The outcomes, however, were different in the latter cases; after expensive litigation, a settlement still had to be paid,[68] and in effect, a posthumous black mark was placed on the muckraker's libel success record. It was simply a matter of economics. After the columnist's death, his family was confronted with the problem of closing the estate.[69]

A third post-1964 reported case involving Pearson was brought in 1966 by U.S. Sen. Thomas Dodd of Connecticut.[70] Dodd sought $5 million in damages for libel, conspiracy, and abstraction of his files.

Dodd's suit evolved from the publication in 1966 and 1967 of more than one hundred "Merry-Go-Round" articles on the senator's misconduct as a public official. Pearson and Jack Anderson essentially alleged that the senator had improperly diverted proceeds of fund-raising testimonial dinners to his personal use. The allegations spurred investigations by the Senate Ethics Committee and the Internal Revenue Service.

Anderson got his initial information on the matter from James Boyd, a former Dodd employee, who got in touch with the columnist about providing him with materials from Dodd's files. Boyd spoke in behalf of himself and several other Dodd workers or former employees—Marjorie Boyd, Terry Golden, and office manager Michael O'Hare. While in the senator's employ, the group had become concerned about several of Dodd's "questionable activities" and decided the public should be made aware of them.

Dodd was held in high esteem; he was particularly well regarded by many special-interest groups. The office workers therefore realized that, if they were to make public much of the information locked within the senator's files, it would require a major effort and commitment. The group decided to go to the media because Dodd had such close relations with the FBI that it would likely not conduct a legitimate investigation. Furthermore, the Senate Ethics Committee was more of a "paper tiger" at that time than it is today. Anderson was contacted because the group decided the "Merry-Go-Round" columnists would be the only journalists willing to complete the job.

O'Hare, nearly a decade later, recalled the "traumatic experience" of deciding to provide Anderson with the information. It was not a rash gesture; O'Hare and his colleagues took ample time to rationalize their actions. O'Hare remembered being confronted with a situation in which he would have to "walk away" or take measures to expose. Obviously, he chose the latter.[71]

Anderson met regularly with the former Dodd aides. He made a list of more than fifty "questionable activities." To substantiate them, two of the former Dodd employees entered Dodd's office during the summer of 1965, without authority and without knowledge of the senator. They removed "numerous documents" from his files, made copies of them, replaced the originals, and gave copies to Anderson. According to the circuit court, Anderson was aware "of the manner in which the copies had been obtained."[72] Extensive follow-up checks were made with people who had dealings with Dodd.

The first column on the Dodd disclosures appeared under Anderson's by-line on January 24, 1966; approximately one hundred twenty columns were devoted to the senator during the next eighteen months. The columns culminated with Dodd's censure, by a ninety-two to five vote of the Senate, on June 23, 1967.

After Dodd brought suit, the federal district court for the District of Columbia held that, since he was a "public official" within the *Times* ruling, he could recover for libel only if he proved "actual malice."[73] The court said that, though it was a "hardship to a high-ranking public official" to have to meet the stringent "actual malice" test, it was, in the eyes of the U.S. Supreme Court, "one of the burdens of public office."[74] Thus, Dodd did not have much of a chance to prove that Pearson or Anderson knew the columns were false, since the information was gleaned from the senator's personal files.

A few months later, however, the same district court granted partial summary judgment to Dodd, finding liability on a theory of conversion; at the same time, the court denied partial summary judgment on the theory of invasion of privacy.[75] This decision was criticized for its chilling effect on press freedom.[76]

The circuit court, however, reversed the lower court's grant of summary judgment for conversion and affirmed the denial of summary judgment for invasion of privacy.[77] In regard to the lower court's denial of summary judgment on invasion of privacy charges, Circuit Court Judge Wright said:

> It has always been considered a defense to a claim of invasion of privacy by publication . . . that the published matter complained of is of general public interest. The columns complained of here . . . clearly bore on appellee's qualifications as a United States Senator, and as such amounted to a paradigm example of published speech not subject to suit for invasion of privacy.[78]

Dodd brought his action under a branch of privacy theory that the late legal scholar Dean Prosser labeled "intrusion." The court stressed that, unlike other types of invasion of privacy, intrusion does not involve as one of its essential elements the publication of the information obtained.[79]

The central question for the circuit court logically became whether Pearson and Anderson improperly intruded into the "protected sphere of privacy" of Dodd in obtaining the information on which their columns were based. Wright stated that, though Dodd's complaint charged the columnists with aiding and abetting the removal of documents, the "indisputed facts" established only that the writers received the documents knowing that they had been removed without the senator's approval. The court concluded that it was not willing to "establish the proposition that one who receives information from an intruder, knowing it has been obtained by improper intrusion, is guilty of a tort."[80] Putting this rationale on a philosophical level, Judge Wright said:

> A person approached by an eavesdropper with an offer to share in the information gathered through the eavesdropping would perhaps play the nobler part should he spurn the offer and shut his ears. However, it seems to us that at this point it would place too great a strain on human weakness to hold one liable in damages who merely succumbs to temptation and listens.[81]

Wright made it clear that, in analyzing a claimed breach of privacy, "injuries from intrusion and injuries from publication should be kept clearly separate." Where there is intrusion, the intruder should be held liable, but the subsequent publication by columnists who played no active role in the intrusion could by itself constitute no invasion of privacy.[82]

The circuit court readily defended its reversal of the partial summary judgment for conversion. It was stressed that conversion consisted essentially in taking something that an individual possessed, and converting it into one's own use. The most "distinctive feature" of conversion in the eyes of the court was "its measure of damages, which is the value of the goods converted."[83] Thus, the court concluded that Pearson and Anderson could not be held liable for conversion because Dodd was not deprived of "property use" of his documents; they were returned to his files undamaged before office operations resumed the morning after the intrusion. The court further reasoned that conversion was meant to protect literary or scientific property; the types of records found in Dodd's files, however, did not fall into either category.[84]

Judge Wright stressed that Dodd was really complaining about publication of materials that proved injurious to his reputation or information that he felt was private. The judge simply said that "injuries of this type" could be redressed at law by suit for libel or invasion of privacy, where a defendant's liability could be established "under limitations created by common law and by the Constitution."[85]

Circuit Court Judge Tamm, in an interesting concurring opinion that illustrated the ironic aspect of the decision, said:

> Conduct for which a law enforcement officer would be soundly castigated is, by the phraseology of the majority opinion, found tolerable; conduct which, if engaged in by government agents would lead to the suppression of evidence obtained by these means, is approved when used for the profit of the press.[86]

Tamm then pointed out the anomaly of the situation: "The news media regard themselves as quasi-public institutions yet they demand immunity from the restraints which they vigorously demand be placed on government."[87]

Pearson always considered the *Dodd* court victory one of his greatest triumphs, but the series of columns was strongly criticized in some circles.[88] The *Dodd* case, however, was not the only legal action initiated against the "Merry-Go-Round" on the basis of alleged removal of documents.

One was an action brought by a political-action organization and its treasurer against Pearson for a permanent injunction and damages. Liberty Lobby sought to prohibit dissemination or publication of information, letters, and documents allegedly illegally obtained by removal from the organization's files by a disgruntled employee.[89] The district court denied the request; the court of appeals affirmed, holding that Liberty Lobby was not entitled to a preliminary injunction, absent a clear showing of ownership of the papers, of unlawful taking, or of participation in removal of the papers or copies.[90]

Circuit Court Judge (later U.S. Supreme Court Chief Justice) Warren Burger, noted that Liberty Lobby did not know precisely which papers Pearson and his associate Anderson had in their possession. He then carefully explained, that for a temporary injunction to be granted, sound reasons would have to be given so as to not offend the First Amendment.

> The First Amendment, of course, protects the free expression and exchange of ideas regardless of their merit because this is considered imperative to open and "robust debate" on matters of public interest. Any claim which seeks prior restraint on publication bears a heavy burden. The validity of any such claim depends on a balance of the interests sought to be protected by the limitation against the injury to free utterance.[91]

Burger went on to explain that, while the right of expression and publication is not absolute, the "balance is always weighted in favor of free expression."[92]

Judge Burger, however, did more than extol the virtues of a free press. He chose to address himself to the activities of Liberty Lobby—political lobbying and dissemination of information on highly controversial subjects, and extensive money-raising campaigns to support various programs of "political education," some of which, according to a footnote in the case, "contain overtones of anti-Semitism and racism."[93] Burger stated:

> While the term "lobbyist" has become encrusted with invidious connotations, every person or group engaged, as this one allegedly has been, in trying to persuade Congressional action is exercising the First Amendment right of petition. Like other Constitutional rights, the right to petition is subject to abuse and misuse and a vigilant press can expose abuses to public view.[94]

Burger acknowledged that "upon a proper showing the wide sweep of the First Amendment might conceivably yield to an invasion of privacy and deprivation of rights of property in private manuscripts," but this was not such a case.[95]

In a concurring opinion, Judge Wright said that "the clandestine character which some lobbying tends to assume makes it imperative that the freedom of speech" is not "paralyzed while the right to petition by lobbying is being exercised."[96] Wright emphasized the "solemn obligation" of the press to keep the public informed on lobbying activities, an "area so vital to the democratic process." Moreover, Wright said that Liberty Lobby, a corporation, had no claim to "privacy."[97]

In another noteworthy suit against Pearson, Louisiana congressman T. Ashton Thompson sought $200,000 in a libel action that evolved from a "Merry-Go-Round" column published on July 26, 1962, in more than six hundred newspapers, including the *Washington Post* and the *Lake Charles American Press* in Louisiana. The column read in part:

> If you want a baby sitter for your second wife's children, get elected to Congress. That seems to be the creed of Rep. T. Ashton Thompson, the Dixiecrat from Ville Platte, La.
>
> For more than a year and a half, Thompson has paid Mrs. Judith Billeaud Coreil a salary of $231 a month of the taxpayers' money supposedly to work in his office and look after the problems of his constituents.[98]

Pearson went on to say that "careful inquiry" had disclosed that Coreil did not work in the congressman's office. Rather, she was being paid taxpayers' dollars for taking care of the children of the congressman's second wife. Furthermore, Pearson said that Coreil was the sister-in-law of the Evangeline Parish sheriff, and "it also helps to have the kinfolk of a local leader on the payroll."[99]

Thompson claimed that the statements were totally false, that Coreil was "one of the most devoted and hardest working public servants employed" in his Washington, D.C., office. He asserted that, had Pearson made the "careful inquiry" he claimed, he would have known that the story was false.[100]

The muckraker's attorney, Donovan, moved to dismiss the suit on the ground that the complaint failed to state a claim upon which relief could be granted. He contended that the words complained of were not libelous per se and that there had been no allegation of special damage or economic loss.[101] Donovan contended that the column did not charge Thompson with crime, corruption, gross immorality, or gross incompetency, and thus no special damage had resulted:

> The article imputes to Congressman Thompson no conduct of a nature generally regarded as disreputable or even discreditable among his fellow members of Congress. Nepotism is constantly imputed to Congressmen whose wives and relatives on the government payroll do very little work or no work at all in a Congressman's Washington office.[102]

The attorney also pointed out that the column concerned political matters, and "to say a person is on one side or the other of a public issue is not libelous. This is horn book law."[103] The columnist's lawyer further maintained that Thompson had in fact suffered no damage as a result of the column; he was renominated at the July 28, 1962, Louisiana primary, had no opposition in the November general election, and was reelected to Congress.[104]

The congressman's attorney naturally challenged Donovan's arguments. The plaintiff's counsel said that Pearson's lawyer assumed the position that no person in public office was entitled to relief for libel unless he lost his employment or suffered economic injury. Making vivid his point, attorney Michael J. Horan stated:

> Plaintiff submits that such a position is patently cruel, unjust, and erroneous, otherwise all persons in governmental service, whether it be in the legislative, judicial, or executive branch, would be at the mercy of slanderers without redress, so long as investigation showed the libelous statements to be false and the person libeled was not impeached and removed from office.[105]

Furthermore, Horan said that it was libelous per se to insinuate that Thompson had improperly used public funds.[106]

Donovan's motion to dismiss the complaint was granted, with prejudice, thus leaving the plaintiff an opportunity to file an amended complaint.[107] Thompson's attorney complied, specifying that his client was seeking special damages of an additional $100,000 for Pearson's claim that he was improperly using public funds.[108] Donovan then moved to dismiss on essentially the same grounds as previously cited. Downplaying the column's impact, he called for a "realistic appraisal." He strongly contended that Thompson had suffered no actual damage.

> Nor has his [Thompson's] reputation been damaged in the District of Columbia or in Louisiana. This Court should not close its eyes to the fact that the ordinary reader of the *Washington Post* probably never heard of Congressman

> Thompson before the column was printed in the *Post*, didn't remember his name five minutes afterwards, and didn't care what his creed was or what he believed. Nor should the Court close its eyes to the fact that the ordinary reader of the *Lake Charles American Press* was tolerant and skeptical, especially of political stories printed in the heat of the campaign, paid little or no attention to them, and reelected him. So plaintiff is not damaged even in Louisiana where he is well known.[109]

Donovan then cited *Sweeney* v. *Patterson*[110] and *Coleman* v. *MacLennan*[111] as cases in which the courts had dealt liberally with those defending remarks they had made concerning public officials.[112]

Donovan, of course, had no way of knowing that the U.S. Supreme Court would establish the "actual malice" rule the following year. Though *New York Times Co.* v. *Sullivan*[113] was handed down before the *Thompson* case was settled, it did not play a prominent role. Rather, the congressman died in July of 1965. Donovan moved to dismiss on the ground that the right of action for alleged libel did not survive the death of the plaintiff.[114] Judge John Sirica ordered that the motion be granted.[115]

Not surprisingly, Coreil filed a libel action, based on the same "Merry-Go-Round" column, in the Western District of Louisiana.[116] She was the only private citizen to file suit against the muckraker during the post-1964 period. She claimed to have been damaged by false and libelous statements written by Pearson and published in two general circulation newspapers in Louisiana. Service of the summons and complaint was attempted in Washington, D.C., on September 13, 1963, by a U.S. marshall, but the columnist was out of the country. On September 22, 1964, however, personal service was made upon him in the nation's capital. Louisiana had only recently enacted a "long-arm" service of process law by which the Louisiana courts were authorized to exercise personal jurisdiction over nonresidents in certain specified instances.[117]

Pearson, however, contended that, since he was not a resident of Louisiana, there was no federal or state statute that provided for service upon him, in a Louisiana libel suit, outside the territorial limits of that state. The district court quickly emphasized, however, that it had jurisdiction on the ground of diversity of citizenship. The inquiry of the court, therefore, consisted of determining whether or not there had been a valid service of process upon Pearson.[118]

The Louisiana statute in question provided for the exercise of personal jurisdiction over a nonresident of Louisiana as to a cause of action arising by virtue of a defendant who transacted any business in Louisiana, contracted to supply service in the state, caused injury or damage by an offense committed through an act in the state, or caused injury or damage in Louisiana by an offense committed outside of the state if the individual regularly did or solicited business in the state.[119]

The district court measured the statute against a dual test: (1) there had to have been some minimum contact with the state that resulted from an affirmative act of the defendant, and (2) it must have been fair and reasonable to require that the defendant journey to the state to defend the action.[120] The court upheld the statute as constitutional and had little difficulty holding that Pearson fell under the umbrella of the statute. The court reasoned that the columnist had contracted to supply "service or things" in Louisiana and had caused injury or damage to Coreil by causing to be published allegedly libelous remarks about her in the state of Louisiana.[121] Furthermore, the court found the "long arm" statute to apply retroactively since there was an "absence of clearly expressed legislative intent to the contrary." Thus, the motion to quash was denied.[122]

Like so many of the Pearson libel cases, however, the *Coreil* action never went to a jury. It was scheduled for trial on September 13, 1965, but on August 2 the date was set aside by consent of parties. The case was not actively pursued, and on November 24, 1969, about three months after Pearson's death, District Court Judge Richard Putnam instructed that the case be dismissed for lack of prosecution.[123]

Though Pearson died in 1969, the flow of libel actions brought against "Merry-Go-Round" writers did not stop. Two actions filed by public officials have been brought against writers of the column in the 1970s.

The first libel suit against Anderson to evolve from a column he wrote after assuming control of the "Merry-Go-Round" was brought by Rankin Fite, speaker of Alabama's House of Representatives. Fite sought $2 million in damages for an April 13, 1970, column.[124] The column, which appeared in the *Tuscaloosa* (Alabama) *News*, among other newspapers, was headlined "IRS Probes Wallace Kin." It pointed out that a special task force of Internal Revenue Service agents had "moved into Alabama to investigate charges of corruption in the administrations of former Governor George Wallace and his late wife, Lurleen."[125] Anderson wrote that the probe focused "on the backdoor activities of Gerald Wallace, the former governor's brother, law partner and political confidant." Furthermore, according to Anderson:

> The government is investigating charges that Gerald Wallace and Rankin Fite, the mighty Speaker of Alabama's House of Representatives, collected kickbacks on state and federal highway contracts. Part of the money is alleged to have been turned over to George Wallace to fuel his 1968 presidential campaign, in which he promised to restore "law and order" to the nation.
>
> Fite allegedly turned the kickback over to Gerald Wallace. Both men vigorously denied any wrongdoing.[126]

The remainder of the column primarily concerned Gerald Wallace's business affairs.

Fite complained that, as a result of the column, he had been "vexed, harassed and annoyed" and was "damaged in his occupation as a lawyer and a public servant."[127] Warren Woods, Anderson's Washington, D.C., attorney, moved to dismiss the action on grounds that the columnist was a resident of Maryland and maintained permanent offices in Washington, D.C. Thus, Woods contended, the muckraker was "not subject to the service of process within the Southern Division of the Northern District of Alabama," and that Anderson had "not been properly serviced with process" in the action.

Woods also requested that the action be transferred, by change of venue, to the District of Columbia federal court.[128] In support of the motion, he asserted that, though jurisdictions of various court systems had undergone great expansion, "the criteria for determining whether a case is to be tried in one jurisdiction or another far distant, are still the 'traditional notions of fair place and substantial justice.' "[129] Woods asked the Alabama court to take "judicial notice" that Washington, D.C., was the "focal point for the gathering of information" Anderson utilized in the column.

> Hence, in terms of the burden of mounting a defense to the instant complaint, the geographical jurisdiction of this court does not provide a fair and convenient place of trial under accepted judicial standards, which warrant the granting of defendant's motion.[130]

As was the case so often during Anderson's late predecessor's numerous libel action experiences, the suit never reached trial. Less than one year after Fite filed it, Chief Judge Seybourn Lynne ordered that the action be dismissed, without prejudice.[131]

Another libel suit against Anderson, together with two of his associates, Les Whitten and Joseph Spear, was brought by Turner B. Shelton, former ambassador to Nicaragua. The action sought $30 million in damages on the basis of three "Merry-Go-Round" columns. Shelton brought the suit on April 18, 1977, about a month after he retired from the U.S. Foreign Service; it was amended on February 10, 1978.[132]

The four-count amended complaint cited an April 1, 1977, "Merry-Go-Round" column that labeled Shelton "probably the worst ambassador of the Nixon era." The column read in part:

> The State Department brought him [Shelton] back from Nicaragua after a disgraceful performance there. But he called on powerful congressional friends who helped him get reappointed as ambassador to the Bahamas. Both the Senate and the Bahamas turned him down. He continued to seek appointments to Bermuda, then to Casablanca. In the end, he had to settle for a position as "Diplomat-in-Residence" at the Navy War College in Newport, R.I. Now the Carter Administration has quietly kicked him out.[133]

Shelton's complaint also quoted from a November 10, 1976, column, which mentioned "the tolerance [Secretary of State Henry] Kissinger has shown for the Foreign Service's foul balls," and said that "the performance of Turner Shelton . . . was so poor that he was rebuked and recalled by the State Department." The columnists also credited Kissinger with the attempts to find other ambassadorial posts for Shelton.[134]

Shelton claimed the column's allegations were false and that the columnists had published the statements knowing them "to be false or having reason to believe" them to be false. The complaint said that Anderson and his associates were aware, or had access to information, that Shelton had received the Distinguished Service Award and the Award of Valor, the latter for superior performance during the earthquake in Nicaragua. Furthermore, Shelton claimed, the columnists knew that President Ford's special coordinator had praised the former ambassador's service to Nicaragua in a memorandum to the president:

> In particular, Ambassador Shelton is deserving of special commendation. Throughout the emergency he performed with exceptional skill and courage a task that would test great generals. Nicaragua and we are fortunate that he was there when the challenge came.[135]

Anderson, after the suit was filed, told the Associated Press that "we have never been sued successfully and this is no exception. We rather welcome the opportunity to lay the record out in court."[136]

After several procedural filings, Shelton's attorneys moved to compel Spear and Anderson to reveal their confidential sources who allegedly supplied the information that served as the basis for the columns in question. U.S. District Court Judge Thomas Flannery, however, denied the motion. Flannery cited *Carey* v. *Hume*, an earlier "Merry-Go-Round" case, and said that the plaintiffs would have to meet two criteria before a columnist would be forced to reveal confidential sources: the information sought would have to "go to the heart" of the claim, and the plaintiff would have to "explore alternative sources" of information. Flannery said that Shelton had "failed to investigate alternate sources of the information, the existence of which sources defendants have freely admitted." Though Anderson gave Shelton the names of twenty nonconfidential individuals who supplied information for the columns, the ambassador or his attorneys had not "made any effort to contact any sources other than the filing of this motion to compel."[137]

On August 1, 1978, before the case could go to trial, it was settled and dismissed with prejudice. Though there was no monetary settlement, Anderson agreed to publish a clarifying column—not a formal retraction—concerning Shelton. In a column released to newspapers on August 12, 1978, Anderson said that certain facts should be added to the series of articles on Shelton. He wrote: "Our criticism of Ambassador Shelton was based upon his close relationship with President [Anastasio] Somoza, but in light of additional facts, we are now convinced he was merely carrying out the Nixon administration policy in Nicaragua." Anderson said that, though he had earlier reported that Shelton was more concerned with personal problems than the plight of Nicaraguans during the earthquake, "we are now persuaded that the Ambassador and his wife were deeply concerned about the devastation. The ambassador worked tirelessly for six days and nights with little more than a few hours sleep and refused to let a broken arm slow him down." In conclusion, Anderson said that, during Shelton's thirty years with the government, he had received several notable awards and had played a "leading role in negotiating the first U.S.-Russian cultural exchange program."[138]

Edward Ashworth, a Washington, D.C., attorney who worked with Anderson's primary attorney of record, Charles Morgan, Jr., said he felt the case had a particular significance to American libel law as a result of the interpretation of the *Carey* v. *Hume* precedent by Judge Flannery. Thus, some twenty confidential sources were protected.[139]

Cases Involving Public Figures

Lobbyist Charles Patrick Clark, who included among his clients the government of Spain and a group of natural gas companies, sought $1 million in damages from Pearson, the Washington Post Company, and the Bell Syndicate, Inc., for allegedly libelous statements in a "Merry-Go-Round" column published in the *Washington Post* on December 1, 1961.[140] Essentially, the article said that Clark and Representative Keogh became "friendly" and at about the same time the congressman reversed his previous opposition to the "natural gas lobby." Pearson also stated that Keogh became a champion of Spain's Franco and "littered" the *Congressional Record* with statements favorable to Spain. Pearson further claimed that Keogh then began to receive checks from Clark, which were listed as payments for legal advice in connection with a specific tax matter. The column also stated that Keogh and Clark were "quizzed" by the FBI.[141]

Clark claimed that the column, in effect, charged him with having committed violations of the criminal law in endeavoring to influence the votes of a member of Congress by paying him money. On the other hand, Pearson's lawyer countered that no such charge could be implied from the article and that the publication merely suggested—at most—an impropriety on the part of the congressman, and an activity of the plaintiff that placed the congressman in an "indiscreet position."[142]

Pearson's counsel listed four defenses: truth, consent by plaintiff, that the plaintiff had failed to plead special damages, and that publication of matters of public interest should be protected through an extension of the *Times* "actual malice" rule as it applied to public officials.[143] It was the final assertion to which District Court Judge Alexander Holtzoff devoted considerable attention. It is important to realize that this suit was decided just a little more than a year after the landmark *Sullivan* case; lower courts were involved in solving many of the unanswered questions posed in the historic decision.[144] Holtzoff stated that—

> [Defense arguments] took a wide range and not only comprised a thorough discussion of the issues of fact and law actually involved in the litigation, but included also a plea for drastic changes in the law of libel, in a manner that would radically devitalize and impair the protection that it affords against defamatory publications.[145]

Holtzoff then decided to make some additional observations "on the basic status of the law of libel in Anglo-American jurisprudence."[146] The opinion emphasized the importance of a right to protect one's reputation. The court said that though it was "intangible and more imponderable" than other rights, it was "equally fundamental and vital."[147] Holtzoff emphasized that the "current trend" in the law was increased protection of individual civil rights, but stated:

> No one is accorded the privilege of maintaining a reputation to which he is not entitled. No one is granted a legal right to sail under false colors without molestation. Consequently the law does not afford any protection against the disclosure of truth, no matter how unpalatable or disagreeable it may be; no matter how unnecessary its revelation; and no matter what the motive or purpose of the disclosure may be. Truth of a defamatory statement is always a complete defense to any action for libel or slander.[148]

The judge then rejected the attempt by Donovan, Pearson's attorney, to prove truth in the column by discussing separately each factual item contained in the article and demonstrating by reference to depositions, affidavits, and exhibits that each individual statement was true and accurate. Rather, Holtzoff said proof of truth "must be as broad as the alleged defamatory statement." He said it was not sufficient to "take every sentence separately and demonstrate its individual accuracy, detached and wrenched out of its context."[149]

The majority also rejected the second defense, consent by plaintiff; Holtzoff said that if the article should be construed by a jury as charging criminality, there was "obviously no consent to its publication."[150] Nor was the judge impressed with Donovan's argument to extend the *Times* doctrine to protect writings that involved public figures and touched on matters of public interest. Holtzoff said that to extend the protection would "abrogate and destroy a large portion of the protection now accorded to persons who have been unjustly defamed."[151] The court then examined the common law precedents of libel law, as well as what it chose to label "two specific and narrow exceptions" that had only recently been introduced: *Barr* v. *Matteo*[152] and *New York Times Co.* v. *Sullivan*.[153] The judge reasoned that the *Matteo* decision merely protected public utterances made by "policy-making officials" of the federal government in connection with their duties and that *Sullivan* simply extended press protection when discussing "high-ranking government officials."[154] The district court said the fact that the *Times* rule was "limited to officials in the high echelons is clearly demonstrated."[155] Though subsequent Supreme Court rulings would prove the district court's interpretation erroneous and narrow,[156] that fact did not help Pearson in this particular case.

Nevertheless, the *Clark* case was one of the early post-*Sullivan* examples of attorneys asking for an extension of the "actual malice" rule to discussion of public figures involved in events of public interest. Lobbyist Clark and his interests in public affairs such as America's stance toward Spain and the natural gas industry certainly belonged in this category. In 1965, however, the Federal District Court for the District of Columbia did not agree. The court denied summary judgment and concluded that a trial was needed to determine whether Pearson's columns were libelous.[157] The majority said that, where newspaper articles concerning Clark were susceptible of two meanings, it was for a jury to determine how the material would be interpreted by the average reader.[158]

Though the court remanded the case, the trial never took place. Clark died. On December 4, 1967, Pearson's lawyer filed a suggestion of death. On April 1, 1968, the district court granted a motion by the defendant to dismiss. That the case never went to trial was gratifying to F. Joseph Donohue, who had been retained by Pearson to represent him at the proceedings. Donohue, who considered himself a friend of both Clark and Keogh in addition to Pearson, later said it would have put him in a precarious position.[159]

Another "Merry-Go-Round" case of the post-1964 era, one of the last in which Pearson was personally involved, was filed in February of 1966 by Lt. Col. Philip J. Corso against the senior muckraker and Anderson.[160] Corso, a decorated twenty-year Army veteran, retired from the military in 1963; he then served Sen. J. Strom Thurmond of South Carolina and Congressman Michael A. Feighan of Ohio as a professional staff member.[161]

The suit evolved from a March 29, 1965, column by-lined exclusively by Anderson. The column reported that Feighan had been "fighting to unload a private investigator from his own payroll and plant him on the Government payroll."[162] Anderson claimed that Feighan wanted the Judiciary Committee to approve Corso as chief counsel of a subcommittee he chaired. However, according to Anderson,

> The FBI has submitted an uncertain report on Corso, a mysterious figure who has been masterminding right-wing

> intrigue on Capitol Hill. The colonel, as he likes to be addressed, worked out of the office of Sen. Strom Thurmond (R.-S.C.), the white supremacy champion, before latching on to Feighan.[163]

The columnist explained that Attorney General Nicholas Katzenbach furnished the House committee with the FBI report. Though the report, according to Anderson, accused Corso of nothing illegal, "it was so disconcerting that Chairman Emanuel Celler (D.-N.Y.) refused to approve the appointment."[164]

Corso charged that the column was false, scandalous, and libelous per se. The career army man said the columnists were "motivated by actual malice, with reckless disregard as to the truth or falsity" of the information.[165] Corso alleged that it was understood by persons reading the column that, among other things, he was "guilty of un-American prejudices against persons of negro and non-Caucasian races," that he was a "political 'right wing extremist' who held subversive and un-American" views, to say nothing of "other odious personal traits."[166]

Donovan, who represented Pearson and Anderson, cited a number of defenses: that the complaint failed to state a claim upon which relief could be granted; that, absent innuendos, the column was true; that the column constituted fair and bona fide comment upon governmental operations and upon the official conduct of public officials; that the information was gathered from trustworthy and reliable sources; and that, most important, under the *Times* "actual malice" rule, the statements were privileged by reason of the First and Fourteenth Amendments.[167]

Like the majority of "Merry-Go-Round" cases, however, the suit was never tried. Instead, just a little more than one year after the complaint was filed, the action was dismissed without prejudice for failure to prosecute.[168]

Carey v. *Hume* was the most widely publicized "Merry-Go-Round" libel case in the post-Pearson years.[169] The action against Brit Hume, then a "Merry-Go-Round" reporter, Anderson, and the Washington Post Company evolved from a "Merry-Go-Round" column published in the *Post* on December 14, 1970. It read, in part:

> Records Stolen?—With the government digging deeper into the financial affairs of the United Mine Workers, the union's President Tony Boyle and General Counsel Ed Carey spent hours recently going through the records. Later, they were seen removing boxfuls of documents from Boyle's office. Not long afterward, Carey made an official complaint to Washington police that burglars had struck at union headquarters. Among the goods reported stolen: a boxful of "miscellaneous items." The Justice Department is investigating.[170]

Hume had written the column, which was published before Carey could rebut the charges. Hume said that he had obtained the information from UMW employees and had established, by inquiry with the police department, that the burglary complaint mentioned in the column had indeed been filed. The reporter said he attempted to call Carey the day before the story was to go to press but, being unable to reach him, went ahead with publication.[171]

After reading the column, Carey called the "Merry-Go-Round" office. The call resulted in the following item, published on December 15:

> Carey's Denial—Our report on the circumstances surrounding the reported burglary of a box of "miscellaneous items" from United Mine Workers headquarters has drawn a belated but angry denial from the union's general counsel Ed Carey. . . . "A contemptible, despicable lie," said Carey. Our report was based upon information supplied by eyewitnesses, and we will not retract.[172]

Carey then filed suit, alleging that the item had been written with "a malicious purpose to damage" his reputation, and with the effect of causing such injury.[173] Authorship was admitted, but liability denied. Since the follow-up column indicated that information concerning removal of the items was based on eyewitness observation, Hume was asked to reveal the identity of his sources. He refused.[174]

The court of appeals, however, affirmed the lower court ruling that had directed the defendants to reveal the names of eyewitnesses to the alleged removal of records in order to escape liability for publishing the statement with "actual malice" or with reckless disregard for the truth.[175]

Carey's counsel had filed a formal motion for Hume to reveal his sources in an effort to possibly discredit them as being unreliable—a necessary step to win the libel suit, since "actual malice" would have to be proved. Attorneys for the "Merry-Go-Round" filed an opposition to the motion pending disposition of *Branzburg* v. *Hayes,* which was then before the U.S. Supreme Court.[176] *Branzburg* concerned the First Amendment privilege of a reporter to refuse to testify before a grand jury investigating criminal activity.

In a footnote, however, the *Hume* court said that *Branzburg* was not controlling because the instant case was a civil libel suit, rather than a grand jury inquiry into a crime; further, the dispute over disclosure was between the press and a private litigant rather than between the press and government.[177] (Later, the Court held in *Branzburg* that a reporter has no First Amendment privilege before such a grand jury.)

In an effort to find a precedent for *Hume,* then, the court cited *Garland* v. *Torre*.[178] The opinion in *Garland*, written by Circuit Court Judge (now Justice) Potter Stewart, involved a suit filed by Judy Garland against the Columbia Broadcasting System, Inc., alleging that the latter had made false and defamatory statements about her and had authorized or induced their publication in newspapers. Some paragraphs written by Marie Torre and printed in the *New York Herald Tribune* contained several statements about Garland that the author attributed to a CBS "network executive." Garland attempted to learn the identity of the executive, but Torre refused. The district court then sentenced the columnist to ten days in jail for criminal contempt. The second circuit court upheld the ruling. The *Hume* court quoted Stewart that, in cases of this nature, a constitutional balance should be struck, that the "concept that it is the duty of a witness to testify in a court of law has roots fully as deep in our history as does the guarantee of a free press."[179]

Reasoning that *Branzburg* would not affect civil litigation and so would not alter the approach taken in *Garland*, the court said that the conditions of *Hume* made it essential for the reporter to release his sources if Carey were to have an opportunity to meet the heavy burden of proving "actual malice":

> Even if he [Carey] did prove that the statements were false, *Sullivan* also requires a showing of malice or reckless disregard of the truth. That further step might be achieved by proof that appellant in fact had no reliable sources, that he misrepresented the reports of his sources, or that reliance upon those particular sources was reckless.[180]

In essence, the court found that the identity of Hume's sources was critical to Carey's claim.[181]

The court further differentiated the critical nature of Carey's request from the request of former St. Louis mayor Alfonso Cervantes in his suit against *Life* magazine, where his main intention was apparently to discover confidential sources upon whom *Life* had relied for part of its story, even though he had little or no hope of establishing "actual malice."[182]

The *Hume* court said that facts disclosed by the record were inadequate to support a "conclusion that appellee is so unlikely to meet the admittedly heavy *Sullivan* burden that no purpose would be served by disclosure of the identity of the sources."[183] Circuit Court Judge Carl McGowan said:

> The courts must always be alert to the possibilities of limiting impingements upon press freedom to the minimum; and one way of doing so is to make compelled disclosure by a journalist a last resort after pursuit of other opportunities has failed. But neither must litigants be made to carry

> wide-ranging and onerous discovery burdens where the path is as ill-lighted as that emerging from appellant's deposition.[184]

In a concurring opinion, Circuit Court Judge George MacKinnon, philosophizing on the enormous power a relatively small number of media owners in America possess, cautioned against total media immunity from revealing sources. He said this would be "contrary to the public interest and not conducive to a responsible press. The news media must be free but it should also be responsible."[185]

The "Merry-Go-Round," however, was cleared of the libel charges on November 14, 1975. The trial lasted five days; the jury deliberated approximately two and one-half hours. According to the *Washington Post,* Carey and his attorney, Gordon Forester, had argued that the "Merry-Go-Round" column "had libeled the then-UMW general counsel by accusing him falsely of the crime of obstruction of justice." Hume had earlier contended that he would not divulge the name of his source; he was not, however, faced with this ultimate decision. The source, a former UMW employee who was related by marriage to a UMW employee at the time of the incident, voluntarily stepped forward to testify at the jury trial.[186] That the source voluntarily testified likely saved Hume from going to jail for contempt. The young reporter, though somewhat frightened at the possibility, was prepared to do so rather than release the name.[187]

Anderson and Hume contended throughout the trial that they had published the information after "checking it as far as they could under the circumstances." They said they based their final decision to print it "on the proven reliability of the informant." Hume, after the verdict, described the case as a "five-year ordeal for me." He said he felt an "enormous sense of vindication and relief."[188] Anderson chose to classify the *Carey* case as a "public relations" suit. He explained that the "Merry-Go-Round" had long been a "thorn in the side" of the UMW and "they wanted us to leave them alone."[189]

As of 1979, Anderson was still involved in a case filed against him in 1970. It promised to be one of the longest-running court battles in "Merry-Go-Round" legal history. The muckraker, through Tacoma, Washington, attorney Patrick Comfort, was defending a libel action brought by Robert O'Brien that sought $500,000 in damages in the Western District of Washington.[190] The suit grew out of a "Merry-Go-Round" column published on October 31, 1968, under a double by-line of Pearson and Anderson, in the *Tacoma News Tribune*. It read in part:

> Robert O'Brien, the $20,000 a year assistant to Rep. Floyd Hicks, D-Wash., has been hit with two unpublicized law suits alleging that he misrepresented himself as an attorney and collected improper legal fees.
>
> One of the plaintiffs, David Hunt, has also charged that O'Brien threatened him with a tax investigation. O'Brien allegedly warned that he would use his position in the Congressman's office to get the Internal Revenue Service to investigate Hunt.[191]

O'Brien charged that he "warned" the newspaper that the article was not true and requested an investigation be made to determine its truth. His request, however, was ignored.[192] O'Brien further alleged that the publication was false, malicious, and defamatory. He said that the portion of the article that accused him of improper practices and misconduct constituted "actual malice as defined by law."[193]

Comfort moved for dismissal, claiming that at the time of the publication O'Brien was either a "public official" or "public figure" and that the column concerned matters of "substantial public or general interest" and was therefore privileged.[194] Comfort later filed an amended answer explaining that he had been advised that Anderson had not, in fact, authored the article in question.[195] There were subsequent filings by attorneys for both parties.

On May 12, 1972, however, Judge Morrell Sharp granted Anderson's motion for summary judgment of dismissal. Sharp said that the publication was not "done with malice";

that it was not published with "knowing falsity or reckless disregard of whether . . . [it] was false or not."[196] Sharp then explained that the plaintiffs had

> failed to produce any evidence from which a jury could find with convincing clarity that said publications had been made with malice on the part of defendant Jack Anderson, within the test set forth in *Rosenbloom* v. *Metromedia, Inc.*[197]

O'Brien appealed the decision. On February 20, 1975, the Ninth Circuit court reversed in an unpublished memorandum opinion.[198] The circuit court reviewed the *O'Brien* case history, emphasizing that the plaintiff had been cleared in the courts of the civil charges alluded to in the "Merry-Go-Round" column.[199] Furthermore, O'Brien had gone to the Tacoma newspaper office, pointed out the alleged inaccuracies of the story, and flatly denied the statements regarding the threat of a tax investigation. Also, neither Pearson nor Anderson had contacted O'Brien to determine the accuracy of the statements.[200]

The circuit court emphasized that the plaintiff had not received an "adequate response to discovery questions," and it was, therefore, an "error to grant summary judgment."[201] The court also pointed out that, though *Rosenbloom* was expressly relied upon by the district court, there had been no finding that O'Brien was a public official. The court then quoted from *Gertz* v. *Robert Welch, Inc.*, stating that there was no "clear evidence of general fame or notoriety in the community, and pervasive involvement in the affairs of society" so that O'Brien could be deemed a public personality.[202] Furthermore, the court said, in *Gertz* the U.S. Supreme Court had withdrawn from the "general or public interest" test of *Rosenbloom*. Based upon this, the circuit court reversed and remanded the case back to trial in order that it be considered "in the light of the new standards" established in *Gertz*.[203]

The remanded case was scheduled for trial in the Western District of Washington on August 30, 1976, but, during pretrial conferences, it was decided that the proceedings should be delayed. Attorney Comfort, at the time of this writing, was not sure when the case might be tried.[204]

Pearson and Anderson Remain Active in the Courts

Though libel cases against writers of the "Merry-Go-Round" column have decreased somewhat since the law of libel was nationalized in 1964, the columnists have found themselves in the courts every year since then. During the post-1964 years, writers of the controversial, muckraking column have been defendants in at least fourteen libel suits[205] and at least two nonlibel cases.[206]

This extensive involvement in litigation illustrates that, though controversial, the writers have been earnestly interested in protecting their First Amendment rights. As was the case before 1964, the columnists have spent considerable money defending themselves—and they have been extremely successful. The courts have not directed damage payments in any actions initiated against "Merry-Go-Round" columnists since 1964, though the Pearson family made out-of-court payments to two plaintiffs after the columnist died to expedite settlement of his estate.[207] Thus, through effective use of available defenses—particularly the "actual malice" rule articulated by the U.S. Supreme Court in *New York Times Co.* v. *Sullivan*—attorneys for "Merry-Go-Round" writers have continued to successfully defend the columnists against libel actions.

Suits against the column, however, have declined noticeably since Pearson's death. Anderson has been sued only four times.[208] Still, he has shown the same tenacious craving of his late predecessor to defend his constitutional rights as a journalist. This stance indicates that the "Merry-Go-Round" column will continue to operate under the aggressive, unwavering principles established by Pearson—despite the threat of libel actions.

7

Fighting Back: Men of the "Merry-Go-Round" as Plaintiffs

The late Drew Pearson's attorneys constantly warned him of the futility of filing libel actions; they insisted that since the muckraker was a defendant in so many, he should save his time, money, and energy. Jack Anderson's primary attorney, Warren Woods, has also advised his client to avoid litigation as a plaintiff. The lawyers' appeals, however, have been largely ignored.

Though Pearson undoubtedly realized the odds against winning, he insisted on filing at least fifteen libel actions during his reporting career. Anderson, who inherited the "Merry-Go-Round" column upon Pearson's death in 1969, has not brought any libel actions, but he has filed two suits with First Amendment overtones.

One of the first libel actions in which Pearson was involved as a plaintiff was brought on June 27, 1940, against the Journal of Commerce Publishing Company of Chicago.[1] The muckraker and his partner, Robert S. Allen, sought $300,000 in damages for an allegedly libelous article published on July

13, 1939, in the *Chicago Journal of Commerce.* The article said in part that "the Corcoranites in Washington also have a very efficient 'Joseph Goebbels' department in the 'Washington Merry-Go-Round' of Pearson and Allen."[2] The complaint emphasized that Goebbels, a German citizen and supporter of Nazism,

> was generally believed to have created and published false reports in order to further the cause of Hitler, and to the majority of the citizens of this country. . . . Goebbels was a despicable character who devised, imagined, wrote, published and disseminated false, scandalous and defamatory libels of and concerning persons opposed to Hitler and also composed and wrote false statements of the accomplishments of the Hitler form of government in order to deceive persons into joining said movement by the means of such false propaganda.[3]

The complaint concluded that the article had been printed with intent to "destroy the good name of the plaintiffs and to cause it to appear" that they "were actively participating in the dissemination of false information and thereby bring them into public contempt, ridicule, and disgrace."[4]

Attorneys for the *Journal of Commerce* answered that the article was not libelous, that it was not stated that the columnists had participated in the dissemination of false information, nor would readers be led to believe this was the case.[5] Attorneys for the defendant cited fair comment on matters of public interest and fair criticism of Pearson and Allen as commentators on public affairs.[6] Furthermore, the defendants claimed that the action was "wholly and altogether frivolous in its nature."[7] The lawyers mentioned that Pearson and Allen had demanded an apology—and received one. Cited was an August 19, 1939, article, which said in part:

> From time to time this column has been handing Messrs. Pearson and Allen, of the "Washington Merry-Go-Round," good natured jibes on the well-understood fact that they are the mouthpiece for the little group of so-called palace politicians in Washington headed by the famous Tommy Corcoran. On one occasion we dubbed them the "Joseph

> Goebbels" of the administration. We did this because after reading their daily output for a long time it was clear beyond peradventure that they were reflecting the point of view of the administration insiders.
>
> Watching this column for a long time one could see that whenever an anti-administration politician began to gain favor with the public the "Merry-Go-Round" boys were quick to print in their column some sort of left-handed compliment.[8]

The *Journal* also said that it had not been the intention of the article in question to aggrieve Pearson and Allen. It was noted that "we hasten to correct the impression in the minds of any of our readers, if any exists, which we doubt very much, that we had any intention of libeling Pearson and Allen. If any such has happened we sincerely apologize."[9]

The article, however, did not end there. It went on to emphasize that it was "common knowledge" in Washington that Pearson and Allen were close to the administration. This was qualified with: "It was going a little too far to call them the 'smear boys' and again we say we are sorry for that."[10] The article concluded with: "Finally it must strike many who do read their column as strange that journalists who have been so adept at imputing bad motives to New Deal opponents, via the left-handed route of faint praise, should be so quick-triggered with libel suit threats."[11]

A trial notice was issued on July 17, 1941, but the case was not aggressively pursued by either party. On January 16, 1948—more than seven years after the complaint was filed—the case was dismissed on the motion of Samuel T. Lawton, attorney for the defendant.[12]

Though Pearson and Allen did not collect damages in the case against the Journal of Commerce Publishing Company, this did not discourage Pearson from filing future suits against others. In a libel action that evolved from some of the more colorful terminology ever aimed at the muckraker, Pearson sought damages from R. J. Funkhouser, editor-in-chief of the weekly West Virginia *Jefferson Republican*, and the Blakeley Corporation, the publisher.[13]

The suit, based on an article by the newspaper's Charleston correspondent, concerned the appearance by Pearson and others before the Charleston Open Forum in April of 1946. Pearson's complaint focused on one paragraph:

> Many of the members of the Open Forum were indignant in their expressions about the communistic and old-word ism [*sic*] type of cheap declaimers that had been foisted upon them in the guise of lecturers, educators and commentators; and attached considerable blame to the members of the forum who were responsible for the booking of these undesirables. This writer has heard them, and known them to be *salmon-bellied propagandists and pink "commy" commentators, and that goes for all of them.*[14]

Pearson claimed that the words implied he was a Communist.

Funkhouser, who was also a state Republican political figure, countered that the article did not convey this impression. Funkhouser's attorneys, in fact, claimed the article

> read as a whole was intended to convey to the readers . . . the fact that [Pearson] is a public character, that his reputation for truth and veracity among people who know him was and is bad, that he is a "smearer" of persons' reputations, that he holds public characters up to ridicule and scorn, knowing that his statements are either false or half truths, and therefore intended to convey false impressions and conclusions, and that he is of radical tendencies.[15]

After numerous filings, the case was scheduled for trial in the Circuit Court of Jefferson County.[16] The trial opened on February 3, 1948, in the Jefferson County courtroom in Charles Town, the same courtroom where John Brown was tried after his raid on the Harper's Ferry arsenal. Funkhouser told the jury that he was not an officer in the corporation, though he owned considerable stock, and that he had not read the article before it was published.[17]

Pearson met with early success as Circuit Court Judge Decatur H. Rodgers ruled that to call a man "a commie" was libel on its face. The Associated Press pointed out that the ruling "was the latest in a series of court opinions which have held that calling a man a Communist is libelous per se." Therefore, under existing common law, lawyers representing both sides were advised that further testimony would have to be restricted to mitigation of damages.[18]

The case, however, never went to the jury. On February 6, the judge announced a settlement that involved a letter from the editor to Pearson. According to the Associated Press, the letter, which was read in open court, said in part: "I have no intention to believe you are a Communist, but feel assured you are neither a Communist or sympathizer with so-called principles of Communists, or ever have been."[19]

Pearson had attended the entire trial, as had his wife, Luvie, who reportedly knitted throughout the proceedings.[20] The muckraker expressed satisfaction the day the case was settled. He said that "all I was interested in was the vindication of my name, and I have received that vindication."[21] Less than a month after he accepted Funkhouser's apology, however, the columnist reevaluated the settlement. Pearson wrote: "I still think we made a mistake in compromising the Funkhouser matter as we did. My first judgment was against it and I wish now that I had not been persuaded to change my mind."[22]

During this post–World War II period, Pearson also brought an action against Time, Inc.[23] The muckraker initiated the suit on January 31, 1947; the filing date indicates that he wasted no time: the *Time* magazine article upon which the complaint was based appeared in the January 27 issue. *Time*'s article, under the headline, "As Drew Pearson Revealed . . .", concerned a libel suit filed by Winston Churchill against author Louis Adamic for a passage in his book *Dinner at the White House*. Churchill, in his suit, cited a footnote on page 151 of the book:

> As Drew Pearson revealed in one of his columns early in 1945, the motives for the British policy in Greece were at least partly linked to the fact that Hambro's Bank of London, the chief British creditors of Greece . . . had bailed Winston Churchill out of bankruptcy in 1912.[24]

Time then made note of the fact that Adamic and his publisher, Harper's,

> had been taken for a ride on Drew Pearson's glittering "Washington Merry-Go-Round." It cost them an estimated $20,000. It was proved in court that Churchill had never been under obligation to the bank. To every person in England who was sent a copy of the book, Harpers promised to send a correction and an apology. Author Adamic had never asked Merry-Go-Round Pearson to prove his statement, and had added the footnote after Harper's had accepted the final proofs.[25]

Pearson claimed that as a result of the *Time* article he had suffered great pain and mental anguish and had been injured in the pursuit of his livelihood.[26]

Time, Inc., moved for dismissal shortly thereafter, contending that the complaint failed to state a claim upon which relief could be granted, that the article constituted a fair report of a judicial proceeding, that it was true, that it consisted of fair comment upon matters of public interest, and that it had been published without malice in reliance upon trustworthy sources.[27]

The case never went to trial; it was dismissed per stipulation of counsel for both parties.[28] One Pearson biographer claimed that New York attorney Morris Ernst helped work out the settlement; Ernst reportedly asked the magazine to do a cover story on the columnist to help patch up differences.[29] There is some evidence to support this claim: *Time* magazine published a generally complimentary article on muckraker Pearson in its December 13, 1948, issue—less than six weeks after the case was settled.[30]

The muckraker was obviously more tenacious in a suit he filed against Sen. Joseph McCarthy. After Pearson's physical encounter with McCarthy and the senator's denouncement of the columnist on the libel-proof Senate floor,[31] the muckraker was determined to sue. He wanted to bring an action immediately after the floor tirade but was reminded that McCarthy had constitutional immunity while speaking on the floor. The muckraker, however, instructed his attorneys to "find a way" to sue. It was Pearson's opinion that McCarthy had circulated the text of his floor speech to the press gallery before he orally delivered it. Pearson also thought other persons who did not have constitutional immunity had helped write the speech. The columnist asked attorneys Woods, William Roberts, Tommy Corcoran, and Harold Ickes to meet one Saturday morning to discuss strategy for the suit. They decided to operate on the assumption that McCarthy had circulated the allegedly defamatory material before his floor speech.[32]

The suit was filed in March of 1951. Pearson's complaint named McCarthy, Fulton Lewis, Jr., the Washington Times-Herald, Inc., Edward K. Nellor, George Waters, Don Surine, Morris A. Bealle, Westbrook Pegler, and J. B. Matthews. The muckraker sought $5 million. Citing four counts, Pearson essentially charged libel and conspiracy to drive him out of business.[33] As was usually the case when the columnist filed suit, he identified himself in complimentary terms:

> The business which the Plaintiff has established and the trade name, "Washington Merry-Go-Round," applicable to and identified with his newspaper column, has become known to one of the world's largest audiences of publishers and readers in the world [*sic*], and has attained high value to newspaper publishers and other publishers *as a means of attracting and holding circulation through the presentation of courageous, unbiased and truthful news matters of great importance and interest.*[34]

Pearson went on to explain that his broadcasts, too, had attained and held a very large listening audience. Further, contracts and agreements concerning his column and radio broadcasts constituted his primary sources of income.[35]

The columnist then alleged that McCarthy, Lewis, the Times-Herald corporation, Nellor, Waters, Surine, and Bealle, all of whom were engaged in the preparation and publication of books, articles, newspaper columns, radio broadcasts, or lectures, "would profit greatly by the elimination of the Plaintiff's business or the destruction of public confidence of editors, publishers, broadcasters and radio and television sponsors in the value" of the publications as an avenue of attracting business and profit to their individual enterprises.[36]

The first count of the complaint concerned the Pearson-McCarthy physical altercation. The complaint alleged that McCarthy planned the incident in order to

> publicize in an untruthful and humiliating manner the injury to the plaintiff and to advertise the defendant who is a United States senator, as the victor of a contest rather than the author and actor in a brutal and unprovoked assault.[37]

The second count also concerned McCarthy—namely, his remarks on the Senate floor and the thirty-seven-page mimeographed statement that he circulated concerning the columnist. In the complaint, Pearson cited various paragraphs of the McCarthy statement that were allegedly libelous.[38]

The third count was essentially a conspiracy charge against the defendants for their alleged efforts to drive the muckraker out of business. The complaint, in part, charged:

> intimidation of public officials by improper and harassing investigation of their personal activities by persons acting purportedly in official capacity and by others, agents of the Defendants, by threats of scurrilous attack and false charges and the abuse of Congressional powers of investigation, so as to cause such public officials and other and proper lawful sources of legitimate news and information to refuse to the Plaintiff and his employees factual and public information normally and customarily supplied to the Defendants and their agents in the performance of their competitive publishing enterprises.[39]

The fourth count alleged that the defendants engaged in widespread publication of libelous statements in an effort to damage the columnist's reputation and deprive him of the rewards of his business.[40]

The case dragged on for nearly five years. Considerable behind-the-scenes maneuvering took place before the case was settled. The Washington Times-Herald Company, one of the defendants, was purchased by the Washington Post in

1954. Thus, the *Post,* which carried the "Merry-Go-Round" column, absorbed both the assets and liabilities of the *Times-Herald.* Obviously, the pending libel suit fell in the latter category. Spokesmen for the newspaper made it clear that they wanted the case dropped, particularly since the *Post* carried Pearson's column. This set in motion a chain of events that resulted in a settlement. There were a number of stipulations. According to Woods, Pearson and Pegler agreed to withdraw other pending suits against each other. As a second condition, the Hearst press, which circulated the Pegler column, agreed to run the "Merry-Go-Round" in all of its newspapers that were not then publishing it. Third, McCarthy was to give Pearson a letter apologizing for and retracting the statements he made on the Senate floor. The letter was to be private; Pearson was not to use it in his column. Woods said he was told the letter was written, but Pearson did not show it to him.[41]

Fellow columnist Pegler, one of the defendants in the *McCarthy* suit, had long been a thorn in Pearson's side. The muckraker filed at least six libel suits against the New York-based writer.[42] Pearson first filed suit in 1945 when Pegler labeled him "a miscalled newscaster specializing in falsehoods and smearing people with personal and political motivation."[43] When Pearson sued Pegler, he clearly pointed out to newspapers distributing the latter's column that he did not want to bring suit against them. He did, however, request a retraction. William A. Roberts, serving as the muckraker's attorney, sent a letter to publishers of twenty-seven newspapers that had carried the Pegler column.[44] Roberts explained that Pearson had "hesitated to sue the various papers . . . because he doubts that they share Pegler's views." Roberts then subtly asked for copies of apologies or corrections.

Though Pearson filed the single action against Pegler, it did not stay in the courts long; it was withdrawn within a year as a result of an exchange of letters. Pegler wrote Pearson a letter, asking that the controversy be dropped, claiming that it would be profitable to no one, and that it could bring unsavory publicity to the newspaper business. Pegler's letter said in part:

> Let bygones be bygones. . . . I do not believe our present course, if pursued, would benefit anyone and I do think we might bring unpleasant attention to the newspaper business, which has been very good to both of us. In fact, I think it is wasteful to devote valuable space to personal controversies between columnists.[45]

Pearson reportedly responded with:

> I appreciate the spirit of your letter and agree that columnists have more important battles to fight than among themselves. I am therefore asking my attorney to withdraw the suit as of this week. This will be a good way to start the new year.[46]

This exchange of letters, however, only temporarily warmed the relationship between the two journalists. Though they had agreed not to criticize each other again openly, Pearson filed a series of suits based on Pegler columns in 1949 and 1950. He claimed that Pegler had broken their pact.

In the first of the series of suits, Pearson brought a libel action against Hearst Consolidated Publications, Inc., in the State Supreme Court for New York County.[47] Citing sixteen causes of action, Pearson's lawyers sought $850,000 in damages.

It was in this complaint that Pearson emphasized that Pegler had broken a January 2, 1946, agreement in which both journalists promised to make no public statements, oral or written, that contained adverse comments about the other. Pearson said that, when the agreement was reached, it was agreed "that a violation and breach . . . by either party would gravely injure, adversely affect, and greatly damage the professional capacity and career of the other."[48] Pearson's second amended complaint further charged that Pegler's violation of the agreement was "willful and deliberate," and that Pegler had intended to cause Pearson "great damage."[49]

The sixth cause of action in the amended complaint concerned remarks made by Pegler about Pearson's then-young protégé, Jack Anderson. The complaint cited a November 23, 1952, Pegler column in which the New York–based writer referred to "a private detective and stooge for Drew Pearson's strange activities, named Jack Anderson."[50] The complaint also made reference to another remark in the same column, that "last year Sen. McCarthy caught up with Pearson in a public resort in Washington and punched him until he squealed for a lavatory attendant to come to his rescue."[51]

Pearson filed a second libel suit against the Hearst Corporation in the same State Supreme Court for New York County. This suit sought damages in excess of $1 million.[52] The muckraker's attorneys listed seventeen causes of action. Excerpts from scores of Pegler columns were said to be libelous. Included in the complaint was a Pegler column published on May 23, 1949, in the *New York Journal-American.* It said in part:

> He [the late James Forrestal, America's first secretary of defense, who was the subject of much Pearson criticism] also was a victim of the wanton blackguardism and mendacity of the radio which has been a professional specialty of Drew Pearson. Pearson has become a man of great power and special privilege because other decent men like Forrestal go in fear of fantastic lies to be spread over the nation by radio, all to stimulate the sale of a brand of hat or laxative [Pearson's radio sponsors]. . . . Pearson was eligible for World War II. His ex-mother-in-law, the late Eleanor (Cissy) Patterson, on the basis of this family intimacy, stated in print that, representing himself to be a Quaker, Pearson "thee'd and thou'd his way out of the war."[53]

The complaint further charged that Pegler wrote and conspired to write the material in order to injure Pearson in his reputation and profession and, simultaneously, to "injure liberal and progressive movements in the United States." The complaint also alleged that Pegler and the Hearst Publishing Company "were further actuated by an intent and hope" that Pegler's column would "provoke and goad" the muckraker into "reciprocal attacks . . . in order that a feud between two such personalities might be advertised and used to defendants' financial advantage."[54]

The thrust of the amended complaint, however, was that Pegler continued to publicly pound away at Pearson after the muckraker filed his initial suit. Pearson's complaint cited a June 8, 1949, column in which Pegler commented on the first libel suit brought that year by Pearson:

> As on a past occasion, Pearson put himself in the position of an injured innocent in the preliminary publicity and immediately began private overtures looking toward a settlement which would permit him to dodge the question whether he is or is not a lying blackguard. He is willing to withdraw his present suit if I would apologize and say publicly that he is neither a liar nor a blackguard. I reiterate that he is both.[55]

Pegler also wrote in a July 21, 1949, column that appeared in the *New York Journal-American*:

> The tragic death of James V. Forrestal, the first Secretary of Defense, whose mental condition Pearson harped upon with gusto until Forrestal jumped out a window, finally brought down on Pearson a storm of resentment by newspapers and magazines. Most of it was gutless generality and therefore as much a reproach to the journals which thus ducked a fight as to the lying blackguard whom they were too yellow to name.[56]

Pearson's complaint stated that the words of the column were understood by readers to mean that he "caused and was responsible for the death of James V. Forrestal."[57]

Pegler's anti-Pearson barbs knew no moderation. His February 6, 1953, column published in the *Journal-American* included these colorful excerpts:

> In recent years, since communism became less popular and profitable, Pearson has sometimes professed to be anti-Communist, a trick used by many others who played with the Reds in the Roosevelt-Truman era. . . .
>
> I would gladly own that I have tried diligently to convince the public that Pearson is a lying faker and scoundrel. . . .

> Perhaps some other lawyer will be reckless enough to take Pearson to trial so that there will be a judicial record that he was held by a "jury of his peers" to be a liar, a faker, and a pro-Communist propagandist.[58]

But Pegler was not through. On February 15, little more than one week after this verbal tirade, the writer was back jabbing away at Pearson:

> I have just amplified my background knowledge of Drew Pearson's systematic resort to the courts to silence persons who have undertaken the difficult and unpleasant task of exposing his lies and fakes and his closeness to the Communists. . . . I believe I might better carry out my determination to destroy Pearson's power for evil by putting him on the stand in a public trial with appropriate publicity and making him admit his lies, one by one.
>
> I would thus shove that proof at newspaper publishers who have continued to print his ill-written lies long after they were fully aware of the character of the man, his methods, his devious, ulterior motives, and his stuff. . . . I will expose Pearson further in the near future.[59]

Columns such as these proved so irritating to Pearson that he filed at least three additional suits, including one in the federal district court for the southern district of New York. In that suit, Pearson sought $1 million in damages from Pegler and others.[60] As in the complaints filed in New York County, Pearson's lawyers outlined several allegedly libelous Pegler columns. One cited was published on December 26, 1950, shortly after McCarthy physically assaulted Pearson:

> Senator Joe McCarthy has started an important public service in going after Drew Pearson. He deserves the support of the patriotic citizens in a fight which inevitably will be rough and dirty. Pearson is a slippery, devious fellow, absolutely insensitive to the inhibitions of truth and ethics, as I intend to prove if he ever brings to trial a suit which he has filed for the purpose of muzzling me in my determined campaign to expose him and break his power. . . . Pearson is a liar and a rogue and I will belt him through the skylight as a service to my country and my honorable profession of journalism.[61]

The muckraker also charged that Pegler had made repeated use of anti-Pearson "information" that had been delivered by McCarthy during his constitutionally protected floor tirade against the columnist.

Pearson was not content, however, to limit his suits based on Pegler's columns to the New York courts. The muckraker sought $250,000 in damages from the San Antonio Light Publishing Company[62] and $500,000 in damages from the Detroit Times Division of the Hearst Publishing Company.[63] Despite the excessive amounts of time and money expended on the cases, all were unspectacularly dropped in either the fall of 1955 or the spring of 1956.[64]

By this time, it should have been evident to Pearson that initiating libel suits was somewhat frivolous and unprofitable. Nevertheless, less than two years after he dropped the Pegler cases, Pearson brought a $352,000 libel action against California attorney Loyd Wright for remarks made by the lawyer in relation to his appointed position as chairman of the Commission on Government Security.[65]

The first of two counts alleged that Wright had written a letter mentioning Pearson to Congressman John E. Moss that was false, defamatory and "entirely outside defendant's line of duty."[66] Moss, chairman of the Government Information Subcommittee on Government Operations, had requested information concerning media disclosures that Wright believed adversely affected the security of the nation. The letter read in part:

> From these cases you will readily ascertain that in many instances the reporter, particularly Drew Pearson, was fully aware of the Secret or Top Secret classification. A couple of weeks ago today the *Washington Post* published his column wherein he stated that he knew the information was confidential but he nevertheless was going to publish it. Your staff undoubtedly knows of the instance. You will readily see from the illustrations given you in the enclosed list that he knew that he was purveying Top Secret information.[67]

Pearson claimed that Wright "intended . . . to injure" his reputation, good name, and profession.[68]

The second count was based on a press release issued by Wright on July 1, 1957, in which he described Pearson and his columns as grave threats to national survival, as well as breaches of security and journalistic ethics.[69] It was made clear that Wright issued the statements from a personal viewpoint, not as spokesman for the commission. In the thirteen-page press release he cited numerous examples of media disclosures of secret documents, which allegedly jeopardized national security. He listed incidents involving metropolitan dailies, trade magazines, weekly magazines, and wire services, but he named names only once. He took Pearson to task:

> Korean War—During the Korean conflict a number of breaches of security and of journalistic ethics occurred. The gravity of the situation can be illustrated beyond cavil simply by reference to the columns of one syndicated newspaperman, Drew Pearson.[70]

Wright then listed seven dates between December 30, 1950, and March 21, 1953, in which the muckraking columnist allegedly published excerpts from classified documents in his "Merry-Go-Round" column.[71]

The district court, in reference to the first count, held that a statement made by a chairman of a federal commission in response to an inquiry from a congressional subcommittee with respect to a matter within the scope of the commission's activities was absolutely privileged. In reference to the second count, however, the court held that a statement made by the chairman in a press release was not. Thus, Wright's motion for summary judgment was granted in part and denied in part.[72] In reference to the press release, District Court Judge Alexander Holtzoff remarked:

> It is no part of the duty of a government official to make statements to the public. It may be desirable for him to do so at times, but it is no part of the functions that are conferred upon him by law, and therefore absolute privilege does not attach.[73]

Holtzoff conceded, however, that there might be a conditional privilege attached to such a statement.[74]

The case dragged on for another two years before it was finally settled. In June of 1959, the U.S. Supreme Court handed down *Barr* v. *Matteo,*[75] a decision that established absolute immunity for public officials to criticize official conduct. This decision spurred Wright's attorneys to file for summary judgment on the second count, which dealt with the press release. Pearson's attorney naturally objected; Donovan contended that *Matteo* was not controlling, that it extended only to "policy making officials below cabinet or comparable rank for actions in the line of duty."[76] Donovan said Wright was not a policy-making official because the commission was not a policy-making body. In summary, Pearson's attorney claimed that the press release was not an official commission statement, that it represented merely a personal statement by Wright, and that the release was not a means of furthering any agency function.[77] Despite Donovan's contentions, the district court granted summary judgment on the second count of the complaint.[78]

Pearson obviously had little success in his role as a libel suit plaintiff during the 1940s and 1950s. One might think that he would have been less likely to continue his court crusades after the *New York Times Co.* v. *Sullivan* "actual malice" rule made it much more difficult for a plaintiff to recover damages in actions that involved public officials or—as a result of later, related rulings—public figures. The muckraker, however, did not hesitate to continue filing suits against newspapers or individuals that were critical of him.

In one of the best-known Pearson cases, the muckraker brought an action against the Fairbanks Publishing Company, Inc., and the editor of its newspaper, C. W. Snedden. Snedden had borrowed a phrase from an anonymous Washington writer and labeled the columnist "the garbage man of the Fourth Estate." Pearson sought $176,000 in damages for the editorial which was published in the *Fairbanks* (Alaska) *Miner.*[79]

Snedden was upset with Pearson's July 7, 1958, column which dealt with Alaska's effort to achieve statehood. The muckraker described the then-governor of Alaska, Mike Stepovich, as a "Johnny-come-lately" to the statehood cause.[80] Snedden printed editorials critical of Pearson. One ended with this comment: "For the time being we'll get a clothespin for our editorial nose while we decide what to do about this free-wheeling garbage man of the Fourth Estate."[81] Much to Pearson's displeasure, the trial court held that the editorials were qualifiedly privileged, that they constituted fair comment, and that they were not made with malice. The Alaska Supreme Court affirmed. In its decision, that court essentially extended the public figure designation to Pearson.[82]

The court said the columnist had made himself a public figure by commenting on matters of extreme public concern in Alaska. Furthermore, the court said that it was unnecessary for it to speculate as to whether the U.S. Supreme Court would "extend the protection of the first amendment so as to encompass situations other than those which involve defamatory falsehoods relating to the official conduct of public officials."[83] The court then simply "adopted" for its jurisdiction the meaning of "actual malice" as articulated in *Sullivan.* Justice John Dimond said that under the meaning of the term, Snedden's statement would have had to have been made with reckless disregard for the truth. In referring to the columnist as a "garbage man," the imputation was that Pearson was inaccurate and that his writings were "literary trash." The court said:

> There was evidence which, if believed by the trial judge, would show that the appellee, Snedden, who caused the editorials of which appellant complains to be published, believed and had a reasonable basis for believing that appellant's writings frequently did not conform with facts and were therefore worthless. The evidence justifies a finding that appellee's characterization of appellant as a garbage man and of his writings as garbage was not made with knowledge that it was false or with a reckless disregard of whether it was false or not.[84]

Though the Alaska court said it was aware that where matters of public concern were involved "the majority of the courts hold that the privilege of public discussion does not extend to misstatements of fact" concerning nonpublic officials, it believed the "actual malice" rule should apply to persons in Pearson's category.[85]

The "garbage man" description proved more than Pearson could endure. He claimed that "I have developed a thickness of skin which is somewhat protective, but some of these criticisms still hurt."[86] Mrs. Pearson was not particularly happy that her husband brought the suit in Alaska—and was forced to travel there to testify—but she nevertheless agreed that he "did not have to take that from an editor."[87]

The Alaska court ruled against Pearson on April 28, 1966, but his combative juices continued to flow. Less than three weeks later, on May 16, the muckraker brought a libel action asking $2,625,000 in damages against George Christopher, former San Francisco Republican mayor, who was seeking his party's gubernatorial nomination. Pearson filed suit in the Superior Court for Los Angeles County. His complaint alleged that Christopher had tried to damage the columnist's business relationships by attempting to halt publication of his May 9 and 10 columns in California newspapers. The muckraker further alleged that Christopher had attempted to intimidate newspapers through a series of letters, telephone calls, telegrams, and personal visits. Christopher had reportedly called Pearson "notoriously unreliable" and claimed that the columns constituted "false statement."[88]

The Associated Press quoted Christopher the day after Pearson filed suit:

> I can only conclude that Mr. Pearson, acting as a worn-out carpetbagger columnist in California to help Pat Brown's governorship race, seeks to gain more publicity for his malicious smear attempts, which hasn't drawn much attention.[89]

Apparently only about half of the thirty-five California papers that regularly carried the "Merry-Go-Round" chose to publish the May 9 and 10 columns. The columns that Christopher worked to suppress compared the former mayor's "ethical standards" to those of Sen. Thomas Dodd of Connecticut, a man under considerable criticism by "Merry-Go-Round" writers at the time. The columns also discussed a technical violation of the State Milk Control Law that Christopher, a dairy business operator, allegedly made in 1940. Pearson further claimed that Christopher had received the benefit of a "public relations job" that had been so effective "the voting public has no idea of his criminal record."[90]

After the columns appeared, Christopher contended that his actions of more than twenty-five years earlier did not have criminal overtones; rather, he was engaged in fighting the milk trust to force lower wholesale milk prices, a common practice of the time.[91]

Two days after Pearson filed suit against Christopher, the gubernatorial candidate brought a $6 million cross-complaint against the columnist. In his countersuit, Christopher contended that the "Merry-Go-Round" columns represented a "scheme" to defame him "in an attempt to prevent his election as the Republican nominee for governor." He labeled Pearson's columns "intentional and malicious." Christopher's cross-complaint further stated that the muckraker "intended by innuendo to accuse" the candidate of "immoral and unethical acts and acts involving moral turpitude." Christopher said he had never accepted "kickbacks," that he had never "watered" any milk, and the 1940 incident referred to by Pearson was a common practice of the day since the constitutionality of the law he had allegedly violated was in doubt.[92]

Christopher later threatened to make Governor Brown a codefendant in the $6 million suit. Christopher had earlier contended that Brown had furnished Pearson with material for the column as part of a political ploy and had purchased a $2 million libel insurance policy for the muckraker.[93] Brown and Christopher, however, reached a public reconciliation, and the latter stated that he would not make the governor a codefendant.[94]

Pearson claimed the allegation that Brown had purchased a $2 million libel insurance policy on the columnist's behalf was categorically untrue. The muckraker said the accusation was obviously false "since it is almost impossible for any newspaper or newspaperman to get a $2 million libel insurance policy." Pearson wrote that he had not carried libel insurance at any time during his career; "the best defense against libel is the truth plus a good lawyer."[95]

Through Los Angeles attorney Irving H. Green, Pearson answered the Christopher cross-complaint by pleading truth, fair comment concerning a candidate for public office, and that the comments were "stated without malice." According to the brief, the columns were meant "to prevent injury and damage to the public who might be unaware of Christopher's history."[96] Like so many libel actions involving Pearson, however, these two cases never reached trial. Less than one year after the initial filings and accompanying publicity, both were quietly dropped by agreement of the concerned parties.[97]

Anderson has been relatively active as a plaintiff since Pearson's death. Both cases he filed have First Amendment overtones.[98] In *Anderson* v. *Nixon,* the columnist sought $22 million in damages from former President Richard Nixon and nineteen subordinates. The action accused Nixon and his aides of conducting a five-year campaign to strip the muckraker of his First Amendment rights and destroy his credibility, citing seventeen allegations of harassment. The case was filed in September of 1976 in the federal district court for the District of Columbia. The action provides evidence that Anderson is willing to invest his time and money to help ensure that journalists' constitutional rights are observed by the government.

Anderson sought damages of $10 million for violation of his First Amendment rights to gather, report, and publish the news; $1 million for violation of his rights of privacy and to be free of unlawful searches and seizures; $1 million for violation of his rights of liberty and property without due process of law; and $10 million as punitive damages.[99]

Among other things, Anderson alleged that after he published a news story relating to President Nixon's secret efforts to have the presidential pension increased, the president directed H. R. Haldeman, his former assistant, and others to investigate the columnist; that the columnist's name appeared on the "enemies" list of names of persons believed by the defendants "to be hostile to them"; that Anderson was a principal target of the "Plumbers," a group that investigated and attempted to prevent "leaks" of information that "defendants wish to keep from U.S. citizens"; that defendants ordered the "Plumbers," as well as other governmental agencies, to investigate Anderson to learn the sources of his information in order to prevent him from gathering and publishing the information; that in early 1972 the defendants, through the CIA, started to conduct "an unlawful investigation, surveillance and interference" with Anderson and his employees, with the "purpose and intent of discovering and punishing persons who were sources" of information for the columnist and his associates; that the defendants made several attempts to "discredit" Anderson and "to destroy his reputation for truth, veracity, and accuracy"; and that through the "Plumbers" the defendants conceived and committed overt acts in a conspiracy to "cause serious physical injury, possibly including death."[100]

In summary, Anderson claimed that as a result of the conspiracy and overt acts allegedly committed by the defendants, he had to "devote considerable time and financial resources to prevent infliction of further harm."[101] In several sections of the suit, Anderson provided vivid details of practices allegedly employed by the defendants. As an illustration of the extent of his sources, the columnist even cited the code names used by the CIA when it investigated him.[102]

Anderson said he felt compelled to file suit against Nixon and the others because the administration's treatment of him was "a classic example of harassment. No other newsman in American history has been harassed by the government to such an extent. You name it, and it happened to us."[103]

On January 26, 1978, however, Anderson was ordered to disclose some confidential sources or face dismissal of his suit. Anderson refused to reveal his sources, claiming constitutional protection; Nixon and the others said they had the right to develop facts for their defense.[104]

Federal District Court Judge Gerhard Gesell agreed with the defense attorneys. Gesell said that, though Anderson's refusal to comply with the court order was "not made in bad faith," it was "willful and deliberate and made with full undertaking of the consequences." Defense attorneys had contended that the columnist had knowledge of many key events in the alleged conspiracy and that therefore the statute of limitations had run. Gesell said that in order for the defendants to prove that Anderson was aware of the alleged conspiracy at an early date—thus contradicting his claim that the conspiracy was concealed—it was "highly material and relevant" that they learn the identity of the columnist's sources. Gesell made it clear that there were no "alternative practical means" of learning who the sources were. As a result, Anderson's complaint was dismissed.[105]

The second case in which Anderson became involved as a plaintiff was filed in 1974. Suit was brought against the American Telephone and Telegraph Company by Anderson, eleven other professional journalists, two publishing corporations, and the Reporters Committee for Freedom of the Press, a legal research and defense fund organization established to protect the freedom-of-information interests of the working press. Essentially, the plaintiffs sought a judicial declaration that it is unlawful for the defendant telephone company and its subsidiaries to release toll records of journalists to government investigative agencies without prior notification to the journalists concerned. In addition, the complaint sought an injunction barring the defendants from releasing records of the plaintiffs without prior notice.[106] Attorneys for the plaintiffs advanced a two-part First Amendment argument: the government's interests must be judicially balanced against the First Amendment rights of journalists, even in good faith investigations; and the judiciary should superintend requests for journalists' records in order to screen out bad faith subpoenas.[107]

Events that led to the suit were initiated in December of 1973. At that time, the plaintiffs wrote to AT&T seeking assurance that their telephone toll billing records—and those of other journalists—would not be turned over to government investigative agencies without reasonable prior notice to the journalists. The plaintiffs expressed concern that the toll records could be used by government investigators to identify confidential sources with whom the plaintiffs communicated by telephone. The plaintiffs pointed out that denial of prior notice made it impossssible for them to invoke otherwise available legal remedies to protect their First Amendment rights. Neither could they raise proper First Amendment issues without such notice, they said.[108]

AT&T refused to comply with the request, and so plaintiffs filed the complaint. After the action was brought, the United States government moved to intervene as a party defendant. The government argued that the courts had no authority to require the telephone companies to give journalists advance notice.[109] Both parties then filed suit for summary judgment. The district court, on August 17, 1976, granted the defendants' motion. The court held that the First and Fifth amendments did not give professional journalists a right to reasonable prior notice from the defendant telephone companies before furnishing government investigative agencies with copies of telephone billing records.[110]

In an appeal, the plaintiffs contended that in approximately 90 percent of the 32,000 instances in which toll records were released to government investigative agencies during the period March 1, 1974, through June 30, 1975, no notice was given to the subscribers.[111] Among the instances cited in the appeal to the District of Columbia's circuit court were two involving Anderson. One subpoena was allegedly issued in an effort to learn the sources of one of his columns regarding the indiscretions of an Agency for International Development official during a visit by Vice-President Spiro Agnew to Kenya.[112] On another occasion, the FBI allegedly obtained toll records of Anderson and one of his employees during the course of investigating reports by an informant that the columnist had arranged to obtain documents that members of a militant American Indian group had removed from the Bureau of Indian Affairs.[113]

Attorneys for the plaintiffs argued that the journalists had a First Amendment interest in maintaining the confidentiality of their sources and that the First Amendment and principles of due process required that the reporters receive prior notice of subpoenas for their toll billing records. It was contended that, under the present operating conditions, the government could "indiscriminately invade reporters' First Amendment rights, totally free from judicial oversight."[114]

In conclusion, the plaintiffs' lawyers conceded that the confidentiality of a newsman's source was not absolutely privileged, but that First Amendment considerations must come into play, and "the competing interests at stake must be duly weighed before forcing disclosure."[115]

On appeal, the circuit court reversed and remanded the case with respect to five plaintiffs, including Anderson, but affirmed the lower court's grant of summary judgment against the other ten plaintiffs.[116] The court held that the federal government's good faith inspection of toll-call records, without prior notice to journalists, does not infringe on their First Amendment rights, but bad faith inspection of long-distance records "in theory" may sometimes abridge First Amendment rights. A journalist, however, would have to show a clear and "imminent threat" that the subpoena would cause substantial and "irreparable harm."[117]

Circuit Court Judge Malcolm Wilkey made it clear that "there is no need for case-by-case balancing where toll record subpoenas have been issued in criminal investigations." He said none of the plaintiffs, Anderson included, had thus far laid an "adequate foundation" to support future judicial intervention when toll records are requested. But Wilkey was willing to give the five plaintiffs the opportunity to "meet this heavy burden on remand."[118]

Wilkey further said that, even if Anderson or the other remaining plaintiffs establish that there have been past instances of abuse, "it does not necessarily mean that [they] will be entitled to prior notice of future subpoenas."[119] The judge said courts have frequently denied "anticipatory relief when plaintiffs have failed to establish . . . a pervasive pattern of past abuse such as will indicate a *continuing* program of misconduct."[120]

Wilkey said journalists could not realistically seek case-by-case judicial scrutiny of all toll-record subpoenas merely because disclosure of the records "might possibly" infringe on First Amendment freedoms:

> If the mere possibility of future government misconduct were sufficient to warrant such prophylactic relief, then the courts would be called upon to superintend virtually all investigative activity. Much more than the mere possibility of future official misconduct is needed to justify this type of judicial intervention.[121]

Circuit Court Judge J. Skelly Wright dissented, claiming that the majority had gone too far in saying that the plaintiffs were not entitled to prior judicial scrutiny unless they met the "difficult if not impossible burden of establishing to a court that they are in imminent danger of having their records disclosed as part of a secret bad faith government investigation to harass them." Wright emphasized that journalists do not enjoy greater First Amendment freedoms than the public, but it is nevertheless the function of journalists to inform the public. That opportunity to inform is diminished, he contended, "when government, however well intentioned, secretly jeopardizes the journalists' sources of information without prior judicial approval."[122]

Reporters Committee sought a review of the decision, but on March 5, 1979, the U.S. Supreme Court denied the petition for a *writ of certiorari.*

A Refusal to Be Intimidated

The late Drew Pearson and Jack Anderson, though constantly defending themselves against libel actions, have not been hesitant to initiate suits as plaintiffs to protect their constitutional rights. Pearson was involved in at least fifteen libel actions[123] and two nonlibel suits[124] as a plaintiff. Anderson, since inheriting the column in 1969, has not been a libel suit plaintiff, but he has initiated two actions that have First Amendment overtones.[125]

Pearson's and Anderson's willingness to enter the legal arena to protect their constitutional rights—to say nothing of their financial livelihoods—is a tribute to them. There are countless reporters and editors who loudly profess their rights; the transformation from lip service to costly litigation is, however, often another matter.

Pearson and Anderson have not vacillated; consistent involvement in the courts as plaintiffs marks their records. Though no more successful as plaintiffs than the scores who filed suits against them, the muckrakers have eagerly given their time, money, and energy to protect and enhance their constitutional rights.

8

The "Merry-Go-Round": Cursed, Sued—but Successful

The "Merry-Go-Round" syndicated opinion column and its primary writers—the late Drew Pearson and Jack Anderson—have occupied a unique role in American journalism during the past half century. The column, launched in 1932, quickly made its presence felt; within two years, more than two hundred newspapers subscribed to it. Today it is published by more than nine hundred newspapers. Conceived by Pearson and Robert S. Allen, the column specializes in the "inside" story; its subjects are often those that other newspapermen shy away from—because of either personal philosophy or publisher pressure.

As might be expected, the column has been controversial from its beginning. Less than two years after the "Merry-Go-Round's" inception, Pearson and Allen were confronted with their first libel action: Gen. Douglas MacArthur, U. S. Army chief of staff, sought $1,750,000 in damages. The suit was eventually dropped; it was a harbinger, however, of scores of libel actions that would be filed against writers of the muckraking, investigative column. It also reflected the attitude many prominent public figures would harbor toward the column during ensuing decades. The list of those who have blatantly criticized the column or its writers reads like a "Who's Who" of influential and important Americans. President Franklin D. Roosevelt, for example, once labeled Pearson a "chronic liar"; President Harry S Truman, drawing from his colorful vocabulary, simply described the columnist as an "S.O.B."; President Dwight D. Eisenhower once said that any newspaper that carried the "Merry-Go-Round" was "irresponsible."

Verbal assaults against Pearson on the libel-proof floors of the House and Senate during the 1940s and 1950s were commonplace. Tennessee Senator Kenneth McKellar once called Pearson "an ignorant liar, a pusillanimous liar, a peewee liar, and a paid liar"; Mississippi Senator Theodore Bilbo said Pearson was "the most notorious liar" in America, that he gathered "slime, mud and slander from all parts of the earth" only to let it "ooze out through his radio broadcasts"; and Rep. James Morrison of Louisiana claimed Pearson was "a downright liar and garbage-can collector of filthy, manufactured, synthetic lies." Pearson controversies, however, went beyond verbal altercations. Wisconsin Senator Joseph McCarthy, for example, once kicked the muckraker in the groin; lobbyist Charles Clark physically attacked the columnist also.

Pearson's successor, Anderson, has also been extremely controversial. The Nixon administration regarded him as an archenemy and allegedly made a strong, concerted effort to discredit him. The columnist responded by filing a $22 million suit against Nixon and nineteen subordinates.

Though one might expect the primary writers of this disputatious column to have hard-nosed personalities, this is not the case. Pearson, a Quaker, was often sensitive to the plight of the poor. Anderson, a devout family man of Mormon upbringing, possesses the unassuming, modest personality of the missionary he once was. Pearson was the catalyst behind the

Friendship Train that carried millions of 'dollars' worth of food to poor, hungry Europeans after World War II; Anderson once volunteered financial aid to Mrs. Charles Colson while her husband was in prison for deeds the muckraker helped disclose.

Contributions of these outwardly subdued "tigers behind the typewriter" to American journalism, however, should not be underestimated. Investigative, muckraking journalism, which became a national phenomenon at the turn of the twentieth century, was nearly dead when Pearson and Allen established the "Merry-Go-Round." Pearson, as evidenced by the strong verbal denouncements of American presidents and U.S. senators, continued this contentious reporting. Day after day, no matter how intense the public or political pressure, Pearson pounded away at the country's prominent elected officials, big business, and other diverse institutions that had come under journalistic attack by a nucleus of crusading writers during this century's first decade. The columnist occupied a precarious position; enemies were numerous and support minimal. Pearson, however, persisted; it was his style of journalism. The powerful did not intimidate him; neither money nor prestige stood in his way when in pursuit of a story. This style of reporting has gained a flood of practitioners during recent years. Still, today's literature indicates that Pearson's successor, Anderson, is the best-known, most effective muckraker of this rapidly expanding breed.

Obviously, men who engage in this inherently debatable writing style can expect their share of enemies. The wrath of Pearson's and Anderson's adversaries has often culminated in the American judicial system; a multitude of lawsuits—primarily for libel—has been brought against "Merry-Go-Round" writers. The precise number of actions filed against writers of the column, or newspapers that publish it, may never be known.

This book, however, has discussed some 126 libel cases that involved writers of the "Merry-Go-Round"; 111 of the suits were brought against one of the column's writers or against newspapers that published the column (including the 68 actions brought by Martin Sweeney against various newspapers); in 15 of the actions, the columnists were plaintiffs. Of the 126 libel actions, 110 were during the pre-*New York Times Co.* v. *Sullivan* years; there were 16 filed after. To further illustrate the involvement of "Merry-Go-Round" writers in litigation, an additional 9 cases not based on libel, ranging from charges of invasion of privacy to assault and battery, have been discussed; "Merry-Go-Round" writers were defendants in 4 of the cases, plaintiffs in the remainder. Thus, this book has considered 135 cases—brought between 1934 and the present—that have involved "Merry-Go-Round" writers. Only 6 of the suits, however, were filed after Pearson's death in 1969.

That writers of the muckraking column have been involved in libel actions every year—without exception—from 1939 to the present is not particularly surprising when one considers the hostile, outspoken attitudes of many of the era's officials toward them. Though the exact figure will likely never be determined, writers of the controversial "Merry-Go-Round" have been sued for at least $118 million since the column's inception.[1] The amount of time, energy, and money expended to defend the suits—particularly by Pearson—is staggering. The muckraker employed a variety of attorneys during his nearly four-decade reporting career; the majority of his legal work, however, was done by John Donovan. Attorneys who specialized in trial law were brought in when a case reached that stage. This, however, was not often: less than 10 percent of the cases examined in this book went to trial. Also, when a suit was brought in a jurisdiction outside the District of Columbia, local counsel was normally retained to handle the procedural aspects, usually in conjunction with Donovan. Anderson, too, has depended primarily on one attorney, Warren Woods. Dollar signs are also prominent in cases where Pearson and Anderson have been plaintiffs. The columnists have sought aggregate damages of at least $34.5 million in suits they have initiated.

It is obvious that changing thrusts in the ever evolving American libel law have been particularly important to the investigative, muckraking columnists. Prior to the landmark *Sullivan* case, the media relied on common law defenses against libel actions: statute of limitations, privilege of a participant, truth, privilege of reporting, fair comment and criticism, consent or authorization, and self-defense or right of reply. Before *Sullivan*, states were categorized according to the libel formulas they followed. The narrow rule, that privilege was confined to comment and criticism based on actual facts, was known as the majority view. The more liberal rule excused false statements about officials that ordinarily would be libelous, provided the statements were published without malice and with probable cause for believing them true. A few jurisdictions—such as the District of Columbia, where many of the suits against "Merry-Go-Round" writers were filed—followed a formula that allowed a more liberal interpretation of privilege in libel cases where there were no charges of crime or gross immorality.

During the 1950s, however, a growing trend toward increased press protection developed. This led to the *Times* "actual malice" rule—that a state cannot, under the First and Fourteenth Amendments, award damages to a public official for defamatory falsehoods relating to his official conduct unless he proves that the statement was made with knowledge of its falsity or with reckless disregard of whether it was true or false.

The constitutional privilege enunciated in *Sullivan* was promptly followed and extended. The U.S. Supreme Court subsequently applied it to prosecutions for criminal libel, to public employees who held positions of responsibility for the control of public affairs, to persons categorized as public figures, and eventually to all discussion involving matters of public or general concern, regardless of the category of individual discussed. Recently, however, the Court has contracted this rule, holding that private individuals are entitled to more protection from defamatory statements than are public officials and figures, even when involved in an event of public concern.

Considering the aggressive writing style of the "Merry-Go-Round," the attitude of powerful people toward it, and the never-static degree of protection accorded journalists by the ever-evolving libel law, the question of how successful the muckraking columnists have been when defending against libel actions is indeed intriguing. This basic query, however, can be succinctly answered: amazingly successful. Pearson personally paid damages ($40,000) in only one suit during his lifetime: *Littell* v. *Pearson.* Littell, a former assistant attorney general who filed the action in 1949, would likely have encountered difficulty proving "actual malice" had the suit been decided after *Sullivan.* Pearson did not pay damages in a single action brought against him after 1964. His family, however, paid settlements on two occasions—*Keogh* v. *Pearson* and *Monitor Patriot Co.* v. *Roy*—in order to close the columnist's estate. Also, though six of the newspapers sued by Sweeney settled out of court, only one of them paid more than $200; the *Reading* (Pennsylvania) *Eagle* paid $900.

It does not stretch the imagination too far, then, to speculate that the muckraker, had he enjoyed the benefits of the "actual malice" rule during his entire writing career (Littell was clearly a public figure and Sweeney was obviously a public official), and had he lived to fight the *Keogh* and *Monitor Patriot* cases to their litigated conclusions, would have boasted a perfect record when defending against libel actions. His successor, Anderson, has not been involved in libel actions to the extent Pearson was, but the junior muckraker has never paid damages.

Why have the muckraking columnists compiled such a successful record in the courts? First of all, Pearson and Anderson obtained outstanding legal advice. John Donovan was Pearson's personal attorney for more than twenty-five years; he coordinated all procedural filings in the multitude of actions brought against the columnist. Warren Woods, Anderson's personal attorney, has also efficiently handled suits brought against his client.

Donovan earned a reputation as one of the outstanding libel attorneys in the East. The lawyer's goal was to get each suit brought against his client dismissed on technical grounds; he often contended that the action should be dropped because the plaintiff had failed to state a claim upon which relief could be granted. Donovan frequently stressed the libel per se–libel per quod distinction. He pointed out that the words in question could have only one meaning to be libelous per se; if they were capable of more than one meaning—which was often the case—he emphasized that they were in fact libelous per quod and required the pleading and proof of special damages.

Pearson's primary attorney relied strongly on two precedents during the common law years: *Sweeney* v. *Patterson* and *Coleman* v. *MacLennan*. *Patterson*, one of the chain libel actions, was brought in the District of Columbia. The court of appeals articulated the relatively liberal rule for the district: that it was not actionable to publish erroneous and injurious statements regarding political conduct and views of public officials so long as no charge of crime, corruption, or gross immorality was made. Associate Justice Henry Edgerton, who wrote the opinion, also emphasized that, if the courts were to uphold claims of public officials, this action would "reflect the obsolete doctrine that the governed must not criticize their governors." This opinion was, of course, later cited in *Sullivan* as recognizing that "erroneous statements are inevitable in free debate" and thus deserving of protection. The *Coleman* decision was handed down by the Kansas Supreme Court in 1908. The court held that, if a story were written in good faith concerning public officials, it was privileged, even though the matters in the article were conceivably untrue in fact and derogatory to the character of the person allegedly defamed.

With these two cases as precedents, Donovan was often able to get actions filed against Pearson dismissed before trial. Donovan, however, relied on more than precedents in his defense strategies. Often, he virtually inundated the courts with procedural filings, attempting to "wear down" the opposition. It was not unusual for an action filed against the muckraker to drag on more than five years; it became a full-time job for the plaintiffs' attorneys to answer motions filed by Donovan. In actions by lobbyist Charles Clark, industrial millionaire Nicolae Malaxa, U.S. Senator Thomas Dodd, California Attorney General Frederick Howser, and Littell, there were more than one hundred entries on the docket sheets.

If, however, Donovan failed to get the case dismissed during its preliminary stages—or the plaintiff did not drop the action out of frustration—Pearson retained an expert trial lawyer—for example, F. Joseph Donohue or William P. Rogers—to argue the case. In the event that a suit advanced to the trial stage in a jurisdiction far removed from the District of Columbia, local counsel was retained to oversee the local court, sometimes working in conjunction with one of the columnist's District of Columbia attorneys. Anderson follows this same practice.

Essentially, then, attorneys for the late Pearson and Anderson have played a major role in the astonishing success the columnists have enjoyed in the courts. Through procedural filings, effective use of common law defenses, retention of outstanding trial attorneys, and the determination to never settle a case in its pretrial stages, "Merry-Go-Round" columnists have proved nearly unbeatable in the courts.

Though many legal scholars and journalists have pointed to the inadequacy of the pre-*Sullivan* common law libel defenses, Pearson's lawyers, particularly Donovan, made prudent use of them. Most of their pre-*Sullivan* defenses were based on truth, fair comment upon matters of public interest, and privilege of reporting. Naturally, Pearson normally wrote about public persons or public events; thus these defenses provided effective protection. The use of truth as a defense in libel actions has been described as illusory at best, but the muckraker, confident of his facts, often insisted that his attorneys cite it. Truth, for example, was sufficient to exonerate the columnist in the well-publicized *Howser* v. *Pearson* case in the early 1950s.

Donovan, who worked in Pearson's office, checked most of the "Merry-Go-Round" columns for potential libel before they were distributed. Pearson was very careful with his wording, since the libelous per se or libelous per quod distinction was so important prior to 1964—but Donovan always double-checked for statements that could provide an avenue for successful libel actions. The attorney occasionally advised the muckraker to "tone down" or eliminate certain passages. The care Pearson took in formulating potentially libelous phrases cannot, however, be overemphasized. *Gariepy* v. *Pearson* provides an excellent example. The action was based on a Pearson column in which he said that the Reverend Charles Coughlin of Royal Oak, Michigan, gave $68,000 to a physician "because of alienation of affection" of the doctor's wife by Father Coughlin. Though the plaintiff's attorneys insisted the words connoted unchastity, the issue at trial became just how the words were to be understood. The jury eventually held for Pearson; the words were capable of other meanings.

Pearson's strong layman's knowledge of the law also aided his success. He likely knew as much about libel law—and the boundaries within which he could legally operate—as most attorneys who do not specialize in it. The combination of a general understanding of the law, an instinct as to how far he could "push" an individual without forcing him to file suit, and his ability to "tone down" potentially libelous passages helped ensure his success.

Since the majority of libel actions brought against Pearson were in the District of Columbia, he also enjoyed the relatively liberal rule established in the *Patterson* case. As a result, the columnist was careful not to accuse people of crimes or gross immorality, though, through innuendo, he often came exceedingly close. Again, however, his general knowledge of the law and his ability to construct a phrase capable of an innocent meaning helped to discourage people from filing libel actions against him and to aid in his defense if a suit were brought.

Effects of Evolving Libel Law on the Column

Writers of the "Merry-Go-Round" have been able to function effectively within the confines of the constantly evolving American libel law since the column's 1932 inception. Pearson, who once said that "the best defense against libel is the truth plus a good lawyer," lost, as mentioned earlier, only one of the libel actions brought against him before *Sullivan*. This impressive record lends support to a 1942 law review commentary by David Riesman which emphasized that, despite the nonuniform jurisdictional common law defenses, journalists were hardly at a great disadvantage. Riesman contended that American juries, often critical of politicians, were not likely to give a plaintiff the "benefit of a doubt." Furthermore, Riesman argued that the procedural technicalities in libel laws were full of "traps for the unwary." He said that lawyers for large newspapers were specialists in libel law while many attorneys for libel action plaintiffs were inexperienced.[2] This contention applied to the multitude of suits brought against Pearson. Some, of course, were "harassment" suits that plaintiffs realistically had little chance of winning. But even in those that appeared legitimate, many attorneys for plaintiffs were simply "outclassed" by the columnist's lawyers, primarily Donovan, who possessed an intricate understanding of libel law technicalities and procedural measures.

Pearson's attorneys in the pre-1964 years did not advance any unique defenses or push for increased press protection through a measure such as the nationalization of the law; they did not have to. The "bread and butter" common law defenses outlined above proved to be quite sufficient.

The landmark *Sullivan* case naturally had an effect on the "Merry-Go-Round." Through the years, many of the persons who filed libel actions against the column were public officials; the vast majority could have at least been categorized as public figures. Despite the increased protection given journalists when discussing public persons as a result of *Sullivan* and its progeny, libel suits—though the rate diminished—continued to be filed against writers of the column. The nationalization of libel laws did not totally discourage public persons from filing suits, but it did limit their chances of winning. Also, *Sullivan* reduced the nonuniform application of common law libel in various jurisdictions, thus making it procedurally easier to defend against actions.

Actually, the reduction in libel suits filed against "Merry-Go-Round" columnists since *Sullivan* has not been dramatically significant. Though it is unlikely that any sixty-eight-suit action, like that filed by Sweeney, would materialize today, "Merry-Go-Round" writers have nevertheless found themselves in the courts every year since 1964. The *Sullivan* rule, however, is not the sole reason suits against the column have tapered off during the past decade. A more noticeable decline occurred after Pearson's death in 1969. Since then, Anderson or his associates have been sued for libel only four times—*O'Brien* v. *The Tribune Publishing Co., Fite* v. *Anderson, Carey* v. *Hume,* and *Shelton* v. *Anderson.*[3] Anderson, however, has been a plaintiff in two additional actions—*Reporters Committee for Freedom of the Press* v. *American Telephone & Telegraph Co.* and *Anderson* v. *Nixon.*

Anderson, without doubt, is more careful with his facts than was his predecessor. This conclusion is based primarily on the fact that, in nearly all instances, Anderson and his associates verify information with the person about whom they are writing. Pearson did not do this; rather than risk losing an exclusive story, he published without extensive efforts toward verification. Pearson's subjects were often "surprised" to see facts about them in print. Anderson, on the other hand, instructs his reporters to obtain responses from subjects of the column. He also insists that his reporters use the "best thing" subjects say on their own behalf. Ironically, however, he does not have his attorney check each column before distribution, even though Anderson admittedly does not understand libel law as well as Pearson did.

There is still another reason why suits against the "Merry-Go-Round" have decreased. It cannot be too strongly emphasized that Pearson, a pioneer in Washington-based investigative reporting, would not likely have been sued so frequently during the current decade. There was so little muckraking practiced during the first twenty years of the "Merry-Go-Round's" existence that Pearson was a prime libel target. Few, if any, other reporters during this period seriously considered printing the controversial material the muckraker regularly produced. During the current decade, conversely, with the burgeoning number of investigative reporters, seldom is one columnist the recipient of such collective disfavor among powerful public persons.

Pearson was bolder than his contemporaries and likely more brazen than Anderson when discussing particularly volatile items. The senior muckraker at times enjoyed "baiting" an individual—almost appearing to "dare" the person to sue. According to his close friends, the columnist relished the feeling of verbal or legal combat with a person on whom he had gathered a great deal of damaging information.

Though Pearson had to operate within a more stringent legal atmosphere during most of his writing career, Anderson and his associates have witnessed, since the mid-1970s, a reverse pendulum swing in regard to press protection. During the first five years Anderson headed the column, the liberal ramifications of *Curtis Publishing Co.* v. *Butts, Time, Inc.* v. *Hill,* and *Rosenbloom* v. *Metromedia, Inc.,* had hoisted the press to its most protected position ever in regard to defamation suits.

Since *Gertz* v. *Robert Welch, Inc.,* in 1974, however, it is conceivable that the apparent contraction in press freedom could make the "Merry-Go-Round" a more attractive target for future actions. Though the effects of the far-reaching decision are not yet clear (states are still groping their way in implementing it), it can be concluded that press freedom has been dampened. Journalists—particularly muckraking columnists who consistently deal with controversial stories—have less constitutional protection from libel actions than they did between 1971 and 1974. The fact remains, however, that writers of the column lost only one libel suit before 1964. Thus, one could hardly conclude that *Sullivan* was a legal savior for "Merry-Go-Round" muckraking writers.

Effects of the Column on Evolving Libel Law

The question of the effects of suits involving "Merry-Go-Round" writers on the evolving law of libel is also challenging. It is not, of course, easy to assess the impact of one man or syndicated column on the perpetually developing American libel law, but it can logically be concluded that "Merry-Go-Round" writers have made their presence felt. Former Supreme Court Justice Arthur J. Goldberg, a member of the Court when the landmark *Sullivan* decision was handed down, emphasized that, though it is "always difficult to say what public events or occurrences influence the Supreme Court," he had "no doubt" that the "strong position taken by Drew Pearson and other courageous journalists in asserting their First Amendment rights was a factor" in the Court's decision to further safeguard the American free press.[4] William P. Rogers, a recognized authority on American libel law who argued *New York Times Co.* v. *Sullivan* and *Associated Press* v. *Walker* before the U.S. Supreme Court, believes that Pearson's style of journalism and his tenacity when defending against libel actions may have contributed as a backdrop for the liberal *Sullivan* decision. Rogers has pointed out that, since Pearson was able to successfully defend against most libel actions before the *New York Times* "actual malice" decision, he "certainly made it a lot safer for other journalists."[5]

Despite the threat of heavy damage suits, Pearson often challenged the country's most powerful persons almost single-handedly. The prestige of his target—whether it was a military hero such as General MacArthur, a U.S. senator such as McCarthy, or a man of the cloth such as Father Coughlin—

was no consideration. The columnist's stepson, attorney Tyler Abell, has contended that Pearson's perseverance in defending against libel actions during the 1940s and 1950s—unparalleled by any other American journalist—served as an example to other reporters. Abell has speculated that, had it not been for the muckraker's willingness and ability to fight—and win—in the courts, newspapers might have become totally dominated by attorneys who routinely instructed editors and reporters to refrain from printing any material even remotely offensive. Pearson—even during the years of lesser legal protection—always had the courage to print his conclusions, apparently without any great fear of libel actions.

Though "Merry-Go-Round" writers have had little difficulty—at least in the eyes of the courts—living within the never-static libel law, many cases in which they were involved have contributed to the development of this American legal phenomenon. The first action in which Pearson was named as a defendant, *MacArthur* v. *Pearson,* was heralded by the national press as providing the case to establish what was legally privileged when reporting on the activities of public persons. This determination, however, never materialized; like so many actions brought against writers of the column, it was dropped.

Some five years later, however, in 1939, one of the most pervasive libel suits in this country's legal history was filed by Ohio right-wing congressman Sweeney against Pearson, Allen, and individual newspapers carrying an allegedly libelous column. This chain libel suit had an appreciable effect on the development of American libel law. Newspaper editors were alerted to the possibility of massive suits that would span jurisdictions across the country; the inconsistencies in the rules of privilege followed by various jurisdictions became glaring; and, most important, the U.S. Supreme Court, for the first time in its history, confronted the possibility of constitutional limitations upon the power to award damages for libel of a public official.

The case in which the U.S. Supreme Court considered this all-important question, *Sweeney* v. *Schenectady Union Pub-*

lishing Co., was one of the few actions filed by the Ohio congressman that was not dismissed in its early stages. The Second Circuit court reasoned that, since Pearson had allegedly accused Sweeney of "anti-Semitism" in newspapers published in New York, where Jews made up a sizable portion of the population, the words were libelous per se and the column should be required to face trial. Historically, however, Justice Charles Clark's dissent provided the basis for the High Court to accept *certiorari.* Clark reasoned that there should be no libel against public officials unless statements were both false and unfair, and unless the aggrieved official proved special damages. He argued, in effect, that the press should have more latitude in discussing a public official than in reporting on a nonpublic person.

The nation's press followed developments in the case. The U.S. Supreme Court was, however, unable to deliver a decision that conceivably could have provided the American press with the equivalent of constitutional privilege some twenty-two years before the Court finally took the bold step in *Sullivan.* The eight justices participating split their vote, Justice Robert Jackson taking no part; the lower court decision, therefore, stood. American libel law could have been dramatically altered had the Court mustered one additional vote to reverse. This case was recognized in *Sullivan* as providing the only previous opportunity for the Court to consider the possibility of constitutional limitations upon the power to award damages for libel of public officials.

One other chain libel case, *Sweeney* v. *Patterson*, was also cited in *Sullivan* as recognizing that "erroneous statements are inevitable in free debate" and thus deserving of protection. In *Patterson*—an action brought in the District of Columbia against Eleanor Patterson, publisher of the *Washington Times-Herald*, Pearson, and Allen—the circuit court held that it was not actionable to publish erroneous and injurious statements regarding political conduct and views of public officials so long as no charge of crime, corruption, or gross immorality was made. This relatively liberal rule was made applicable to the District of Columbia; it extended protection to "Merry-Go-Round" writers in suits brought by public officials during the common law years.

Thus, through perpetual involvement of "Merry-Go-Round" columnists, primarily Pearson, in libel suits during the common law years, the need for the proper balancing between a free, aggressive press and the equally important interest in providing safeguards for wrongful injury by defamation became a legal issue that could not be ignored. In addition, though Pearson's attorneys during the pre-1964 years did not openly advocate that a constitutional privilege be extended to journalists when discussing public officials, the Sweeney chain libel suit played an important part in the judicial recognition of the nonuniform common law applications across the country. Also, two of the Sweeney decisions were later cited in *Sullivan* as primary examples of early cases that brought to the forefront questions that were answered in the landmark 1964 decision.

"Merry-Go-Round" writers, primarily Pearson, were also involved in at least three post-1964 decisions that further amplified the *Sullivan* "actual malice" rule. In the first case, *Clark* v. *Pearson*, Pearson's lawyer, Donovan, listed four defenses; the one that received considerable attention by the federal court for the District of Columbia, however, was the attorney's contention that the *Times* rule should be extended to include writings that involved public figures and touched on matters of public interest. Though the district court refused to accommodate the request, the *Clark* case was one of the earliest post-*Sullivan* actions in which defense attorneys asked for an extension of the "actual malice" rule.

A District of Columbia circuit court ruling in 1966 extended increased protection against libel judgments to newspapers that published syndicated columns. In *The Washington Post Co.* v. *Keogh,* an action filed by New York congressman Eugene Keogh against Pearson, Anderson, and the Washington Post Company, the court ruled that newspapers could not be held legally responsible for writings about public officials by syndicated columnists unless the editors had reason to believe the facts in the column were false. Though the U.S. Supreme Court denied *certiorari,* the decision has provided a guiding principle to other courts.

The "actual malice" rule was further extended in a third post-1964 libel case, *Monitor Patriot Co.* v. *Roy*, a suit brought against a New Hampshire newspaper that published a "Merry-Go-Round" column in which Pearson was critical of Alphonse Roy, a candidate for the U.S. Senate in his party's 1960 primary election. The Court ruled that facts about a political candidate's early life—no matter how remote—were relevant to the discussion of public affairs and thus deserving of constitutional protection.

As emphasized earlier, it is difficult to evaluate the effects of one column on the developing American libel law. "Merry-Go-Round" writers, particularly Pearson, however, have undoubtedly had an appreciable effect. During the past half century, writers of the column have compiled an amazing litigation odyssey. The more than one hundred court cases that have involved the writers—either as defendants or plaintiffs—are likely unmatched by any other American syndicated column. Most of the "Merry-Go-Round" suits have been more than small, local feuds; they have a certain historical significance because of the national attention gained. The adversaries were often familiar names—congressmen, army chiefs of staff, state officials, gubernatorial candidates, and lobbyists. These powerful figures, however, had one thing in common: they were not particularly successful in their actions against "Merry-Go-Round" writers. During the past five decades, litigation involving the column's writers has helped entrench in the public mind the role of a free press. If nothing else, the sheer volume of litigation, and aggregate dollars running into millions, emphasize the active role of the columnists in libel encounters.

Pearson and Anderson have indeed operated successfully within the perpetually changing American libel law; their unceasing battle, however, has not been free from worry, apprehension, and legal fees. When defending against libel actions, the muckrakers have not merely cited common law defenses or majestically pointed to the *Times* "actual malice" rule. Much more has been required. Law books succinctly list defenses against libel actions; they don't emphasize the time, money, and energy necessary to successfully utilize them.

The columnists have repeatedly offended—sometimes carelessly—the country's most powerful persons and exposed wrongdoing in high places; their impact has been poignant and pervasive. Like the impact of prominent turn-of-the-century muckrakers, Pearson's and Anderson's influence has not been a localized phenomenon. Nearly one thousand newspapers subscribe to the column; it reaches approximately fifty million readers daily. This huge readership has likely been a factor in the extreme number of libel actions filed against the columnists; it has also amplified the muckrakers' contribution to American press freedom. Disgruntled subjects of the column have often sought satisfaction through the American judicial system. Pearson's and Anderson's successful tenacity in defending against the suits has likely helped instill a similar desire in other journalists and made an imprint on those justices who are called upon to define the proper relationship between the need for a vigorous, uninhibited press and the legitimate interest in redressing wrongful injury by defamation. Without doubt, the successful record of "Merry-Go-Round" writers during the past half century in defending press freedom through court involvement is a saga unmatched by any other American syndicated columnists.

Appendix

List of Suits Filed

by

Martin L. Sweeney

(as compiled by Pearson's office in 1942)

State	Newspaper Sued	Damages Sought
Arizona:		
	Prescott Courier	$250,000
	Tucson Publishing Co.	250,000
	Douglas Daily Dispatch	250,000
Arkansas:		
	Little Rock Gazette	$ 25,000
	Pine Bluff Commercial	25,000
District of Columbia:		
	Washington Times-Herald	$250,000
	Pearson and Allen	250,000
Florida:		
	Jacksonville Times-Union	$250,000
Idaho:		
	Boise Capital News	*
Illinois:		
	Joliet Herald News	$250,000
	Dixon Evening Telegram	250,000
	Chicago American	250,000

State	Newspaper Sued	Damages Sought
Kansas:		
	Atchison Globe	$ 50,000
	Concordia Blade-Empire	50,000
	El Dorado Times	50,000
	Garden City Telegram	50,000
	Great Bend Tribune	50,000
	Hutchinson Herald	50,000
	Ottawa Herald	50,000
	Junction City Daily Union	50,000
	Topeka State Journal	50,000
	Winfield Daily Courier	50,000
Massachusetts:		
	Chelsea Evening Record	$250,000
	Greenfield Recorder	50,000
	Holyoke Transcript-Telegram	50,000
	Quincy Patriot-Ledger	50,000
	Worcester Telegram	*
	Gardner News	*
Missouri:		
	Joplin Globe	*
	Springfield Newspapers, Inc.	$ 50,000
New York:		
	Buffalo Courier-Express	$250,000
	Jamestown Post	250,000
	Schenectady Union	*
	United Feature Syndicate	*
Ohio:		
	Beacon Journal (Akron)	$250,000
	Ashtabula Printing Co.	250,000
	Coshocton Tribune	250,000
	Dayton Evening News	250,000
	Dover, The Tuscarawas Publishing Co.	250,000
	Elyria Chronicle-Telegram	*
	Hamilton Journal-News	*
	Ironton News	250,000
	Uhrichsville Chronicle	250,000
	Columbus Dispatch	*
Panama:		
	Panama American Publishing Co. (Ancon)	*

State	Newspaper Sued	Damages Sought
Pennsylvania:		
	Allentown Chronicle & News	*
	Philadelphia Record	$250,000
	Philipsburg Daily Journal	50,000
	Pittsburgh Press	*
	Ridgeway Publishing Co.	100,000
	Schuykill Reporter	50,000
	Lock Haven Express	250,000
	Jersey Shore Herald	25,000
South Carolina:		
	Greenwood Index-Journal	$250,000
Tennessee:		
	Chattanooga Free Press	$250,000
Texas:		
	Corpus Christi Caller-Times	$250,000
Virginia:		
	Bristol Publishing Co.	$ 25,000
	Fredericksburg Free Lance Star	35,000
	Martinsville Bulletin	25,000
	Newport News Daily Press	250,000
	Petersburg Newspaper Corp.	*
	Richmond News Leader	10,000
	Suffolk News Co.	250,000
Washington:		
	Seattle Times	*
West Virginia:		
	Charleston Gazette	$250,000
	Clarksburg Exponent	250,000
	Huntington Publishing Co.	250,000
Wisconsin:		
	Milwaukee Publishing Co.	$250,000

*No damages listed.

About the Notes

The notes that follow are based on legal methods of citation. Since so many of the book's notes refer to court cases, it was determined that references to general sources, such as books, magazines, newspapers, and scholarly journals, should also conform to this style. A word of explanation, then, may be in order. *New York Times Co.* v. *Sullivan*, 376 U.S. 254 (1964), means that the reported court decision can be found in volume 376 (on page 254) of the *United States Reports*, the official government reporter for cases decided by the U.S. Supreme Court; 1964 refers to the year in which the case was decided. Federal court of appeals decisions are found in the *Federal Reporter* system. *Carey* v. *Hume*, 492 F.2d 631 (D.C. Cir. 1974), means that the decision can be found in volume 492 (on page 631) of the second series of the *Federal Reporter*. The parenthetical (D.C. Cir. 1974) indicates that the case was decided by the Court of Appeals for the District of Columbia in 1974. *Howser* v. *Pearson*, 95 F. Supp. 936 (D.D.C. 1951), means that the decision can be found in the *Federal Supplement* (federal district court decisions). The volume number is 95, the page number is 936, and the date of decision by the U.S. District Court for the District of Columbia is 1951.

Many of the Drew Pearson cases discussed in this book were not officially reported in the volumes that appear on law library shelves; they are called unreported decisions. This does not mean that newspapers did not report the case, but merely that the decision was not chosen for inclusion in any of the official court reports that are published, bound, and distributed to libraries. Materials from the cases are, however, on file in the appropriate courthouses. For example, if one wanted to examine materials in the suit Pearson filed against Sen. Joseph McCarthy, the following would lead him to the information: *Pearson* v. *McCarthy*, Civil No. 51-897 (D.D.C., Feb. 15, 1956). This citation gives the name of the case, the civil action number, the court in which it was filed (Federal District Court for the District of Columbia), and the date the case was decided.

Articles in law reviews are cited by last name of author, title, volume and name of the review, page, and date: Donnelly, "The Law of Defamation: Proposals for Reform," 33 *Minn. L. Rev.* 632 (1949). Articles in general circulation publications are footnoted using the same system. Books are cited by first initial and last name of the author, title, page, and copyright date: B. Hume, *Inside Story* 7 (1974).

The use of *supra* is the equivalent of *op. cit.* under traditional citation methods. The word *at* is used in place of *p.* for page numbers. Hume, *supra* note 4, at 10, means that the information can be found on page 10 of Hume's book, cited in note number 4. Authors' full names and complete publication details of books and articles can be found in the bibliography.

Notes

1. The "Merry-Go-Round" and Its Men

1. Pearson, "Confessions of an 'S.O.B.' " 229 *Saturday Evening Post* 23 (Nov. 3, 1956).

2. In 1949 President Truman was speaking at the Army-Navy Country Club in honor of his military aide, Gen. Harry Vaughan, when the president publicly placed the "S.O.B." label on Pearson.

3. Pearson and Robert S. Allen launched the "Washington Merry-Go-Round" column in November of 1932.

4. Pearson, "Confessions of an 'S.O.B.,' " Part II: My Life in the White House Doghouse," 229 *Saturday Evening Post* 76 (Nov. 10, 1956).

5. "Judging the Fourth Estate: A *Time*–Louis Harris Poll," 94 *Time* 39 (Sept. 5, 1969).

6. "The Press," 94 *Time* 82 (Sept. 12, 1969).

7. "The Square Scourge of Washington," 99 *Time* 40 (April 3, 1972).

8. Harrison and Stein, "Muckraking: Present and Future," in *Muckraking: Past, Present and Future* 156, ed. J. Harrison and H. Stein (1973).

9. B. Hume, *Inside Story* 31 (1974).

10. O. Pilat, *Drew Pearson: An Unauthorized Biography* 39 (1973).

[11] " 'Merry-Go-Round' Moves," 44 *Time* 62 (Nov. 27, 1944).

[12] "Pearson Smears Again," 10 *National Review* 11 (Jan. 14, 1961).

[13] 90 Cong. Rec. 3683–88 (1944).

[14] "Querulous Quaker," 52 *Time* 71 (Dec. 13, 1948).

[15] 91 Cong. Rec. 2010–11 (1945).

[16] Washington Post, Sept. 2, 1969, at A-11, col. 2.

[17] New York Times, Sept. 2, 1969, at 44, col. 6.

[18] Alexander, "Pugnacious Pearson," 217 *Saturday Evening Post* 11 (Jan. 6, 1945).

[19] "Querulous Quaker," *supra* note 14, at 75.

[20] Interview with Mrs. Drew Pearson, in Washington, D.C., Jan. 13, 1977.

[21] New York Times, *supra* note 17.

[22] Telephone interview with Ernest Cuneo, Washington, D.C., writer, lawyer, Aug. 30, 1977.

[23] Alexander, *supra* note 18, at 66.

[24] Pearson first learned of the divorce when he noticed the headline in another man's newspaper while riding a State Department elevator. One daughter, Ellen Cameron, was born to the couple. Pilat, *supra* note 10, at 89–91.

[25] Pilat, *supra* note 10, at 80.

[26] Alexander, *supra* note 18, at 64.

[27] Washington Post, *supra* note 16, at A-11, col. 2. Pearson later stipulated in his will that Abell, an attorney, would be the executor of his estate, and would also edit the columnist's diaries. The first edition of his diaries, covering the years between 1949–59, was published in 1974. Abell is currently in the process of editing the second volume, which will cover the years between 1959 and 1964. Abell, before attending law school, worked as a reporter on the Pearson staff. Abell served in the Johnson administration as U.S. chief of protocol with the rank of ambassador and now practices law in Washington, D.C.

[28] "Querulous Quaker," *supra* note 14, at 75–76.

[29] "Cissie and Drew," 39 *Time* 68 (May 18, 1942).

[30] "Here Is My Prediction," 68 *Time* 80 (Nov. 26, 1956).

[31] Washington Post, *supra* note 16.

[32] Interview with William Neel, longtime Pearson staff member, in Washington, D.C., Jan. 10, 1977.

[33] Interview with George Vournas, attorney and longtime Pearson friend, in Washington, D.C., Jan. 18, 1977.

[34] Interview with Mrs. Drew Pearson, *supra* note 20.

[35] Interview with William Neel, *supra* note 32.

[36] Interview with Mrs. Drew Pearson, *supra* note 20, and William Neel, *supra* note 32.

[37] Interview with George Vournas, *supra* note 33.

[38] Interview with Tyler Abell, Pearson's stepson and Washington, D.C., attorney, in Washington, D.C., Jan. 11, 1977.

[39] Interview with Mrs. Drew Pearson, *supra* note 20.

[40] "Querulous Quaker," *supra* note 14, at 71.

[41] *Id.* at 70.

[42] C. Fisher, *The Columnists* 225–30 (1944).

[43] "*'Merry-Go-Round' Goes Round,*" 24 *Newsweek* 84 (Nov. 27, 1944).

[44] Anderson received the Pulitzer Prize in 1972 for national reporting of America's stance in the Indo-Pakistan War.

[45] Pilat, *supra* note 10, at 19.

[46] One of Pearson's most satisfying series of columns centered upon Khrushchev. Mrs. Pearson accompanied her husband on the trip, which came about because the Pearsons were going on a cruise with Mrs. Eugene Meyer of the *Washington Post,* who had chartered a boat in Norway. Pearson decided that perhaps he could go on to Russia and get an exclusive interview with Khrushchev. Though the columnist did not think the chances were particularly good that he would get to see the Soviet leader, he kept his hopes up. One day, when the Pearsons were going through a Leningrad museum, they received word that Khrushchev would receive the columnist in his cottage on the Black Sea. Both the columnist and his wife came away with warm regard for the Soviet leader. The talk ranged from politics to farming. Interview with Mrs. Drew Pearson, *supra* note 20.

[47] H. Klurfeld, *Behind the Lines: The World of Drew Pearson* 221 (1968).

[48] *Id.* at 147–54.

[49] "Querulous Quaker," *supra* note 14, at 75.

[50] Klurfeld, *supra* note 47, at 161.

[51] New York Times, May 28, 1948, at 26, col. 2.

[52] New York Times, Nov. 25, 1948, at 2, col. 3.

[53] New York Times, Feb. 24, 1949, at 1, col. 7.

[54] New York Times, Feb. 25, 1949, at 19, col. 1.

[55] Interview with William Neel, *supra* note 32.

[56] New York Times, Sept. 2, 1969, at 1, col. 6.

[57] Washington Post, Sept. 2, 1969, at 1, col. 4.

[58] New York Times, Sept. 5, 1969, at 37, col. 3.

[59] Washington Post, *supra* note 57, at col. 2.

[60] Sheehan, "The Anderson Strategy: 'We Hit You—Pow! Then You Issue a Denial, and Bam—We Really Let You Have It,'" *New York Times Magazine* at 79, cols. 1–2 (Aug. 13, 1972).

[61] C. Moritz, ed., *Current Biography* 10 (1972).

[62] Sheehan, *supra* note 60, at 79, cols. 2–3.

[63] *Id.* at 10, col. 3.

[64] *Id.* at 79, col. 3.

[65] *Id.* at 11, col. 1.

[66] Interview with Jack Anderson, in Washington, D.C., Jan. 12, 1977.

[67] Neary, "Jack Anderson, Improbable New Folk Hero of the Young," 72 *Life* 93 (April 21, 1972).

[68] New York Times, Jan. 6, 1972, at 17, col. 6.

[69] Hume, *supra* note 9, at 165–66.

[70] Neary, *supra* note 67, at 93.

[71] Sheehan, *supra* note 60, at 77, col. 2.

[72] Interview with Jack Anderson, *supra* note 66.

[73] C. Colson, *Born Again* 242 (1976).

[74] Interview with Jack Anderson, *supra* note 66.

2. The Muckraking "Merry-Go-Round" and Its World

[1] Complaint for Plaintiff at 3, Anderson v. Nixon, Civil No. 76-1794 (D.D.C., April 4, 1978).

[2] "A Muckraker with a Mission," 79 *Newsweek* 53 (April 3, 1972).

[3] "The Press," 94 *Time* 82 (Sept 12, 1969).

[4] B. Hume, *Inside Story* 7 (1974).

[5] Allen, "My Pal, Drew Pearson," 124 *Collier's* 14 (July 30, 1949).

[6] *Id.*

[7] C. Fisher, *The Columnists* 237–38 (1944).

[8] H. Klurfeld, *Behind the Lines: The World of Drew Pearson* 4 (1968).

[9] After Pearson and Allen completed work on their first book, they began considering titles for it. Possibilities included *On the Potomac* and *Under the Capitol Dome.* Allen said he had seen a British movie called *Carrousel.* Tom Smith, who edited the book, seized upon the idea and decided on *Washington Merry-Go-Round.* It was only natural that the column that followed would keep the name. O. Pilat, *Drew Pearson: An Unauthorized Biography* 116 (1973).

[10] Washington Post, Sept. 2, 1969, at 1, col. 2.

[11] Fisher, *supra* note 7, at 214.

12. *Id.* at 243.

13. T. Abell, ed., *Drew Pearson Diaries, 1949–1959* xiii (1974).

14. Warner, *"The Terrors of Washington,"* 103 *Collier's* 11 (April 22, 1939).

15. " 'Merry-Go-Round' Goes Round," 24 *Newsweek* 84 (Nov. 27, 1944).

16. "Querulous Quaker," 52 *Time* 70 (Dec. 13, 1948).

17. Warner, *supra* note 14, at 85.

18. Fisher, *supra* note 7, at 238, 240.

19. Warner, *supra* note 14, at 11.

20. Interview with George Vournas, attorney and longtime Pearson friend, in Washington, D.C., Jan. 18, 1977.

21. Warner, *supra* note 14, at 86.

22. Pilat, *supra* note 9, at 187.

23. "He Kept Them Honest," 74 *Newsweek* 65 (Sept. 15, 1969).

24. *Id.*

25. "Pearson's Hot Potato," 202 *Nation* 410 (April 11, 1966).

26. As quoted in "He Kept Them Honest," *supra* note 23, at 65.

27. Interview with Jack Anderson, in Washington, D.C., Jan. 12, 1977.

28. "The Square Scourge of Washington," 99 *Time* 40 (April 3, 1972).

29. Hume, *supra* note 4, at 8.

30. Pilat, *supra* note 9, at 4.

31. New York Times, Jan. 6, 1972, at 17, cols. 5–6.

32. 16 H. Hagedorn, ed., *The Works of Theodore Roosevelt* 415 (1926). Though President Roosevelt first publicly affixed the "muckraker" label on April 14, 1906, he had used the term earlier during an off-the-record informal speech at the Gridiron Club in Washington.

33. C. Regier, *The Era of the Muckrakers* 2 (1932).

34. F. Hudson, *Journalism in the United States, 1690–1872,* 642–43 (1873), as cited in W. Francke, "Investigative Exposure in the Nineteenth Century: The Journalistic Heritage of the Muckrakers," Ph.D. dissertation at 190, University of Minnesota, 1974. A nineteenth-century writer also pointed to the investigative articles of exposure during his era: "I imagine that the brilliant success of these attacks on the Tweed Ring has had something to do with the newspaper tendency which has developed so strongly in the last 25 years—that, namely, of finding something to expose." "Reminiscences of An Editor," 14 *Printer's Ink* 18 (Jan. 15, 1896).

35. Francke, *supra* note 34, at 358. *See* Francke's study for an excellent analysis of pre-twentieth-century investigative exposure.

[36.] Filler, "The Muckrakers and Middle America," in *Muckraking: Past, Present and Future* 29, ed. J. Harrison and H. Stein (1973).

[37.] J. Wood, *Magazines in the United States* (1956), as cited in McWilliams, "The Continuing Tradition of Reform Journalism," in *Muckraking: Past, Present and Future* 121, ed. J. Harrison and H. Stein (1973).

[38.] Stein, "The Muckraking Book in America, 1946–1973," 52 *Journalism Quarterly* 297 (Summer 1975).

[39.] Pearson also coauthored a fifth book in the 1930s, *The American Diplomatic Game* (1935), with Constantine Brown. It was essentially an account of America's foreign relations from 1928 to 1934.

[40.] *See* e.g., Stein, *supra* note 38, at 297–303, for a review of some of the most prominent post–World War II muckraking books.

[41.] *See* L. Downie, *The New Muckrakers* (1976) for an extensive report on the most prominent current-era muckrakers. *See also* J. Behrens, *The Typewriter Guerrillas* (1977).

[42.] Harrison and Stein, "Muckraking: Present and Future," in *Muckraking: Past, Present and Future* 159, ed J. Harrison and H. Stein (1973).

[43.] Stein and Harrison, "Muckraking Journalism in Twentieth-Century America," in *Muckraking: Past, Present and Future* 16, ed. J. Harrison and H. Stein (1973).

[44.] L. Filler, *Crusaders for American Liberalism* 12 (1950).

[45.] "Patriotism," 21 *McClure's* 336 (July 1903).

[46.] Hastings (Neb.) Daily Tribune, April 17, 1973, at 12, cols. 1–2.

[47.] Interview with F. Joseph Donohue, Pearson trial lawyer, in Washington, D.C., Jan. 19, 1977.

[48.] Washington Post, Sept. 2, 1969, at 13-D, col. 5.

[49.] New York Times, Sept. 2, 1969, at 46, cols. 1–2.

[50.] *Id.* at col. 2.

[51.] *Id.* at 44, col. 5.

[52.] As quoted in "The Tenacious Muckraker," 94 *Time* 82 (Sept. 12, 1969).

[53.] Pilat, *supra* note 9, at 19.

[54.] Washington Post, *supra* note 48, at cols. 6–7.

[55.] Pilat, *supra* note 9, at 22.

[56.] " 'Merry-Go-Round' Goes Round," 24 *Newsweek* 84 (Nov. 27, 1944).

[57.] *See,* e.g., "The Muckraker," 67 *Newsweek* 87 (June 27, 1966) for an account of Pearson's graphic report on Rep. Mendel Rivers's drinking habits.

58. Harrison and Stein, *supra* note 42, at 156.

59. "The Square Scourge of Washington," *supra* note 28, at 42.

60. "Jack Anderson—Biography," issued by his office in 1976, at 1–2.

61. *See,* e.g., Linsley, "Working for Jack Anderson," 111 *Editor & Publisher* 15 (Aug. 12, 1978).

62. Neary, "Jack Anderson, Improbable New Folk Hero of the Young," 72 *Life* 93 (April 21, 1972).

63. "Anderson's Brass Ring," 99 *Time* 34 (Jan. 17, 1972).

64. Hume, *supra* note 4, at 105.

65. *Id.* at 281.

66. "A Muckraker with a Mission," *supra* note 2, at 53.

67. Interview with Jack Anderson, *supra* note 27.

68. Jack Anderson, University of Nebraska–Lincoln Seminar; November 1972.

69. *Id.*

70. "The Square Scourge of Washington," *supra* note 28, at 44.

71. All of these books, with the exception of *The Kefauver Story* (which was primarily a laudatory political biography of Estes Kefauver of Tennessee, an aspirant for the Democratic Presidential nomination in 1956), could logically be placed in the "muckraking" category.

72. "Battle of the Billygoats," 56 *Time* 11 (Dec. 25, 1950).

73. *Id.*

74. "McCarthy v. Pearson," 36 *Newsweek* 21 (Dec. 25, 1950).

75. "Mayflower Punch," 59 *Time* 53 (June 30, 1952).

76. Interview with Warren Woods, Jack Anderson's attorney, in Washington, D.C., Jan. 14, 1977.

77. 96 Cong. Rec. 16634–41 (1951).

78. As quoted in Klurfeld, *supra* note 8, at 175.

79. New York Times, Dec. 25, 1950, at 31, col. 6.

80. As quoted in "McCarthy v. Pearson," *supra* note 74, at 21.

81. As quoted in "Mayflower Punch," *supra* note 75, at 53.

82. "The Price of Freedom," 53 *Time* 43 (June 6, 1949).

83. Pilat, *supra* note 9, at 212–13.

84. Abell, *supra* note 13, at 50, 51.

85. "Press Is Sharply Criticized for Attacks on Forrestal," 82 *Editor & Publisher* 4 (May 28, 1949).

86. Abell, *supra* note 13, at 53.

87. As quoted in "Columny," 33 *Newsweek* 50 (June 6, 1949).

88. Abell, *supra* note 13, at 51. *See* chapter 7 *infra* for details of the libel suits Pearson filed against Pegler.

89. "The Price of Freedom," *supra* note 82.

90. Abell, *supra* note 13, at 52.

91. Interview with Mrs. Drew Pearson, in Washington, D.C., Jan. 13, 1977.

92. Pilat, *supra* note 9, at 125–26.

93. Interview with Tyler Abell, Pearson's stepson and Washington, D.C., attorney, in Washington, D.C., Jan. 11, 1977.

94. "The Tenacious Muckraker," *supra* note 52.

95. As quoted in New York Times, Sept. 1, 1943, at 4, col. 2.

96. "V for Vituperation," 157 *Nation* 286 (Sept. 11, 1943).

97. "Chronic Liar," 42 *Time* 18–19 (Sept. 13, 1943).

98. "Whipping Boy," 27 *Newsweek* 34 (Jan. 21, 1946).

99. As quoted in "Who's Boss Around Here?" 53 *Time* 24 (March 7, 1949).

100. *Id.*

101. Washington Post, Feb. 23, 1949, at 1, col. 8.

102. New York Times, Feb. 23, 1949, at 1, cols. 6–7.

103. As quoted in New York Times, Feb. 25, 1949, at 19, col. 1.

104. St. Louis Post-Dispatch, Feb. 24, 1949, at B-2, col. 2.

105. Washington Post, Feb. 24, 1949, at 10, col. 1.

106. *Id.* at 1, col. 2.

107. Interview with William Neel, longtime Pearson staff member, in Washington, D.C., Jan. 10, 1977.

108. "H-Bomb Misfire," 63 *Time* 93–94 (April 12, 1954).

109. "Ten Simple Facts," 48 *Newsweek* 70 (Nov. 5, 1956).

110. "A Bipartisan Liar?" 47 *Newsweek* 78 (Feb. 6, 1956).

111. Pilat, *supra* note 9, at 228.

112. Interview with Tyler Abell, *supra* note 93.

113. Interview with Mrs. Drew Pearson, *supra* note 91.

114. Interview with Tyler Abell, *supra* note 93.

115. Interview with Mrs. Drew Pearson, *supra* note 91.

116. Interview with Tyler Abell, *supra* note 93.

117. J. Magruder, *An American Life* 205 (1975).

118. *Id.* at 206.

119. Anderson v. Nixon, *supra* note 1. *See* chapter 7 *infra* for details.

120. Washington Post, Nov. 19, 1975, at C-10, cols. 1–4.

121. Washington Post, Nov. 11, 1975, at B-26, col. 1.

122. "He Kept Them Honest," 74 *Newsweek* 65 (Sept. 15, 1969).

123. Sherrill, "Drew Pearson: An Interview," 209 *Nation* 15 (July 7, 1969).

124. New York Times, Sept. 2, 1969, at 44, col. 2.

125. Wall Street Journal, May 25, 1966, at 9, col. 2.

126. Interview with Jack Anderson, *supra* note 27.

127. Interview with Tyler Abell, *supra* note 93.

128. *See Carey* v. *Hume,* 492 F.2d 631 (D.C. Cir. 1974), *cert. denied,* 417 U.S. 938 (1974); *Fite* v. *Anderson,* Civil No. 70-405 (N.D., Ala., Apr. 19, 1971); *O'Brien* v. *The Tribune Publishing Co.,* Civil No. 4183 (W.D., Wash., May 12, 1972), *rev'd and remanded,* No. 72-2312 (9th Cir., Feb. 20, 1975); *Shelton* v. *Anderson,* Civil No. 77-0666 (D.D.C., Aug. 1, 1978) for cases in which Anderson has been involved as a defendant since 1969.

129. *See Anderson* v. *Nixon,* Civil No. 76-1794 (D.D.C., April 4, 1978); Reporters Committee v. AT&T, 4 Med. L. Rptr. 1177 (D.C. Cir., Aug. 11, 1978), *cert denied,* 4 Med. L. Rptr. 2536 (1979) for cases in which Anderson has been involved as a plaintiff since 1969.

130. Of the 126 suits, the columnists were plaintiffs in 15. Of the remaining 111, "Merry-Go-Round" writers were not formal defendants in all the actions, though each case evolved from a "Merry-Go-Round" column. For example, though Congressman Sweeney filed 68 actions against individual newspapers, Pearson was named a defendant in only one. However, whenever a suit evolved from one of his columns, Pearson lent whatever legal or financial assistance he could to the defendant newspaper. Thus, he was very much involved in all suits arising from his column—whether or not he was a formal defendant. *See* chapters 4–7 for details.

131. Pearson, "Confessions of an 'S.O.B.,' " 229 *Saturday Evening Post* 24 (Nov. 3, 1956).

132. Alexander, "Pugnacious Pearson," 217 *Saturday Evening Post* 10 (Jan. 6, 1945).

133. "Columnist and Kennedy," 74 *Newsweek* 75 (Aug. 25, 1969). Anderson took the course at George Washington University.

134. M. Beale, *Washington Squirrel Cage* 17 (1944).

135. Telephone interview with Ernest Cuneo, Washington, D.C., lawyer-writer, Aug. 30, 1977.

136. "The Muckraker," *supra* note 57 at 87.

137. "Hundreds of Washington Bylines Daily," 58 *Newsweek* 68 (Dec. 18, 1961).

138. *See* chapter 7 *infra* for details of cases in which "Merry-Go-Round" writers were plaintiffs.

139. The Pearson family, however, paid settlements to two plaintiffs after the columnist's death in order to expedite the closing of his estate.

140. Pearson, "Confessions of an 'S.O.B.,' Part IV: How To Make Enemies," 229 *Saturday Evening Post* 150 (Nov. 24, 1956).

141. H. Klurfeld, *supra* note 8, at 26.

[142]. Interview with William Neel, *supra* note 107.
[143]. Interview with George Vournas, *supra* note 20.
[144]. Interview with Tyler Abell, *supra* note 93.
[145]. Washington Post, Sept. 2, 1969, at A-8, col. 1.
[146]. Interview with Mrs. Drew Pearson, *supra* note 91.
[147]. Interview with George Vournas, *supra* note 20.
[148]. Interview with William Neel, *supra* note 107.
[149]. Interview with George Vournas, *supra* note 20.
[150]. Telephone interview with Ernest Cuneo, *supra* note 145.
[151]. "Querulous Quaker," *supra* note 16.
[152]. Letter from Drew Pearson to Joseph Tumulty, Washington, D.C., attorney, Oct. 19, 1940.
[153]. Telephone interview with William P. Rogers, attorney general in the Eisenhower administration and secretary of state in the Nixon administration, New York City, Sept. 9, 1977.
[154]. Interview with William Neel, *supra* note 107.
[155]. Interview with Tyler Abell, *supra* note 93.
[156]. Pearson v. Mayflower Washington, Civil No. 59-2652 (D.D.C., filed Sept. 24, 1959).
[157]. Interview with Tyler Abell, *supra* note 93.
[158]. Interview with F. Joseph Donohue, *supra* note 47.
[159]. Telephone interview with Ernest Cuneo, *supra* note 135.
[160]. Interview with Mrs. Drew Pearson, *supra* note 91.
[161]. W. Rivers, *The Opinion Makers* 115 (1965).
[162]. Wall Street Journal, *supra* note 125, at 1, col. 1.
[163]. *Id.* at 9, col. 2.
[164]. Interview with F. Joseph Donohue, *supra* note 47. Donohue was aware of Donovan's tactics because he served as Pearson's trial counsel on three occasions in the 1950s and 1960s.
[165]. Interview with Tyler Abell, *supra* note 93.
[166]. Interview with F. Joseph Donohue, *supra* note 47.
[167]. Memo from John Donovan to Drew Pearson, March 20, 1951.
[168]. Interview with F. Joseph Donohue, *supra* note 47.
[169]. Interview with William Neel, *supra* note 107.
[170]. Interview with Mrs. Drew Pearson, *supra* note 91.
[171]. Interview with F. Joseph Donohue, *supra* note 47.
[172]. 376 U.S. 254, 279–80 (1964).
[173]. *See* chapter 3 *infra* for the effects of *Sullivan* and its progeny, as well as the retrenchment of press protection under the libel laws that started with *Gertz* v. *Robert Welch,* 418 U.S. 323 (1974).
[174]. Interview with Jack Anderson, *supra* note 27.
[175]. *See* chapter 6 *infra* for details of *Pearson* v. *Dodd,* 410 F.2d 701 (D.C. Cir. 1969), *cert. denied,* 395 U.S. 947 (1969).

3. The "Merry-Go-Round" and Its Libel Law Boundaries

[1] W. Prosser, *Handbook of the Law of Torts* 737 (4th ed. 1971).

[2] 376 U.S. 254, 279–80 (1964). Though, to some degree, American newspapers have always claimed the right to criticize government and public officials, it was really not until the Alien and Sedition Acts of 1798 expired when the Jefferson administration took office at the turn of the nineteenth century that American editors had a relative immunity to do so. *See* e.g., L. Levy, *Legacy of Suppression: Freedom of Speech and Press in Early American History* (1960).

[3] *See* C. Lawhorne, *Defamation and Public Officials* (1971) for an analysis of the perpetually evolving American libel law.

[4] R. Phelps and E. Hamilton, *Libel: Rights, Risks, Responsibilities* 1 (1966).

[5] *Id.* at 3.

[6] *Id.* at 4–5.

[7] Prosser, *supra* note 1, at 739.

[8] Whitby v. Associates Discount Corp., 59 Ill. App. 2d 337, 340–41 (1965).

[9] Prosser, *supra* note 1, at 739.

[10] A. Hanson, *Libel and Related Torts* 21–22 (Vol. 1 1969).

[11] Kimmerle v. New York Evening Journal, 186 N.E. 217, 218 (1933).

[12] Phelps and Hamilton, *supra* note 4, at 12.

[13] H. Black, *Black's Law Dictionary* 1060 (4th ed. 1968).

[14] *Id.* at 1062.

[15] 418 U.S. 323 (1974).

[16] Hanson, *supra* note 10, at 23.

[17] Black, *supra* note 13, at 1062.

[18] Lawhorne, *supra* note 3, at 126.

[19] Phelps and Hamilton, *supra* note 4, at 12.

[20] Prosser, *supra* note 1, at 773, as quoted in Brosnahan, "From *Times* v. *Sullivan* to *Gertz* v. *Welch:* Ten Years of Balancing Libel Law and the First Amendment," 26 *Hast. L.J.* 777, 778–79 (1975).

[21] H. Nelson and D. Teeter, *Law of Mass Communications* 139 (2d ed. 1973).

[22] Phelps and Hamilton, *supra* note 4 at 100–1.

[23] Nelson and Teeter, *supra* note 21, at 100.

[24] *See* Prosser, *supra* note 1; Phelps and Hamilton, *supra* note 4; Nelson and Teeter, *supra* note 21; Gillmor and Barron, *infra*

note 26; and D. Pember, *Mass Media Law* (1977) for extensive discussions of statutory and common law libel defenses.

25. Prosser, *supra* note 1, at 792.

26. D. Gillmor and J. Barron, *Mass Communication Law: Cases and Comment* 280–84 (2d ed. 1974).

27. *Id.* at 190 92.

28. A. Kelly and W. Harbison, *The American Constitution* 1036 (4th ed. 1970).

29. T. Emerson, *The System of Freedom of Expression* 519 (1970).

30. 283 U.S. 697, 715 (1931).

31. 315 U.S. 568, 571–72 (1942), as cited in Emerson, *supra* note 29, at 520.

32. Lawhorne, *supra* note 3, at xiii.

33. 59 Fed. 530 (6th Cir. 1893).

34. 98 Pac. 281 (Kan. 1908). *See* Lawhorne, *supra* note 3, at 122–27 for a good discussion of the effects of *Hallam* and *MacLennan* on various state definitions of privilege.

35. Post Publishing Co. v. Hallam, 59 Fed. at 540.

36. *Id.* at 540 41.

37. Coleman v. MacLennan, 98 Pac. at 281–82.

38. *Id.* at 285.

39. Lawhorne, *supra* note 3, at 127.

40. State jurisdictions accepting this rule were Alabama, Arkansas, Florida, Illinois, Kentucky, Louisiana, Maine, Maryland, Massachusetts, Mississippi, New Jersey, New York, North Dakota, Ohio, Oregon, South Carolina, Tennessee, Vermont, Virginia, Washington, and Wisconsin. *See* Lawhorne, *supra* note 3, at 128–42.

41. State jurisdictions accepting this doctrine were Arizona, California, Colorado, Connecticut, Iowa, Kansas, Michigan, Minnesota, Montana, Nebraska, New Hampshire, North Carolina, Pennsylvania, South Dakota, Utah, and West Virginia. *See* Lawhorne, *supra* note 3, at 152–65.

42. State jurisdictions in this category were Idaho, Nevada, New Mexico, and Rhode Island. *See* Lawhorne, *supra* note 3, at 165–66.

43. Jurisdictions accepting some form of "middle ground" doctrine were Delaware, the District of Columbia, Georgia, Indiana, Missouri, Oklahoma, Texas, and Wyoming. *See* Lawhorne, *supra* note 3, at 142–52. This relatively liberal rule proved to be an advantage to the "Merry-Go-Round" since many of the suits filed against its writers were in the U.S. District Court for the District of Columbia.

44. *Id.* at 190.

45. *Id.* at 194.

46. *See* chapter 4 *infra* for a comprehensive account of treatments given the Sweeney cases in various jurisdictions.

47. *See* Noel, "Defamation of Public Officers and Candidates," 49 *Colum. L. Rev.* 903 (1949).

48. *See* Riesman, "Democracy and Defamation: Fair Game and Fair Comment, Part II," 42 *Colum. L. Rev.* 1285 (1942).

49. *Id.* at 1282.

50. *Id.* at 1284 85.

51. Donnelly, "The Law of Defamation: Proposals for Reform," 33 *Minn. L. Rev.* 632 (1949).

52. Donnelly, "The Right of Reply: An Alternative to an Action for Libel," 34 *Va. L. Rev.* 870 (1948).

53. 343 U.S. 250 (1952).

54. *Id.* at 263–64.

55. 360 U.S. 564 (1959).

56. *Id.* at 571.

57. R. McCloskey, *The American Supreme Court* 227 (1960).

58. New York Times Co. v. Sullivan, 376 U.S. at 256–57.

59. *Id.* at 257–58.

60. *Id.* at 258.

61. *Id.* at 256. Eleven other suits filed against the *Times* were pending when the *Sullivan* decision was handed down; they sought damages totaling $5,600,000. In a concurring opinion, Justice Black made note of the excessive monetary amounts: "Moreover, this technique for harassing and punishing a free press—now that it has been shown to be possible—is by no means limited to cases with racial overtones; it can be used in other fields where public feelings may make local as well as out-of-state newspapers easy prey for libel verdict seekers." *Id.* at 295 (Black, J., concurring). Black also said that state libel laws, such as those in Alabama, "threaten the very existence of an American press virile enough to publish unpopular views on public affairs and bold enough to criticize the conduct of public officials." *Id.* at 294 (Black, J., concurring).

62. *Id.* at 279–80.

63. *Id.* at 280.

64. P. Kurland, ed., *The Supreme Court Review* 193–94 (1964).

65. *Id.* at 209.

66. New York Times Co. v. Sullivan, 376 U.S. at 282–83.

67. *Id.* at 283.

68. Garrison v. Louisiana, 379 U.S. 64 (1964).

69. *Id.* at 65–66.

70. *Id.* at 67.

71. *Id.* at 77.

72. 98 Pac. 281, 291 (1908), as quoted *id.* at 77.

73. The Court, however, in 1965, in a per curiam opinion, reversed a lower court decision in which a man was held liable for stating that his arrest for disturbing the peace was "the result of a diabolical plot" in which the county attorney and chief of police were involved. The Court said that, under the circumstances, the "actual malice" standard was applicable, thus permitting recovery by public officials (which the county attorney and chief of police clearly were) only upon proof that a false statement was made "with knowledge that it was false or with reckless disregard of whether it was false or not." *Henry* v. *Collins,* 380 U.S. 356 (1965).

74. 383 U.S. 75 (1966).

75. *Id.* at 94.

76. *Id.* at 85.

77. *Id.* at 87.

78. Time, Inc. v. Hill, 385 U.S. 374 (1967).

79. Notes, "*New York Times* Rule—the Awakening Giant of First Amendment Protections," 62 *Kentucky L.J.* 832 (1973–74).

80. Time, Inc. v. Hill, 385 U.S. at 374.

81. *Id.* at 388.

82. The lower courts, in the immediate years after *Sullivan,* applied the "actual malice" rule in a number of cases. For example, in *Washington Post Co.* v. *Keogh,* 365 F.2d 965 (D.C. Cir. 1966), the circuit court made it clear that false statements made with hostility, vindictiveness, or negligent disregard for reputations were not actionable by public officials, and, no matter how gross the untruth, a defamed public official had no hope of legal redress without proving actual malice. *See* chapter 6 *infra* for details. In another lower court ruling, *Piracci* v. *The Hearst Corp.,* 263 F. Supp. 511 (D. Md. 1966), the court held that a newspaper article that gave the name of a minor and said that he had been arrested and charged with possession of marijuana was substantially accurate and hardly "wanton and reckless." Also, the alleged longstanding policy of the newspaper against publishing names of juveniles under police investigation did not justify an inference of "actual malice" when the newspaper printed an article about this particular minor.

83. 388 U.S. 130 (1967).

84. *Id.* at 134.

85. *Id.* at 138.

86. *Id.* at 140–41.

87. *Id.* at 146.

88. *Id.* at 154.
89. *Id.* at 155.
90. *Id.* at 157.
91. *Id.* at 158–59.
92. *Id.* at 164. (Warren, C.J., concurring.)
93. Beckley Newspapers Corp. v. Hanks, 389 U.S. 81 (1967).
94. *Id.* at 84.
95. Garrison v. Louisiana, 379 U.S. at 74.
96. Curtis Publishing Co. v. Butts, 388 U. S. at 153.
97. 390 U.S. 727 (1968).
98. *Id.* at 731.
99. *Id.* at 728–29.
100. *Id.* at 731.
101. *See* Comments, "Constitutional Law: Defamation of Private Individuals," 14 *Washburn L.J.* 646 (Fall 1975).
102. 398 U.S. 6 (1970).
103. 401 U.S. 265 (1971).
104. 401 U.S. 295 (1971).
105. 401 U.S. 279 (1971).
106. Greenbelt Cooperative Publishing Assn. v. Bresler, 398 U.S. at 7–8.
107. *Id.* at 11.
108. *Id.* at 13.
109. *Id.* at 14.
110. Monitor Patriot Co. v. Roy, 401 U.S. at 277. *See* chapter 6 *infra* for details.
111. *Id.* at 266.
112. *Id.* at 273.
113. Ocala Star-Banner Co. v. Damron, 401 U.S. at 295–96.
114. *Id.* at 298.
115. *Id.* at 299.
116. *Id.* at 300–1.
117. 365 U.S. 167 (1961).
118. Time, Inc. v. Pape, 401 U.S. at 279.
119. *Id.* at 290.
120. *Id.*
121. 403 U.S. 29 (1971).
122. *Id.* at 44.
123. 403 U.S. at 31–32.
124. *Id.* at 33.
125. *Id.* at 34–35.
126. *Id.* at 36.
127. *Id.* at 40.
128. *Id.* at 43–44.

[129]. *Id.* at 57.
[130]. Gertz v. Robert Welch, Inc., 418 U.S. 323 (1974).
[131]. Rosenbloom v. Metromedia, Inc., 403 U.S. at 63.
[132]. *Id.* at 64 (Harlan, J., dissenting).
[133]. *Id.* at 79 (Marshall, J., dissenting).
[134]. *Id.* at 84 (Marshall, J., dissenting).
[135]. Giampietro, "The Constitutional Rules of Defamation, Or It's Libel but Is He Liable?" 64 *Illinois B.J.* 10, 12 (September 1975). Wayne Giampietro was Gertz's lawyer.
[136]. Comments, "The Law of Libel—Constitutional Privilege and the Private Individual: Round Two," 12 *San Diego L. Rev.* 464 (March 1975).
[137]. 418 U.S. 323 (1974).
[138]. *Id.* at 325–26.
[139]. *Id.* at 329–32.
[140]. *Id.* at 343.
[141]. *Id.* at 345.
[142]. *Id.* at 351–52.
[143]. *Id.* at 345.
[144]. *Id.* at 349.
[145]. *Id.* at 354 (Blackmun, J., concurring).
[146]. *Id.* at 361–62 (Brennan, J., dissenting).
[147]. Time, Inc. v. Hill, 385 U.S. at 388, as quoted *Id.* at 362.
[148]. Brosnahan, *supra* note 20, at 778.
[149]. Notes, "Constitutional Law—Reformulation of the Constitutional Privilege to Defame," 24 *Kansas L. Rev.* 416 (Winter 1976).
[150]. Cases Noted, "Libel: A Two-Tiered Constitutional Standard," 29 *Miami L. Rev.* 369 (Winter 1975).
[151]. Comments, *supra* note 136, at 473–74.
[152]. Giampietro, *supra* note 135, at 15.
[153]. *Id.*
[154]. 424 U.S. 448 (1976).
[155]. *Id.* at 463–64.
[156]. Gertz v. Robert Welch, Inc., 418 U.S. at 345.
[157]. Time, Inc. v. Firestone, 424 U.S. at 453.
[158]. *Id.* at 457.
[159]. Herbert v. Lando, 4 Med.L.Rptr. 2575 (April 18, 1979).
[160]. Herbert v. Lando, 3 Med.L.Rptr. 1241, 1249 (2d Cir., Nov. 7, 1977).
[161]. Herbert v. Lando, *supra* note 159, at 2582.
[162]. *Id.* at 2584.
[163]. Notes, *"Gertz* v. *Robert Welch, Inc.:* Defamation and Freedom of the Press—the Struggle Continues," 28 *Sw. L.J.* 1050 (Winter 1974)

[164]. Anderson, "Libel and Press Self-Censorship," 53 *Texas L. Rev*. 423–24 (March 1975).

[165]. *Id.* at 458.

[166]. Brosnahan, *supra* note 20, at 796.

[167]. Stonecipher and Trager, "The Impact of *Gertz:* How the States Have Defined the Standard of Liability for the Private Libel Plaintiff" (paper presented before the Association for Education in Journalism, University of Maryland, College Park, 1976), 18–19.

[168]. Stonecipher and Trager, "The Impact of *Gertz* on the Law of Libel," 53 *Journalism Quarterly* 617 (Winter 1976). This article combines the primary observations from two unpublished papers that were presented at the annual convention of the Association for Education in Journalism, University of Maryland, College Park, in August 1976: Stonecipher and Trager, *supra* note 167, and Trager and Stonecipher, *"Gertz* and *Firestone:* How Courts Have Construed the 'Public Figure' Criteria."

[169]. Trager and Stonecipher, *id.* at 20.

[170]. Stonecipher and Trager, *supra* note 167, at 20.

[171]. Stonecipher and Trager, *supra* note 168, at 618.

[172]. Jacobellis v. Ohio, 378 U.S. 184, 197 (1964) (Stewart, J., concurring).

[173]. Phelps and Hamilton, *supra* note 4, at 368.

[174]. Id.

4. Initial Libel Challenges to the "Merry-Go-Round"—MacArthur and Sweeney

[1]. MacArthur v. Pearson (D.C. Sup. Ct. 1934), in New York Times, May 17, 1934, at 20, col. 4.

[2]. In July of 1932, some twenty thousand unarmed veterans encamped on the Anacostia Flats in Washington, D.C., in an effort to persuade Congress to vote them a bonus.

[3]. New York Times, *supra* note 1.

[4]. Pearson, "Confessions of an 'S.O.B.,' Part II: My Life in the White House Doghouse," 229 *Saturday Evening Post* 38 (Nov. 10, (1956).

[5]. "Gossip Columns: 'Tidbits' Raise General MacArthur's Ire," 3 *Newsweek* 22 (May 26, 1934).

[6]. *Id.*

[7]. "General MacArthur's Libel Suit against Newspaper and Authors of Syndicated Column May Draw Legal Line between What Washington News Is Privileged and What Is Not," 117 *Literary Digest* 112 (June 2, 1934).

[8] *Id.*

[9] Pearson had gained access to Helen Robinson, a former chorus girl in Singapore who was the daughter of a Chinese woman and a Scottish businessman living in Manila. Pearson biographer Oliver Pilat said the woman had a packet of letters that traced in detail her liaison with General MacArthur. The letters would have been extremely embarrassing to MacArthur. For example, one four-page letter from MacArthur pledged unlimited devotion so long as he lived and after his death. He would die, he reportedly declared, if she did not return to him. Fearing embarrassment, MacArthur withdrew the suit. Pearson and Allen returned the original to MacArthur but kept several copies of the letters as protection against any resumption of legal activities by the general. *See* O. Pilat, *Drew Pearson: An Unauthorized Biography* 141–146 (1973).

[10] *See* e.g., chapter 3 *supra* for details of the common law defenses.

[11] In the *Sullivan* case, 376 U.S. 254, 279–80 (1964), the Court held that a state cannot, under the First and Fourteenth Amendments, award damages to a public official for defamatory falsehoods relating to his official conduct unless he proves "actual malice"—that the statement was made with knowledge of its falsity or with reckless disregard of whether it was true or false. *See* chapter 3 *supra* for details.

[12] Donnelly, "The Law of Defamation: Proposals for Reform," 33 *Minn. L. Rev.* 626 (May 1949).

[13] The sixty-eight suit figure is based on a list compiled by Pearson's office in 1942. There were numerous other estimates; since the sixty-eight suit figure can be documented, however, it will be cited as authority for purposes of this book. Warren Woods, Washington, D.C., attorney who helped defend Pearson against some of the actions, recalled that there were 151 suits filed; Donnelly estimated sixty-eight, *supra* note 12, at 627; Pilat said "nearly 150" suits were filed, *supra* note 8 at 12; and David Riesman gave a range of between seventy-five to two hundred in "Democracy and Defamation: Fair Game and Fair Comment, Part II," 42 *Colum. L. Rev.* 1291 (1942). Neither Pearson nor Allen was listed as a formal defendant in most of the actions, but Pearson played an active role by advising newspapers during the course of the various cases. Suffice to say, however, the Sweeney action was one of the most pervasive libel suits in American legal history.

[14] Interview with Warren Woods, Jack Anderson's attorney, in Washington, D.C., Jan. 13, 1977.

[15.] Interview with Mrs. Drew Pearson, in Washington, D.C., Jan. 13, 1977.

[16.] Letter from Drew Pearson to Roy Anderson, editor of the *Ketchikan* (Alaska) *Chronicle,* Jan. 22, 1940.

[17.] *Id.*

[18.] *Id.*

[19.] As quoted in Sweeney v. Patterson, 128 F.2d 457, 458 (D.C. Cir. 1942), *cert. denied,* 317 U.S. 678 (1942).

[20.] There was considerable speculation on the matter in the press. For example, a 1942 article in the *Nation* stated that Pearson and Allen's allegations that Sweeney was Father Coughlin's spokesman and an anti-Semite "seem supported by substantial evidence." The authors said newspaper files revealed that Sweeney, as early as 1933, was extolling the priest as the "great crusader of the air." He also supposedly aided several Coughlin political efforts. It was further pointed out that Sweeney's congressional district had a significant Jewish vote, and so it was understandable that he filed suit. Chasan and Riesel, "Keep Them Out! Martin L. Sweeney of Ohio, Candidate for a Democratic Congressional Nomination," 154 *Nation* 627–28 (May 30, 1942). The label "anti-Semite" had been affixed to Father Coughlin prior to the "Merry-Go-Round" column. A *New Republic* article, for example, labeled the radio priest "the leading anti-Semite in America." Seldes, "Father Coughlin: Anti-Semite," 96 *New Republic* 353 (Nov. 2, 1938).

[21.] 84 Cong. Rec. 6163 (1939) (remarks of Representative Sweeney).

[22.] *Id.* at 6164.

[23.] *Id.*

[24.] *Id.*

[25.] *Id.*

[26.] The exception was Sweeney v. Schenectady Union Publishing Co., 122 F.2d 288 (2d Cir. 1941), *aff'd by an equally divided court,* 316 U.S. 642 (1942).

[27.] Sweeney v. United Feature Syndicate, Civil No. 2880 (D.D.C., April 11, 1941).

[28.] Complaint for Plaintiff at 1, Sweeney v. United Feature Syndicate, Civil No. 2880 (D.D.C., April 11, 1941).

[29.] Deposition of Ernest Cuneo, taken in U.S. District Court for the District of Columbia on Jan. 28, 1941; filed with the court on Feb. 14, 1941.

[30.] The firm appeared on behalf of Pearson and Allen in many of the chain libel cases, including: Sweeney v. Citizen Publishing Co., Civil No. 82, U.S. District Court for the District of Arizona; Sweeney v. Gazette Publishing Co., Civil No. LR-229, U.S. District

Court for the Eastern District of Arkansas, Western Division; Sweeney v. the Hutchinson Publishing Co., Civil No. 1876, U.S. District Court for the District of Kansas, Second Division; Sweeney v. Worcester Telegram Publishing Co., Inc., Civil No. 497, U.S. District Court for the District of Massachusetts; Sweeney v. Robie, Civil No. 488, U.S. District Court for the District of Massachusetts; Sweeney v. Buffalo Courier Express, Civil No. 335, U.S. District Court, Western District of New York; Sweeney v. Post Publishing Co., Civil No. 336, U.S. District Court for the Western District of New York; Sweeney v. the Tribune Co., Court of Common Pleas, Coshocton County, Ohio; Sweeney v. the Evening News Publishing Co., Civil No. 90279, Court of Common Pleas, Montgomery County, Ohio; Sweeney v. Chronicle and News Publishing Co., Civil No. 695, U.S. District Court for the Eastern District of Pennsylvania; Sweeney v. J.H. Zerbey Newspapers, Civil No. 676, U.S. District Court for the Eastern District of Pennsylvania; Sweeney v. Lock Haven Express Printing Co., Civil No. 368, U.S. District Court for the Middle District of Pennsylvania; Sweeney v. Jersey Shore Herald Publishing Co., Civil No. 367, U.S. District Court for the Middle District of Pennsylvania; Sweeney v. E.F. Bair, Civil No. 366, U.S. District Court for the Middle District of Pennsylvania; Sweeney v. Petersburg Newspaper Corp., Civil No. 65, U.S. District Court for the Eastern District of Virginia; Sweeney v. Milwaukee Publishing Co., Civil No. 212, U.S. District Court for the Eastern District of Wisconsin; Sweeney v. Daily Gazette Co., Civil No. 68, U.S. District Court for the Southern District of West Virginia; Sweeney v. Huntington Publishing Co., Civil No. 82, U.S. District Court for the Southern District of West Virginia; Sweeney v. Caller-Times Publishing Co., Civil No. 62, U.S. District Court for the Southern District of Texas; Sweeney v. Freeman, docketed in the U.S. District Court of the Eastern District of Arkansas, Western Division. Cuneo deposition, *id.* at 6–10.

31. Brief for Plaintiff at 1, Sweeney v. United Feature Syndicate, Civil No. 2880 (D.D.C., April 11, 1941).

32. *Id.* at 1.

33. *Id.* at 3.

34. *Id.* at 5.

35. Sweeney v. Milwaukee Publishing Co., Civil No. 212, U.S. District Court for the Eastern District of Wisconsin; Sweeney v. the Blade-Empire Publishing Co., Civil No. 4411, U.S. District of Kansas, First Division; Sweeney v. Gazette Publishing Co., Civil No. LR-229, U.S. District Court for the Eastern District of Arkansas, Western Division; Sweeney v. Citizens Publishing Co., Civil No. 82, U.S. District Court for the District of Arizona; Sweeney

v. Illinois Publishing and Printing Co., Civil No. 1201, U.S. District Court for the Northern District of Illinois, Eastern Division; Sweeney v. Joliet Printing Co., Civil No. 1204, U.S. District Court for the Northern District of Illinois, Eastern Division; Sweeney v. the Lorain County Printing and Publishing Co., Civil No. 41623, Lorain County (Ohio) Court of Common Pleas; Sweeney v. Clarksburg Publishing Co., Civil No. 81-C, U.S. District Court for the Northern District of West Virginia; and Sweeney v. United Feature Syndicate, Civil No. 4-119, U.S. District Court for the Southern District of New York. As cited *id.* at 5–6.

36. Brief for Plaintiff, *supra* note 31, at 8.

37. *Id.* at 9.

38. District court order, April 11, 1941.

39. Sweeney v. Patterson, 128 F.2d 457 (D.C. Cir. 1942), *cert. denied,* 317 U.S. 678 (1942).

40. *Id.* at 458.

41. *Id.*

42. *Id.*

43. Memo from Drew Pearson to attorneys and editors involved in the Sweeney action, May 27, 1942.

44. 376 U.S. at 271–72.

45. Sweeney v. Beacon Journal Publishing Co., 35 N.E.2d 471 (C.A. Ohio 1941).

46. *Id.* at 472.

47. *Id.* at 473.

48. *Id.*

49. Sweeney v. Caller-Times Publishing Co., 41 F. Supp. 163 (S.D. Tex. 1941).

50. "A libel is a defamation expressed in printing or writing, or by signs and pictures, or drawings tending to blacken the memory of the dead, or tending to injure reputation of one who is alive, and thereby expose him to public hatred, contempt or ridicule, or financial injury, or to impeach the honesty, integrity, or virtue or reputation of any one, or to publish the natural defects of any one and thereby expose such person to public hatred, ridicule, or financial injury." Art. 5430, Vernon's Civil Statutes of the State of Texas, as quoted *id.* at 166.

51. *Id.*

52. *Id.* at 167.

53. *See* note 26, *supra.*

54. Sweeney v. Caller-Times Publishing Co., 41 F. Supp. at 167.

55. *Id.*

56. *Id.* at 168.

57. *Id.* at 169.

58. 37 F. Supp. 355 (S.D. Idaho 1941).
59. *Id.* at 356.
60. *Id.*
61. *Id.* at 357.
62. Sweeney v. Newspaper Printing Corp., 147 S.W. 2d 406 (Tenn. 1941).
63. *Id.* at 407.
64. *Id.*
65. *Id.*
66. Sweeney v. Philadelphia Record Co., Sweeney v. Chronicle & News Publishing Co., Sweeney v. Steinman & Steinman, Inc., 126 F.2d 53 (3d Cir. 1942).
67. *Id.* at 54.
68. *Id.*
69. *Id.* at 55.
70. *Id.*
71. *Id.*
72. Sweeney v. Schenectady Union Publishing Co., 122 F.2d at 289. The case, however, was never tried. An order of discontinuance was issued by the district court on Feb. 5, 1943.
73. *Id.* at 291.
74. 304 U.S. 64 (1938).
75. Sweeney v. Schenectady Union Publishing Co., 122 F.2d at 289.
76. 186 N.E. 217, 218 (1933), as quoted *id.* at 290.
77. Sweeney v. Schenectady Union Publishing Co., 122 F.2d at 290.
78. *Id.* at 291.
79. *Id.* (Clark, J., dissenting).
80. *Id.*
81. *Id.* at 291–92.
82. Schenectady Union Publishing Co. v. Sweeney, 314 U.S. 605 (1942).
83. Notes, "Libel Actions Brought by Public Officials," 51 *Yale L.J.* 693 (1942).
84. Notes, "Libelous Publications Affecting Public Officials," 36 *Illinois L. Rev.* 793 (1942).
85. Gertz v. Robert Welch, Inc., 418 U.S. 323 (1974). *See* chapter 3 *supra* for details.
86. Notes, *supra* note 83, at 696–97.
87. *Id.* at 699.
88. 87 Cong. Rec. App. A3794 (1941) (remarks of Representative Sweeney).
89. *Id.*

90. *Id.*

91. *Id.*

92. As quoted in New York Times, March 1, 1942, at 24, col. 2.

93. *Id.*

94. *Id.*

95. New York Times, March 3, 1942, at 11, col. 5.

96. New York Times, March 10, 1942, at 14, col. 3.

97. New York Times, March 17, 1942, at 16, col. 6.

98. Letter from Jonathan Daniels, editor, *Raleigh* (North Carolina) *News and Observer,* to Drew Pearson, Nov. 4, 1941.

99. As quoted in New York Times, April 1, 1942, at 17, col. 3.

100. *Id.*

101. As cited in *Sullivan,* the *Schenectady* suit was "the only previous case that did present the question of constitutional limitations upon the power to award damages for libel of a public official." New York Times v. Sullivan, 376 U.S. at 268.

102. Schenectady Union Publishing Co. v. Sweeney, 316 U.S. 642 (1942).

103. New York Times, April 14, 1942, at 19, col. 1.

104. Preliminary draft, Pearson's thoughts on the importance of the Supreme Court's rehearing the *Schenectady Union Publishing Company* case.

105. 316 U.S. 710 (1942). *See also* New York Times, June 2, 1942, at 15, col. 4.

106. Letter from Paul L. Gross, general manager of the *Schenectady* (New York) *Union Star,* to Drew Pearson, May 20, 1942.

107. 129 F.2d 904 (2d Cir. 1942).

108. *Id.* at 906.

109. *Id.* at 907.

110. *Id.*

111. *Id.*

112. Letter from Drew Pearson to C.E. Palmer, editor of the *Hot Springs* (Arkansas) *Sentinel-Record,* Aug. 14, 1941.

113. Letter from Drew Pearson to A.M. Crawford, Prescott, Arizona, attorney, Nov. 23, 1942.

114. *Id.*

115. Letter from Drew Pearson to A.M. Crawford, Prescott, Arizona, attorney, Dec. 11, 1942.

116. Memo from Drew Pearson to editors and attorneys interested in the Sweeney case, Jan. 18, 1943.

117. *Id.*

118. *Id.*

119. A reasonably accurate estimate of damages, however, would place the figure in excess of $8 million. This total is computed by

adding the damages on a list compiled by Pearson's office. No figures are listed for fourteen of the cases. Thus, the total is likely more than $10 million. The exact figure will probably never be known; even law review articles and newspaper accounts at the time of the suit could only estimate total damages sought.

120. Pearson v. O'Connor, Civil No. 9630 (D.D.C., July 16, 1942).

121. Complaint for Plaintiff at 2, Pearson v. O'Connor, Civil No. 9630 (D.D.C., July 16, 1942).

122. *Id.* at 2.

123. *Id.* at 2–3.

124. *Id.* at 3.

125. *Id.* at 4.

126. *Id.* at 5.

127. *Id.*

128. *Id.* at 8–9.

129. Order granting defendants' motion for judgment on the pleadings, May 28, 1942.

130. *See,* e.g., Donnelly, "The Law of Defamation: Proposals for Reform," 33 *Minn. L. Rev.* 626–28 (1942); Noel, "Defamation of Public Officers and Candidates," 49 *Colum. L. Rev.* 882–903 (1949); Riesman, "Democracy and Defamation: Fair Game and Fair Comment, Part II," 42 *Colum. L. Rev.* 1290–94, 1298–1300 (1942); Notes, "Libel Actions Brought by Public Officials," 51 *Yale L.J.* 693–99 (1942); and Notes, "Libelous Publications Affecting Public Officials," 36 *Illinois L. Rev.* 791–96 (1942).

131. *See,* e.g., progress coverage of *Sweeney* v. *Schenectady Union Publishing Co.,* 122 F.2d 288 (2d Cir. 1941), *aff'd by an equally divided Court,* 316 U.S. 642 (1942), in various editions of the *New York Times* in March and April of 1942.

132. Though chain libel suits had long been feared by newspaper publishers, editors, syndicated columnists, and publishing syndicate executives, the problem never seemed so close at hand or formidable until Sweeney launched his massive campaign.

133. Sweeney attempted to keep his colleagues informed of outcomes of his various suits through periodic entries in the *Congressional Record. See,* e.g., Cong. Rec. 6163 (1939) (remarks of Representative Sweeney) and 87 Cong. Rec. App. A3794 (1941) (remarks of Representative Sweeney).

134. In *Schenectady Union Publishing Co.* v. *Sweeney,* 316 U.S. 642 (1942), the justices split four to four on the issue. This case was later cited in *New York Times Co.* v. *Sullivan,* 376 U.S. at 268, as the only previous instance in which the Court considered the question.

5. The "Merry-Go-Round" and the Years of Common Law Defenses

1. The law of libel was not nationalized until the U.S. Supreme Court decided *New York Times Co.* v. *Sullivan*, 376 U.S. 254 (1964). Prior to 1964, there was little uniformity in common law libel among jurisdictions. *See* chapter 3 *supra* for details.

2. *See* chapter 3 *supra* for details of the common law libel defenses.

3. Placement of plaintiffs in these three categories is not, of course, automatic or ironclad, as evidenced by post-1964 libel decisions by the courts. For purposes of organization and synthesis, however, the writer has created these categories for pre-1964 cases though the courts did not do so until *New York Times* v. *Sullivan* and its progeny.

4. Howser v. Pearson, 95 F. Supp. 936 (D.D.C. 1951).

5. *Id.* at 937.

6. Complaint for Plaintiff at 1–2, Howser v. Pearson, Civil No. 49-1245 (D.D.C., Jan. 22, 1951). Historically, many nations established a three-mile territorial limit. However, in the 1940s the question of whether the federal government or the states could claim ownership over the three-mile belt became an explosive political issue in the United States. The U.S. Supreme Court in *United States* v. *California,* 322 U.S. 19 (1947), *United States* v. *Louisiana*, 399 U.S. 699 (1950), and *United States* v. *Texas*, 399 U.S. 707 (1950), upheld the claim of the federal government to be paramount regarding the territorial waters. However, in 1953 Congress enacted the Submerged Lands Act, which provided for state ownership of the three-mile marginal belt, though the federal government retained paramount rights over the area for purposes of navigation, commerce, national defense, and international affairs. *See,* e.g., Notes, "Territorial Waters—Ownership and Control," 8 *Case W. Res. J. Int'l Law* 240–56 (Winter 1976).

7. Complaint for Plaintiff at 3, Howser v. Pearson, Civil No. 49-1245 (D.D.C., Jan. 22, 1951).

8. *Id.* at 4.

9. Howser v. Pearson, 95 F. Supp. at 937–38.

10. *Id.* at 940. The plaintiff, however, called Irvine as a witness. He denied the transaction in toto. *Id.* at 941.

11. *Id.* at 939.

12. *Id.* at 943.

13. *Id.*

14. Interview with George Vournas, longtime Pearson friend and a Washington, D.C., attorney, in Washington, D.C., Jan. 18, 1977.

[15.] Telephone interview with William Rogers, former cabinet level official and attorney for Drew Pearson, New York City, Sept. 9, 1977.

[16.] "Unbroken Record," 57 *Time* 43 (Feb. 5, 1951).

[17.] Pearson v. Howser, Civil No. 50-3529 (D.D.C., Dec. 11, 1951).

[18.] Complaint for Plaintiff at 2–4, Pearson v. Howser, Civil No. 50-3529 (D.D.C., Dec. 11, 1951).

[19.] Brief for Defendant at 1–5.

[20.] Brief for Plaintiff at 2.

[21.] Brief for Defendant at 1.

[22.] *Id.* at 7.

[23.] Order Denying Plaintiff's Motion to Consolidate Civil No. 50-3529 with Civil No. 49-1245, Nov. 27, 1950.

[24.] Stipulation of Dismissal, Dec. 11, 1951.

[25.] Duncan v. Pearson, 135 F.2d 146 (4th Cir. 1943).

[26.] *Id.* at 147.

[27.] *Id.*

[28.] *Id.* at 147–48.

[29.] *Id.* at 148.

[30.] *Id.*

[31.] *Id.* at 147.

[32.] *Id.* at 149.

[33.] *Id.*

[34.] *Id.* at 150.

[35.] Suits included Earl v. Pearson, Civil No. 58-339 (D.D.C., Nov. 10, 1958); Earl v. Times, Inc., Civil No. 20545 (Coos County, Ore., Cir. Ct., April 12, 1958); Earl v. Hearst Publishing Co., Civil No. 4443 (W.D. Wash., Oct. 3, 1958). Earl also sued the Journal Publishing Company of Portland and reporter Arthur Williams for libel. He sought $500,000 in damages and charged that the Portland newspaper and Williams had provided Pearson with material for his allegedly libelous columns. The case, however, was eventually dismissed for want of prosecution. Earl v. Journal Publishing Co., Civil No. 243-908 (Multnomah County, Ore., Cir. Ct., Jan. 5, 1960).

[36.] Complaint for Plaintiff at 1–2, Earl v. Pearson, Civil No. 58-339 (D.D.C., Nov. 10, 1958).

[37.] *Id.* at 3.

[38.] *Id.* at 4–5.

[39.] *Id.* at 7.

[40.] *Id.* at 8.

[41.] Brief for Defendant at 2-4.

[42]. Dismissal Notice, Nov. 10, 1958, Earl v. Pearson, Civil No. 58-339 (D.D.C., Nov. 10, 1958).

[43]. Earl v. Times, Inc., Civil No. 20545 (Coos County, Ore., Cir. Ct., April 12, 1958).

[44]. Complaint for Plaintiff at 1, Earl v. Times, Inc., Civil No. 20545 (Coos County, Ore., Cir. Ct., April 12, 1958).

[45]. Telephone interview with Forest Amsden, Portland, Oregon, television executive, Feb. 4, 1977.

[46]. The morning *Oregonian* and afternoon *Portland Journal* "were going at each other tooth and claw over the so-called vice investigation in Portland." There was a great deal of investigative reporting by staffs of both newspapers. Local politics were volatile. The two Pearson columns fell into this boiling pot. Letter from Forest Amsden to the author, Feb. 18, 1977.

[47]. Motion for Change of Judge, June 11, 1957, Earl v. Times, Inc., Civil No. 20545 (Coos County, Ore., Cir. Ct., April 12, 1958).

[48]. Order Assigning Case, June 11, 1957.

[49]. Brief for Defendant at 2.

[50]. Motion for Change of Venue, Feb. 25, 1958.

[51]. Affidavit of Helen W. Johnson, Feb. 25, 1958.

[52]. *Id.* at 2.

[53]. Answer to Defendant's Motion for a Change of Venue, Feb. 27, 1958.

[54]. Motion for Postponement by Defendant, Feb. 28, 1958.

[55]. Answer to Defendant's Motion for Continuance, March 3, 1958.

[56]. Order of Judge Fort, March 10, 1958.

[57]. Interview with Jack Anderson, in Washington, D.C., Jan. 12, 1977. *See also Coos Bay World*, April 11, 1958, at 1, col. 5, and at 5, cols. 1–4, for an account of progress in the trial, particularly Anderson's testimony. In this testimony, Anderson stated that, during his telephone interview with Earl, the Portland politician had questioned his identity. Anderson testified that in answer to one of his questions Earl said, "Yes, Elkins gave me a great big chunk and I chewed on it and chewed on it until it spilled out baloney." *Id.* at 5, col. 3. There was also, according to the newspaper account, some "give-and-take" between Earl's attorney and Anderson about dates when Elkins disposed of his pinball interests in relation to the time when Earl changed his city council position on the devices from favoring them to disfavoring them. *Id.*

[58]. Letter from Forest Amsden, *supra* note 46. *See also Coos Bay World,* April 12, 1958, at 1, col. 6, and at 2, cols. 1–3. Ac-

cording to the newspaper account of the trial, the jury returned its verdict one hour and twenty-six minutes after receiving the case from Judge Fort. Final arguments were particularly colorful. Earl's attorney Dwight Schwab, for example, argued the case for an hour and forty-one minutes, making frequent allusions to Old Testament verses. He said that the jury should bring a big verdict "to teach these people" that they should follow the Ninth Commandment: Thou shall not bear false witness. In an obvious reference to the Eastern press, particularly muckraker Pearson, Schwab stated: "Make your verdict sufficiently large so that it can be heard loud and clear back to the East Coast. A little verdict won't stop this besmirching. A big verdict will prevent the next innocent victim from being vilified. If you bring in a small verdict, you'll be able to hear Drew Pearson laughing clear out here." The paper, however, noted that Pearson was not a defendant in the Oregon case. In his final summation, local attorney Walsh asked the jurors if they wanted a newspaper that "runs for cover" every time someone shouted "lawsuit." Walsh praised the executive editor of the *Times,* Amsden, and asked, "Did he sound like a man who wanted to vilify anybody?"

59. Wallace v. Pearson, Civil No. 56-710 (D.D.C., May 29, 1956).

60. Complaint for Plaintiff at 2.

61. *Id.*

62. Brief for Defendant at 1.

63. *Id.*

64. 128 F.2d 457, 458 (D.C. Cir. 1942), as quoted *id.* at 2.

65. Sweeney v. Caller-Times Publishing Co., 41 F. Supp. 163 (S.D. Tex. 1941), as quoted *id.* *See* chapter 4 *supra* for details of the *Caller-Times* case.

66. Brief for Plaintiff at 2, Wallace v. Pearson, Civil No. 56-710 (D.D.C., May 29, 1956).

67. *Id.* at 3.

68. Order Dismissing Complaint, filed May 29, 1956.

69. McGonigle v. Pearson, Civil No. 58-2725 (D.D.C., March 27, 1961).

70. Statement made by Drew Pearson to the Associated Press and United Press International, Oct. 30, 1958.

71. Complaint for Plaintiff, Exhibit "A," McGonigle v. Pearson, Civil No. 58-2725 (D.D.C., March 27, 1961).

72. *Id.*

73. Complaint for Plaintiff at 2–5.

74. Motion to Dismiss, filed by Defendant, Dec. 16, 1958. This was precisely the motion utilized in the *Wallace* case *supra.*

[75.] *See* text and note 65 *supra*.

[76.] Coleman v. MacLennan, 98 Pac. 281 (Kan. 1908), as cited in Brief for Defendant at 2, McGonigle v. Pearson, Civil No. 58-2725. *See* chapter 3 *supra* for details of the *Coleman* decision and the liberal impact it had on libel law protection for journalists. It will also be recalled that the *Coleman* case was cited in *New York Times Co.* v. *Sullivan,* 376 U.S. 254 at 280–82, as establishing the liberal rule relied upon by a number of state courts prior to *Sullivan*. *See also* chapter 3 *supra* for a breakdown of which jurisdictions adhered to which pre-1964 basic libel law rules.

[77.] Brief for Defendant at 2, Pearson v. McGonigle, Civil No. 58-2725 (D.D.C., March 27, 1961).

[78.] *Id.* at 3. It will be recalled that, in *Sweeney* v. *Patterson,* 128 F.2d 457 (D.C. Cir. 1942), the circuit court affirmed a district court ruling that a plaintiff who was a public official had to be falsely charged with crime, corruption, gross immorality, or gross incompetence to collect libel damages. Donovan, in numerous pre-1964 libel cases, cited the *Patterson* holding as controlling.

[79.] Memorandum from U.S. District Judge Matthew S. McGuire, Jan. 23, 1959.

[80.] Brief for Defendant at 2–3, Pearson v. McGonigle, Civil No. 58-2725 (D.D.C., March 27, 1961).

[81.] Voluntary Dismissal of Cause by Plaintiff, March 27, 1961.

[82.] Letter from Drew Pearson to Stephen B. Narin, Philadelphia attorney, April 5, 1961.

[83.] Bramblett v. Pearson, Civil No. 32000 (N.D. Calif., June 4, 1953).

[84.] Complaint for Plaintiff at 2.

[85.] *Id.* at 3.

[86.] *Id.*

[87.] *See* explanation of *Patterson* holding in note 78 *supra* and details of the *Coleman* precedent in note 76 *supra.*

[88.] Complaint for Plaintiff at 1–2, Littell v. Pearson, Civil No. 49-2959 (D.D.C., May 15, 1953).

[89.] *Id.* at 1, italics added.

[90.] *Id.* at 2. Under the Foreign Agents Registration Act of 1938, willful failure of a propagandist for a foreign government, political party, or group to register as a foreign agent was punishable by a fine of up to $10,000, five years in prison, or both.

[91.] Brief for Defendant at 2–3, Littell v. Pearson, Civil No. 49-2959 (D.D.C., May 15, 1953).

[92.] Brief for Plaintiff at 1–2.

[93.] Memorandum of the District Court, Feb. 2, 1950.

94. Amended Answer for Defendant, March 2, 1950.

95. Littell v. Pearson, Civil No. 50-2505 (D.D.C., Sept. 30, 1953).

96. Memo from John Donovan to Drew Pearson, May 8, 1951.

97. Complaint for Plaintiff at 1, Littell v. Pearson, Civil No. 50-2505 (D.D.C., Sept. 30, 1953).

98. *Id.* at 1–2.

99. *Id.* at 2.

100. *Id.* at 2–3.

101. Interview with Mrs. Drew Pearson, in Washington, D.C., Jan. 13, 1977.

102. T. Abell, ed., *Drew Pearson Diaries, 1949–1959* 267 (1974).

103. *Id.* at 267–68.

104. *Id.* at 268.

105. Verdict of Jury for Plaintiff, U.S. District Court, District of Columbia, May 15, 1953.

106. Order Discharging Jury on Disagreement, Littell v. Pearson, Civil No. 50-2505 (D.D.C., Sept. 30, 1953). The case, however, was never retried. It was dismissed with prejudice per attorneys for the plaintiff on Sept. 30, 1953.

107. O. Pilat, *Drew Pearson: An Unauthorized Biography* 255 (1973).

108. Abell, *supra* note 102, at 271. *See* this volume generally at 267–69 for all of Pearson's diary entries concerning the trial.

109. Interview with William Neel, longtime Pearson employee, in Washington, D.C., Jan. 10, 1977.

110. Interview with Mrs. Drew Pearson, *supra* note 101.

111. Letter from Drew Pearson to Lee F. Payne, executive editor of the *Los Angeles Daily News,* Oct. 2, 1953.

112. Interview with Tyler Abell, Pearson's stepson and editor of the Pearson diaries, in Washington, D.C., Jan. 11, 1977.

113. Rockwell v. Pearson, Civil No. 59-699 (D.D.C., May 18, 1959). *See* note 90 *supra* for an explanation of the Foreign Agents Registration Act.

114. Brief for Defendant at 5, Rockwell v. Pearson, Civil No. 59-699 (D.D.C., May 18, 1959).

115. *Id.*

116. *Id.*

117. Motion to Dismiss, Rockwell v. Pearson, Civil No. 59-699 (D.D.C., May 18, 1959).

118. Brief for Defendant at 1.

119. *Id.* at 2.

[120] *Id.* at 3.

[121] *Id.*

[122] *Id.* at 4.

[123] Order Dismissing Complaint, May 18, 1959.

[124] *See,* e.g., Koehne v. Radio Corporation of America, Civil No. 21309 (D.D.C., Nov. 12, 1945); Anderson v. Allen, Civil No. 8592 (D.D.C., Jan. 31, 1941); Dennett v. Pearson, Civil No. 37711 (D.D.C., Nov. 19, 1949); Laughlin v. Pearson, Civil No. 24362 (D.D.C., Feb. 15, 1945); Rumely v. Pearson, Civil No. 48-1348 (D.D.C., June 23, 1948). Defense strategies were similar in the latter four cases of this group: "Merry-Go-Round" attorneys claimed the plaintiffs failed to state a claim upon which relief could be granted.

[125] Koehne v. Radio Corporation of America, Civil No. 21309 (D.D.C., Nov. 12, 1945).

[126] Complaint for Plaintiff at 9.

[127] *Id.* at 15–18.

[128] Consolidated Motion to Dismiss, Nov. 9, 1943. Basis for the request was largely procedural; it was claimed that the complaint should be stricken for failure to comply with certain requirements of the Federal Rules of Civil Procedure governing class actions.

[129] Order to Dismiss, Nov. 12, 1945.

[130] Dennett v. Pearson, Civil No. 37711 (D.D.C., Nov. 19, 1949).

[131] Complaint for Plaintiff at 2.

[132] Amendment to Complaint for Damages at 1.

[133] Brief for Defendant at 1–2.

[134] Notice of Dismissal, Nov. 19, 1949. The most interesting phase of this case, however, occurred after it had been dismissed for want of prosecution. On March 21, 1950, attorneys for Dennett moved to reinstate action, claiming that they were not notified of the dismissal until more than three months had elapsed. It was emphasized, however, that the rules did not require such notice. Dennett's attorneys nevertheless contended, in a hearing before Judge Tamm, that their client was not to blame for the lack of prosecution, that it was their "inadvertence" and that they were "somewhat embarrassed." Dennett's lawyers further emphasized that their client was a veteran and was "entitled to his day in court." Pearson's attorney, John Donovan, naturally disagreed. During the hearing, he told Judge Tamm that the item that was the source of the complaint was aired approximately six years previous, that the case was filed in 1946, but after the pleadings

were closed in 1948 nothing was done by the plaintiff. Donovan said that, under Rule 15 (basis for the dismissal), lack of prosecution merits dismissal. Donovan insisted that the rule should be enforced. Judge Tamm agreed: he said that in fairness to both sides, "since the onus of the break-down" of the case was upon the plaintiff, he felt compelled to deny the motion to reinstate action. *See* account of proceedings on May 31, 1950, at 1–14. Dennett's attorneys then moved that the order denying the motion to reinstate action be vacated. Motion by Plaintiff to Vacate Order, June 13, 1950. In a memorandum opinion, however, Judge Tamm denied the motion to vacate. Memorandum Opinion of Judge Tamm, July 26, 1950.

135. Complaint for Plaintiff at 2, Laughlin v. Pearson, Civil No. 24362 (D.D.C., Feb. 15, 1945).

136. Brief for Defendant at 2, Laughlin v. Pearson, Civil No. 24362 (D.D.C., Feb. 15, 1945).

137. *Id.* at 1–3.

138. Praecipe Dismissing Action, Feb. 15, 1945.

139. Anderson v. Allen, Civil No. 8592 (D.D.C., Jan. 31, 1941).

140. Brief for Plaintiff, Exhibit "A," Anderson v. Allen, Civil No. 8592 (D.D.C., Jan. 31, 1941).

141. Complaint for Plaintiff at 2.

142. Motion for Defendants to Dismiss and Strike, Nov. 18, 1940.

143. Brief for Defendant at 1–3.

144. *Id.* at 3.

145. *Id.* at 4.

146. Judgment of Dismissal, Jan. 31, 1941.

147. Rumely v. Pearson, Civil No. 48-1348 (D.D.C., June 23, 1948).

148. Complaint for Plaintiff at 2, Rumely v. Pearson, Civil No. 48-1348 (D.D.C., June 23, 1948).

149. *Id.* at 3–4.

150. Brief for Defendant at 1.

151. Order to Dismiss, June 23, 1948.

152. Ware v. Pearson, Civil No. 22580 (D.D.C., May 2, 1944); Ross v. Pearson, Civil No. 49-778 (D.D.C., Feb. 27, 1952); Franzino v. Pearson, Civil No. 49-1848 (D.D.C., Jan. 26, 1953).

153. Complaint for Plaintiff at 1, Ware v. Pearson, Civil No. 22580 (D.D.C., May 2, 1944).

154. *Id.* at 1–2.

155. *Id.* at 2.

156. *Id.* at 3.

[157] *Id.* at 4.

[158] *Id.*

[159] Brief for Defendant at 3, Ware v. Pearson, Civil No. 22580 (D.D.C., May 2, 1944).

[160] *Id.* at 3–4.

[161] *Id.* at 4.

[162] *Id.* at 5.

[163] *Id.*

[164] *Id.*

[165] *Id.*

[166] Stipulation of Dismissal, May 2, 1944.

[167] Complaint for Plaintiff at 1, Ross v. Pearson, Civil No. 49-778 (D.D.C., Feb. 27, 1952).

[168] Complaint for Plaintiff at 1, Franzino v. Pearson, Civil No. 49-1848 (D.D.C., Jan. 26, 1953).

[169] Complaint for Plaintiff at 2, Ross v. Pearson, Civil No. 49-778 (D.D.C., Feb. 27, 1952).

[170] *Id.* at 2–3.

[171] Brief for Defendant at 2–3.

[172] Praecipe, Feb. 27, 1952.

[173] Complaint for Plaintiff at 2–3, Franzino v. Pearson, Civil No. 49-1848 (D.D.C., Jan. 26, 1953).

[174] *Id.* at 3.

[175] Brief for Defendant at 2–3.

[176] Praecipe, Jan. 26, 1953.

[177] Malaxa v. Pearson, Civil No. 55-5549 (D.D.C., May 29, 1962); Monroe v. Pearson, Civil No. 20241 (D.D.C., March 31, 1944); Dall v. Pearson, 246 F. Supp. 812 (D.D.C. 1963).

[178] Monroe v. Pearson, Civil No. 20241 (D.D.C., March 31, 1944).

[179] Monroe v. Meyer, Civil No. 20242 (D.D.C., March 31, 1944).

[180] Complaint for Plaintiff at 1–10, Monroe v. Pearson, Civil No. 20241 (D.D.C., March 31, 1944).

[181] *Id.* at 4.

[182] *Id.*

[183] *Id.* at 4–5.

[184] *Id.* at 3.

[185] *Id.* at 9.

[186] Brief for Defendant at 2, Monroe v. Pearson, Civil No. 20241 (D.D.C., March 31, 1944).

[187] *Id.* at 3.

[188] Pre-Trial Proceedings at 3, Monroe v. Pearson, Civil No. 20241 (D.D.C., March 31, 1944).

[189] Verdict and Judgment, March 31, 1944, Monroe v. Pearson, Civil No. 20241 (D.D.C., March 31, 1944), and Monroe v. Meyer, Civil No. 20242 (D.D.C., March 31, 1944).

[190] Malaxa v. Pearson, Civil No. 55-5549 (D.D.C., May 29, 1962). Malaxa, to justify his claim for the additional $45 million in special damages, contended that over a ten-year period, from 1956 projected to 1966, he would be prevented from concluding contracts with the Argentine government for manufacture of railroad cars and drilling for oil in Argentina, as a result of publication of the Pearson column in the Argentine press. Malaxa did not recall when the publication occurred. Pearson's attorney, Donovan, questioned the claim for special damages. He pointed out that individuals and companies not domiciled in Argentina were not allowed to hold petroleum rights even under a new policy announced in 1958 that permitted use of foreign capital in development of that country's industries and resources. Brief for Defendant at 2–5.

[191] Order Dismissing Case, May 29, 1962.

[192] Complaint for Plaintiff at 1–3, Malaxa v. Pearson, Civil No. 55-5549 (D.D.C., May 29, 1962).

[193] *Id.* at 3. Malaxa claimed that the 1955 column was part of an "anti-Nixon campaign" that the muckraker had been waging since 1952, and that he (Malaxa) had been "caught as an innocent victim in its crossfire."

[194] *Id.* at 5.

[195] *Id.,* Exhibit "A."

[196] *Id.*

[197] *Id.*

[198] *Id.,* Exhibit "B."

[199] *Id.*

[200] *Id.,* Exhibit "C."

[201] *Id.,* Exhibit "D."

[202] *Id.*

[203] *Id.*

[204] Motion for Summary Judgment by Defendant, May 3, 1961.

[205] Brief for Defendant at 2.

[206] *Id.* at 2–3.

[207] *Id.* at 3–5. *See* note 190 *supra* for details about the $45 million sought in special damages.

[208] *See* Brief for Defendant at 1–28.

[209] Request for Continuance by Plaintiff, May 15, 1962.

[210] Letter from Marc Vechsler, New York medical doctor, dated May 9, 1962. Filed in the District Court on May 15, 1962, as part of plaintiff's request for continuance.

[211] Interview with F. Joseph Donohue, Drew Pearson's trial attorney, in Washington, D.C., Jan. 19, 1977.

[212] 246 F. Supp. 812 (D.D.C. 1963).

[213] *Id.* at 813.

[214] *Id.* at 813–14.

[215] *Id.* at 813.

[216] *Id.*

[217] *Id.*

[218] *Id.* at 814.

[219] Silver Motors v. Pearson, Civil No. 48-2411 (D.D.C., Dec. 10, 1948).

[220] Complaint for Plaintiff at 1, Silver Motors v. Pearson, Civil No. 48-2411 (D.D.C., Dec. 10, 1948).

[221] *Id.* at 2.

[222] Certificate of Dismissal, Dec. 10, 1948.

[223] Gariepy v. Pearson, 104 F. Supp. 681 (D.D.C. 1952), *rev'd,* 207 F.2d 15 (D.C. Cir. 1953).

[224] Complaint for Plaintiff at 2, Gariepy v. Pearson, Civil No. 50-437 (D.D.C., Feb. 2, 1955), italics added.

[225] *Id.* at 3.

[226] *Id.*

[227] *Id.* at 4–5.

[228] Rough draft statement by Drew Pearson; in Pearson papers at Lyndon Baines Johnson Library, Austin, Texas.

[229] *Michigan Catholic* (newsletter), Feb. 3, 1949, at 1.

[230] *Id.*

[231] *Id.*

[232] *Id.*

[233] Draft copy of Drew Pearson statement prepared for distribution by Western Union; in Pearson papers at Lyndon Baines Johnson Library, Austin, Texas.

[234] *Id.*

[235] Brief for Defendant at 2–3, Gariepy v. Pearson, Civil No. 50-437 (D.D.C., Feb. 2, 1955).

[236] Gariepy v. Pearson, 104 F. Supp. at 683.

[237] *Id.* at 683–84.

[238] *Id.* at 684.

[239] *Id.* at 685.

[240] Notice of Appeal Docketed with the District of Columbia Court of Appeals, June 4, 1952.

[241] Gariepy v. Pearson, 207 F.2d 15 (D.C. Cir. 1953).

[242] *Id.* at 16.

[243] *Id.*

[244] Order Discharging Jury on Disagreement, Oct. 30, 1954, Gariepy v. Pearson, Civil No. 50-437 (D.D.C., Feb. 2, 1955).

[245] Interview with F. Joseph Donohue, *supra* note 211.

[246] Form letter from Drew Pearson to interested parties in the *Gariepy* case, Nov. 2, 1954.

[247] Interview with F. Joseph Donohue, *supra* note 211.

[248] Verdict and Judgment, U.S. District Court, District of Columbia, Feb. 2, 1955.

[249] Order of Judge Tamm, March 11, 1955.

[250] Letter from Drew Pearson to F. Joseph Donohue, trial attorney, Feb. 7, 1955.

[251] Howard v. the Washington Post Co., Civil No. 49-2611 (D.D.C., April 12, 1951).

[252] Complaint for Plaintiff at 2–3.

[253] *Id.* at 10.

[254] *Id.*

[255] Brief for Defendant at 1–4.

[256] *Id.* at 3.

[257] Howard v. the Washington Post, Civil No. 50-1088 (D.D.C., May 25, 1953).

[258] Motion for Summary Judgment, filed for Defendant, May 27, 1952.

[259] *Id.* at 1–2.

[260] *Id.* at 2.

[261] *Id.* at 3.

[262] *Id.* at 4.

[263] *Id.* at 5–6.

[264] Brief for Plaintiff at 1, Howard v. the Washington Post, Civil No. 50-1088 (D.D.C., May 25, 1953).

[265] Brief for Defendant at 1.

[266] Notice of Dismissal, May 25, 1953.

[267] Kefalos v. Pearson, Civil No. 57-720 (D.D.C., May 9, 1957).

[268] Complaint for Plaintiff at 1–2, Kefalos v. Pearson, Civil No. 57-720 (D.D.C., May 9, 1957).

[269] *Id.* at 2.

[270] *Id.* at 3.

[271] Brief for Defendant at 1, Kefalos v. Pearson, Civil No. 57-720 (D.D.C., May 9, 1957).

[272] *Id.* at 3.

[273] *Id.* at 8.

[274] *Id.* at 3–4.

[275] Order Dismissing Complaint, May 9, 1957.

276. Washingtonian Publishing Co. v. Pearson, 306 U.S. 30 (1939). The Washingtonian Publishing Co., publisher of the *Washingtonian,* a monthly magazine, brought suit against Pearson and Allen for alleged unauthorized use of a copyrighted magazine article in their 1932 book, *More Merry-Go-Round.* Focus of the U.S. Supreme Court's decision was whether a copyrighted article had to be promptly deposited in the Copyright Office in order to recover for infringement. Fourteen months had elapsed between the time the required statutory notice was printed over the magazine article and when the copies of the article were actually deposited. The trial court sustained the *Washingtonian*'s claim, but the court of appeals reversed, holding that lack of promptness, as stipulated by the Copyright Act, precluded any recovery of damages by the corporation. The U.S. Supreme Court, however, reversed, holding that the right to sue was not lost by mere delay in depositing copies of the copyrighted work and that the Copyright Act of 1909 was not designed to burden those seeking protection, but to protect them. It was a six to three decision with Justices Hugo Black, Stanley Reed, and Owen Roberts dissenting.

277. Elmhurst v. Pearson, 153 F.2d 467 (D.C. Cir. 1946). Ernest M. Elmhurst brought a $100,000 suit alleging trespass and invasion of privacy against the Shoreham Hotel, Pearson, the Blue Network Company, Radio Station WMAL, and O. John Rogge in 1944. Elmhurst was a defendant in a sedition trial that had been in progress nearly four months when he filed suit. He had obtained employment as captain in the Shoreham Terrace of the Shoreham Hotel, but he alleged that when Rogge, who was with the Justice Department, learned that he was working at the hotel he tried to get him fired. Elmhurst claimed he overheard Rogge tell a third party over the telephone that he would get Pearson to broadcast that Elmhurst had found employment at the hotel, and, if the word got out, the hotel would feel obligated to fire him. Pearson broadcast the information on his July 30, 1944, news show. The district court held for the defendants, emphasizing that, when an individual became involved in a nationally publicized sedition trial, there could be no invasion of privacy. The circuit court affirmed. Associate Justice Wilbur Miller said that "it is clear that the District Court properly held that the right of privacy does not include protection from publication of matters of legitimate public or general interest." *Id.* at 468. The court's decision closely paralleled a statement made by Pearson during the early stages of the case. Pearson said: "Some people sue for publicity's sake. Elmhurst is one of them. The American press and radio have every right to report the whereabouts and job of any man

accused of sedition and I shall continue do so—regardless of threats. I would be neglecting my job as a newspaperman otherwise." Statement by Drew Pearson, sent via Western Union, Aug. 12, 1944.

278. Pearson settled a $15,290 tax claim against him for $7,592 in U.S. Tax Court. The columnist had contended that $30,500 the Lee Hat Company paid to him in 1950 and 1951 after terminating sponsorship of his news broadcasts was not taxable. New York Times, Dec. 6, 1955, at 74, col. 2.

279. *See* chapter 4 *supra* for details.

280. Pre-1964 libel cases in which Pearson was a defendant include: Anderson v. Allen, Civil No. 8592 (D.D.C., Jan. 31, 1941); Bramblett v. Pearson, Civil No. 32000 (N.D. Calif., June 4, 1953); Dall v. Pearson, 246 F. Supp. 812 (D.D.C. 1963); Dennett v. Pearson, Civil No. 37711 (D.D.C., Nov. 19, 1949); Duncan v. Pearson, 135 F.2d 146 (4th Cir. 1943); Earl v. Pearson, Civil No. 58-339 (D.D.C., Nov 10, 1958); Franzino v. Pearson, Civil No. 49-1848 (D.D.C., Jan. 26, 1953); Gariepy v. Pearson, 207 F. 2d 15 (D.C. Cir. 1953), *cert. denied,* 346 U.S. 909; Howard v. the Washington Post Co., Civil No. 50-1088 (D.D.C., May 25, 1953); Howard v. the Washington Post Co., Civil No. 49-2611 (D.D.C., April 12, 1951); Howser v. Pearson, 95 F. Supp. 936 (D.D.C. 1951); Kefalos v. Pearson, Civil No. 57-720 (D.D.C., May 9, 1957); Koehne v. Radio Corporation of America, Civil No. 21309 (D.D.C., Nov. 12, 1945); Laughlin v. Pearson, Civil No. 24632 (D.D.C., Feb. 15, 1945); Littell v. Pearson, Civil No. 49-2959 (D.D.C., May 15, 1953); Littell v. Pearson, Civil No. 50-2505 (D.D.C., Sept. 30, 1953); MacArthur v. Pearson (D.C. Sup. Ct. 1934), in New York Times, May 17, 1934, at 20, col. 4; McGonigle v. Pearson, Civil No. 58-2725 (D.D.C., March 27, 1961); Malaxa v. Pearson, Civil No. 55-5549 (D.D.C., May 29, 1962); Monroe v. Pearson, Civil No. 20241 (D.D.C., March 31, 1944); Rockwell v. Pearson, Civil No. 59-699 (D.D.C., May 18, 1959); Ross v. Pearson, Civil No. 49-778 (D.D.C., Feb. 27, 1952); Rumely v. Pearson, Civil No. 48-1348 (D.D.C., June 23, 1948); Silver Motors v. Pearson, Civil No. 48-2411 (D.D.C., Dec. 10, 1948); Wallace v. Pearson, Civil No. 56-710 (D.D.C., May 29, 1956); Ware v. Pearson, Civil No. 22580 (D.D.C., May 2, 1944).

281. Earl v. Times, Inc., Civil No. 20545 (Coos County, Ore., Cir. Ct., April 12, 1958); Earl v. Hearst Publishing Co., Civil No. 4443 (W.D. Wash., Oct. 3, 1958); Monroe v. Meyer, Civil No. 20242 (D.D.C., March 31, 1944).

282. Littell v. Pearson, Civil No. 49-2959 (D.D.C., May 15, 1953). *See* discussion this chapter *supra.*

6. The "Merry-Go-Round" and the Years of Protection for "Robust, Wide-Open" Reporting

1. 376 U.S. 254 (1964). This decision, as discussed *supra,* nationalized the law of libel. The U.S. Supreme Court held that a state cannot, under the First and Fourteenth Amendments, award damages to a public official for defamatory falsehoods relating to his official conduct unless he proves "actual malice." *Id.* at 279–80.

2. The majority opinion, written by Justice William Brennan, Jr., included the following: "Thus we consider this case against the background of a profound national commitment to the principle that debate on public issues should be uninhibited, robust, and wide-open, and that it may well include vehement, caustic, and sometimes unpleasantly sharp attacks on government and public officials." *Id.* at 270.

3. This expansion, however, came to a halt in 1974, when the U.S. Supreme Court decided *Gertz* v. *Robert Welch, Inc.,* 418 U.S. 323 (1974). This decision is particularly important in terms of momentum; for nearly a decade after *Sullivan,* the Court's libel decisions all moved toward greater press protection. *Gertz,* however, focused, not on whether the publication concerned an event of public interest, but upon the status of the person defamed, pre-*Rosenbloom* v. *Metromedia, Inc.,* 403 U.S. 29 (1971). *See* chapter 3 *supra* for details.

4. New York Times Co. v. Sullivan, 376 U.S. at 279–80.

5. The exception was Coreil v. Pearson, 242 F. Supp. 188 (W.D. La. 1965).

6. Keogh v. Pearson, Civil No. 62-3788 (D.D.C., July 9, 1974); Keogh v. Pearson, Civil No. 64-1274 (D.D.C., July 9, 1974); Keogh v. Pearson, Civil No. 64-C940 (E.D. N.Y., Dec. 16, 1965). The first case, filed in 1962, was reported as Keogh v. Pearson, 244 F. Supp. 482 (D.D.C. 1966).

7. The suit Keogh filed in New York, *supra* note 6, sought damages of $1 million, but was dismissed without prejudice on Dec. 16, 1965, just a little more than one year after the congressman filed it.

8. The Washington Post Co. v. Keogh, 365 F.2d 965, 969 (D.C. Cir. 1966), *cert. denied,* 385 U.S. 1011 (1967).

9. Keogh v. Pearson, 244 F. Supp. at 483.

10. 379 U.S. 64, 74 (1965), as quoted *id.* at 484.

11. Keogh v. Pearson, 244 F. Supp. at 486.

12. *Id.* at 483.

13. *Id.* at 484.

14. *Id.* at 485.
15. *Id.* at 486.
16. The Washington Post Co. v. Keogh, 365 F.2d 965 (D.C. Cir. 1966), *cert. denied,* 385 U.S. 1011 (1967).
17. *Id.* at 972.
18. *Id.*
19. *Id.* at 968.
20. 360 U.S. 564 (1959). *See* chapter 3 *supra* and chapter 7 *infra* for details.
21. The Washington Post Co. v. Keogh, 365 F.2d at 968.
22. *Id.* at 969.
23. *Id.*
24. *Id.*
25. *Id.* at 971.
26. *Id.*
27. *Id.*
28. *Id.* at 972–73.
29. Keogh v. Pearson, Civil No. 64-1274 (D.D.C., July 9, 1974).
30. Complaint for Plaintiff, Exhibit "A," Keogh v. Pearson, Civil No. 64-1274 (D.D.C., July 9, 1974).
31. *Id.*
32. *Id.*
33. Complaint for Plaintiff at 3.
34. 128 F.2d 457 (D.C. Cir. 1942), *cert. denied,* 317 U.S. 678.
35. Brief for Defendant at 2–5, Keogh v. Pearson, Civil No. 64-1274 (D.D.C., July 9, 1974).
36. 376 U.S. 254 (1964).
37. Brief for Defendant at 6, Keogh v. Pearson, Civil No. 64-1274 (D.D.C., July 9, 1974).
38. New York Times Co. v. Sullivan, 376 U.S. at 270, as quoted *id.*
39. Brief for Plaintiff at 4, Keogh v. Pearson, Civil No. 64-1274 (D.D.C., July 9, 1974).
40. *Id.* at 7.
41. *Id.* at 9.
42. *See* note 6 *supra.*
43. Brief for Defendant at 10.
44. *See* chapter 3 *supra* for a discussion of these cases.
45. Affidavit of Drew Pearson at 3, Keogh v. Pearson, Civil No. 64-1274 (D.D.C., July 9, 1974).
46. Interview with Tyler Abell, Drew Pearson's stepson and Washington, D.C., attorney, in Washington, D.C., Jan. 11, 1977.
47. *Id.*

48. New York Times, Jan. 10, 1967, at 28, col. 1.

49. C. Lawhorne, *Defamation and Public Officials* 249 (1971).

50. Monitor Patriot Co. v. Roy, 401 U.S. 265 (1971).

51. *Id.* at 266.

52. *Id.* at 266–67. Pearson became personally involved in the case because he had an indemnity contract with the distributor.

53. *Id.* at 268.

54. *Id.*

55. *Id.* at 269.

56. *Id.* at 268–69. The trial judge gave the jury the following definition of a "lawful occasion": "If the end to be attained by the publication is justifiable, that is, to give useful information to those who have a right and ought to know in order that they may act upon such information, the occasion is lawful. Where, however, there is merely the color of a lawful occasion and the defendant, instead of acting in good faith, assumes to act for some justifiable end merely as a pretense to publish and circulate defamatory matter, or for other unlawful purpose, he is liable in the same manner as if such pretense had not been resorted to." *Id.* According to the trial judge, "conditional privilege" could prevail even if the jury found the article to be false, but only if it also found that its publication was "on a lawful occasion, in good faith, for a justifiable purpose, and with a belief founded on reasonable grounds of the truth of the matter published." *Id.* at 269.

57. *Id.* at 270.

58. *Id.* at 271.

59. *Id.* at 273.

60. *Id.* at 277.

61. *Id.*

62. *Id.* at 272.

63. Garrison v. Louisiana, 379 U.S. at 76–77, as quoted *id.* at 273–74.

64. *Id.* at 275.

65. *Id.* at 278 (Black, J., separate opinion).

66. Interview with Tyler Abell, *supra* note 46.

67. Lawhorne, *supra* note 49, at 258.

68. Interview with Tyler Abell, *supra* note 46.

69. Telephone interview with Tyler Abell, March 17, 1976.

70. Pearson v. Dodd, 410 F.2d 701 (D.C. Cir. 1969), *cert. denied,* 395 U.S. 947 (1969).

71. Telephone interview with Michael O'Hare, former office manager for Sen. Thomas Dodd of Connecticut, Arlington, Virginia, Jan. 26, 1977.

72. Pearson v. Dodd, 410 F.2d 703.

[73] Dodd v. Pearson, 277 F. Supp. 469, 470-71 (D.D.C. 1967).

[74] *Id.* at 471.

[75] Dodd v. Pearson, 279 F. Supp. 101 (D.D.C. 1968).

[76] *See,* e.g., Recent Decisions, "Conversion As a Remedy for Injurious Publication—New Challenge to the *New York Times* Doctrine? *Dodd* v. *Pearson,*" 56 *Geo. L. J.* 1223–30 (1968). The author concluded that the *Dodd* decision was "an unwarranted infringement on the first amendment's protection of the public's right to know through the freedom of the press." *Id.* at 1230. *See also* Recent Cases, "Constitutional Law—Freedom of the Press—Judgment for Conversion against Journalists Who Acquire and Publish Information with Knowledge that It Was Stolen from U.S. Senator's File Does Not Violate Freedom of the Press—*Dodd* v. *Pearson,*" 82 *Harv. L. Rev.* 926–31 (1969). The author stated that "by permitting recovery against the newspapermen, the *Dodd* court may have effectively curtailed dissemination of some valuable information by making it extremely costly for journalists to obtain information from those who have acquired it improperly. This limitation conflicts with the interest found critical in *Sullivan* and *Hill* [Time, Inc. v. Hill, 385 U.S. 374 (1967). *See* chapter 3 *supra* for details], the people's right to be informed about all matters of public interest in order that they may 'cope with the exigencies of their period.' " *Id.* at 930.

[77] Pearson v. Dodd, 410 F.2d 701.

[78] Pearson v. Dodd, 410 F.2d at 703.

[79] *Id.* at 704.

[80] *Id.* at 705.

[81] *Id.*

[82] *Id.* at 705–06.

[83] *Id.* at 706.

[84] *Id.* at 707–08.

[85] *Id.* at 708.

[86] *Id.* (Tamm, J., concurring).

[87] *Id.*

[88] An article in the *National Review,* for example, chastised Pearson for his role in the affair. The article implied that the Senate voted to censure Dodd, not because of hard, solid evidence of wrongdoing, but rather because the senators were likely a bit intimidated by the muckraker. It was said that "it is not just any senator who is willing to disobey the Quaker scavenger whose lies and contumely have been deplored by every American President within living memory." In a strong conclusion, the article stated: "The pietistic Mr. Pearson must hope, deep in the recesses of his shriveled heart, that there will be no

Final Judgment after we are all dead. Imagine the chances he would have. . . . He will have to hope that in the beyond, all is charity, much as he loathes that virtue in this world." *See* "Pearson the Conquerer," 19 *National Review* 507–08 (May 16, 1967).

89. Liberty Lobby v. Pearson, 390 F.2d 489 (D.C. Cir 1968).

90. *Id.* at 489–91.

91. *Id.* at 490–91.

92. *Id.* at 491.

93. *Id.*

94. *Id.*

95. *Id.*

96. *Id.* at 492 (Wright, J., concurring).

97. *Id.*

98. Complaint for Plaintiff at 1, Thompson v. Pearson, Civil No. 62-3133 (D.D.C., Sept. 14, 1965).

99. *Id.* at 2.

100. *Id.*

101. Brief for Defendant at 1, Thompson v. Pearson, Civil No. 62-3133 (D.D.C., Sept. 14, 1965).

102. *Id.* at 3.

103. *Id.* at 4.

104. *Id.* at 1.

105. Brief for Plaintiff at 1–2.

106. *Id.* at 1.

107. Order of the Court, Jan. 23, 1963.

108. Amended Complaint for Plaintiff at 2.

109. Brief for Defendant at 4.

110. 128 F.2d 457 (D.C. Cir. 1942), *cert. denied,* 317 U.S. 678. *See* chapter 3 *supra* for details.

111. 98 Pac. 281 (Kan. 1908). *See* chapter 3 *supra* for details.

112. Brief for Defendant at 7–9.

113. The case was decided March 9, 1964.

114. Motion to Dismiss, July 30, 1965.

115. Order to Dismiss, Sept. 14, 1965.

116. Coreil v. Pearson, 242 F. Supp. 802 (W.D. La. 1965).

117. *Id.* at 803–04.

118. *Id.* at 804.

119. *Id.*

120. *Id.* at 805.

121. *Id.*

122. *Id.* at 806.

123. Order to Dismiss, Coreil v. Person, Civil No. 9626 (W.D. La., Nov. 24, 1969).

[124] Fite v. Anderson, Civil No. 70-405 (N. D. Ala., April 19, 1971).

[125] Complaint for Plaintiff, Exhibit "1," Fite v. Anderson, Civil No. 70-405 (N.D. Ala., April 19, 1971).

[126] *Id.*

[127] Complaint for Plaintiff at 2.

[128] Motion to Dismiss or Change Venue, Fite v. Anderson, Civil No. 70-405 (N.D. Ala., April 19, 1971).

[129] Brief for Defendant at 2.

[130] *Id.* at 3.

[131] Order of Dismissal, April 19, 1971.

[132] Shelton v. Anderson, Civil No. 77-0666 (D.D.C., Aug. 1, 1978).

[133] Amended Complaint for Plaintiff, at 6.

[134] *Id.* at 4.

[135] *Id.* at 5.

[136] Jack Anderson, statement to the Associated Press, April 18, 1977.

[137] Order of Judge Thomas Flannery, May 20, 1978, at 1–2. See also the discussion of *Carey* v. *Hume,* this chapter, *infra.*

[138] "Merry-Go-Round" column for release on August 12, 1978.

[139] Telephone interview with Edward Ashworth, Washington, D.C., attorney, Sept. 1, 1978. Leonard Appel, Washington, D.C., attorney of record for "Merry-Go-Round" columnists in *Carey* v. *Hume,* also expressed satisfaction with Judge Flannery's interpretation of the *Carey* precedent. Telephone interview with Leonard Appel, Aug. 31, 1978.

[140] Clark v. Pearson, 248 F. Supp. at 188.

[141] *Id.* at 190.

[142] *Id.*

[143] *Id.* at 191–96.

[144] *See* chapter 3 *supra* for details.

[145] Clark v. Pearson, 248 F. Supp. at 190–91.

[146] *Id.* at 191.

[147] *Id.*

[148] *Id.*

[149] *Id.*

[150] *Id.* at 192.

[151] *Id.*

[152] 360 U.S. 564 (1959). *See* chapter 3 *supra* and chapter 7 *infra* for details.

[153] 376 U.S. 254 (1964). *See* chapter 3 *supra* for details.

[154] Clark v. Pearson, 248 F. Supp. at 193.

[155] *Id.* at 194.

[156] *See,* e.g., Rosenblatt v. Baer, 383 U.S. 75 (1966); Curtis Publishing Co. v. Butts, 388 U.S. 130 (1967); Rosenbloom v. Metromedia, 403 U.S. 29 (1971).

[157] Clark v. Pearson, 248 F. Supp. at 196.

[158] *Id.* at 188.

[159] Interview with F. Joseph Donohue, Pearson trial attorney, in Washington, D.C., Jan. 19, 1977.

[160] Corso v. Pearson, Civil No. 66-482 (D.D.C., April 21, 1967).

[161] Complaint for Plaintiff at 2.

[162] Complaint for Plaintiff, Exhibit "A."

[163] *Id.*

[164] *Id.*

[165] Complaint for Plaintiff at 3.

[166] *Id.*

[167] Brief for Defendant at 2–6.

[168] Notation of Dismissal, April 21, 1967.

[169] 492 F.2d 631 (D.C. Cir. 1974).

[170] *Id.* at 632.

[171] *Id.*

[172] *Id.* at 633.

[173] *Id.* at 632.

[174] *Id.* at 633.

[175] *Id.* at 632.

[176] 408 U.S. 665 (1972), as cited *id.* at 636.

[177] *Id.*

[178] 259 F. 2d 545 (2d Cir. 1958), *cert. denied,* 358 U.S. 910 (1958).

[179] Carey v. Hume, 492 F.2d at 634–35.

[180] *Id.* at 637.

[181] *Id.*

[182] Cervantes v. Time, Inc., 464 F.2d 986 (8th Cir. 1972), as discussed *id.* at 637–38.

[183] Carey v. Hume, 492 F.2d at 638.

[184] *Id.* at 639.

[185] *Id.* at 640 (MacKinnon, J., concurring).

[186] Washington Post, Nov. 15, 1975, at A-13, col. 1.

[187] Interview with Warren Woods, Jack Anderson's personal attorney, in Washington, D.C., Jan. 14, 1977.

[188] Washington Post, *supra* note 186, at col. 2.

[189] Interview with Jack Anderson, in Washington, D.C., Jan. 12, 1977.

[190]. O'Brien v. the Tribune Publishing Co., Civil No. 4183 (W.D. Wash., May 12, 1972), *rev'd and remanded,* No. 72-2312 (9th Cir., Feb. 20, 1975).

[191]. Complaint for Plaintiff at 3.

[192]. *Id.*

[193]. *Id.* at 5.

[194]. Brief for Defendant at 3.

[195]. Brief for Defendant at 2.

[196]. Order for Dismissal at 2.

[197]. *Id.* As discussed *supra,* in *Rosenbloom,* 403 U.S. 29 (1971), the U.S. Supreme Court made the "actual malice" rule applicable to "all discussion and communication involving matters of public or general concern, without regard to whether the persons involved are famous or anonymous." *Id.* at 44.

[198]. O'Brien v. the Tribune Publishing Co., No. 72-2312 (9th Cir., Feb. 20, 1975).

[199]. *Id.* at 2.

[200]. *Id.* at 3.

[201]. *Id.* at 5.

[202]. 418 U.S. 323, 352 (1974), as quoted *id.* at 7.

[203]. *Id.* at 8.

[204]. Telephone interview with Patrick C. Comfort, Tacoma, Washington, attorney who represents Jack Anderson, June 5, 1979.

[205]. Post-1964 libel cases in which Pearson or Anderson were defendants include: Carey v. Hume, 492 F.2d 631 (D.C. Cir. 1974), *cert. denied,* 417 U.S. 938; Christopher v. Pearson, Civil No. 885082 (Super. Ct., Los Angeles, Calif., County, March 3, 1967); Clark v. Pearson, 248 F. Supp. 188 (D.D.C. 1965); Coreil v. Pearson, 242 F. Supp. 802 (W.D. La. 1965); Corso v. Pearson, Civil No. 66-482 (D.D.C., April 21, 1967); Fite v. Anderson, Civil No. 70-405 (N.D. Ala., April 19, 1971); Keogh v. Pearson, 244 F. Supp. 482 (D.D.C. 1966); Keogh v. Pearson, Civil No. 64-1274 (D.D.C., July 9, 1974); Keogh v. Pearson, Civil No. 64-C940 (E.D. N.Y., Dec. 16, 1965); O'Brien v. the Tribune Publishing Co., Civil No. 4183 (W.D. Wash., May 12, 1972), *rev'd and remanded,* No. 72-2312 (9th Cir., Feb. 20, 1975); Pearson v. Dodd, 410 F.2d 701 (D.C. Cir. 1969), *cert. denied,* 395 U.S. 947; Roy v. Monitor Patriot Co., 254 A.2d 832 (N.H. 1969), *rev'd and remanded,* 401 U.S. 265 (1971); Shelton v. Anderson, Civil No. 77-0666 (D.D.C., Aug. 1, 1978); Thompson v. Pearson, Civil No. 62-3133 (D.D.C., Sept. 14, 1965).

206. Liberty Lobby v. Pearson, 390 F.2d 489 (D.C. Cir. 1968); Ortiz v. Pearson, Civil No. 69-1711 (D.D.C., Feb. 12, 1970). The *Ortiz* case was not discussed in the text of this chapter. It involved a $115,000 suit filed in June of 1969 by George G. Ortiz against Pearson. The charge: assault and battery. Ortiz, a photographer, was allegedly assaulted by Pearson when Ortiz tried to photograph Pearson during a pretrial court session in which there was an agreement that there would be no pictures. *See,* e.g., O. Pilat, *Drew Pearson: An Unauthorized Biography* 306 (1973). Ortiz, in his complaint, was graphic about the circumstances. He claimed that Pearson, "without just cause and provocation maliciously grabbed plaintiff by the neck with his left hand with great force and pressure, and while holding the plaintiff helpless in this position proceeded to viciously pound the plaintiff in the stomach with an object held in his right hand." Complaint for Plaintiff at 1, Ortiz v. Pearson, Civil No. 69-1711 (D.D.C., Feb. 12, 1970). In one of the more vivid complaints against the muckraker, it was further emphasized that Ortiz "sustained painful bruises, contusions and damages to his neck muscles and soft tissues as well as pain and injury to his abdominal region." *Id.* at 2. There were no extensive proceedings in the case; the columnist died about ten weeks after the complaint was filed. On Feb. 12, 1970, the case was dismissed per Ortiz's counsel.

207. *See* discussion of Keogh v Pearson, Civil No. 64-1274 (D.D.C., July 9, 1974); Keogh v. Pearson, Civil No. 62-3788 (D.D.C., July 9, 1974); and Roy v. Monitor Patriot Co., 254 A.2d 832 (N.H. 1969); *rev'd and remanded,* 401 U.S. 265 (1971) this chapter *supra.*

208. Carey v. Hume, 492 F.2d 631 (D.C. Cir. 1974), *cert. denied,* 417 U.S. 938; Fite v. Anderson, Civil No. 70-405 (N.D. Ala., April 19, 1971); O'Brien v. the Tribune Publishing Co., Civil No. 4183 (W.D. Wash., May 12, 1972), *rev'd and remanded,* No. 72-2312 (9th Cir., Feb. 20, 1975); and Shelton v. Anderson, Civil No. 77-0666 (D.D.C., Aug. 1, 1978). It should be noted, however, that though the *O'Brien* case was brought after Pearson's death, it was based on a column written by the senior muckraker before his death. Anderson did not write it, though it carried the double by-line of Pearson and Anderson.

7. Fighting Back: Men of the "Merry-Go-Round" as Plaintiffs

1. Allen v. the Journal of Commerce Publishing Co., Civil No. 40S-8696 (Super. Ct., Cook County, Ill., Jan. 16, 1948).

2. Complaint for Plaintiff at 2–3. The term *Corcoranites* referred to followers of a well-known adviser to President Franklin D. Roosevelt, Tommy Corcoran, who was a good friend of Pearson's.

3. *Id.* at 2.

4. *Id.* at 3–4.

5. Brief for Defendant at 4.

6. *Id.* at 5.

7. *Id.* at 6.

8. *Id.* at 7.

9. *Id.*

10. *Id.* at 8.

11. *Id.*

12. Order to Dismiss, Jan. 16, 1948, Super. Ct., Cook County, Ill.

13. Pearson v. Funkhouser (Cir. Ct., Jefferson County, W. Va., Feb. 6, 1948). According to a spokesperson from the circuit court's office, cases prior to 1950 in Jefferson County did not have civil action numbers. Suit was filed in 1946. According to records in the circuit court, the suit was dismissed by agreement of parties on Feb. 6, 1948; the court costs were paid by the Blakeley Corp.

14. Complaint for Plaintiff at 4, italics added.

15. Brief for Defendant at 3.

16. Charleston Gazette, Feb. 3, 1948, at 5, col. 7.

17. Charleston Gazette, Feb. 4, 1948, at 17, col. 3. Charles Town should not be confused with Charleston.

18. Charleston Gazette, Feb. 5, 1948, at 18, col. 5.

19. Charleston Gazette, Feb. 7, 1948, at 1, col. 4.

20. Charleston Gazette, Feb. 4, 1948, at 17, col. 3.

21. Charleston Gazette, Feb. 7, 1948, at 1, col. 4.

22. Letter from Drew Pearson to Lee Bushong of Charles Town, W. Va., Feb. 28, 1948.

23. Pearson v. Time, Inc., Civil No. 47-411 (D.D.C. Nov. 5, 1948).

24. As quoted in Complaint for Plaintiff at 2, Pearson v. Time, Inc., Civil No. 47-411 (Nov. 5, 1948).

25. Complaint for Plaintiff at 3.

26. *Id.*

27. Brief for Defendant at 2, Pearson v. Time, Inc., Civil No. 47-411 (Nov. 5, 1948).

28. Notice of Dismissal, Nov. 5, 1948.

29. O. Pilat, *Drew Pearson: An Unauthorized Biography* 13 (1973).

30. *See* "Querulous Quaker," 52 *Time* 72 (Dec. 13, 1948).

31. *See* chapter 2 *supra* for details.

32. Interview with Warren Woods, Jack Anderson's personal attorney, in Washington, D.C., Jan. 14, 1977.

33. Pearson v. McCarthy, Civil No. 51-897 (D.D.C., Feb. 15, 1956).

34. Complaint for Plaintiff at 2, Pearson v. McCarthy, Civil No. 51-897 (D.D.C., Feb. 15, 1956), italics added.

35. *Id.*

36. *Id.* at 3.

37. *Id.* at 5.

38. *Id.* at 5–7.

39. *Id.* at 9.

40. *Id.* at 12.

41. Interview with Warren Woods, *supra* note 32.

42. Pearson v. Pegler, Civil No. 45-3205 (N.Y. County Sup. Ct., Jan. 7, 1946); Pearson v. Hearst Consolidated Publications, Civil No. 49-31541 (N.Y. County Sup. Ct., Oct. 19, 1955); Pearson v. Pegler, Civil No. 97-344 (S.D. N.Y., May 22, 1956); Pearson v. the Detroit Times Division, Hearst Publishing Co., Civil No. 9479 (E.D. Mich., Sept. 28, 1955); Pearson v. the Hearst Corp., Civil No. 49-31542 (N.Y. County Sup. Ct., Oct. 19, 1955); Pearson v. the San Antonio Light Publishing Co., Civil No. F-54905 (57th Jud. Dist., Bexar County, Texas, Oct. 14, 1955).

43. Pearson v. Pegler, Civil No. 45-3205 (N.Y. County Sup. Ct., Jan. 7, 1946).

44. Letter from William A. Roberts, Drew Pearson's attorney, to newspapers carrying the column in question, Nov. 20, 1945.

45. Letter from Westbrook Pegler to Drew Pearson, as quoted in "From A to Z," 54 *Time* 35 (Dec. 19, 1949).

46. Letter from Drew Pearson to Westbrook Pegler, as quoted in O. Pilat, *Pegler: Angry Man of the Press* 237 (1963).

47. Pearson v. Hearst Consolidated Publications, Civil No. 49-31541 (N.Y. County Sup. Ct., Oct. 19, 1955).

48. Second Amended and Supplemental Complaint for Plaintiff at 5.

49. *Id.* at 6.

[50] *Id.* at 8.

[51] *Id.*

[52] Pearson v. the Hearst Corp., Civil No. 49-31542 (N.Y. County Sup. Ct., Oct. 19, 1955).

[53] Second Amended and Supplemental Complaint for Plaintiff at 2.

[54] *Id.*

[55] *Id.* at 4.

[56] *Id.* at 5.

[57] *Id.*

[58] *Id.* at 10.

[59] *Id.* at 11.

[60] Pearson v. Pegler, Civil No. 97-344 (S.D. N.Y. May 22, 1956). The suit was filed on Dec. 22, 1954, against Pegler, the Hearst Corporation, Hearst Consolidated Publications, Inc., and King Features Syndicate. On Oct. 20, 1955, there was a stipulation of discontinuance filed in regard to the two Hearst enterprises and King Features. A stipulation of discontinuance for Pegler was filed May 22, 1956.

[61] Complaint for Plaintiff at 12.

[62] Pearson v. The San Antonio Light Publishing Co., Civil No. F-54905 (57th Jud. Dist., Bexar County, Tex., Oct. 14, 1955).

[63] Pearson v. The Detroit Times Division, Hearst Publishing Co., Civil No. 9479 (E.D. Mich., Sept. 28, 1955).

[64] *See* text accompanying note 41 *supra.*

[65] Pearson v. Wright, 156 F. Supp. 136 (D.D.C. 1957).

[66] Complaint for Plaintiff at 3, Pearson v. Wright, Civil No. 57-2118 (D.D.C., Oct. 14, 1959).

[67] Complaint for Plaintiff, Exhibit "A."

[68] Complaint for Plaintiff at 5.

[69] *Id.*

[70] Complaint for Plaintiff, Exhibit "B" at 6. Pearson's attorney contended that the intent of Wright to injure the columnist was apparent, based on the fact that he alone was singled out from "among nineteen well known national magazines, newspapers and writers"; the others were not named.

[71] *Id.*

[72] Pearson v. Wright, 156 F. Supp. at 137.

[73] *Id.*

[74] *Id.*

[75] 360 U.S. 564 (1959). *See* chapter 3 *supra* for details.

[76] Brief for Plaintiff at 5, Pearson v. Wright, Civil No. 57-2118 (D.D.C., Oct. 14, 1959).

[77] *Id.* at 8–9.

78. Grant of Motion to Dismiss, Oct. 14, 1959.

79. Pearson v. Fairbanks Publishing Co., 413 P.2d 711 (Alaska 1966).

80. *Id.* at 712.

81. *Id.*

82. *Id.* at 714.

83. *Id.* at 713–14.

84. *Id.* at 715.

85. *Id.* at 713–14.

86. As quoted in "Fairbanks Syllogism," 64 *Newsweek* 48 (Dec. 14, 1964).

87. Interview with Mrs. Drew Pearson, in Washington, D.C., Jan. 13, 1977.

88. Brief for Plaintiff at 13–15, Pearson v. Christopher, Civil No. 885082 (Super. Ct., Los Angeles, Calif., County, March 3, 1967).

89. San Francisco Chronicle, May 17, 1966, at 12, col. 6.

90. Brief for Plaintiff at 5–12, Pearson v. Christopher, Civil No. 885082 (Super. Ct., Los Angeles County, Calif., March 3, 1967).

91. San Francisco Chronicle, May 18, 1966, at 1, col. 5, and at 11, col. 6.

92. Cross-complaint by Christopher at 6–7.

93. San Francisco Chronicle, June 30, 1966, at 7, col. 1.

94. *Id.* at 1, col. 1.

95. San Francisco Chronicle, July 2, 1966, at 6, col. 1.

96. Answer to cross-complaint for Pearson at 13–14.

97. Dismissal with Prejudice, March 3, 1967.

98. Anderson v. Nixon, Civil No. 76-1794 (D.D.C., April 4, 1978), and Reporters Committee for Freedom of the Press v. American Telephone & Telegraph Co., No. 76-2057 (D.C. Cir., Aug. 11, 1978).

99. Complaint for Plaintiff at 12, Anderson v. Nixon.

100. *Id.* at 6–12.

101. *Id.* at 12.

102. *Id.* at 9.

103. Interview with Jack Anderson, in Washington, D.C., Jan. 11, 1977.

104. 3 Med. L. Rptr. 2050 (D.D.C., April 4, 1978).

105. *Id.* at 2051.

106. Brief for Appellants at 5, Reporters Committee for Freedom of the Press v. American Telephone & Telegraph Co., No. 76-2057 (D.C. Cir., Aug. 11, 1978).

107. Reporters Committee v. AT&T, 4 Med. L. Rptr. 1177 (D.C. Cir., Aug. 11, 1978), *cert. denied,* 4 Med. L. Rptr. 2536 (1979), at 1188–1207.

[108]. Brief for Appellants, *supra* note 106, at 3–5.

[109]. *Id.* at 6.

[110]. *Id.* at 1.

[111]. *Id.* at 8.

[112]. *Id.* at 9.

[113]. *Id.* at 9–10.

[114]. *Id.* at 28.

[115]. *Id.* at 45.

[116]. Reporters Committee v. AT&T, *supra* note 107, at 1178. The circuit court also remanded the case for plaintiffs Richard Dudman, James R. Polk, David E. Rosenbaum, and Knight Newspapers.

[117]. *Id.* at 1202.

[118]. *Id.* at 1207.

[119]. *Id.* at 1203–4.

[120]. *Id.* at 1204 (italics in original).

[121]. *Id.* at 1202.

[122]. *Id.* at 1229 (Wright J., dissenting).

[123]. Allen v. the Journal of Commerce Publishing Co., Civil No. 40S-8696 (Super. Ct., Cook County, Ill., Jan. 16, 1948); Pearson v. Christopher, Civil No. 885082 (Super. Ct., Los Angeles County, Calif., March 3, 1967); Pearson v. Funkhouser (no civil action number) (Cir. Ct., Jefferson County, W. Va., Feb. 6, 1948); Pearson v. Fairbanks Publishing Co., 413 P.2d 711 (Alaska 1966); Pearson v. Hearst Consolidated Publications, Civil No. 49-31541 (N.Y. County Sup. Ct., Oct. 19, 1955); Pearson v. Howser, Civil No. 50-3529 (D.D.C., Dec. 11, 1951); Pearson v. McCarthy, Civil No. 51-897 (D.D.C., Feb. 15, 1956); Pearson v. O'Connor, Civil No. 9630 (D.D.C., July 16, 1942); Pearson v. Pegler, Civil No. 45-3205 (N.Y. County Sup. Ct., Jan. 7, 1946); Pearson v. Pegler, Civil No. 97-344 (S.D. N.Y., May 22, 1956); Pearson v. the Detroit Times Division, Hearst Publishing Co., Civil No. 9479 (E.D. Mich., Sept. 28, 1955); Pearson v. the Hearst Corp., Civil No. 49-31542 (N.Y. County Sup. Ct., Oct. 19, 1955); Pearson v. the San Antonio Light Publishing Co., Civil No. F-54905 (57th Jud. Dist., Bexar County, Tex., Oct. 14, 1955); Pearson v. Time, Inc., Civil No. 47-411 (D.D.C., Nov. 5, 1948); Pearson v. Wright, 156 F. Supp. 136 (D.D.C. 1957).

[124]. Pearson v. Time, Inc., Civil No. 21314 (D.D.C., Nov. 13, 1945). The columnist brought suit against Time, Inc., for allegedly printing material that was original to the plaintiff, or obtained through his exclusive sources. The article in question concerned

Thurman Arnold, who had resigned as assistant attorney general in charge of the Antitrust Division of the Department of Justice to accept an appointment to a federal judgeship. Pearson claimed *Time* "stole" a direct quotation from his column that Arnold had privately made to him. The *Washington Post,* with Pearson's permission, had published the Pearson story ahead of the scheduled release, since it was so newsworthy and had inadvertently left off Pearson's by-line and copyright notice. *Time* had picked up the story from the *Post.* However, the columnist claimed the magazine should have been aware of the by-line and copyright notice anyway since they had accompanied the story in numerous other newspapers. The court held for Time, Inc., pointing out that the facts were not subject to copyright. A key factor in the decision, however, was *Time*'s clip file pertaining to Arnold, which contained the *Post*'s story that did not include Pearson's by-line or copyright notice. There was no copy of the "Merry-Go-Round" column, which was duly copyrighted. Pearson v. Mayflower Washington, Inc., Civil No. 59-2652 (D.D.C., May 20, 1960). Pearson unsuccessfully attempted to try his own automobile damages case. *See* chapter 1 *supra* for details.

[125.] Anderson v. Nixon, Civil No. 76-1794 (D.D.C., April 4, 1978); Reporters Committee v. AT&T, 4 Med. L. Rptr. 1177 (D.C. Cir., Aug. 11, 1978), *cert. denied,* 4 Med. L. Rptr. 2536 (1979).

8. The "Merry-Go-Round": Cursed, Sued—but Successful

[1.] This estimate is the aggregate damages sought against "Merry-Go-Round" writers in cases examined in this book. The total does not include an estimated $8 million in damages sought in the sixty-eight Sweeney cases. The estimate for the Sweeney suits is conservative. It is based on figures listed by Pearson's office in a compilation of the suits. No amount was listed for fourteen of the suits; thus it is likely Sweeney sought more than $10 million in aggregate damages. Damages in other cases brought directly against "Merry-Go-Round" writers conservatively total $118 million. This figure is based on known damages in cases discussed in this book. Individual amounts sought ranged from $100,000 to $50 million. To realize the staggering significance of these totals, it is important to remember that the vast majority of the suits were brought long before excessive dollar amounts were sought in most libel cases.

[2.] *See* Riesman, "Democracy and Defamation: Fair Game and Fair Comment, Part II," 42 *Colum. L. Rev.* 1284–85 (1942).

[3]. The *O'Brien* case was not brought until 1970, but it was based on a 1968 "Merry-Go-Round" column written by Pearson. Since the suit was filed after Pearson's death, Anderson, who shared the by-line, was named a defendant.

[4]. Letter from Arthur J. Goldberg, U.S. Supreme Court associate justice, 1962–65, to the author, Feb. 2, 1977.

[5]. Telephone interview with William P. Rogers, former cabinet-level official and Drew Pearson attorney, New York City, Sept. 9, 1977.

Selected Bibliography

Table of Cases Involving "Merry-Go-Round" Writers

Allen v. the Journal of Commerce Publishing Co., Civil No. 40S-8696 (Super. Ct., Cook County, Ill., Jan. 16, 1948).

Anderson v. Allen, Civil No. 8592 (D.D.C., Jan. 31, 1941).

Anderson v. Nixon, Civil No. 76-1794 (D.D.C., April 4, 1978).

Bramblett v. Pearson, Civil No. 32000 (N.D. Calif., June 4, 1953).

Carey v. Hume, 492 F.2d 631 (D.C. Cir. 1974), *cert. denied,* 417 U.S. 938.

Christopher v. Pearson, Civil No. 885082 (Super. Ct., Los Angeles County, Calif., March 3, 1967).

Clark v. Pearson, 248 F. Supp. 188 (D.D.C. 1965).

Coreil v. Pearson, 242 F. Supp. 802 (W.D. La. 1965).

Corso v. Pearson, Civil No. 66-482 (D.D.C., April 21, 1967).

Dall v. Pearson, 246 F. Supp. 812 (D.D.C. 1963).

Dennett v. Pearson, Civil No. 37711 (D.D.C., Nov. 19, 1949).

Duncan v. Pearson, 135 F.2d 146 (4th Cir. 1943).

Earl v. Hearst Publishing Co., Civil No. 4443 (W.D. Wash., Oct. 3, 1958).

Earl v. Journal Publishing Co., Civil No. 243908 (Multnomah County, Ore., Cir. Ct., Jan. 5, 1960).

Earl v. Pearson, Civil No. 58-339 (D.D.C., Nov. 10, 1958).

Earl v. Times, Inc., Civil No. 20545 (Coos County, Ore., Cir. Ct., April 12, 1958).

Elmhurst v. Pearson, 153 F.2d 467 (D.C. Cir. 1946).

Fite v. Anderson, Civil No. 70-405 (N.D. Ala., April 19, 1971).

Franzino v. Pearson, Civil No. 49-1848 (D.D.C., Jan. 26, 1953).

Gariepy v. Pearson, 207 F.2d 15 (D.C. Cir. 1953), *cert. denied,* 346 U.S. 909.

Howard v. the Washington Post Co., Civil No. 49-2611 (D.D.C., April 12, 1951).

Howard v. the Washington Post Co., Civil No. 50-1088 (D.D.C., May 25, 1953).

Howser v. Pearson, 95 F. Supp. 936 (D.D.C. 1951).

Kefalos v. Pearson, Civil No. 57-720 (D.D.C., May 9, 1957).

Keogh v. Pearson, Civil No. 64-C940 (E.D. N.Y., Dec. 16, 1965).

Keogh v. Pearson, 244 F. Supp. 482 (D.D.C. 1966).

Keogh v. Pearson, Civil No. 64-1274 (D.D.C., July 9, 1974).

Koehne v. Radio Corporation of America, Civil No. 21309 (D.D.C., Nov. 12, 1945).

Laughlin v. Pearson, Civil No. 24632 (D.D.C., Feb. 15, 1945).

Liberty Lobby v. Pearson, 390 F.2d 489 (D.C. Cir. 1968).

Littell v. Pearson, Civil No. 49-2959 (D.D.C., May 15, 1953).

Littell v. Pearson, Civil No. 50-2505 (D.D.C., Sept. 30, 1953).

MacArthur v. Pearson (D.C. Sup. Ct. 1934), in N.Y. Times, May 17, 1934, at 20, col. 4.

McGonigle v. Pearson, Civil No. 58-2725 (D.D.C., March 27, 1961).

Malaxa v. Pearson, Civil No. 55-5549 (D.D.C., May 29, 1962).

Monroe v. Meyer, Civil No. 20242 (D.D.C., March 31, 1944).

Monroe v. Pearson, Civil No. 20241 (D.D.C., March 31, 1944).

O'Brien v. The Tribune Publishing Co., Civil No. 4183 (W.D. Wash., May 12, 1972), *rev'd and remanded,* No. 72-2312 (9th Cir., Feb. 20, 1975).

Ortiz v. Pearson, Civil No. 69-1711 (D.D.C., Feb. 12, 1970).

Pearson v. Christopher, Civil No. 885082 (Super. Ct., Los Angeles County, Calif., March 3, 1967).

Pearson v. The Detroit Times Division, Hearst Publishing Co., Civil No. 9479 (E.D. Mich., Sept. 28, 1955).

Pearson v. Dodd, 401 F.2d 701 (D.C. Cir. 1969), *cert. denied,* 395 U.S. 947.

Pearson v. Fairbanks Publishing Co., 413 P.2d 711 (Alaska 1966).

Pearson v. Funkhouser (no civil action number) (Cir. Ct., Jefferson County, W. Va., Feb. 6, 1948).

Pearson v. Hearst Consolidated Publications, Civil No. 49-31541 (N.Y. County Sup. Ct., Oct. 19, 1955).

Pearson v. The Hearst Corp., Civil No. 49-31542 (N.Y. County Sup. Ct., Oct. 19, 1955).

Pearson v. Howser, Civil No. 50-3529 (D.D.C., Dec. 11, 1951).

Pearson v. McCarthy, Civil No. 51-897 (D.D.C., Feb. 15, 1956).

Pearson v. Mayflower Washington, Civil No. 59-2652 (D.D.C., May 20, 1960).

Pearson v. O'Connor, Civil No. 9630 (D.D.C., July 16, 1942).

Pearson v. Pegler, Civil No. 45-3205 (N.Y. County Sup. Ct., Jan. 7, 1946).

Pearson v. Pegler, Civil No. 97-344 (S.D. N.Y., May 22, 1956).

Pearson v. The San Antonio Light Publishing Co., Civil No. F-54905 (57th Jud. Dist., Bexar County, Tex., Oct. 14, 1955).

Pearson v. Time, Inc., Civil No. 21314 (D.D.C., Nov. 13, 1945).

Pearson v. Time, Inc., Civil No. 47-411 (D.D.C., Nov. 5, 1948).

Pearson v. Wright, 156 F. Supp. 136 (D.D.C. 1957).

Reporters Committee v. AT&T, 4 Med. L. Rptr. 1177 (D.C. Cir., Aug. 11, 1978), *cert. denied,* 4 Med. L. Rptr. 2536 (1979).

Rockwell v. Pearson, Civil No. 59-699 (D.D.C., May 18, 1959).

Ross v. Pearson, Civil No. 49-778 (D.D.C., Feb. 27, 1952).

Roy v. Monitor Patriot Co., 254 A. 2d 832 (N.H. 1969), *rev'd and remanded,* 401 U.S. 265 (1971).

Rumely v. Pearson, Civil No. 48-1348 (D.D.C., June 23, 1948).

Shelton v. Anderson, Civil No. 77-0666 (D.D.C., Aug. 1, 1978).

Silver Motors v. Pearson, Civil No. 48-2411 (D.D.C., Dec. 10, 1948).

Sweeney v. Beacon-Journal Publishing Co., 35 N.E. 2d 471 (C.A. Ohio 1941).

Sweeney v. Buffalo Courier Express and Sweeney v. Post Publishing Co., 35 F. Supp. 446 (W.D. N.Y. 1940).

Sweeney v. Caller-Times Publishing Co., 41 F. Supp. 163 (S.D. Tex. 1941).

Sweeney v. Capital News Publishing Co., 37 F. Supp. 355 (S.D. Idaho 1941).

Sweeney v. Newspaper Printing Corp., 147 S.W.2d 406 (Tenn. 1941).

Sweeney v. Patterson, 128 F.2d 457 (D.C. Cir. 1942), *cert. denied,* 317 U.S. 678.

Sweeney v. Philadelphia Record Co., Sweeney v. Chronicle & News Publishing Co., Sweeney v. Steinman & Steinman, Inc., 126 F.2d 53 (3d Cir. 1942).

Sweeney v. Schenectady Union Publishing Co., 122 F.2d 288 (2d Cir. 1941), *aff'd by an equally divided Court,* 316 U.S. 642 (1942).

Sweeney v. United Feature Syndicate, Inc., 129 F.2d 904 (2d Cir. 1942).

Thompson v. Pearson, Civil No. 62-3133 (D.D.C., Sept. 14, 1965).

Wallace v. Pearson, Civil No. 56-710 (D.D.C., May 29, 1956).

Ware v. Pearson, Civil No. 22580 (D.D.C., May 2, 1944).

Washington Post Co. v. Keogh, 365 F.2d 965 (D.C. Cir. 1966), *cert. denied,* 385 U.S. 1011 (1967).

Washingtonian Publishing Co. v. Pearson, 306 U.S. 30 (1939).

Libel Law Development

Table of Cases

Post Publishing Co. v. Hallam, 59 Fed. 530 (6th Cir. 1893).

Coleman v. MacLennan, 98 Pac. 281 (Kan. 1908).

Beauharnais v. Illinois, 343 U.S. 250 (1952).

Barr v. Matteo, 360 U.S. 564 (1959).

New York Times Co. v. Sullivan, 376 U.S. 254 (1964).

Garrison v. Louisiana, 379 U.S. 64 (1964).

Henry v. Collins, 380 U.S. 356 (1965).

Rosenblatt v. Baer, 383 U.S. 75 (1966).

Associated Press v. Walker, 388 U.S. 130 (1967).

Curtis Publishing Co. v. Butts, 388 U.S. 130 (1967).

Beckley Newspapers Corp. v. Hanks, 389 U.S. 81 (1967).

Time, Inc. v. Hill, 385 U.S. 374 (1967).

St. Amant v. Thompson, 390 U.S. 727 (1968).

Greenbelt Cooperative Publishing Assn. v. Bresler, 398 U.S. 6 (1970).

Time, Inc. v. Pape, 401 U.S. 279 (1971).

Ocala Star-Banner Co. v. Damron, 401 U.S. 295 (1971).

Rosenbloom v. Metromedia, 403 U.S. 29 (1971).

Gertz v. Robert Welch, Inc., 418 U.S. 323 (1974).

Time, Inc. v. Firestone, 418 U.S. 448 (1976).
Herbert v. Lando, 4 Med. L. Rptr. 2575 (April 18, 1979).

Books

Abell, Tyler, ed. *Drew Pearson Diaries: 1949–1959*. New York: Holt, Rinehart and Winston, 1974.

Allen, Robert S., and Pearson, Drew. *More Merry-Go-Round*. New York: Liveright, 1932.

———. *Washington Merry-Go-Round*. New York: Liveright, 1931.

Anderson, Jack. *The Anderson Papers*. New York: Random House, 1973.

———. *Washington Exposé*. Washington, D.C.: Public Affairs Press, 1967.

Anderson, Jack, and Blumenthal, Frederick G. *The Kefauver Story*. New York: Dial Press, 1956.

Anderson, Jack, and Kalvelage, Carl. *American Government . . . Like It Is*. Morristown, N.J.: General Learning Press, 1972.

Anderson, Jack, and May, Ronald. *McCarthy: The Man, the Senator, the "Ism."* Boston: Beacon Press, 1952.

Beale, Morris A. *Washington Squirrel Cage*. Published by the author, 1944.

Behrens, John C. *The Typewriter Guerrillas*. Chicago: Nelson-Hall, 1977.

Black, H. C., *Black's Law Dictionary*. 4th ed. St. Paul: West Publishing Co., 1968.

Colson, Charles W. *Born Again*. Lincoln, Va.: Chosen Books, 1976.

Downie, Leonard, Jr. *The New Muckrakers*. Washington, D.C.: New Republic Book Co., 1976.

Emerson, Thomas I. *The System of Freedom of Expression*. New York: Random House, 1970.

Filler, Louis. *Crusaders for American Liberalism*. Yellow Springs, Ohio: Antioch Press, 1950.

Fisher, Charles. *The Columnists*. New York: Howell, Soskin, 1944.

Gillmor, Donald, and Barron, Jerome. *Mass Communication Law: Cases and Comment*. 2d ed. St. Paul: West Publishing Co., 1974.

Hagedorn, Herman, ed. *The Works of Theodore Roosevelt*. Vol. 16. New York: Charles Scribner's Sons, 1926.

Hanson, Arthur B. *Libel and Related Torts*. Vol. 1. New York: American Newspaper Publishers Association Foundation, 1969.

Harrison, John M., and Stein, Harry H., eds. *Muckraking, Past, Present and Future.* University Park, Pa.: Pennsylvania State University Press, 1973.

Hofstadter, Richard. *The Age of Reform.* New York: Alfred A. Knopf, 1972.

———. *The Progressive Historians.* New York: Alfred A. Knopf, 1968.

Hume, Brit. *Inside Story.* Garden City, N.Y.: Doubleday, 1974.

Kelly, Alfred H., and Harbison, Winfred A. *The American Constitution.* New York: W. W. Norton, 1970.

Klurfeld, Herman. *Behind the Lines: The World of Drew Pearson.* Englewood Cliffs, N.J.: Prentice-Hall, 1968.

Kurland, Philip B., ed. *The Supreme Court Review.* Chicago: University of Chicago Press, 1964.

Lawhorne, Clifton O. *Defamation and Public Officials: The Evolving Law of Libel.* Carbondale: Southern Illinois University Press, 1971.

Levy, Leonard W. *Freedom of the Press from Zenger to Jefferson.* Indianapolis: Bobbs-Merrill, 1966.

———. *Legacy of Suppression: Freedom of Speech and Press in Early American History.* Boston: Belknap Press, 1960.

McCloskey, Robert G. *The American Supreme Court.* Chicago: University of Chicago Press, 1960.

Magruder, Jeb Stuart. *An American Life.* New York: Pocket Books, 1975.

Moritz, Charles, ed. *Current Biography.* New York: H. W. Wilson Co., 1972.

Nelson, Harold L., ed. *Freedom of the Press from Hamilton to the Warren Court.* Indianapolis: Bobbs-Merrill, 1967.

Nelson, Harold L., and Teeter, Dwight L., Jr., *Law of Mass Communications.* 2d ed. Mineola, N.Y.: Foundation Press, 1973.

Pearson, Drew, and Allen, Robert S. *Nine Old Men at the Crossroads.* Garden City, N.Y.: Doubleday, Doran, 1936.

———. *The Nine Old Men.* Garden City, N.Y.: Doubleday, Doran, 1937.

Pearson, Drew, and Anderson, Jack. *The Case against Congress.* New York: Simon & Schuster, 1968.

———. *U.S.A.—Second-Class Power?* New York: Simon & Schuster, 1958.

Pearson, Drew, and Brown, Constantine. *The American Diplomatic Game.* Garden City, N.Y.: Doubleday, Doran, 1935.

Pember, Don R. *Mass Media Law.* Dubuque, Iowa: Wm. C. Brown, 1977.

Phelps, Robert H., and Hamilton, E. Douglas. *Libel: Rights, Risks, Responsibilities.* New York: Macmillan Co., 1966.

Pilat, Oliver. *Drew Pearson: An Unauthorized Biography.* New York: Harper's Magazine Press, 1973.

———. *Pegler: Angry Man of the Press.* Boston: Beacon Press, 1963.

Prosser, William L. *Handbook of the Law of Torts.* 4th ed. St. Paul: West Publishing Co., 1971.

Regier, C. C. *The Era of the Muckrakers.* Chapel Hill: University of North Carolina Press, 1932.

Rivers, William L. *The Opinion Makers.* Boston: Beacon Press, 1965.

Law Review Articles

Anderson, David A. "Libel and Press Self-Censorship." *Texas Law Review* 53 (March 1975): 422–81.

Brosnahan, James J. "From *Times* v. *Sullivan* to *Gertz* v. *Welch:* Ten Years of Balancing Libel Law and the First Amendment." *Hastings Law Journal* 26 (January 1975): 777–96.

Case Notes. "*Gertz* v. *Welch:* Reviving the Libel Action." *Temple Law Quarterly* 48 (Winter 1975): 450–70.

Cases Noted. "Libel: A Two-Tiered Constitutional Standard." *University of Miami Law Review* 29 (Winter 1975): 367–72.

Comments. "Constitutional Law: Defamation of Private Individuals." *Washburn Law Journal* 14 (Fall 1975): 645–49.

Comments. "Defamation Law in the Wake of *Gertz* v. *Robert Welch, Inc.*: The Impact on State Law and the First Amendment." *Northwestern University Law Review* 69 (January–February 1975): 960–82.

Comments. "The Law of Libel—Constitutional Privilege and the Private Individual: Round Two." *San Diego Law Review* 12 (March 1975): 455–74.

Donnelly, Richard C. "The Law of Defamation: Proposals for Reform." *Minnesota Law Review* 33 (May 1949): 609–33.

Giampietro, Wayne B. "The Constitutional Rules of Defamation; Or, It's Libel but Is He Liable?" *Illinois Bar Journal* 64 (September 1975): 10–15.

Noel, Dix W. "Defamation of Public Officers and Candidates." *Columbia Law Review* 49 (November 1949): 875–903.

Notes. "Constitutional Law—Reformulation of the Constitutional Privilege to Defame." *University of Kansas Law Review* 24 (Winter 1976): 406–21.

Notes. "*Gertz* v. *Robert Welch, Inc.*: Defamation and Freedom of the Press—the Struggle Continues." *Southwestern Law Journal* 28 (Winter 1974): 1043–50.

Notes. "New York *Times* Rule—the Awakening Giant of First Amendment Protections." *Kentucky Law Journal* 62 (1973–74): 824–43.

Recent Cases. "Constitutional Law—Freedom of the Press—Judgment for Conversion against Journalists Who Acquire and Publish Information with Knowledge that It Was Stolen from U.S. Senator's File Does Not Violate Freedom of the Press—*Dodd* v. *Pearson*." *Harvard Law Review* 82 (February 1969): 926–31.

Recent Decisions. "Conversion as a Remedy for Injurious Publication—New Challenge to the *New York Times* Doctrine?—*Dodd* v. *Pearson*." *Georgetown Law Journal* 56 (June 1968): 1223–30.

Riesman, David. "Democracy and Defamation: Fair Game and Fair Comment, Part I." *Columbia Law Review* 42 (1942): 1085–1123.

———. "Democracy and Defamation: Fair Game and Fair Comment, Part II." *Columbia Law Review* 42 (1942): 1282–1318.

Periodicals and Newspapers

"Aggressive Inheritor." *Time* 94 (September 12, 1969): 82.

Alexander, Jack. "Pugnacious Pearson." *Saturday Evening Post* 217 (January 6, 1945): 9–11, 64, 66–68.

Allen, Robert S. "My Pal, Drew Pearson." *Collier's* 124 (July 30, 1949): 14–16, 55–56.

"Anderson's Brass Ring." *Time* 99 (January 17, 1972): 34.

"Anti-Jewish Acts Held Not Always Racial." *New York Times* 91 (April 1, 1942): 17.

"A.V.C. Urges Senate to Impeach McCarthy." *New York Times* 100 (December 25, 1950): 31.

"Backs Right of Press." *New York Times* 91 (March 10, 1942): 14.

"Battle of the Billygoats." *Time* 56 (December 25, 1950): 11.

"Bipartisan 'Liar'?" *Newsweek* 47 (February 6, 1956): 78.

"B'nai B'rith Wins Plea." *New York Times* 91 (March 3, 1942): 11.

"Brown, Aides, Blamed in Pearson 'Smear.'" *San Francisco Chronicle* 102 (May 18, 1966): 1, 11.

"Brown Confirms Pearson Pipeline." *San Francisco Chronicle* 102 (May 25, 1966): 12.

Buckley, William F., Jr., "The Theory of Jack Anderson." *National Review* 24 (May 12, 1972): 545.

Chasan, Will, and Riesel, Victor. "Keep Them Out! Martin L. Sweeney of Ohio, Candidate for a Democratic Congressional Nomination." *Nation* 154 (May 30, 1942): 626–28.

"Chile Honors Newsmen." *New York Times* 98 (November 25, 1948): 2.

"Christopher Now Suing Pearson." *San Francisco Chronicle* 102 (May 19, 1966): 6.

"Christopher, Pearson Suits To Stay in L.A." *San Francisco Chronicle* 102 (June 1, 1966): 6.

"Chronic Liar." *Time* 42 (September 13, 1943): 18–19.

"Cissie and Drew." *Time* 39 (May 18, 1942): 68–69.

"Code-Breaker?" *Time* 57 (January 22, 1951): 72.

"Columnist and Kennedy." *Newsweek* 74 (August 25, 1969): 75.

"Columnist Wins in Libel Action." *Washington Post* 98 (Nov. 15, 1975): A-13.

"Columny." *Newsweek* 33 (June 6, 1949): 50.

" 'Commie' Labeling Ruled Libel Basis." *Charleston* (W.Va.) *Gazette* (February 5, 1948): 18.

"Crusading Columnist Drew Pearson Dies at 71: An Appreciation: Muckraker with a Quaker Conscience." *Washington Post* 92 (September 2, 1969): 1, A-8.

"Crusading Columnist Drew Pearson Dies at 71: Heart Attack Ends Long Career as Gadfly of Government." *Washington Post* 92 (September 2, 1969): 1, A-11.

"Denies Newspaper's Plea." *New York Times* 91 (June 2, 1942): 15.

"Drew Pearson." *Life* 24 (June 28, 1948): 115.

"Drew Pearson." *Nation* 209 (September 15, 1969): 237–38.

"Drew Pearson, Columnist, Dies: Was Often a Center of Conflicts." *New York Times* 118 (September 2, 1969): 1, 44.

"Drew Pearson Named 'Father of the Year.' " *New York Times* 98 (May 28, 1948): 26.

"Epithet Reaction Pleases President." *New York Times* 98 (February 25, 1949): 19.

"Fairbanks Syllogism." *Newsweek* 64 (December 14, 1964): 48.

Felt, Jeremy P. "The Progressive Era in America: 1900–1917." *Societas* 3 (Spring 1973): 103–14.

"Fight Press 'Shackling.' " *New York Times* 91 (March 17, 1942): 16.

"Fights for 'the Right' to Criticize 'Rulers.' " *New York Times* 91 (March 1, 1942): 24.

"Free-For-All." *Time* 57 (January 8, 1951): 38.

Friendly, Alfred. "In Slander's Field." *New Republic* 127 (November 3, 1952): 20–21.

"From A to Z." *Time* 54 (December 19, 1949): 34, 36.

"General MacArthur's Libel Suit against Newspaper and Authors of Syndicated Column May Draw Legal Line between What Washington News Is Privileged and What Is Not." *Literary Digest* 117 (June 2, 1934): 112.

"Gets Review in Libel Suit." *New York Times* 91 (December 24, 1941): 14.

"Gossip Columns: 'Tidbits' Raise General MacArthur's Ire." *Newsweek* 3 (May 26, 1934): 22–23.

"Guest in the House." *Time* 60 (September 8, 1952): 86.

"H-Bomb Misfire." *Time* 63 (April 12, 1954): 93–95.

"He Kept Them Honest." *Newsweek* 74 (September 15, 1969): 65.

"Here Is My Prediction." *Time* 68 (November 26, 1956): 80.

"High Court Backs Press on Privacy." *New York Times* 116 (January 10, 1967): 28.

Holborn, Frederick L. "All the News That's Safe to Print." *Saturday Review* 50 (March 4, 1967): 31–32.

"Honor Eisenhower, Bradley." *New York Times* 95 (February 4, 1946): 10.

"How Many Angels?" *Time* 55 (March 6, 1950): 72.

"Hundreds of Washington Bylines Daily . . . And Here Are Some Big Ones." *Newsweek* 58 (December 18, 1961): 68.

"Ill Wind." *Time* 61 (April 27, 1953): 56.

"It will be Denied, but . . ." *Time* 68 (November 5, 1956): 89.

"Judging the Fourth Estate: A *Time*-Louis Harris Poll." *Time* 94 (September 5, 1969): 39.

"Know-It-Alls." *Time* 43 (March 27, 1944): 56–57.

"Libel Demand Increased." *New York Times* 99 (December 17, 1949): 10.

Linsley, Jean. "Working for Jack Anderson." *Editor & Publisher* 111 (August 12, 1978): 15, 16, 42.

"MacArthur Charges Libel." *New York Times* 83 (May 17, 1934): 20.

"McCarthy vs. Pearson." *Newsweek* 36 (December 25, 1950): 19–21.

"Mayflower Punch." *Time* 59 (June 30, 1952): 53.

" 'Merry-Go-Round' Goes Round." *Newsweek* 24 (November 27, 1944): 84–85.

" 'Merry-Go-Round' Moves." *Time* 44 (November 27, 1944): 62.

Mitford, Jessica. "Muckraking a la Mode." *New Republic* 169 (October 20, 1973): 29–30.

"Muckraker." *Newsweek* 67 (June 27, 1966): 87.

"Muckraker with a Mission." *Newsweek* 79 (April 3, 1972): 53–55.

Neary, John. "Jack Anderson, Improbable New Folk Hero of the Young." *Life* 72 (April 21, 1972): 93.

"Newsletter News." *Newsweek* 41 (February 16, 1953): 86–88.

"Nixon's 'Anderson Conspiracies.' " *Washington Post* 98 (November 11, 1975): A-13.

"No Firing Aides for 'Any S.O.B.' Truman Asserts." *Washington Post* No. 26,550 (February 23, 1949): 1.

"Old Foes and a Herring." *Newsweek* 43 (January 18, 1954): 51.

"Patriotism." *McClure's* 21 (July 1903): 335–36.

"Pearson Accuser Loses." *New York Times* 100 (January 23, 1951): 53.

"Pearson Charges Libel." *New York Times* 99 (December 2, 1949): 23.

Pearson, Drew. "Confessions of an 'S.O.B.' " *Saturday Evening Post* 229 (November 3, 1956): 23–25, 87–91, 94.

———. "Confessions of an 'S.O.B.' Part II: My Life in the White House Doghouse." *Saturday Evening Post* 229 (November 10, 1956): 38, 72–76.

———. "Confessions of an 'S.O.B.' Part III: My Mother-in-Law Troubles." *Saturday Evening Post* 229 (November 17, 1956): 44–45, 87–89, 91–92.

———. "Confessions of an 'S.O.B.' Part IV: How to Make Enemies." *Saturday Evening Post* 229 (November 24, 1956): 36, 148, 150.

"Pearson Feared, Defense Charges." *Charleston* (W. Va.) *Gazette* (February 6, 1948): 13.

"Pearson Go-Round." *Newsweek* 32 (November 22, 1948): 58.

"Pearson Loses Libel Suit." *New York Times* 102 (May 16, 1953): 9.

"Pearson Settles for Costs, Apology." *Charleston* (W. Va.) *Gazette* (February 7, 1948): 1.

"Pearson Settles Tax Claim." *New York Times* 105 (December 6, 1955): 74.

"Pearson Smears Again." *National Review* 10 (January 14, 1961): 10–11.

"Testimony Starts in Pearson Action." *Charleston* (W. Va.) *Gazette* (February 4, 1948): 17.

"Pearson Sued for $300,000." *New York Times* 98 (July 13, 1949): 29.

"Pearson Sues Christopher for Libel." *San Francisco Chronicle* 102 (May 17, 1966): 12.

"Pearson Sues McCarthy." *New York Times* 100 (March 3, 1951): 5.

"Pearson the Conquerer." *National Review* 19 (May 16, 1967): 507–8.

"Pearson v. Hearst." *Newsweek* 28 (September 30, 1946): 62.

"Pearson v. Reagan." *Newsweek* 70 (November 27, 1967): 88.

"Pearson's Communication." *Newsweek* 30 (July 21, 1947): 21–22.

"Pearson's Hot Potato." *Nation* 202 (April 11, 1966): 410–11.

"Pearson's Libel Suit Opens Today." *Charleston* (W.Va.) *Gazette* (February 3, 1948): 5.

"Pearson's Side—Libel Insurance." *San Francisco Chronicle* 102 (July 2, 1966): 6.

"Peron on Nobel List with Pearson." *New York Times* 98 (February 24, 1949): 1.

"Presidency." *Time* 32 (September 12, 1938): 21, 23.

"President Brands Columnist a Liar." *New York Times* 92 (September 1, 1943): 1, 4.

"Press." *Time* 94 (September 12, 1969): 82.

"Press Is Criticized Sharply for Attacks on Forrestal." *Editor & Publisher* 82 (May 28, 1949): 4, 52.

"Price of Freedom." *Time* 53 (June 6, 1949): 43.

"Professed 'Muckraker' Anderson Doesn't Enjoy Exposing People." *Hastings* (Neb.) *Daily Tribune* 68 (April 17, 1973): 12.

"Project Mudhen, or Tracking Jack." *Washington Post* 98 (November 19, 1975): C-10.

"Public Reconciliation by Brown and Christopher." *San Francisco Chronicle* 102 (June 30, 1966): 1, 7.

"Querulous Quaker." *Time* 52 (December 13, 1948): 70–72, 75–76.

"Reminiscences of an Editor." *Printer's Ink* 14 (January 15, 1896): 17–20.

"Roosevelt Blast at Pearson as 'Liar' Climaxes Longtime Feud with Press." *Newsweek* 22 (September 13, 1943): 79–80.

"Rules Bias Charge Libelous if False." *New York Times* 91 (April 14, 1942): 19.

"Save Our Brethren." *Washington Post* No. 26,551 (February 24, 1949): 10.

"Say Pegler Broke Pact." *New York Times* 99 (December 8, 1949): 44.

"Scoop!" *Time* 66 (October 31, 1955): 34.

Sedgwick, Ellery. "The Man with the Muck Rake." *American Magazine* 62 (May, 1906): 111–12.

Seldes, George. "Father Coughlin: Anti-Semite." *New Republic* 96 (November 2, 1938): 353–54.

"Senator's Round." *Time* 57 (January 1, 1951): 47–48.

Sheehan, Susan. "The Anderson Strategy: 'We Hit You—Pow! Then You Issue a Denial, and—Bam!—We Really Let You Have It.'" *New York Times Magazine* (August 13, 1972): 10–11, 76–82, 84.

Sherrill, Robert G. "Drew Pearson: An Interview." *Nation* 209 (July 7, 1969): 7–16.

"S.O.B.?" *St. Louis Post-Dispatch* 101 (February 24, 1949): B-2.

"Square Scourge of Washington." *Time* 99 (April 3, 1972): 40–44.

Stein, Harry H. "The Muckraking Book in America." *Journalism Quarterly* 52 (Summer 1975): 297–303.

Stone, I. F. "V for Vituperation." *Nation* 157 (September 11, 1943): 286–87.

Stonecipher, Harry W., and Trager, Robert. "The Impact of *Gertz* on the Law of Libel." 53 *Journalism Quarterly* (Winter 1976): 609–18.

"Sweeney Libel Suit Fails." *New York Times* 90 (February 27, 1941): 21.

"Sweeney Loses a Round." *New York Times* 91 (May 26, 1942): 42.

"Sweeney Loses Libel Suit." *New York Times* 91 (November 30, 1941): 62.

"Sweeney Loses Libel Suit Plea." *New York Times* 92 (November 10, 1942): 20.

"Ten Simple Facts." *Newsweek* 48 (November 5, 1956): 70.

"Tenacious Muckraker." *Time* 94 (September 12, 1969): 82.

"Testifies in Libel Suit." *New York Times* 90 (February 19, 1941): 18.

"Time to Clear Air of Pearson Poison." *Michigan Catholic* (February 3, 1949): 1.

"Times, Inc. Innocent of Charge." *Coos Bay* (Ore.) *World* 52 (April 12, 1958): 1–2.

"Truman in Strong Language Assails Critics of His Aides." *New York Times* 98 (February 23, 1949): 1.

"TV Show Drops Pearson." *New York Times* 109 (July 14, 1960): 55.

"Unbroken Record." *Time* 57 (February 5, 1951): 43.

"U.S. Officials Ruled Open to Libel Suit." *New York Times* 107 (November 9, 1957): 12.

"Vaughan Gets News Medal from Mexico; Church Head Calls on Truman to Apologize for Use of 'S.O.B.'" *Washington Post* No. 26,551 (February 24, 1949): 1.

Warner, Eugene. "The Terrors of Washington." *Collier's* 103 (April 22, 1939): 11, 85–86.

"Watchdog of Virtue." *New York Times* 118 (September 2, 1969): 44.

"Wayne Morse Lauds Pearson at Services." *New York Times* 118 (September 5, 1969): 37.

Wecter, Dixon. "Hearing Is Believing." *Atlantic* 176 (July 1945): 37–43.

"When Is News?" *Newsweek* 43 (April 12, 1954): 86–87.

"Whipping Boy." *Newsweek* 27 (January 21, 1946): 33–34.

"Who's Boss Around Here?" *Time* 53 (March 7, 1949): 23–24.

"Witnesses Link Earl-Elkins." *Coos Bay* (Ore.) *World* 52 (April 11, 1958): 1, 5.

"Writer Drew Pearson Stirs New Storms as He Probes Officials' Acts." *Wall Street Journal* 157 (May 25, 1966): 1, 9.

"Wrong Again." *Time* 42 (July 12, 1943): 70.

Interviews

Abell, Tyler. Drew Pearson's stepson, editor of *Drew Pearson's Diaries 1949–1959,* and Washington, D.C., attorney. Telephone interview, March 17, 1976.

———. Interview, January 11, 1977.

Amsden, Forest. General manager and executive vice-president, KGW-TV, Portland, Ore., and former executive editor of the *Coos Bay* (Ore.) *Times.* Telephone interview, February 4, 1977.

Anderson, Jack. "Merry-Go-Round" columnist, Washington, D.C. Telephone interview, March 30, 1976.

———. Interview. January 11, 1977.

Appel, Leonard. Washington, D.C., attorney. Telephone interview, August 31, 1978.

Ashworth, Edward. Washington, D.C., attorney. Telephone interview, September 1, 1978.

Comfort, Patrick. Jack Anderson's attorney, Tacoma, Wash. Telephone interviews, January 24, 1977, June 5, 1979.

Cuneo, Ernest. Lawyer-writer and longtime Drew Pearson personal friend, Washington, D.C. Telephone interview, August 30, 1977.

Donohue, F. Joseph. Former trial attorney for Drew Pearson, Washington, D.C. Interview, January 19, 1977.

Neel, William. Longtime Drew Pearson employee, Washington, D.C. Interview, January 10, 1977.

O'Hare, Michael. Former office manager for Sen. Thomas Dodd of Connecticut, Arlington, Va. Telephone interview, January 26, 1977.

Pearson, Luvie. Drew Pearson's widow, Washington, D.C. Interview, January 13, 1977.

Rogers, William P. Former cabinet-level official and Drew Pearson attorney, New York City. Telephone interview, September 9, 1977.

Vournas, George. Attorney and longtime Drew Pearson personal friend, Washington, D.C. Interview, January 18, 1977.

Woods, Warren. Jack Anderson's personal attorney, Washington, D.C. Telephone interview, February 3, 1976.

———. Interview, January 13, 1977.

Letters

Amsden, Forest. General manager and executive vice-president, KGW-TV, Portland, Ore., and former executive editor of the *Coos Bay* (Oregon) *Times*. Letter to the author, February 18, 1977.

Comfort, Patrick. Jack Anderson's attorney, Tacoma, Wash. Letter to the author, January 28, 1977.

Daniels, Jonathan. Editor, *Raleigh* (N.C.) *News and Observer*. Letter to Drew Pearson, November 4, 1941.

Goldberg, Arthur. Former U.S. Supreme Court Justice, Washington, D.C. Letter to the author, February 2, 1977.

Gross, Paul L. General manager, *Schenectady* (N.Y.) *Union Star*. Letter to Drew Pearson, May 20, 1942.

Pearson, Drew. Letter to Roy Anderson, editor, *Ketchikan* (Alaska) *Chronicle*, January 22, 1940.

———. Letters to Albert M. Crawford, Prescott, Ariz., attorney, November 23, 1942, December 11, 1942.

———. Letter to F. Joseph Donohue, Washington, D.C., attorney, February 7, 1955.

———. Form letters to attorneys and editors interested in the *Sweeney* case, May 27, 1942, January 18, 1943.

———. Form letter to interested parties in the *Gariepy* case, November 2, 1954.

———. Letter to Sam Hahn, Los Angeles attorney, June 18, 1948.

———. Letter to Stephen B. Narin, Philadelphia attorney, April 5, 1961.

———. Letter to C. E. Palmer, *Hot Springs* (Ark.) *Sentinel-Record,* August 14, 1941.

———. Letter to Lee F. Payne, executive editor, *Los Angeles Daily News,* October 2, 1953.

———. Letter to David E. Scoll, New York attorney, September 23, 1955.

———. Letter to Joseph Tumulty, Washington, D.C., attorney, October 19, 1940.

Roberts, William A. Attorney for Drew Pearson. Form letter to twenty-seven newspaper publishers, November 20, 1945.

Congressional Reports and Documents

U.S. Congress. House. Representative Bennett speaking about Drew Pearson. 87 *Congressional Record,* 77th Cong., 1st sess., 1941: 9943–44.

U.S. Congress. House. Representative Morrison speaking about Drew Pearson. 89 *Congressional Record*, 78th Cong., 1st sess., 1943: 4722–24.

U.S. Congress. House. Representative Sweeney speaking about the "Washington Merry-Go-Round" syndicated column. 84 *Congressional Record,* 76th Cong., 1st sess., 1939: 6163–64.

U.S. Congress. House. Representative Sweeney speaking about the "Washington Merry-Go-Round" syndicated column. 84 *Congressional Record* Appendix, 77th Cong., 1st sess., 1941: A3794–96.

U.S. Congress. Senate. Senator Bilbo speaking about Drew Pearson. 91 *Congressional Record,* 79th Cong., 1st sess., 1945: 2010–12.

U.S. Congress. Senate. Senator McCarthy speaking about Drew Pearson. 96 *Congressional Record,* 81st Cong., 2d sess., 1951: 16634–41.

U.S. Congress. Senate. Senator McKellar speaking about Drew Pearson. 90 *Congressional Record,* 78th Cong., 2d sess., 1944: 3683–87.

Unpublished Materials

Francke, Warren T. *"Investigative Exposure in the Nineteenth Century: The Journalistic Heritage of the Muckrakers."* Ph.D. dissertation, University of Minnesota, 1974.

"Jack Anderson—Biography." Issued by his office, 1976.

Stonecipher, Harry W., and Trager, Robert. "The Impact of *Gertz:* How the States Have Defined the Standard of Liability for the Private Libel Plaintiff." Paper presented at the annual convention of the Association for Education in Journalism, University of Maryland, College Park, 1976.

Trager, Robert, and Stonecipher, Harry W. *"Gertz* and *Firestone:* How Courts Have Construed tre 'Public Figure' Criteria." Paper presented at the annual convention of the Association for Education in Journalism, University of Maryland, College Park, 1976.

Index

Abell, Tyler, vii, 6, 44, 50, 188-89, 192, 258, 269(n 27); quoted, 41-42
"Actual malice" rule, 61, 71-74, 192, 194, 234, 249, 250, 261, 76-95, 181, 182-83, 187, 190, 192, 194, 208, 234, 249, 250, 261, 281(n 82), 306(n 1), 313(n 197). *See also New York Times Co.* v. *Sullivan*
Adamic, Louis, 223-24
Agency for International Development, 241-42
Agnew, Spiro, 242
Akron Beacon Journal, 108
Alabama Supreme Court, 73
Alaska, 235
Alaska Supreme Court, 235, 236
Alien and Sedition Acts of 1798, 278(n 2)
Alienation of affection, defined, 172
Allen, Robert S., 5, 6, 9-10, 16, 18-19, 24, 46, 99, 100, 101, 103-27 passim, 153-54, 219-21, 245, 247, 258, 259, 271(n 9), 285(n 13), 286(n 20); quoted, 17
Allen v. *Journal of Commerce Publishing Co.,* 219-21
Allred, James, quoted, 110-11
American Broadcasting Company, 151, 168, 169
American Civil Liberties Union, 118, 150, 151
American Friends Service Committee, 4
American Government . . . Like It Is(Anderson and Kalvelage), 30
American Jewish Committee, 118
American Jewish Congress, 118
American Opinion, 87

American Telephone & Telegraph, 240-43
American Veterans Committee, 33
Amsden, Forest W., 136, 137
An American Life(Magruder), 42
Anderson, Agnes Mortensen, 12
Anderson, Franklin, 153-55
Anderson, Jack Northman, iv, vii, 2, 10, 22, 24, 25, 27, 28-30, 44, 45, 55, 56, 67, 135, 136, 137, 193-94, 260, 261-62, 294(n 57); and controversy, 245-46; current column status, 20-22; freedom of the press cases filed by, 219, 229, 238-44; infrequency of legal actions against, 255-56; libel cases against, 197, 203-7; libel cases by public figures, 210-18; and libel insurance, 53-54; life of, 12-15; and Nixon administration, 42-44; summary of libel suits, 247-54; quoted, 26, 29-30
Anderson, Orlando N., 12
Anderson, Roy, 103
Anderson Papers, 30
Anderson v. *Allen,* 153-55
Anderson v. *Nixon*, 238-40, 255
Arnold, Thurman, 320(n 124)
Ashworth, Edward, 207
Associated Press, 222, 223
Associated Press v. *Walker*, 77-80, 257
Atlantic Monthly, 93
Attorneys' role in libel suits, 251-53

Bachman Bakeries(Reading, Pa.), 140
Baer, Frank, 76, 78
Bailey, Jennings, 127, 173
Baltimore Sun, 5-6, 17
Barr, William G., 70
Barr v. *Matteo,* 70, 74, 185, 209, 234
Bealle, Morris A., 225
Beauharnais v. *Illinois*, 69
Bell Syndicate, 18, 143, 174-77, 207
Bernardo O'Higgins Order of Merit, 11
Berry, Albert S., 65
Bickel, Karl, 17
Biggs, John, quoted, 112-13
Bilbo, Theodore, 246; quoted, 3-4
Black, Hugo, 90, 192, 304(n 276)
Blackmun, Harry, 88, 96
Black's Law Dictionary, 59
Blakeley Corporation, 221
Blue Network Company, Inc., 151
B'nai B'rith, 118
Bonus march of 1932, 284(n 2)
Born Again(Colson), 14
Boyd, James, 193
Boyd, Marjorie, 193
Boyle, Tony, 212
Bramblett, Ernest, 27, 141-42
Bramblett v. *Pearson*, 141-42
Branzburg v. *Hayes*, 213-14
Braunstaupt, Victor, 151
Brehm, Walter, 27
Brennan, William, Jr., 88-89; quoted, 74, 306(n 2)
Bresler, Charles, 81-82
Brewster, Owen, 33
Bridgeport, Ohio, 177-78
Bristol News Courier(Va.), 122
Britton, George, 177
Broenstrup, Howard V., 150
Brown, Edmund "Pat", 236, 237
Brown, George, vii
Bryant, Paul, 78
Bunyan, John, 22
Bureau of Indian Affairs, 242
Burch, Rousseau, quoted, 66
Burger, Warren E., quoted, 197-98
Burnett, George, 78
Butts, Wallace, 78, 79

Buzzard Roost power project So. Carolina), 132-33

Cameron, Ellen, 269(n 24)
Camp Peary, Va., 157-58
Carey, Ed, 212-16
Carey v. *Hume,* 206, 207, 211-16, 255, 263
Carlin, George, 103-4
Carrott, M. Browning, vii
Case Against Congress(Pearson and Anderson), 24
Castro, Fidel, 28, 186
Cavanah, Charles, quoted, 111
CBS, Inc., 93
Celler, Emanuel, 211
Central Intelligence Agency (CIA), 28, 43, 239
Cervantes, Alfonso, 214
Cervantes v. *Time*, 214
Chaplinsky v. *New Hampshire*, 64-65
Charleston, West Virginia, 123
Charleston Open Forum(W. Va.), 222
Chase, Harrie, 114; quoted, 121
Chautauqua circuit, 4
Chelsea Record(Mass.), 122
Chicago Journal of Commerce, 220-21
Christian Science Monitor, 9, 16-17
Christopher, George, 236-38
Churchill, Winston, 223-24
Cincinnati Post, 65
Circuit Court for Coos County (Ore.), 135
Circuit Court for the District of Columbia, 184
Circuit Court for Jefferson County(W. Va.), 222
Citizens' Civil Liberties Union, 150
Civil Rights Commission report (1961), 83
Clark, Charles, 117, 259; quoted, 114-15
Clark, Charles Patrick, 30, 33-34, 186, 207-10, 246, 252
Clark, Frank W., 150
Clark v. *Pearson*, 207-10, 260
Cohens v. *Virginia*, 71
Coleman, C. C., 66
Coleman v. *MasLennan*, 65-68, 73, 75, 201, 251, 296(n 76); quoted, 141, 142
Colorado, 96
Colson, Charles, 14-15
Colson, Mrs. Charles, 247
Columbia Broadcasting System, 213
Columbia Law Review, quoted, 68
Comfort, Patrick, 216-18
Commission on Government Security, 232
Committee for Constitutional Government, 155
Committee to Impeach Governor Almond, 148
Common law, 58-61; libel cases, 65-68, 128-80, 249
Common Pleas Court of Summit County(Ohio), 108
Concord Monitor(New Hampshire), 190
Confessions of a Muckraker (Anderson), 30
Congressional Record, 3, 4, 31, 35, 117, 207
Consent/authorization, 61
Consolidated Press v. *New York World Telegram*, 49
Cook, Marlow, 28
Coos Bay, Oregon, 135-37
Coos Bay Times, 136-37
Copyright Act, 304(n 276)
Corcoran, Tommy, 220, 225
Coreil, Judith Billeaud, 199, 201-3
Coreil v. *Pearson*, 201-3
Corpus Christi Caller-Times, 110
Corso, Philip J., 210-11
Corso v. *Pearson*, 210-11

Coughlin, Charles E., 47, 104, 112, 169-74, 253, 257, 286(n 20)
Court of Appeals for the Second Circuit, 113
Court of Appeals for the Third Circuit, 112
Cuneo, Ernest, 49, 105; quoted, 5, 46, 51
Curtis Publishing House v. *Butts*, 77-80, 94, 256

Dall v. *Pearson*, 167-68
Damron, James, 83
Damron, Leonard, 82-83
Daniel, Price, 155
Daniels, Jonathan, quoted, 118
Defamation, defined, 58
Dennett, Prescott, 151-52, 298-99(n 134)
Dennett v. *Pearson*, 151-52
Deseret News, 12
Detroit Times Division of the Hearst Publishing Co., 232
Dies Committee, 153-54
Dimond, John, quoted, 235
Dinner at the White House (Adamic), 223
District Court for the District of Columbia, 107
District Court for the Northern District of Virginia, 117
District Court for the Southern District of Texas, 109
District of Columbia, 67, 178, 179, 251, 252; Court of Appeals, 124
Dodd, Thomas, 10, 20, 27, 28, 47, 54, 193-97, 237
Dodd v. *Pearson*, 309(n 76)
Donohue, F. Joseph, 166-67, 173, 174, 210, 252; quoted, 51-52
Donovan, John, 51, 129, 138-39, 140, 141, 142, 143-45, 165-67, 173, 175, 178-79, 187, 188, 209, 211, 234, 248, 250, 251-53, 254, 260, 298-99(n 134), 301(n 190); quoted, 149-50, 190-201, 298-99(n 134), 301(n 190)
Doyle, Arthur, quoted, 108-9
Duncan, Daniel T., 132-34
Duncan v. *Pearson*, 132-34

Eagleton, Thomas, 29
Earl, Stanley, 134-37, 293(n 35), 294(n 57), 294-95(n 58)
Earl v. *Pearson*, 134-37
Edgerton, Henry, 172, 251; quoted, 107-8
Eisenhower, Dwight D., 11, 40-41, 138, 139, 246
Eisler, Gerhardt, 145
Eldorado Times(Ark), 122
Elkins, Jim, 134-35
Elmhurst v. *Pearson*, 304-5(n 277)
Eniwetok atoll, 40
Erie Railroad v. *Tompkins*, 114
Ernst, Morris, 118-19, 224
Evening Star Broadcasting Co., 151

Fairbanks Miner(Alaska), 234
Fairbanks Publishing Co., 234-36
Fair comment/criticism, 62
Farley, Olivia(Mrs. Jack Anderson), 13
"Fascists in Capitol," 153
Federal Bureau of Investigation (FBI), 193, 242
Federal Communications Commission, 170
Federal District Court for the District of Columbia, vi, 210
Federal District Court for the Southern District of Idaho, 111
Federal Reporter system, 263
Federal Supplement, 264
Feighan, Michael A., 210, 211
Fifth Amendment, 241
Firestone, Mary Alice, 90

First Amendment, v, 53, 56, 64, 65, 70, 73, 81-82, 89, 90, 93, 95, 167, 179, 184, 187, 191, 192, 197-98, 213, 238-44, 249, 257, 306(n 1)
Fish, Hamilton, 152
Fisher, Charles, quoted, 17-18
Fite, Rankin, 203-4
Fite v. *Anderson*, 203-04,255
Flannery, Thomas, 206
Florida, 97; Court of Appeals, 83; Supreme Court, 91
Ford, Gerald, 205
Foreign Agents Registration Act of 1938, 148, 149, 296(n 90)
Forester, Gordon, 215
Forrestal, James V., 33, 34-36, 229, 230
Fort, William S., 136
Fourteenth Amendment, v, 53, 56, 64, 82, 187, 191, 249, 306(n 1)
Fourth Circuit Court, 133
Francke, Warren T., vii; quoted, 23
Franco, Francisco, 33, 186, 207
"Franco Lobby"(Pearson), 186, 187
Frankfurter, Felix, quoted, 69-70
Franzino, Joseph B., 159-61
Franzino v. *Pearson*, 159-61
Freed, Emerich B., 104, 106, 118
Freedom Balloons, 10
Freedom of the press. *See* First Amendment; Fourteenth Amendment
Friendship Train, 10-11, 247
Funkhouser, R. J., 221-23

Gariepy, Bernard F., 169, 171
Gariepy, Mary G., 169-74
Gariepy v. *Pearson*, 169-74, 253
Garland, Judy, 213
Garland v. *Torre*, 213-14
Garrison, James, 74
Garrison v. *Louisiana*, 75, 76, 80, 183, 191
Gertz, Elmer, 87-90
Gertz v. *Robert Welch, Inc.*, 59-60, 85-90, 91, 92, 95, 96, 97, 116, 217, 256, 306(n 3)
Gesell, Gerhard, 240
Gizycka, Felicia(Drew Pearson's first wife), 5, 100
Goebbels, Joseph, 220
Goering, Albert, 164
Goering, Herman, 164
Goldberg, Arthur J., 257
Golden, Terry, 193
Green, Grafton, 111-12
Green, Irving H., 238
Greenbelt Cooperative Publishing Association, Inc. v. *Bresler*, 81-82
Greenbelt News Review (Md.), 81
Gross, Paul L., 120

Hagerty, James C., 40
Haldeman, H. R., 28, 239
Hallam, Theodore F., 65
Hambro's Bank of London, 223
Hamilton, E. Douglas, 61, 62; quoted, 57-58
Hancock, Frank, 174, 176
Hand, Learned, 114
Handelman, Philip, 182; quoted, 187-88
Harbison, Winfred A., quoted, 64
Harlan, John Marshall, quoted, 70, 85-86, 90
Harris, Louis, 1-2
Headline Club(Chicago), 48
Hearst Consolidated Publications, Inc., 228-32
Herbert, Anthony, 92-94
Herbert v. *Lando*, 92-94
Hicks, Floyd, 216
Hill, James, 76-77
Hillings, Pat, 163
Hoey, Clyde, 174-75
Hoge, Ludwig, 177

Holtzoff, Alexander, 131, 150; quoted, 208, 233-34
Hoover, Herbert, 5, 16, 36
Hoover, J. Edgar, 164
Horan, Michael J., quoted, 200
House Military Affairs Committee, 162
House Un-American Activities Committee, 32, 149
"How a Supersoldier Was Fired from His Command," 92
Howard Ernest, 174-77
Howard, Mrs. Ernest, 174, 175-77
Howard v. *The Washington Post*, 174-77
Howser, Fred N., 129-32, 252
Howser v. *Pearson*, 129-32, 133, 263
Hudson, Frederick, quoted, 23
Hull, Cordell, 37
Hume, Brit, 29, 212-16; quoted, 21. *See also Carey* v. *Hume*
Hunt, David, 216
Huntington, W. Va., 123

Ickes, Harold, 225
Idaho libel law, 111
Illinois, 97; libel/slander laws, 58-59
Indiana, 96
Indo-Pakistani War, 28, 29
Internal Revenue Service(IRS), 193, 203
International Telephone and Telegraph Co., 21, 28
"IRS Probes Wallace Kin," 203
Irvine, Joseph A., 130

Jackson, Robert, 119, 120, 259
Jefferson Republican(W. Va.), 221
Jensen, Robert C., quoted, 7
Jewish Labor Committee, 118
John Birch Society, 87
Johnson, Helen W., quoted, 136-37
Johnson, Lyndon B., 41-42
Johnson, Ralph, vii
Jones, William, 189
Journal of Commerce Publishing Co.(Chicago), 219-21

Kalven, Harry, Jr., quoted, 73
Kansas, 97; Supreme Court, 66, 142, 251
Katzenbach, Nicholas, 211
Kefalos, Sam, 177-79
Kefauver Story(Anderson & Blumenthal), 30
Kelley, Alfred H., quoted, 64
Kennedy, John F., 41
Keogh, Eugene, 33, 182-89, 207, 210, 260
Keogh v. *Pearson* cases, 182-89, 192, 250
Ketchikan Chronicle(Alaska), 103
Khrushchev, Nikita, 10, 41, 270(n 46)
Kimmerle v. *New York Evening Journal*, quoted, 114
King, Dal M., 136
King, Martin Luther, Jr., 71, 72
Kissinger, Henry, 205
Klassen, Ted, 28
Koehne, Ira Chase, 150-51
Koehne v. *Radio Corporation of America*, 150-52
Korean War, 233

Lake Charles American Press, 201
Lando, Barry, 92-93
Lane County(Oregon), 136
Laughlin, James J., 152-53
Laughlin v. *Pearson*, 152-53
Lawhorne, Clifton, 189; quoted, 60
Lawrence, David, 5, 11
Lawton, Samuel, 221
Lee, Kathie, vii
Lewis, Fulton, Jr., 225
Libel, defined, 59, 288(n 50)
Libel actions, defenses against, 61-65

Libel cases: against Pearson/ Anderson summed up, 247-54; filed by Pearson/Anderson, 219-45; involving public figures, 143-69, 207-18; involving public officials, 129-43, 182-207; Pearson and, 44-54; by private persons, 169-80; post-*Sullivan* ruling, 181-218; results of recent, 95-98
Libel law, 55-58; common law cases, 65-68, 128-80; common law origins, 58-61; effect of column on, 257-62; effect of Sweeney cases, 127; effects of evolution on column, 254-57; evolution of, 249-50; trends in 1940s/50s, 68-71
Libel limits, court sanctioned, v-vi
Libel per quod, defined, 60
Libel per se, defined, 59-60
Libel rulings, post-*Sullivan*, 74-95
Liberty Lobby v. *Pearson*, 197-98
Liddy, G. Gordon, 42
Life, 14, 28, 76-77, 92, 214
Literary Digest; quoted, 101
Littell, Norman, 143-48, 252
Littell v. *Pearson*, 143-48, 250
Little Green House on K Street, 161
Los Angeles Daily News, 148
Louisiana, 201-2; Court of Appeals, 80; Criminal Defamation Statute, 75
Louisville Courier-Journal, 9
Lyndon Baines Johnson Library, vii, 42, 102
Lynne, Seybourn, 204

MacArthur, Douglas, 2, 6, 47, 99-101, 128, 245, 257, 285(n 9)
MacArthur v. *Pearson*, 99-102, 258
McCarthy, Joseph, 27, 30-33, 47, 145, 224-27, 229, 230, 246, 257, 264
McCarthy: The Man, the Senator, the Ism(Anderson and May), 30
McCarthy, W. Marvin, quoted, 157
McClellan, John, 134
McCloskey, Robert, quoted, 70-71
McClure, S. S., quoted, 25
McCracken, Alan R., quoted, 164
McGonigle, Arthur J., 139-41
McGonigle v. *Pearson*, 139-41
McGowan, Carl, quoted, 214-15
McGuire, Matthew, 141
McIntire, Carl, 39
McKellar, Kenneth, quoted, 3, 246
MacKinnon, George, 215
McLaughlin, Charles, 146
MacLennan, F. P., 66
Madison Capital Times, 9
Madole, James, 148
Magruder, Jeb Stuart, 42
Malaxa Nicolae, 163-67, 252, 301(n 190)
Malaxa v. *Pearson*, 163-67
Marbury v. *Madison*, 71
Marshall, John, 71
Marshall, Thurgood, quoted, 85-86
Martin's Ferry Ledger(Ohio), 178
Maryland Court of Appeals, 81
Matthews, Burnita, 132
Matthews, J. B., 225
May, Andrew, 27
Mayflower Hotel(Washington, D.C.), 50
Medill, Joseph, 5
Mellett, Lowell, vii

Mellett Fund for a Free and Responsible Press, vii
Meredith, James, 78
Meyer, Eugene, 157, 161
Meyer, Mrs. Eugene, 270(n 46)
Michigan Catholic, quoted, 170
Miller, Wilbur, quoted, 304(n 277)
Milwaukee Sentinel, 122
Mitchell, John, 28
Monitor Patriot Co. v. *Roy*, 82, 190-92, 250, 261
Monroe, James, 83
Monroe, John, 161-63
Monroe v. *Pape*, 83
Monroe v. *Pearson*, 161-63
Montgomery, Ala., 71, 72
Moore, Luvie, 6. *See also* Mrs. Drew Pearson
More Merry-Go-Round(Allen and Pearson), 17, 24, 304(n 276)
Morgan, Charles, Jr., 207
Morrison, James, 246
Morse, Wayne, 11
Moss, John E., 232
Muckraking, 2, 6-7, 22-30, 256
Mulloy, James T., 130
Murphy, Frank, quoted, 64-65
Murphy, George, 28
Murphy, James, 175

Nader, Ralph, 24, 168
Nasser, Gamal, Abdel, 149, 150
Nation, 23, 286; quoted, 20
National Broadcasting Co., 151
National Press Club, 18
National Renaissance party, 149
National Review, quoted, 2, 309-10(n 88)
Near v. *Minnesota*, 64
Neel, William, 147
Nellor, Edward K., 225
Nelson, Donald, 162
New Deal, 17, 18. *See also* Franklin D. Roosevelt
New Hampshire Supreme Court, 191, 192
New Orleans, 74, 75
New Republic, 23
Newspaper Guild, vii
Newsweek, 40, 44, 46; quoted, 19, 29, 38, 100
New York, 97; libel law, 114-17
New York Daily Mirror, 165
New York Herald, 23
New York Journal American, quoted, 229, 230, 231
New York Law Journal, 49
New York Post, quoted, 33
New York State Publishers Association, 118
New York Times, 23, 44, 92, 117; quoted, 26, 39
New York Times Co. v. *Sullivan*, v, vi, 53, 56-67, 61, 95, 96, 108, 234, 236, 248, 249, 251, 254-55, 257, 259, 260, 264, 280(n 61), 285(n 11), 292(n 1); analysis of, 71-74; libel cases after, 181-218; post-ruling developments, 74-95
Nicaragua, 205
Nine Old Men(Allen and Pearson), 24
Nine Old Men at the Crossroads (Allen and Pearson), 24
Nixon, Richard M., 30, 42-43, 163, 165, 238-40
Nixon administration, 205, 206, 246
North American Newspaper Alliance, 190, 191
Northern District of New York, 113
Nuccio, Richard, 87

O'Brien, Robert, 216-18
O'Brien v. *the Tribune Publishing Co.*, 216-18, 255, 314(n 208)
Ocala Star Banner Co. v. *Damron*, 82-83
O'Connor, John J., 105, 125-27; quoted, 119

O'Hare, Michael, 193-94
Ohio, 97
Opinion Makers (Rivers), 51
Oregonian, 294(n 46)
Ortiz v. *Pearson*, 314(n 206)

Pakistan, 28
Panama American 103
Pape, Frank 83
Parade magazine, 13
Partin, E. G., 80
Patterson, Eleanor "Cissy," 5, 6, 100, 105, 124, 153, 229, 259
Patton, George S., 27
Paul, Randolph, 148
Pearson, Andrew Russell "Drew," iv, vii, 2, 13, 15, 29, 55, 56, 60, 67, 82, 99, 101, 276(n 130), 285(n 9, n 13), 295(n 58); assessment of, 22, 23-24, 25-27; assessment by Jack Anderson, 20-21; common law libel cases, 128-80; controversy about, 245-46; effects on evolving libel law of, 257-62; and evolution of libel law, 254-57; launching column, 16-20; libel cases, 44-45; libel cases after *Sullivan* ruling, 181-218; libel cases filed by, 219-44; libel cases involving public figures, 207-18; life of, 4-12; personal controversies, 30-42; summary of libel suits, 247-54; and Sweeney libel suits, 102-27; quoted, 1, 3, 100, 304(n 277)
Pearson, Edna Wolfe, 4
Pearson, Mrs. Drew, 7, 42, 50, 51, 103, 146, 147, 188-89, 223, 236. *See also* Luvie Moore
Pearson, Paul Martin, 4
Pearson v. *Christopher*, 236-38
Pearson v. *Dodd*, 193-97
Pearson v. *Fairbanks Publishing Co.*, 234-36
Pearson v. *Funkhouser*, 221-23
Pearson v. *Hearst Consolidated Publications*, 228-32
Pearson v. *McCarthy*, 224-27, 264
Pearson v. *Pegler*, 227-28, 231-32
Pearson v. *Time, Inc.*, 223-24
Pearson v. *Wright*, 232-34
Pegler, Westbrook, 35, 225, 227-32
Pelley, William D., 153-54
Peterson, Cate, vii
Phelps, Robert, 61, 62; quoted, 57-58
Philadelphia Record, 17
Philadelphia Record Co., 112
Pilat, Oliver, 21, 285(n 9)
Pilgrim's Progress(Bunyan), 22
Piracci v. *The Hearst Corporation*, 281(n 82)
Portland (Ore.) City Commission, 134
Portland Journal, 294(n 46)
Post Publishing Co., 65
Post Publishing Co. v. *Hallam*, 65-68
Powell, Adam Clayton, Jr., 10, 27
Powell, Lewis, 90
Pravda, quoted, 33
Prescott Courier(Arizona), 122
Press, current state of the, 95-98
Private persons, libel cases by, 169-80
Privilege of participant, 62
Privilege of reporting, 62-63
Prosser, Dean, 59, 195; quoted, 56, 61, 63
Public figures, libel cases by, 143-69, 207-18
Public officials, libel cases involving, 129-43, 182-207
Public Works Administration (PWA), 133

Raleigh News and Observer, 118

Reading Eagle(Pa.), 122, 250
Reading Times(Pa.), 139
Rehnquist, William, 90; quoted, 91-92
Reporters Committee for Freedom of the Press v. *American Telephone & Telegraph Co.,* 240-43, 255
Reserve Officers' Association, 38
Riesman, David, 254; quoted, 68-69
Right of reply, 61-62
Rivers, William, quoted, 51
Roberts, Owen, 304(n 276)
Roberts, William A., 105, 225, 227
Robert Welch, Inc., 87-90
Robinson, Helen, 285(n 9)
Rockwell, George Lincoln, 148-50
Rockwell v. *Pearson,* 148-50
Rodgers, Decatur H., 222
Rogers, William P., 49, 130, 131, 252, 257
Rogge, O. John, 304(n 277)
Rooney, John, 186
Roosevelt, Eleanor, 11
Roosevelt, Franklin D., 2, 30, 36, 45, 48, 100, 133, 134, 246
Roosevelt, Theodore, 22
Roosevelt administration (FDR's), 117
Rosenblatt, Alfred, 76
Rosenblatt v. *Baer,* 76
Rosenbloom, George, 84-85
Rosenbloom v. *Metromedia, Inc.,* 84-86, 88-90, 95, 217, 256
Ross, Kenwood, 159-61
Ross v. *Pearson,* 159-61
Roy, Alphonse, 82, 190-92, 261
Rumely, Edward, 155-56
Rumely v. *Pearson,* 155-56

Sackett, Sheldon, 136, 137
St. Amant, Phil, 80
St. Amant v. *Thompson,* 80-81, 85
St. Louis Post-Dispatch, quoted, 39
Salt Lake Tribune, 12
San Antonio Light Publishing Co., 232
Saturday Evening Post, 78, 170; quoted, 47
Schenectady Union Publishing Co., 118, 120
Schenectady Union Star, 120
Schwab, Dwight, 295(n 58)
Seabees, 158-69
Second Circuit Court of Appeals, 93, 109
Selft defense/right of reply, 61-62
Senate Ethics Committee, 54, 193
Serbia, 4-5
Serutan Company, 151
Sharp, Morrell, quoted, 216-17
Shelton, Turner B., 204-7
Shelton v. *Anderson,* 204-7, 255
Shoreham Hotel(Washington, D.C.), 304(n 277)
Shrine of the Little Flower (Royal Oak, Mich.), 169
Silver Motors, Inc. v. *Pearson,* 168
Sinclair, Upton, 26
Sirica, John, 201
"60 Minutes," 92-93
Slander, defined, 58
Smith, Gerald K., 152
Smith, Tom, 271(n 9)
Smythe, Charles, 152, 153
Snedden, C. W., 234-35
Soldier(Herbert), 93
Somoza, Anastasio, 206
Southern District of New York, 120
Spear, Joseph, 204, 206
Stassen, Harold, 139
State Milk Control Law(Calif.), 237
State Supreme Court for New York County, 229

Statute of limitations, 62
Steffens, Lincoln, 9, 26
Stepovich, Mike, 235
Stewart, Potter, 97, 213, 214; quoted, 191
Stone, I. F., quoted, 37
Stonecipher, Harry W., xii
Submerged Lands Act of 1953, 292(n 6)
Sulgrave Club(Washington, D.C.), 30
Sullivan, L. B., 71-74
Superior Court for Los Angeles County, 236
Supreme Court of Louisiana, 80
Supreme Court of New Hampshire, 76
Surine, Don, 225
Swarthmore College, 4
Sweeney, Martin L., 44, 47, 68, 128, 152, 248, 250, 255, 258, 260, 276(n 130), 286(n 20), 291(n 133), 320(n 1); libel suits against Pearson, 102-27, 263-65
Sweeney v. *Caller-Times Co.*, 140
Sweeney v. *California News Publishing Co.*, 111
Sweeney v. *Illinois Publishing and Printing Co.*, 106-7
Sweeney v. *Patterson*, 138, 141, 143, 187, 201, 251, 253, 259-60, 296(n 78)
Sweeney v. *Schenectady Union Publishing Co.*, 113-20, 121, 258-59
Sweeney v. *United Feature Syndicate*, 120-22
Tacoma News Tribune, 216
Tamm, Edward, 174, 188, 298-99(n 134); quoted, 196-97
Tarbell, Ida M., 9
Taft, William Howard, quoted, 65-66
Tennessee Supreme Court, 111-12
Territorial waters claims, 292(n 6)
Texas libel law, 109-11
Thomas, J. Parnell, 27
Thompson, Herman A., 80
Thompson, T. Ashton, 198-201
Thompson v. *Pearson*, 198-201
Thorkelson, Jacob, 153-54
Thurmond, J. Strom, 210, 211
Tidelands oil lobby, 130, 155
Time, 2, 21, 35, 83-84, 131; quoted, 9, 27, 28, 31, 37, 33-34, 49, 223-24
Time, Inc., 223-24
Time, Inc. v. *Firestone*, 90-92
Time, Inc. v. *Hill*, 76-77, 89, 256
Time, Inc. v. *Pape*, 83-84, 92
Times, Inc.(Oregon), 136-37
"Time to Clear Air of Pearson Poison," 170
Tito, Josip B., 5
Topeka Star Journal, 66
Torre, Marie, 213
Trager, Robert, vii
Truman, Harry S, 1, 11, 31, 34, 35, 37-40, 45, 48, 246, 268(n 2)
Truth defense, 62
Tucker Corporation, 168
Tumulty, Joseph, 49
Turlock Journal(Calif.), 122
Tuscaloosa News(Ala.), 203
Tweed, William Marcy, 23
24th Infantry Division, 159-60

United Feature Syndicate, iv, 17, 18
United Mine Workers, 212, 215
U. S. Court of Appeals, Seventh District, 88
United States Daily, 5
U.S. District Court, Northern District of Illinois, 87
U.S. District Court for the Eastern District of South Carolina, 133

U.S. News and World Report, 5
United States Reports, 263
United States Supreme Court, v, 53, 56, 61, 64, 65, 101, 114, 115, 119-20, 127, 180, 183, 189, 191-92, 194, 209, 213, 234, 235, 243, 249, 257, 258, 259, 261; libed cases of the 1950s, 69-71; libel rulings, 73, 75, 76-95
United States v. *California,* 292 (n 6)
United States v. *Louisiana,* 292 (n 6)
United States v. *Texas,* 292(n 6)
University of Alabama, 78
University of Mississippi, 78
USA-Second Class Power? (Pearson & Anderson), 24

Vaughan, Harry, 33, 38, 39, 268(n 2)
Vetter, Charles, 160
Vietnam, 92
Vournas, George, 7, 131

Walker, Edwin, 78-79
Wallace, Gerald, 203
Wallace, George, 203
Wallace, Lew, 138-39
Wallace, Lurleen, 203
Wallace, Mike, 93
Wallace v. *Pearson*, 138-39, 140
Wall Street Journal, 44; quoted, 51
Walsh, Leonard, quoted, 183
Walsh, William, 137
Walter Reed General Hospital, 3
Ware, James G., 156-59
Ware v. *Pearson*, 156-59
Warren, Earl, 79, 130; Court, 95
Washington Exposé(Anderson), 30
Washington Herald, 100
Washingtonian, 304(n 276)
Washingtonian Publishing Co., 304(n 276)
Washington Merry-Go-Round (Allen and Pearson), 5, 16, 24, 36, 271(n 9)
Washington Merry-Go-Round column, 225-28, 236-37; aggregate damages against, 320(n 1); Anderson joins, 12-13; common law libel cases, 128-80; current status, 20-22; effects of evolution of libel law on, 254-57; effects on libel law of, 257-62; first libel suit, 99-102; launched, 6, 16-20; libel cases involving public figures, 207-18; libel suits summed up, iv-vi, 44-45; muckraking tradition, 20-30; place in American journalism, 245-54; post-*Sullivan* libel cases, 181-218; summary of libel actions, 247-54; Sweeney's libel suits against, 102-27
Washington Post, 6, 35, 37, 38-39, 157, 158, 159, 161, 174-77, 182, 184, 185, 186, 200, 207, 212, 215, 226-27, 232; quoted, 48
Washington Post Co. v. *Keogh,* 260, 281(n 82)
Washington Post Publishing Co., 182, 184, 207
Washington Rent Commission, 162
Washington Social List, 2
Washington Times-Herald, 6, 105, 225, 226
Watergate, 28
Waters, George, 225
Welch, Robert, 87-90
Western District of Washington, 217
Wheeling News Register(W. Va.), 178
White, Byron, R., quoted, 94

White House "plumbers," 239
Whitten, Les, 204; quoted, 14
Whittier, Calif., 165
Wilkey, Malcolm, quoted, 242-43
Williams, Arthur, 293(n 35)
Williams, Edward Bennett, 146, 147
Winchell, Walter, 34, 35
WIP radio station, 84, 85
WMAL radio station, 151, 304(n 277)
Woodring, Harry H., 99
Woods, Warren, 54, 132, 203-4, 219, 225, 227, 248, 250, 285(n 13)
Wright, J. Skelly, 185-86, 195, 196, 198, 243; quoted, 184
Wright, Lloyd, 232-34

Yale Law Journal, quoted, 116
Yugoslavia, 5